German Chronicle

IN THE
HISTORY OF THE OHIO VALLEY
AND ITS CAPITAL CITY
CINCINNATI
IN PARTICULAR

By
Emil Klauprecht

Translated by
Dale V. Lally, Jr.

Edited by
Don Heinrich Tolzmann

HERITAGE BOOKS
2007

HERITAGE BOOKS
AN IMPRINT OF HERITAGE BOOKS, INC.

Books, CDs, and more—Worldwide

For our listing of thousands of titles see our website
at
www.HeritageBooks.com

Published 2007 by
HERITAGE BOOKS, INC.
Publishing Division
65 East Main Street
Westminster, Maryland 21157-5026

Copyright © 1992 Dale V. Lally, Jr. and
Don Heinrich Tolzmann

Cover illustration from *German Achievements in America*
by Rudolph Cronau

— English Translation —

Original Copyright Information:
Entered according to Act of Congress in the year 1864 by G. Hof & M. A. Jacobi, in the Clerks
Office of the District Court of the United States for the Southern District of Ohio.

All rights reserved. No part of this book may be reproduced or transmitted in any form or by any means,
electronic or mechanical, including photocopying, recording or by any information storage and retrieval system
without written permission from the author, except for the inclusion of brief quotations in a review.

International Standard Book Number: 978-1-55613-703-7

TABLE OF CONTENTS

Preface by Don Heinrich Tolzmann vii

Introduction by Don Heinrich Tolzmann ix

Translator's Note by Dale V. Lally, Jr. xv

Forward by Emil Klauprecht 3

Chapter 1 The French Sovereignty - The wars of independence of the Ohio Indians with the Iroquois. - The Miami Confederation. - The Wyandots, Delawares and Shawnees. - Homan's Map of the Ohio Valley. - Meaning of the name "Ohio". - The Company of the West. - The Germans, the First Settlers in the Mississippi Valley. - New Orleans in 1722. - The First French Settlements on the Ohio. - The Bear Hunt at Fort Massac. - The Woodsmen. - Vincennes. - Ancient parapets and mounds on the site of today's Cincinnati. 6

Chapter 2 The first English on the Ohio. - Captain Batte. - The Knights of the Golden Horseshoe. - Germanna. - The Plans of Spotswood and Keith to use the Germans to force out the French. - German Regiments. - The Chickasaws. - Fiery death of Captain de Vincennes. - Johann Salling's Adventures. - The French Hunt the English Traders. - Conrad Weiser. - The Treaty and Drinking Bout at Lancaster. 14

Chapter 3 The Ohio Company. - Lorenz Washington seeks German settlers for their lands. - French trade. - French and English legal titles to the river area. - Celeron de Bienville formally takes possession of it (the river area) for France. - Pickawillany and its Destruction. - Christopher Gist. - Fortifying the Ohio. - St. Pierre and George Washington. 20

Chapter 4 Crevecour seizes the Ohio Company fort. - De Jumonville's death. - Washington's Capitulation. - Benjamin Franklin's Plan for Conquering and Fortifying the Ohio Valley. - Braddock's March and Defeat. - Barbaric Victory Celebration in Fort Duquesne. - Destruction of the German settlements. 26

Chapter 5 The Moravians and their Missions. - Persecution and Expulsion of the German Missionaries. - Germans Naturalized as Iroquois. - Schikellimus. - The Burning of Gnadenhütten. - Bethlehem. - German Indian Villages. - Christian Delawares and Mohicans. 33

Chapter 6 Post convinces the Indians of the upper Ohio to desert France. - The French destroy Fort Duquesne. - The decisive Battle at Upper Piqua. - Defeat of the French Indians. - The Miamis depart the Ohio Valley. - The English occupy the Fork of the Ohio with German Troops. 40

Chapter 7 The English Sovereignty - Advance of the Anglo-Americans to the West. - Ohio one hundred years ago. - Post and Heckewelder, the only settlers. - Their adventures and tribulations. - Pontiac's Conspiracy. - Captain Schlosser. - Ensign Pauly.
.... 43

Chapter 8 The Treaty of Fort Stanwix. - George Washington seeks German Farmers for the Ohio Valley. - Boone's German Companions. - George Jäger, Kenton's Mentor. - The German Long Hunters. - Michael Schuck. - David Zeisberger Establishes Friedensdorf. - the First Community. - Johann Herrmann Plants the First Corn in Kentucky. -Glikhican's Vision. - A German-Indian National Church in the Ohio Valley.
.... 51

Chapter 9 The 3rd of May 1772. - David Zeisberger founds Schönbrunn, the First City in Ohio. - Terrible Fate of its Inhabitants. - The Evacuation of Friedenshütten and Friedensdorf. - An Ancient Indian Saga. - The First Municipal Regulations of Ohio. - Founding of Gnadenhütten, Ohio's Second City by Johann Jacob Schmick.
.... 56

Chapter 10 Connolly captures Pittsburg for Virginia. - His Blood Letter to the Inhabitants of the Ohio Valley. - The Murder of Logan's Family. - The Battle of Point Pleasant. - Captain Johann Nieswanger. - German Marksmen from Tennessee. - Colonel Christian. - Cornstalk and Zeisberger. - The German Cities during Dunmore's Campaign.
.... 61

Chapter 11 The German Pioneers and Stations in Kentucky. - Meyers, the Land Agent. - German Village Life in Schönbrunn. - The Beginning of the Revolutionary War in the Ohio Valley. - Zeisberger Prevents a General Alliance of the Indian Tribes Against the American Colonists. - The Founding of Lichtenau. - The Murder of Cornstalk. - Dangers to the German Cities.
.... 65

Chapter 12 The First Settlement in the Ohio Valley. - Character of the Pioneers. - Belief in Witches and Magic. -Professional Sorcerers. - Old and Young in German Homesteads. - The German Immigrants. - Indian Attacks. - Colonel Peter Nieswanger. - Six German Spartans. - The Intrigues of British Agents in the German Cities.
.... 70

Chapter 13 Clark's Victories in the West. - Leonard Helm. - The Capture of Hamilton. - Girty's Murder Attempt against Zeisberger. - The Battle on the Licking. - The Claims of Spain on the Ohio Valley. - Fort Jefferson. - The Wars of Destruction on both Sides of the Ohio. - Destruction of Loramy's Store.
.... 74

Chapter 14 Founding of Salem. - King Schingask's Warning. - Birth of Marie Heckewelder and Christian David Sensemann, the First White Children in the State of Ohio. - Plundering of the German Cities. - Capture and Deportation of their Inhabitants.
.... 80

Chapter 15 The Massacre at Gnadenhütten. - The Revenge of the Delawares and Wyandots against the Murderers. -Death of Colonel Crawford at the Stake.
.... 89

Chapter 16 The Battle of Blue Licks. - Major George W. Bedinger. - Clark's Campaign Against the Shawnees. - A Dying Person's Vision on a Cincinnati Hill. - The Praise of the Kentuckians. - End of the Revolutionary War. - Gen. Steuben's Mission to the West to Take Over the British Military Posts. 95

Chapter 17 Captain Elholm. - Captain David Ziegler. - The Organization of the Northwest Territory. - The Founding of Marietta. - Governor St. Clair. - Ludwig Wetzel. 101

Chapter 18 The American Sovereignty - John Cleves Symmes. - The Founding of Cincinnati. - The Pesthal Family. -Fort Washington. - The Wetzel Mob. - Karl Bilderbach. 106

Chapter 19 The First Popular Assembly in Cincinnati. - The First Court Session. - Conflict Between the Civil and Military Authorities. - The Change of the Name of the City. - The Cincinnati. - Stations Around the City. - Indian Attacks. - Jakob Wetzel and his Dog. - Harmar's Campaign. 112

Chapter 20 Major David Ziegler defends Marietta. - St. Clair's Defeat. - Ziegler Commandant of Fort Washington. -Colonel Schaumburg. - Gen. Wayne's Campaign. - Major Rudolph. 119

Chapter 21 Secession Attempts in Kentucky. - The Intrigues of Spain and France in the Ohio Valley. - The Whiskey Rebellion. - Ludwig Wetzel's Captivity and Death. 126

Chapter 22 The Founding of Gallipolis, Chillicothe, and Dayton. - Volney and Brissot (write about) the German Settlers. - The First Church and School in Cincinnati. - The first Jail - The First Sheriff and the First Execution. - The Courts and Lawyers. - Distribution of the Northwest Territory. - The End of St. Clair. 132

Chapter 23 Cincinnati in 1800. - David Ziegler, Mayor of the City. - The Founding of Vevay. - German Wolf Hunters. - Burr's Conspiracy. - Justus Erich Vollmann. - The First German Property Owners in Cincinnati. 138

Chapter 24 German Boatsmen on the Ohio. - Michel Fink. - Martin Baum. - Settlement of the State of Ohio. - German Pioneers in the Various Counties. - The First German Newspaper. 144

Chapter 25 Zeisberger's Return to Ohio. - A Moravian Settlement in Indiana. - Fiery Death of a German Mohican. - The End of Zeisberger and Ziegler. - The Earthquake of 1811. - Growth of Cincinnati. - The War of 1812. - Introduction of Steam Navigation. - German Arrivals in Cincinnati. - The First German Congregation. 149

Chapter 26 Cincinnati as a City. - The First Catholic Churches in Ohio. - Fr. Friedrich Rese. - German Life in 1825. - The Swiss Colony at Vevay. - Lafayette in Cincinnati. - The First German Newspaper. - The First Synagogue. 157

Chapter 27 Columbus and its German pioneers. - Goshen and Zeisberger's Grave. - The Rappists and Zoarites. - The First German Settlers of Pittsburg. - Lenau's Farm. 163

Chapter 28 German Citizens of Cincinnati from 1790 to 1830. - The Immigration of 1830. - Cholera and Floods. - German Newspapers. - Schools and Churches. - Julius Weise. - Friedrich Gerstäcker. - The Explosion of the Moselle. - Expansion of the German Sectors of the City across the Canal. - German Military Corps and Wine Planters. 171

Chapter 29 The period from 1848 to 1860. - Development and expansion of German culture in the Ohio Valley. - Its struggles and achievements. 180

List of early German Cincinnati families (from page 159)
.... 199

Index of Family Names
.... 201

Index of Place Names & Organizations
.... 230

Index of Periodicals/Publications and Dissertations cited by Klauprecht
.... 261

Preface

The purpose of this work is to make available for the first time a translated edition of Emil Klauprecht's *German Chronicle in the History of the Ohio Valley and its Capital City Cincinnati in Particular...* Klauprecht published this valuable pioneer history in 1864, which focussed on and recorded the German-American dimension in the history of the Ohio Valley.

Dale V. Lally, Jr., St Lawrence University in Canton, NY, has here provided an excellent translation of the old German Fraktur text. Moreover, he also consulted with Professor Kurt Jankowsky, Georgetown University, with regard to translation matters. Mr. Lally's work is, hence, one that is finely crafted to remain true to the spirit of the German original, but is rendered into a readable and graceful translation. After reading the text, it was my belief that such a valuable work needed to attain publication. Indeed, I was quite aware of the significance of Klauprecht's work, having first cited it in my *German-Americana: A Bibliography* (1975). Also, I had just completed work on a translated edition of the Cincinnati German urban mystery novel published by Klauprecht in 1854, and it, therefore, seemed a logical step for both Mr. Lally and I to collaborate on this work. The goal has been to see this important history reach publication, since it certainly will be of interest to many in the Ohio Valley, as well as elsewhere. A special word of gratitude is in order here to the German-American Studies Program at the University of Cincinnati for assistance in the completion of this manuscript. Here then is the first German-American history of the Ohio Valley in over a century.

DHT

Introduction:

The First Ohio Valley German-American History

by

Don Heinrich Tolzmann

If Emil Klauprecht's novel dealing with German-American life, *Cincinnati, or, the Mysteries of the West* (1854), can be called "the most important piece of creative literature produced by a German-American during the nineteenth century," then his *German Chronicle in the History of the Ohio Valley and its Capital City Cincinnati in Particular* (1864) may be viewed with equal importance in the writings of German-American history.[1] It was the first history of the topic, and clearly laid the foundations for the later general histories of the German element in the Ohio Valley, and especially for works dealing with the Cincinnati Germans. Who was the man, who in the 1850s/60s acquired a reputation not only as the major German-American novelist in the Ohio Valley, but also as the foremost historian of the German element?

Klauprecht and the Immigration of the 1830s

Klauprecht was one of the many German liberal refugees who came to the U.S. in the 1830s, and were, hence, known as the *Dreissiger* (the Thirtyers). They had come to America after the protest gathering, the Hambacher Festival, held in May 1832 at the ruins of the old castle at Hambach. Here "students, burghers, craftsmen, farmers, and officials assembled...to listen to speeches about liberty and reform and the tyranny of the petty princes."[2] This protest gathering was followed by arrests, dismissals, censorship, and police surveillance, thus forcing many into the emigration from Germany. The German immigration to the U.S. in 1832 exceeded 10,000; in 1834 it reached 17,000, and by 1837 had soared to 24,000. Although somewhat less radical than the Forty-Eighters, the refugees of the failed revolution of 1848 in Germany, the Thirtyers exerted a profound influence on the social, cultural, and political life of the German element. A number of them found their way to Cincinnati: Heinrich Roedter became the editor of the *Cincinnati Volksblatt*, the first German-language daily newspaper in the West; Johann Bernhard Stallo became a judge and a political leader, and helped to organize the all-German Ninth Ohio Turner Regiment in 1860; Karl Rümelin was elected to the State Senate; Friedrich Eckstein organized the Academy of Fine Arts; Heinrich A. Rattermann built a reputation as a historian by editing the historical journal, *Der Deutsche Pionier*. Among this illustrious group which came to Cincinnati in the 1830s was Emil Klauprecht, who arrived in America in 1832 at the age of seventeen.[3]

---

[1] 1. George C. Schoolfield, "The Great Cincinnati Novel", Cincinnati Historical Society Bulletin, 20 (1962): 44. For an introduction to German-American literature see Don Heinrich Tolzmann, *German-American Literature*, (Metuchen, NJ: Scarecrow Press, 1977), and for a survey of historical writings see Don Heinrich Tolzmann, "German-American Studies: History and Development," *Monatshefte*, 80:3(1988): 278-88. DHT

[2] 2. Carl F. Wittke, *Refugees of Revolution: The German Forty-Eighters in America*, (Philadelphia: University of Pennsylvania, 1952), p. 10. DHT

[3] 3. The best general history of the Dreissiger immigration and its impact on the German-American community can be found in Heinrich A. Rattermann, *Gesamelte ausgewählte Werke: Band 12: Deutsch-Amerikanisches Biographikon und Dichter-Album der ersten Hälfte des 19. Jahrhunderts*, (Cincinnati: Selbstverlag des Verfassers, 1911). DHT

The facts surrounding Klauprecht are few, but his place was assured early on in German-American history. Gustav Koerner in 1880 included him in his history of the German element covering the years from 1818 to 1848, and Rattermann does also in his biographical encyclopedia. Klauprecht was also included in a 1927 Hessian biographical directory, an indication of continued interest in his life and work.[4] From these works we know that he was born on 11 September 1815 in Mainz as Emil Karl Eduard Klauprecht.[5] His parents were Daniel Ernst Klauprecht (1769-1850) and Eva Josepha, nee Müller (1776-1850). Klauprecht himself came to the U.S. alone in 1832 and settled in Paducah, Kentucky, located several hundred miles west from Cincinnati along the Ohio River. That he would find his way to the Ohio Valley region is not at all surprising, since it was at that time well on its way to becoming a major destination point of the German immigration. Cincinnati itself would become, along with St. Louis and Milwaukee, one of the three corners in the German Triangle.[6]

German-American Journalism

After five years of work as a farm laborer in Paducah, Kentucky, he then moved to Cincinnati where he settled in the German district known as Over-the-Rhine. In Cincinnati he established a lithographic firm with Adolph Menzel, under the name of "Klauprecht und Menzel's Lithographie," one of the first in the West.[7] Among the many fine works which they produced were a series of lithographs for the German-American home: "German Poets" featured Goethe, Schiller, Wieland, Klopstock, Lessing, and Herder; "German Composers" portrayed Mozart, Beethoven, Haydn, Weber, Schubert, and Mendelssohn; "German Patriots" depicted Robert Blum, Gottfried Kinkel, Friedrich Hecker, Franz Sigel, Gustav, Struve, and Ferdinand Freiligrath; as well as other lithographs, especially ones dealing with scenes from Ohio, Indiana, and Kentucky. The lithographic business also marked Klauprecht's entrance into the world of German-American journalism, when the firm commenced publication of a weekly, *Fliegende Blätter*, from 1846 to 1847.[8] The journal consisted of the first German-American illustrated publication in the U.S. It contained Klauprecht's literary writings, essays, reviews together with his sketches and caricatures. He clearly displayed a penchant and talent for satire. Early on he developed an avid interest in German-American history, and the pages of the journal were filled with his articles and essays on historical topics, especially those of the German element of the Ohio Valley. The journal also contained high quality socio-political criticism on contemporary issues.

---

[4] 4. See Gustav Koerner, *Das deutsche Element in den Vereinigten Staaten von Nordamerika, 1818-1848*, (Cincinnati: Verlag von A.E. Wilde & Co., 1880), pp. 192-92, and Rattermann, Werke, pp. 321- 24. DHT

[5] 5. For bio-bibliographical data on Klauprecht see Robert E. Ward, *A Bio-Bibliography of German-American Writers, 1670-1970*, (White Plains, New York: Kraus, 1985). DHT

[6] 6. For a general survey of German-American history, especially with regard to the Midwest, see LaVern J. Ripley, *The German-Americans*, (Boston: T, 1976). DHT

[7] 7. For further information on the Over-the-Rhine district see Don Heinrich Tolzmann, "Festschrift for the German-American Tricentennial Jubilee: Cincinnati 1983", (Cincinnati: Cincinnati Historical Society, 1982), pp. 2-21. For a survey of the district in the twentieth century see Don Heinrich Tolzmann, *The Cincinnati Germans after the Great War*, (New York: Peter Lang, 1987). DHT

[8] See Karl J.R. Arndt, *The German Language Press of the Americas: Vol. 1: History and Bibliography, 1732-1968: United States of America*, (München: Verlag Dokumentation, 1976), p. 443. DHT

Each issue of the journal numbered 12-22 pages, and included several of Klauprecht's lithographs.[9] In 1849 Klauprecht then became editor of the daily Whig newspaper, *Der Deutsche Republikaner*, which he edited until 1851, and then again from 1852 to 1856. He made it a nonmilitant, lively newspaper and expanded its influence and "improved its literary offerings and in general contributed to the elevation of German journalism."[10] Under his direction the newspaper became the major German-American Whig newspaper in the West.

At the same time, Klauprecht was engaged with his lithographic business as well as his newspaper work, he established with another journalist, Fenner von Fenneberg, a weekly belletristic Sunday journal, *Westliche Blätter*, which he published from 1851 to 1852. It contained about eight pages of text and was clearly modelled along the lines of his earlier journal, *Fliegende Blätter* (1846-47). After it ceased publication, Klauprecht returned to his former editorial position at the *Republikaner*. Although busy with his lithographic business and his newspaper position, Klauprecht was clearly interested in writing works of a literary and historical nature, and his two journals in the 1840s and 1850s reflected this interest. It was also quite clear that Klauprecht was interested deeply not only in the German-American experience, but also in seeking out German-American historical roots. These interests and concerns found expression, first, in his literary works, and then, thereafter, in his major historical work, the *German Chronicle*.

Politics and the Return to Germany

A word is in order here about the newspaper battles carried on in the 1850s between various German-American editors. Papers which supported either the Democratic or the Whig/Republican parties were naturally hostile to one another, but the German-American press at that time acquired a negative reputation for its often vicious, personal attacks. In Klauprecht, however, such editors encountered an individual without equal, who had the reputation of being able to "annihilate" any opponent in the press.

In 1852 the Democratic paper, *Der Alte Hickory*, became involved in such a heated campaign against the leader of the German-American Whig/Republican element, Emil Klauprecht. After a long series of hostile articles, the *Hickory*, published a savage series of sketches against "the youth with blond locks," which everyone knew was supposed to be Klauprecht. The series reached a climax when an article appeared, which Klauprecht felt had besmirched the honor of his family. In a fit of rage, he and three friends marched to the home of Dr. Wilhelm Albers, editor of the *Hickory*, and demanded to know the name of the author of the anti-Klauprecht articles. Naturally, Albers refused. Enraged by the refusal, Klauprecht then drew a pistol, shot Albers in the chest, and stormed out with his associates. After being found guilty of shooting with intent to kill, Klauprecht was sentenced to one year in prison, but was pardoned by the governor. In the whole affair, Klauprecht was strongly supported by the German community in Cincinnati, which felt that Klauprecht had only intended to defend the honor of his family. There was no question that his strong Republican affiliations assisted in the pardon by the governor.[11]

In 1856 Klauprecht moved from the *Republikaner* to take over as editor of the major newspaper not only in Cincinnati, but in the entire West, the venerable *Volksblatt*. His strong support for the Republican cause, and especially for Lincoln in the 1860 and 1864 elections, was rewarded in 1864 when he was appointed by the President to serve as US Consul in Stuttgart, a position he held until 1869, when he was replaced by a Grant appointee.

---

[9] Ibid, p. 441. DHT

[10] Koerner, *Element*, pp. 192-93. DHT

[11] Note that five of the six German Patriots were Forty-Eighters involved in the 1848 revolution. DHT

Thereafter, Klauprecht remained in Stuttgart and later on moved to Vienna, where he resided until his death in 1896. In these years he continued to write extensively for the German, Austrian, and the German-American press.[12]

Klauprecht was a recognized political leader in Cincinnati and throughout the Ohio Valley, exerting substantial political influence through the various newspapers he edited. His support of the Republican party going back to the 1850s was rewarded by Lincoln in 1864. Given his background, connections, publications, one can readily see that Klauprecht was ideally suited to produce the first attempt at a comprehensive history of the Ohio Valley with particular attention to the role of the German element in the region. His historical interests were first reflected in his many literary works which dealt with the German-American experience, which can be regarded as a prelude to his historical work.

Klauprecht's Literary Work

Especially noteworthy among the author's literary works were two historical novellas. His *Mississippi Wasser und Ohio Wein (Mississippi Water and Ohio Wine)* was set in the Ohio and Mississippi River valleys, and deals in a literary manner with the role of the German-American settler in the region. His *Aus dem Tagebuch eines Reisenden in Texas (From the Diary of a Traveler in Texas)* deals with the experience of a German traveler in the Texas hill country. However, most well known of his literary works was the major novel he published in 1854 entitled *Cincinnati, oder Geheimnisse des Westens (Cincinnati, or, the Mysteries of the West)*. This novel dealt with the issues of ethnicity and life in the New World, but was especially concerned with defining the role of the German-American in the history of the state of Ohio. He, therefore, discusses the early German Moravian missionaries in Ohio including Heckewelder, Zeisberger and other Ohio German pioneers in considerable detail.[13]

Klauprecht also authored a number of plays and songs. Among the former was his three act farce entitled *Das Sängerfest auf dem Bald Hill, oder, die weissen und rothen Rosen: Bildergallerie aus dem deutschen Leben Cincinnatis (The Sängerfest on BaldHill, or, the White and Red Roses: A Picture Gallery from the German Life of Cincinnati)*. Among the many songs which Klauprecht composed, the ones which proved to be the most popular were those he wrote for the Cincinnati German singing societies, such as the *Liedertafel*. Especially popular was his song *Deutsch-Amerikanischer Festchor (German-American Festival Choir)*. In 1849 and 1851 his songs were presented at Singing festivals in Cincinnati.[14]

Klauprecht's Historical Work

Klauprecht's journalistic and literary work displayed a deep and abiding interest in German-American history. Among all of his writings one finds historical themes, allusions, etc. pertaining mainly to the Ohio Valley. Moreover, since the 1840s Klauprecht had written numerous historical and biographical essays for the publications

---

[12] Regarding Klauprecht's work with the Volksblatt see Henry John Groen, "A History of the German-American Newspapers of Cincinnati before 1860," (Ph.D., Dissertation, Ohio State University, 1944). DHT

[13] As mentioned in the Preface, I have just completed work on a translated edition of Emil Klauprecht, *Cincinnati, or, the Mysteries of the West*, translated by Steven Rowan, University of Missouri-St. Louis. For a discussion of Klauprecht's literary work see my "Introduction: The Great Cincinnati German Novel." The novel is now in the final stages of preparation for publication. DHT

[14] For information on German-American societies and their festivities see Tolzmann, "Festschrift", pp. 36-41. DHT

he edited. His 1854 novel was basically a literary attempt to locate the German element within the framework of the history of the state of Ohio. It is, therefore, not altogether surprising that Klauprecht would then take the next step, and produce the first systematic attempt at a history of the Ohio Valley with a particular focus on the German element. Rattermann referred to Klauprecht's pioneer history as a "valuable source," and there is no question that it became the basis for later German-American histories of the region.[15]

Klauprecht's work was produced during the pioneer period of German-American historical writing. This period began in the mid-nineteenth century and continued into the 1880s. The pioneer historians were not professional scholars, of course, but rather businessmen, journalists, and politicians. They, however, produced for the first time histories of the German element in America, and they provided the invaluable service of having uncovered and preserved source material for the early period of German-American history. Since the role of the immigrants and their offspring was largely ignored by Anglo-American scholars until the 1920s, the pioneer historians were motivated by the desire to rectify this situation. It is important to note that they began to write in a period of nativism, i.e. the Know-Nothing Movement of the 1850s. They, therefore, aimed to awaken ethnic pride and a sense of group consciousness in the face of this nativist attitude. They also aimed to define what their role would be in America. It was clear that they saw the group as a permanent factor in American life, and one that would survive beyond the immigrant generation.[16]

The period receives its name from the well known pioneer society, *Der Deutsche Pionier-Verein von Cincinnati*, which published the major nineteenth century German-American historical journal, *Der Deutsche Pionier*, from 1869 to 1887. Its editor, Heinrich A. Rattermann, aimed "to prove that the Germans had played their honorable part in the development of the United States and that they had been very strong supporters of the American Revolution and had also helped to win the Civil War." He also exclaimed that "The future will have no more serious doubts as to the reality or existence of German-American history. By means of our publications we are enabled to hand down a record of our deeds to later generations."[17]

Klauprecht's work typifies the works of this period. Klauprecht himself was not a professional historian, but rather a self-educated journalist and politician. However, his professional activities provided him with the opportunity to become thoroughly versed in the history of the Ohio Valley and his numerous historical essays and articles in the press reflected his interest going back to the 1840s. Writing as he did in the nativist 1850s, he without question was also motivated by the desire to firmly establish and identify the role of the German-American in American history. As an active and leading participant in the German-American community, he was uniquely equipped to focus on the Ohio Valley region. There is no question also that he viewed the German element as playing an important role within the multiethnic fabric of American society. Indeed, he himself was one of the major proponents and practitioners of ethnic politics, along with Carl Schurz and others of the time.[18]

---

[15] Cited in Tolzmann, **German-American Studies: History and Development**, pp. 279-81. DHT

[16] The pioneer period is discussed in Tolzmann, "German-American Studies: History and Development," 278-88. DHT

[17] Ibid. DHT

[18] For an understanding of German-American political life and their community leaders see Hans Trefousse, "Carl Schurz: Myth and Reality," *Yearbook of German-American Studies, 19(1984)*: 1- DHT

Like Rattermann, he also aimed to document the role German-Americans had played in the development of the country, especially leading up to the time of the Civil War. It is significant that Klauprecht's book was published during this war, since it was the war which provided German-Americans with the opportunity to demonstrate their solid patriotism for the Union, which in effect brought the nativist movement of the 1850s to an abrupt halt. The importance of the German vote in the election of 1860 and of the German-American regiments in the Civil War were major topics of discussion at the time. It is in this time period which Klauprecht's work should be placed.[19] The history which he wrote and the definition of the role of the German-American in the history of the Ohio Valley which he provided awakened ethnic pride and focussed interest on pioneer history. Indeed, five years after his history was published, *Der Deutsche Pionier Verein* was founded in Cincinnati to collect and record German-American history.

Klauprecht's history is invaluable not only because of the sources which he uncovered, but because he assembled them into a structural framework of German-American history in the Ohio Valley, which he conceived and constructed. This framework would become the foundation on which all later German-language histories by Armin Lenner, Gustav Koerner, Anton Eickhoff, Max Burgheis, H.H. Fick, and H.A. Rattermann would be based.[20] These works in turn would become the basis for the standard English-language history, published in 1909, Albert B. Faust's *The German Element in the U.S.*.[21] With regard to the history of the German element in the Ohio Valley the historical framework can be traced back from Faust through the German-language histories directly to Klauprecht. However, none of them could recount in such depth and detail the history of the period leading up to the Civil War, as did Klauprecht's work.

The German-American history by Klauprecht will, hence, be of value not only to those interested in the region and period covered, but also to those concerned with immigration/ethnic history in general and German-American history in particular.

---

[19] With regard to the role of the Cincinnati Germans in the Civil War see Constantin Grebner, *We Were the Ninth: A History of the Ninth Regiment, Ohio Voluntary Infantry, April 17, 1861 to June 7, 1864*. Translated and edited by Frederic Trautmann, (Kent: Kent State University, 1987). DHT

[20] These authors and their works are analyzed and annotated in Don Heinrich Tolzmann, **Catalog of the German-Americana Collection, University of Cincinnati**, (München: Verlag K.G.Saur, 1990). DHT

[21] See Albert B. Faust, *The German Element in the U.S.*, (Boston: Houghton Mifflin, 1909). DHT

TRANSLATOR'S NOTE

In mid-1985, while browsing through the Civil War section in the library of the University of Louisville (KY), it seemed that the Klauprecht text literally jumped into my hand.

What first caught my eye, after the apparent age of the book, was the old German Fraktur script. But right after that came the words "Geschichte des Ohio Thals" or "History of the Ohio Valley". Now that really caught my attention. I already had a severe case of "Civil War Fever" and the fact that the Klauprecht text was published during the Civil War made it even more interesting. I have never for even one second regretted finding that text.

Reading the Fraktur script, initially a challenge, soon became second nature. As a matter of fact, after several months of working on the text, I started anticipating what was going to come. Klauprecht's style was very clear and the language very efficient. The descriptions of the various personalities and locations soon led me to start visiting some of the sites mentioned in the text. During the course of the next several years I cycled through the old part of Louisville, following Klauprecht's description of the Bloody Monday riots of 1855. I then went further afield, visiting the Point Pleasant battlefield in West Virginia. One unusual occurrence happened around 1987 when I was came home from reserve duty in Washington DC. While following the civil war trails from Fredericksburg to Chancellorsville VA, I happened to find Germanna Ford, which Klauprecht described in detail. Strangely enough I also came upon an archeologist who was excavating the famous hall of mirrors. The person in charge of the dig was absolutely amazed at Klauprecht's description, for he himself pointed out that he had never before read such a detailed description of the structure as contained in Klauprecht's book.

Time and time again I came upon personalities or locations mentioned in the book. I began to feel that fate had ordained me to find and translate it. I also got the idea of making a faithful reproduction of the text, retaining the original page layout and numbering. So if the reader thinks that my translation looks old fashioned, then that person is absolutely right. Except for one instance, I have maintained the original layout. That one exception is on page 159, where Klauprecht, being the good newspaperman he was, sought to name as many of Cincinnati's early German pioneers as possible. He knew that every family mentioned in his book would probably buy a copy. Therefore, he included as many names as possible. Unfortunately, this meant literally stuffing all the names onto one page using very small type. In my solitary concession to modern day sensitivities, I placed all of those names at the end of the text, where they can be easily found and read. Otherwise, except for the choice of easy to read Times Roman font, the book is as faithful a reproduction of the original work as I could make it.

I do wish to express a note of gratitude to my Doris and our two sons who had to put up with years of Dad's taking his translation along on every family trip and working on it at every available opportunity with a Tandy Model 100 computer propped on my lap. I also wish to extend a note of sincere gratitude to Professor Kurt Jankowsky of Georgetown University in Washington DC. I spend many a pleasant evening in his comfortable suburban home, sipping a glass of wine and discussing the myriad ideas and events in Klauprecht's book. Professor Jankowsky also corrected several glaring translation errors, for which I will be eternally grateful. It was through his coaching and patience that I was able to literally get into Klauprecht's mind and know intuitively exactly what he intended to write.

This work also made me much more appreciative of my own German heritage. This went so far as to take me back to the ancestral family farm in northern Germany, where I met some of my German cousins. Finally, back in Louisville itself, and directly because of the interest generated by the Klauprecht text, I found myself in the exact same physical location that my great grandfather, Herman Heinrich Raming, had occupied during the census of 1880. It was a strange but wonderful feeling. I sincerely hope that this book will have similar effects on other readers anxious to discover more about their ancestors.

Dale V. Lally, Jr.
Canton NY
1992

GERMAN CHRONICLE

in the

History of the Ohio Valley

and its

Capital City Cincinnati

in Particular

including an extensive Description of the Adventures, Settlements and the overall Effect of the Germans in the River Areas from the Discovery of the Mississippi Valley to the Present Days.

Collected from authentic sources by

Emil Klauprecht

Translated by Dale V. Lally, Jr.

and

Edited by Don Heinrich Tolzmann

Cincinnati, Ohio
Printed and Published by G. Hof and M. A. Jacobi
Publisher of the "Cincinnati Volksblatt"

FOREWORD

The Valley of the Ohio, blessed with the richest fruits of nature, offers in its history a rich treasure of romantic sagas and great historical memories.

Even though to the world it appears to be young and new, the diverse petrified tropical plants and oceanic organisms, the fossilized skeletons of gigantic animals, which lie beneath the earth of its hills and valleys, the man-made mounds, parapets and burial sites of a vanished and puzzling people, testify that nature, as well as human beings, have had at that place fabulous times[1].

The appearance of the Europeans in this new area re-inflamed the old battle between the Romanic and the Germanic people for its mastery. A myth of the Indians of Hispaniola about the discovery of a fountain of youth, which would make old people young again, led the Spaniards as the first explorers to the Mississippi Valley. The French followed them with dreams of a "New France," which encompassed almost the entire North American continent. But it was not to be the Romanic people-neither Spaniards nor French, but rather the *Germanic* people-Britons and Germans, for whom the invigorating atmosphere of the huge valley would become the fountain of youth, which de Soto had sought in vain. From that they have emerged as the young and impetuous nation, which, with magical swiftness, has transformed that huge wilderness between the Alleghenies and the Pacific Ocean into a chain of thriving states. The settlement of the Ohio Valley, that most blessed branch of the Mississippi region, and the founding and amazing growth of its capital city Cincinnati, whose trade and industry, no less than its natural beauty and charm, won for it the honored title of "Queen of the West", both crystalize this titanic activity. The history of both extends through all the great epochal periods from the rise of the far west out of its mythical epoch to its modern state and business life, with its enormous advances in population, culture, industry, and trade.

Has any segment of the earth ever advanced with stronger momentum? This transformation of a wilderness, inhabited by a

---

[1] About the demise of the giant animals, the Indians of Ohio had a symbolic myth, which resembles the battle between Jupiter and the Titans. They explained that the herds of mammoths were destroyed by the great father, Winnitou, in order to permit the rise of the red sons of the forest and give them rich hunting grounds. The battle between him and the giants was said to have been terrible. There was one he could not defeat. This last one was able to shake off the lightning bolts from his (Winnitou's) armored head. Finally he was wounded in the side and fled to the great lakes, where he remains to this day. About the vanished people, whose remains are the above noted edifices, the Indians have absolutely no tradition. Even the experts remain puzzled about that, since that ancient people was evidently composed partially of dwarfs and partially of giants. In 1830, below the county seat Coshockton in Ohio, an old burial ground was discovered, described by Dr. Hildreth in Silliman's Journal. The skeletons all lay in coffins, none of which were longer than 3 to 4 1/2 feet. A large number were opened and all of them contained pygmies, with the heads to the west and the feet to the east. Iron nails were found in one coffin. The graves, laid out in neat rows with a space for walking in between, occupying an area of 10 acres, suggest that a large city was nearby. At the time of discovery, midget oaks covered the site, at the foot of which stood a mighty mound. On the eastern side of Conneaut, the Plymouth of the "Western Reserve," a similar ancient burial site was found. However, the bones found there were of gigantic structure, with skulls large enough to easily contain the head of a normal man. In some of the colossal jawbones, false teeth were found. (Howe's Ohio Historical Collection, page 40.) This contrastive body structure points to a collective people which is older than our own history.

few Indians, into an area of millions and equipped with all the achievements of the century, is the result of 80 years of work? This time span joins a pioneer people, not only courageous and sacrificial, but also partially sharing the barbarism and superstition of the ancient Romanic and Germanic sagas with our effeminate, fashionable, money-making present time. Did these ancient founders of the state in the wilderness have a reason to complain about the ungratefulness of the republics? The truth is that Boone, Kenton, Clarke, St. Clair, Symmes, and others went to their grave, ignored, impoverished, and almost forgotten by their contemporaries. The wild conflict of pioneer life did not permit one to grieve over the fallen. But the Anglo-American descendants have not forgotten these honored dead. Their memory lives on in the names of counties, cities and lakes of the Ohio Valley. Their statues stand in the niches of the capitols. Their deeds are recorded in history books and made famous in poetry and paintings. Historical societies make an effort to immortalize the victories of each of their co-fighters in the dangers and traps of the wilderness. But how different are the German pioneers treated by their descendants. Today, who thinks about a Weiser or Post, those strong giants of the primeval forest, who had such a massive effect on securing the Ohio Valley for European immigration? And what about the pilgrim fathers Zeisberger, Heckewelder, Schmick, Sensemann and their cities, the Golgathas of German humanity and culture in Ohio? Who remembers that glorious August morning, when Johann Ettwein, in the shadows of the Muskingum oaks, after an Indian choir sang in German, proclaimed the first community rules in Ohio, which the historian Taylor calls the Constitution of 1772? Who recalls those lionhearted pathfinders of the wilderness such as Salling, Bilderbach, Jäger, Wetzel, Nieswanger, Funk, Hof, Knoop, and others, whose adventures weave a red thread through the history of the first settlements? Who remembers the likes of Bedinger, Ziegler, Schaumburg, Womeldorf, Vischer and other brave ones, whose swords protected the homes of the Ohio. The names of these pioneers disappeared with their lives. The great treasure of their combined activities lies scattered, buried in decayed old English historical works, magazines and newspapers.

In comparison, do our German forefathers lack the character and effectiveness of their English brethren? Certainly not. Among them one could not find men of more cordial spirit, tougher energy, and victorious efforts. Their language was heard in the blockhouses and villages of the river region even before English. Their educational efforts among the Indians puts the German pilgrim fathers of Ohio far above the intolerant zealots of Plymouth Rock. But is it any wonder that the old pioneer figures, shrouded in the fog of the previous century, remain unknown to today's generation, since most of us today are not even aware of a newer and closer field, the history of the development of German life in and around Cincinnati?! Numerous German churches of all denominations glitter in every section of the city. From their towers, Sunday bells ring far into the valley, calling festively dressed families in large numbers to worship. Which of these, crowded into pews during a colorful and imposing high mass, might even think about the modest, schoolhouse with wooden sidings on Arch Street, where the first German congregation gathered in harmony for prayer, regardless of denomination.

According to the latest monthly reports of the school board, at least 6364 children are currently learning German in the German-American public schools. How many remember the years of fighting against the narrow-mindedness and misunderstanding of that same body, which 22 years ago finally introduced a few hundred children to the "introductory German-English school"?! And today, on holidays, when glasses glowing with the fiery spirit of Catawba or Isabella are raised to German songs, who thinks to give praise to the old and honest vintners of Vevay, in whose roughly hewed cellars the first Ohio wine was poured. Everywhere beneath the soft hills of the Ohio valley, our pioneers, in the midst of deprivation and harassment, built splendid seats of German life. Thousands of our sons, now grown men, could join in A. Grün's "Greetings to the Ohio River":

> You have grasped the house from my fatherland and
> had like an angel in heavenly flight
> as once Loretto's favored house over the sea
> had from the Rhein borne it here.

For me it has become an affair of the heart to refresh the memory of those brave German forebearers in the minds of us, their descendants. The so-inclined reader should judge this "Chronicle" from this aspect and not from a desire for literary worth. On a patriotic note, the reader will agree with me that a people can expect respect from their neighbors and sacrificing friends and benefactors among them, only when they themselves honor the great deeds and merits of their forefathers and pass them on from generation to generation. In the following pages, I have considered every German whose effect on the community, whose individual ability, and strength or characteristic feature, have raised him above the ordinary events of history. Naturally, in order to maintain continuity, it was necessary to go back to the earliest period, in order to give new meaning to the general history of the country, which is already wellknown to various readers. The history of the Ohio valley includes the three epochs of French, English and American sovereignty. The latter is divided into three periods: the territorial, the beginnings of statehood, and the life as a state. The most valuable sources used for this "Chronicle" were the historical works and manuscripts of the pioneers themselves, the Zeisberger diaries, the stories of Heckewelder, Loskiel, Rundthaler and others, the collected traditions contained in the English (language) county histories of the Atlantic seaboard states, in newspapers and monthly publications of various periods, the written collections of the local historical society, and, above all, oral reports. Almost until the second period of the third historical epoch, the Indians remain the central focus of occurrences and interests. Therefore a clear grasp of their changing relationship to the original German settlers demands that we give them our first attention in the chain of events.

With the wish that it might become the measure of their constantly advancing spiritual development, of their successful nurturing of the sciences and arts, of their business energy and trade, as well as of their general well-being and happiness, this Chronicle is respectfully dedicated to his beloved countrymen by

the Author.

The French Sovreignty

Chapter 1

The wars of independence of the Ohio Indians with the Iroquois. - The Miami Confederation. - The Wyandots, Delawares and Shawnees. - Homan's Map of the Ohio Valley. - Meaning of the name "Ohio". - The Company of the West. - The Germans, the First Settlers in the Mississippi Valley. - New Orleans in 1722. - The First French Settlements on the Ohio. - The Bear Hunt at Fort Massac. - The Woodsmen. - Vincennes. - Ancient parapets and mounds on the site of today's Cincinnati.

On April 9, 1682, on one of the three estuaries of the Mississippi, there arose a column with the insignia of France and a wooden cross. A *Te Deum* was sung and salutes were fired by a group of wizened adventurers. In their midst stood the cavalier (Robert) de la Salle, in his hand a roll of parchment, the official declaration of his discovery. After both tokens of civil and spiritual authority had been erected, he formally took possession of the entire region of the Mississippi, including the huge area between the Alleghenies and the Rocky Mountains, in the name of the "elder son of the Church, Louis the XIV."

At the same time as this ceremony was going on, the triumphant native opponent of the French hegemony, namely the mighty Iroquois Confederation, which included the five tribes of the Mohawks, the Oneidas, Onondagas, the Cayugas and the Senecas, who resided mostly in New York and Pennsylvania, had conquered almost the entire Ohio valley with fire and sword and placed it under their control. Having grown overconfident due to 50 years of victories, the Confederation had attacked every western tribe, which did not belong to an alliance. One after the other, the Confederation partially destroyed or drove away those who would not recognise their authority, even though the victims were, on an individual basis, stronger than each of their five opponents. Thus the Wyandots, along with their allies the Ottawas, were driven to the headwaters of the Mississippi and towards the Sioux. The Eries (or Cats) who lived on the south shore of Lake Erie were attacked in their strong fortifications and almost totally wiped out. The Andastes, who had occupied the valleys of the upper Ohio, suffered a similar fate. Around the same time (1672) even the Shawnees were driven out of the forests of the Scioto and as far away as the Gulf of Mexico[1]. However, the military might of the Eastern alliance would finally be broken by a Western alliance, namely the Miami Confederation, whose tribes included the Piankeshaws, the Tawightees, the Piquans and others. Their territory stretched from the Big Miami to the south shore of Lake Michigan and to the Illinois river. The Miami's were a warrior people, very proud of their heritage. While the other Indian tribes - the Iroquois as well as

---

[1] On the south side of Kelly's Island in Sandusky Bay, one finds a notable memorial to the victorious period of the Iroquois Confederation. Deeply inscribed in a granite ledge (32 x 21 feet) are numerous figures of Indian warriors, groups smoking at a council fire, and a number of curious figures all in the normal pictographs of the natives. Schoolcraft writes about these: "It is not only the most extensive but also the best inscription of the pre-historic period of North America. Apparently the drawings are related to the inhabitation of the lake basin by the Eries, the arrival of the Wyandots, the ultimate triumph of the Iroquois, and the flight of the people, who left behind their name on the lake." *History of the Indian Tribes* by H.R. Schoolcraft, II, Pag. 86-8.

their opponents, who historically had all been grouped under the name of Algonquin, and, according to tradition, had immigrated from the West, the Miamis, true to their name[2], maintained that the Great Spirit had created them on their Ohio valley hunting grounds[3]. A large number of refugees from the Iroquois had sought refuge in Miami territory and in that manner increased the Miamis military might. In 1680, according to reports of French missionaries and quoted by Schoolcraft, the angry Iroquois attacked a camp of Miami and Illinois Indians on the Maumee river, killed 30 and took 300 prisoners. However, in a surprise move, the Miamis and their allies surrounded the enemy camp, ambushed their overconfident enemies, killed them in droves, and freed their captives.

That initial defeat of the Iroquois in the west marked the turn of their former fortune. In 1696, France exacted a bloody revenge for the martyr death of the Jesuit priests Jouges, Breboeuf and Lallemand, and even more so for the massacres of St. Ignatius and Montreal, where 1400 French perished under the tomahawks of the Mohawks. In that year, Governor Frontenac of Canada, with his entire provincial military force, invaded the territory of the Five Nations, and defeated them soundly, destroying their villages and fields. After repeated defeats, the cocky Iroquois had no choice but to make peace in the year 1700. Notable among the French officers for their bravery and victories in subduing a stubborn enemy, the provincial annals and those of New England mentioned Captain Hertel, his two sons, and a nephew, a family probably from the Alsace, who gave to the settlement of New France a sizeable contingent[4]. In 1726, after the French had erected a permanent military station on the most important pass of the Niagara, within the borders of ther confederation, the power of the Five Nations was broken completely and they sought the protection of Great Britain.

Shortly after the peace treaty of 1701, de la Motte Cadillac built the fortress Ponchartrain (named after the current Minister of the Navy) on the route from Lake Erie to Lake Huron, and thus laid the basis for Detroit. In that year Detroit had a population of one Jesuit priest along with 100 French mercenaries and farmers. It would become a city whose future, as it will be told here, would become intimately entwined with the history of the Ohio valley and even the German pioneers. The Wyandots (whom the French called Hurons) returned to the surrounding forests from their fifty years of exile. They had been the major and mightiest pillar of the Algonquin tribes in their long wars of freedom and independence from the Iroquois[5]. The extent of their prestige and influence was evident in the honor of the title of "Uncle" accorded them by the Delawares, the predecessors of the Algonquins. Not only were they wise in the councils and the bravest in battle, but were also more civilized than the other Ohio Indians in that they engaged in extensive farming and raised livestock. In 1639, small pox had devastated them to such an extent that a census taken by the Jesuit missionaries counted only 2000 families in 700 huts. The Jesuits had much earlier (Champlain in 1614 and Sigourd in 1624) established missions among them and won many more converts to the church than among any other tribe outside of the French settlements. Whether as a result of

---

[2] In the Ottawa language, *Miami* means: mother.

[3] During his trip along the Wabash, Volney mentioned to Little Turtle, their chief, that the Miamis were probably the offspring of the Tartars. The chief replied: "Why could it not be that the Tartars, who resemble us so much, did not originate in our land. Is there any proof against this?!"

[4] Perkin's *Annals of the West*, p. 77.

[5] Charlevoir, the historian of New France, states that in 1721 they were still the very soul of all councils of the western Indians.

the horrible destruction of the Eries and Andastes, or based upon some ancient title, the Wyandot's ownership of the entire region between Lake Erie and the Ohio river, from the Alleghenies to the Big Miami, was never contested by any of the Ohio tribes and only by the Five Nations[6].

On July 16, 1843, a horde of impoverished Indians - children, men, women, and the elderly, dressed like gypsies in the dirty, tattered clothes of the white man, camped on the landing at Cincinnati, surrounded by a crowd of sympathetic and charitable whites. Most of the Indians spoke English and Pennsylvania Dutch. It was the last remnant of the proud master tribe of Wyandots, the former owners of the state of Ohio. What few lands remaining to them after the wars with the Americans were sold to the government for a pittance. Accompanied by the Federal Commissioner, Colonel Johnson, they were shipped to their new lands in the far west.

What a hard fate! What a change of fortune a hundred years will bring! Great had been the prestige of the tribe, when the name of every Huron chief was highly honored by the French. A hundred years before, the Wyandots had sent out French messengers from Detroit with their powerful invitation to return to the tribute-laden waters of the Ohio. They offered asylum and the use of the fabled, rich hunting grounds in Kentucky not only to those tribes driven out by the Iroquois, but also to those related tribes being pressured by the British in the east. At the same time that the reverse migration was taking place, the heralds of the impending massive migration of whites, namely the canoes of English and German traders, were plowing the Ohio, and the bark of the rifles of daring pioneers was heard in the forests. First in 1740-50 came a large group of Delawares or Leni Lenape, whom the white settlers had driven from their homes on the waters of the Delaware and its tributaries within the state of present-day New Jersey and eastern Pennsylvania. As indicated above, they were forerunners of the Algonquins, and, with the exception of the Wyandots and the Five Nations, who bore the title of "uncle", they addressed all the other tribes as younger brothers, children, grandchildren, or relatives[7]. According to a tradition of the tribe, which Heckewelder reports in his "History of the Indian Nations," the Leni Lenape had originally lived in the far west of the American continent and had gradually migrated eastward to the Allegheny river, which had its name from a nation of giants, the Allegewis, who lived along its banks. Together, the Wyandots and the Iroquois (who had also come from the west) destroyed the Allegewi's in a murderous battle. They then settled on the Delaware, the Hudson, the Susquehanna and the Potomac. The Delaware river, in the midst of their hunting grounds, gave them their name. They then split into three branches: the Turtles, the Welch Cocks and the Wolves. The novelist Cooper immortalized them as his poetic favorites. For us they are more interesting than all the other tribes, since it was the Germans who came among them as the apostles of civilization. The Indians eagerly adopted the (German) language and religion as their own. After their return, they settled in the forests of the Muskingum, where they blossomed into a mighty and influential tribe whose hunting grounds soon extended to over half of present-day Ohio.

About the same time as the Delawares, in 1755, the Shawnees returned from their exile on the Savannah river, from whence they had their name. They chose the land on the Scioto upstream to Sandusky, and westwards to the Big Miami where they engaged in extensive cattle and horse farming. They bitterly defended their old hunting grounds in Kentucky against the intruding whites. During the next

---

[6] Taylor's *History of Ohio*, 1-4 p. 31.

[7] Parkman's *Conspiracy of Pontiac*, p. 26.

40 years of Ohio valley history, no other tribe showed their bloody hatred against the Americans so much as they. After their return, the Wyandots restricted their settlements to the land south of Detroit along Lake Erie, eastwards to Sandusky Bay. They carefully maintained their image as the owners of the land, in contrast to the Delawares, Shawnees, Ottawa and others who only appeared to be tenants, whose lease could be broken at any time.

In spite of their humiliation and defeat by the French, the animosity of the Iroquois towards the Ohio Indians did not end. For that reason, almost a century after the Jesuit priest Marquette discovered the Ohio (1673), the banks remained uninhabited. With the exception of a deserted Shawnee village at the mouth of the Scioto, and an Indian trading post 20 miles south of the Forks of the Ohio, which the English called Logtown, no wigwam, no clearing interrupted the belt of forests along the clear streams. The tribes living on the north side maintained a belt of land, 60 miles wide on each side of the river, exclusively as a hunting ground[8]. The reason for this deserted wilderness appears to be the continuing hostility of the Iroquois. Every year a squadron of countless canoes would descend the river bringing death and destruction upon its inhabitants, in order to maintain their usurping rights on the Ohio valley. The Senecas and the Cayugas appear to have been the guardians of the river. The latter even later had a station on the Ohio, below the spot where Steubenville now stands.

It was the maps of the copper engraver Johann Baptist Homann in Nürnberg that first made the Ohio valley known to the world. Homann was born in 1664 in the Swabian village of Kambach near Mendelheim. Somewhat ill-disposed towards the clerical vocation which his parents wanted for him, he fled the seminary for the city where Behaim was born, where he became a notary[9]. In his spare time he took up copper engraving and became the most renowned map engraver of the century. The Kaiser appointed him his geographer, and Peter the Great made him his scientific agent. Even though he had converted to Protestantism, he remained highly interested in the journeys of discovery of his former seminary colleagues, that group of devout missionaries who had renounced the worldly pleasures for the Indian areas of North America. He published the first map of the Flemish Franciscan, Father Louis Hennepin[10], who on August 7, 1679, together with La Salle and the Italian Tonti crossed Lake Erie in Griffin's bark. These relics show that the French adventurers were totally ignorant about the Ohio river area. On the west side of "Lake Erie or the Cat" there is a bend, one side of which extends down to almost 36 degrees latitude into the area of Nashville and thus encompasses one third of the present-day states of Ohio and Kentucky. One degree below the lake's southwest corner winds the "Sohio", (described on earlier French maps as a tributary of the Ouabache, Wabash) between the Appalachian hills, on the south side of which there is a lake, about as large as Lake Ontario, evidently the source of the Savannah river. It appears that the Ohio runs only 60 miles south of Lake Erie, and that West Virginia, Kentucky and Tennessee do not even exist. On the map of Father Charlevoir, the historian of New France, produced in 1722, the route of the "Oyo" and its distance from the northern lakes and the ocean is more accurate, even though the huge wildernesses of Ohio and Indiana are portrayed much better than (those) in Illinois. The territory of the French missionaries, including the main river between Canada and Louisiana, was much more traveled and well-known than the Ohio valley described in the Indian legends.

---

[8] *Transactions of the Historical Society of Ohio, Vol. II*, pag. 237. Hildreth's *Pioneer History*, p. 1.

[9] In 1491-92 Martin Behaim fashioned a globe in Nüremberg, which is still preserved there as one of the most interesting relics of cosmographic art prior to the Columbian discovery of 1492. He is representative of the great interest in the New World in the German-speaking countries. For a bibliography of the earliest works on America in German see Paul Baginsky, *German Works Relating to America, 1493-1800: A List Compiled from the Collections of the New York Public Library*, (New York: New York Public Library, 1942). DHT

[10]*Amplissimae Regiones Mississippi, seu Provinciae Ludovicianae a R. P. Hennepin. Fran. Miss. anno 1687 edita p. J. B. Homann, Geograph Noribergae. Regio. Mexic. Novae Hispaniae, Ludoviciannae N. Angliae, Caroliniae, Virginiae et Pennsylvaniae. J. B. Homan, 1712, u. A.*

The French called the Ohio the *La belle Riviere*, the beautiful river, the origin of which is disputed. Colonel John Johnson, for many years the Federal Commissioner among the Wyandots, maintained that the name originated in that tribe. The Wyandots supposedly called the Ohio the "Ohezu" which means "large and beautiful river". In contrast, both Heckewelder and Duponceau, who was versatile in the Indian languages, were of the opinion that it was originally the Delaware name "Ohiopeckhanne", which means "deep and white bubbling river." It was shortened by the French whose nasals must have sounded horrible in contrast to the beautiful Indian names.

Father Joseph Soucaire had accompanied the appropriately costumed chiefs of the returned Ohio Indians to the governor in Montreal, where they formally placed their tribes under the protection of France. A most lively exchange developed between the two. While the Puritan zealots of New England were using the hatred of the Old Testament to preach a crusade against the red heathens, the positive graycoats, the cheerful Franciscans, went along on their hunts and fishing expeditions, taught the squaws to cook tasty soups, played with the children and entertained them, as had Fathers Hennepin and Pierson, with ice skating. Later, in Ghent, Hennepin boasted that he had become quite adept at ice skating. The easy-going attitude of the French farmers and soldiers to get the most out of life with the least amount of work found a ready outlet in the pristine forest life, where about the only real work was lucrative fur hunting and the days of rest were filled with loving the Indian maidens and drinking the abundant brandy. While the Puritans destroyed the natives with fire and sword, the French not only totally adopted the Indians' customs, but united with them to create a new mixed race. Thus grew up the adept and gifted as well as courageous bastards of the North American wilderness, the French Indians, who, during the many feuds with the English, extracted horrible revenge for the mistreatment of their related tribes in the east. There is an explanation why, given such material, the French villages and stations did not thrive and increase. It was primarily the German immigration, unfortunately under miserable conditions, that would be the key to a thriving culture in the Mississippi valley.

John Law, the notorious Minister of Finance under the immoral and extravagant Count of Orleans, had acquired the territory as the basis of a gigantic project, that was supposed to save France from bankruptcy and lead to fabulous wealth. Due to the unique misadministration of finances under the Louis', French currency had sunk to about 60-70% of its former value. Law then opened his "Royal Bank" with capital of six million francs based on 12,000 shares of stock, each worth 500 francs. Only a fourth of the amount was backed up (with gold) while the rest was secured with devalued currency, which was declared to be of full value. In order to increase the bank's credit, the "Company of the West" was founded, which had a 25 year trade monopoly in the Mississippi valley, and also included the rich canadian beaver fur trade. Exaggerated descriptions of gold and silver wealth and of the fertility and heavenly beauty of the new western French empire were published simultaneously in France and Germany, in order to attract farmers and miners for the speculators. In the Palatinate, the sinister Karl Philipp, the last of the bigoted Neuburg line, had assumed power and harassed the Protestants with very stern measures. That unhappy region had, due to changes in ruling houses, changed religions four times and was now again being forced into Catholicism. Law's descriptions found here a fertile ground, similar to a proclamation years before from Queen Ann to the Scottish adventurers, promising free passage and citizenship[11]

---

[11] The basic history of the Palatine immigration can be found in Walter Allen Knittle, *Early Eighteenth Century Palatine Immigration*, (Baltimore, Maryland: Genealogical Pub. Co., 1976). DHT

in America after homesteading for 3 years. Of the more than 15,000 Palatines who were enticed to embark on the trip to America, barely half arrived. Along with the scum of the French cities, swindlers, whores and criminals[12], an additional 2000 Palatinate farmers were shipped to New Orleans, the newly founded capital of Law's El Dorado. After arriving, many of the unfortunates died of sickness and adversity in the marshes of the Mississippi estuary, since absolutely no preparations had been made for their arrival. Those who survived settled in St. Bernhard Parish, where, with a bit of luck, they were able to engage in raising tobacco, indigo, rice and silk. The "Sea Allemand" or the "German Coast" as well as a large number of German speaking descendants reminds us today of these founders of the first thriving agriculture in the Mississippi valley. At the same time in St. Charles parish, a Mr. von Aaronburg led a company of Wuertemburgers and Alsassers, whose settlements took root and lasted a long time. In a missionary report of November 17,1750, Father Vivier wrote that "these German colonies were, at the time, the most significant in the entire river region." Meanwhile, based on its continued favor with the government, the Company of the West furthered its criminal activities in gigantic dimensions. In addition to its earlier extensive privileges, the government had also granted the company a tobacco monopoly, trade rights in Asia, coinage, taxation, and others. Given this greenhouse system, the stocks had risen by 2000%. The money in circulation increased to over 1 billion francs, and this excess of paper money caused a fantastic increase in the price of staples. The whole facade finally disappeared, when people began demanding cash money rather than notes. The finance minister frantically attempted to prevent his house of cards from falling. It was forbidden to maintain more than 500 francs in cash in the cash register. Anything over that was to be turned into notes. Later another useless regulation ordered all debts of over 100 francs, and later of over 10 francs, to be paid with notes. There was even a hollow threat to confiscate notes and cash if someone tried to change a note into cash. The notes continued to sink to a final value of 2 cents per franc. The bank eventually collapsed and many went into poverty. In order to escape the wrath of the people, Law fled from France with the remainder of his huge fortune[13].

Given the administration of such a swindlous company, it is no wonder that the natural support for trade and farming did not materialize in the new area. In regards to the highly praised capital city of New Orleans, laid out with much pomp in 1718, Father Charlevoir wrote upon his arrival in 1722: "The 800 beautiful buildings and five parish churches, which the journals described in some detail two years ago, have shrunk to about 100 randomly constructed shacks, one wooden magazine, and 2 or 3 houses which would do little justice to a French village. The church is constructed from the remains of an old warehouse, so unsafe that the priest must soon move out of it and into his tent, which would better pass for a church. Just imagine 200 persons sent out to build a city, camped on the bank of a river, barely protected against the rigors of the weather, and you will have an accurate picture of New Orleans. There is no lack of grandiose, well ordered construction plans. However, carrying them out is much more difficult than their conception." Further astute predictions of the devout historian about the increase of the city were not borne out by 1750. In that year, his missionary brother Vivier counted a population of only 1200 persons, including women, children, and negroes.

---

[12] Father Poisson in the *Lettres edifiantes*. Paris 1781, p. 393.

[13] For further information on the German Coast of New Orleans see John F. Nau, *The German People of New Orleans*, (Leiden, The Netherlands: Brill, 1958). Note that in this chapter Klauprecht is appropriately connecting the settlement of the Ohio Valley to the earlier settlement of the Mississippi Valley, and that he has traced the German involvement in this area, beginning early on with Behaim and others. DHT

The initial French attempt to settle and fortify the Ohio was not crowned with great success. A terrible fever wiped out the first settlement at the mouth of the river and an even more gruesome end awaited the occupants of the fort[14], built on the north side of the river 40 miles away. One day the lookouts spotted a herd of bear on the opposite bank. Fired by a hunting fever, a group climbed into canoes and crossed to the other side. At the same time, those left behind gathered on the river bank to watch the hunt. What the unfortunates thought were bear were actually Cherokees, clothed in bear skins crawling about on all fours to lure the soldiers out to the hunt. The trick worked. The group had barely landed when the Indians attacked and wiped them out to a man. At the same time, another group seized the empty fort and killed the helpless onlookers on the shore[15].

As pioneers of the French on the Ohio, the so-called "Runners of the Woods" or *Coureurs des Bois* arrived. They were half-breeds, wild and hardened by their Indian lifestyle, talented bootsmen, fishermen, and expert shots, whose bullets never missed "the buffaloe's right eye." They gathered the loads for the fur traders. They knew every rock, island, harbor and stream in the western waters. Using leather straps fastened to their forehead or shoulders they carried the freight from the boats around the "portages", the swamps and unnavigable areas of the river. Any mosaic of the people of "New France on the Ohio" must include these persons. Next would come the Canadian fur trader in a leather cap, a loose brightly striped smock or flannel skirt, (molton) deerskin trousers, seamed with fringes and bright red sash, into which was sticking a wide hunting knife. Then there was the French farmer in a red cap, a long outer skirt and deerskin leggings and moccasins. Then there was the government official in a fancy-striped costume in the style of Louis XIV, with a dagger and full bottomed wig. Around them would group the remainder of the society, pipe-smoking soldiers in tri-cornered hats, long pigtails, blue and white-open uniforms and short trousers; the missionary in his long, black or gray habit, and, to complete the contrast, the post Indians in the wild garb of the tribes, with eagle feathers in their hair, necklaces and bear claws, moccasins decorated with porcupine quills and a coat of colorful blanket or a bearskin. The clergy had the greatest influence in this society. Very often a lonely altar with wooden cross and heavy, rough candle holders made of Michigan copper would be constructed in a forest chapel covered with tree bark. Indian boys would swing the incense burners and the hymns of the Roman Catholic church would come from the mouths of the colorful congregation, mixed with the wail of panthers and wolves[16].

Vincennes in present-day Indiana was the first post from whence the French traveled the Ohio. Its founder, the young and brave Captain de Vincennes arrived there in 1734 with soldiers, fur hunters and cattle herders. A few feel that he was the first one to follow the Maumee into the Wabash and then into the Ohio rather than take the long detour of the Mississippi. In 1663, Father Hennepin had already heard of the Ohio as the shortest route from the lakes to the Mississippi. La Salle also mentioned this in the journal which he sent to Count Frontenac. It certainly appears that the French had a much greater knowledge of the states of Ohio and Indiana than the remaining reports of missionaries would indicate. In the first state, trees with ax marks have been found, whose rings point to 1660[17]. In Lorain county, near the Lamb farm, a moss-covered, four-sided stone pillar was found, on three sides of which was inscribed the date 1533 and the name Louis Vagard. L. France. At the

---

[14] Today still called Fort Massac after the massacre.

[15] *History of Illinois* by Henry Brown, p. 170. Hall's *Sketches of the West*, V. I, p. 181.

[16] Lanman's *History of New France*.

[17] Whittlesey's Disc. before the Historical Society of Ohio p. 8.

point of the pillar there was also a relatively well-inscribed rendering of a sailing ship[18].

Even before 1725, "New France" was divided into Departments, each with its own local Governor or Commander and Judge. They all, however, were subject to the authority of the general council of Louisiana. One of these Departments included northwest Ohio and its capital was Detroit. After the French, with their forts on French Creek off the Allegheny and Fort Duquesne at the forks of the Ohio, had secured the connection between Lake Erie and the Mississippi, the area of our immediate interest, central Ohio, witnessed the traffic between the French stations. In the forests, the marching of troops and the songs of the traders echoed against the splashes of the Indian servants, who were traveling in barks and canoes. In the early museums of Letton and Dorfeuille, in the early twenties, there was a collection of bizarre buttons from the Rococo period, tailoring tools and old-style dishes and other materials, which had been found on the present-day landings in Ohio, and, according to tradition, came from a French bark that had been stranded here. An old Indian warpath crossed a military road from the Ohio to Detroit. This later became the route on which the Indians from the north first harassed the first English stations in Kentucky.

Even in those days, the broad area on which Cincinnati now stands was the object of much mythology. As a silent witness to an ancient battle, two circular ramparts of 600 feet circumference stretched between the current intersections of Race and Vine streets, Sycamore and Broadway, and the 4th and 5th Streets. Where today Pike's opera house stands, began a long lateral trench which was connected to a 35 to 40 foot artificial mound on the northwest corner of Main and 3rd Street. The mound was cut open during the construction of Main street. Inside were found shells, uniquely shaped tools and earthenware, a male skeleton in a stone coffin, and an ivory statue of the Virgin Mary with Child[19], probably the treasures of a Christian Indian family, hidden in the face of an expected attack by some marauding enemy. There were additional and similar mounds in the area. One on the corner of Mound and 5th Street and two smaller ones at the head of Central Avenue, where only bones were found. Birch and oak trees all of similar size growing out of the crests of these earthen walls testified as to the age of this massive vestige of a people who had vanished long before the Indian period.

---

[18] Jacob Cartier, the first French explorer of Canada, traveled the St. Lawrence for the first time in 1540, and it is difficult to believe that this Vangard might have been a member of Verrazano's expedition, sent by Franz I to North America in 1524. The first English colony, Jamestown was founded in 1606.

[19] *Transactions of the Historical Society of Ohio, Vol. II*, p. 36.

Chapter 2

The first English on the Ohio. - Captain Batte. - The Knights of the Golden Horseshoe. - Germanna. - The Plans of Spotswood and Keith to use the Germans to force out the French. - German Regiments. - The Chickasaws. - Fiery death of Captain de Vincennes. - Johann Salling's Adventures. - The French Hunt the English Traders. - Conrad Weiser. - The Treaty and Drinking Bout at Lancaster.

The barriers erected against Americans by the French expansion in the west were naturally viewed with hostility both by the provincial governments and the population. England claimed this segment of the North American continent based on the discoveries of the two Cabots. Its kings had granted to several colonies, such as Connecticut[1], Massachusetts, Virginia, et al., all the land between the degrees of latitude which fell within their borders between the Atlantic and Pacific Oceans. And, based on a treaty arranged by the Governor of New York in 1684, the government assumed guardianship over the Five Nations, and, through their ownership, claimed control over the Ohio valley. In addition, it was well known that all of the chiefs of the Iroquois federation had, after their humiliation at the hands of the French in 1726, in their own names and in the names of all their descendants formerly placed all of their lands under the protection of England. In contrast to the motherland and the other provinces, and based on its royal charter, an ambitious Virginia would not merely be a hostile spectator, but rather early on tried to compete with the French in swindling the Indians from their lands. Already in 1667, Governor William Beverly had sent out an expedition commanded by Captain Batte and accompanied by Indian scouts to explore the west. According to Beverly's report, the explorers reached an initial mountain chain (the Blue Ridge) which was easily crossed. However, crossing the second chain (the Alleghenies), whose peaks reached into the clouds, was full of hardship and danger. However, they finally got across and traversed magnificent valleys with game-filled forests towards the west, until they reached a river which hindered their progress, whose waters, in their own words, "ran backwards", i.e., in a direction away from the Atlantic. Without a doubt, Captain Batte was standing on the shore of the Ohio, and thus saw the river several years before Father Marquette. Upon hearing his report, Beverly himself desired to embark upon a second and more ambitious expedition; however, the revolt against his authority led by the lawyer Nathaniel Bacon delayed its departure. The huge immigration of Palatines and Swabians during the years 1709-10, a result of the famous proclamation by Queen Anne, convinced the subsequent governor of Virginia, Spotswood, to reinstate the plan for royal colonial grants. Spottswood was an innovative aristocrat, who obviously had a few bizarre ideas, but nevertheless a man of restless energy and activity. It did not escape his shrewd eye, that the German immigrants, so badly treated in the coastal cities, would provide excellent material for an expansion of Virginia sovereignty towards the Ohio. After sending scouts to explore the passes of the Blue Ridge, he himself, with a large retinue and ceremonial pomp, undertook an expeditionary trip through the west-

---

[1] Connecticut's so-called "Western Reserve" in northeast Ohio resembles an older charter of Charles II from the year 1662. It stretches 120 miles from east to west and an average of 50 from north to south. Only after an extended dispute with the U.S. did Connecticut relinquish its jurisdiction over this area, but not its right of ownership.

ern regions of the Alleghenies. Upon his return he founded the "Order of Tramontines." Everyone who had participated in the expedition received a golden horseshoe as a medal and remembrance for successfully finding several trails for packhorses. In order to initially concentrate the Germans in one outpost, he founded the city of Germanna on the Rapidan, in Spotsylvania county, which was named after him, and which the Germans soon understood as all of Virginia[2]. Hugh Jones, who visited the city, wrote in his "Present Condition of Virginia" published in 1724: "Governor Spotswood has here established extensive iron works, which employs many of the Germans sent here by Queen Anne. There are craftsmen of every sort among them. Right next to the city is a colony of Palatines, on good land, who are happy, thriving and hospitable. They cultivate wine from domestic, French, Spanish and German vines. In the midst of this German settlement the governor has erected an imposing palace." Even Colonel Byrd, who visited Germanna in 1732, was full of praise for the Germans, the governor, and his charming wife. He writes: "The famous city Germanna compliments the no less famous palace of the governor, whose energy and actions have earned for him the name "Tubal Cain of Virginia." One interesting aspect of this palace is an elegant hall, whose walls are covered with enormous mirrors. There I was introduced to Mrs. Spotswood. The lady raises several pet animals, including a cute deer, which she was feeding as I entered. The intruder's movements startled the animal and, to my horror, it jumped into one of the expensive mirrors. The highly educated lady eased my shock with polite conversation[3]." Germanna is still there on the east side of the Blue Ridge. Soon the westbound German pilgrims had crossed this branch of the Alleghenies. They then spread out over the glorious and fruitful Shenandoah valley on both sides of the Peaked mountains, until they had filled almost all of the glorious flat lands between the east and west Alleghenies up to a diameter of 60 miles. Winchester, the oldest city in the valley, was the outpost of the English until they drove the French out of the Ohio valley. An almost entirely German population[4] stretched that far, and even further to the south branch of the Potomac. In 1734, the Germans had four Lutheran congregations - Winchester, Woodstock, Strassburg and Staunton.

As with Spotswood in Virginia, so too did Governor Keith of Pennsylvania have a plan to use the Germans, flooding into his state every year in increasing numbers, to seize the Ohio valley and there establish an independent state[5]. But, unlike Spotswood, who wanted an army of farmers, Keith wanted to send a militarily equipped force, under officers speaking their own language, who would drive out the French, using force if necessary. Logan, the provincial secretary, who was at the same time the agent for the Pennsylvania homesteads, supported the plan, and he seems to have had some sympathy for the Germans, since they were no longer seeking to buy land from him. At least he wrote in 1729: "Seldom do the Germans come to me to buy land. At their own discretion, they choose some wild stretch of land, build their homes and begin clearing the land. At any attempt to legitimize ownership based on the royal grant, one is just laughed at, and one hears the reply that a European King had also promised them free land. They have come to take the land, not with pockets full of money, but rather to build and defend it with strong arms. Many are former soldiers. These masses could soon establish a German nation, possibly similar to that founded by the Saxons in Old England[6].

The English government took a long time to consider Keith's plan, but rejected it, since they did not want, just then, to use blatant force against the French.

---

[2] For the background of Germanna see John Wayland, *Germanna: Outpost of Adventure, 1714-1956*, Harrisonburg, Virginia: Memorial Foundation of the Germanna Colonies, 1956. DHT

[3] *Progress to the Mines of Virginia* by J. Byrd 1732.

[4] Howe's History Coll. of Virginia p. 451.

[5] Rupp's *History of Berks & Lebanon* pp. 91, 92.

[6] Rupp's *History of Berks & Lebanon* pp. 91, 92.

Parliament later adopted it with an intolerant amendment. The law in question mandated the formation of a German regiment to be called the "Royal Americans" consisting of four battalions of 1000 men each. The junior officers were to speak German. Furthermore, the Germans, or foreigners in general, could aspire to the senior officer and engineer positions, if they were Protestants[7].

Since intensive diplomatic negotiations with the French were unsuccessful, Great Britain then tried murderous intrigue. At Great Britain's instigation, British agents in the Chickasaw area of the lower Mississippi, drove the Natchez Indians to a mass slaughter of their French competitors. On November 28, 1729, the Indians raised their tomahawks, forced their way into the colony of Natchez, and murdered all of the settlers with the exception of two workers. Even though the French and their allies, the Chocktaws, were able to avenge the bloodbath in a horrible manner by defeating a large part of the Chickasaws several months later, and selling those remaining, with their chief, "Great Sun," into slavery in Santo Domingo, the French could still not deny that, over a period of years, the Chickasaws were able to seriously obstruct navigation and make it difficult on the Mississippi. The patience of the French government finally came to an end, and they decided to end the problem with one blow. The order went out from Detroit down to New Orleans to all those in New France able to bear arms, to assemble on May 10, 1736, at a specified location in the land of the Chickasaws, in order to wipe out England's red servants.

The sound of drums and the clatter of weapons now resounded through the emptiness of the Ohio valley. The contingent from the Northwest Department, in a group of barks and canoes led by Captain de Vincennes, came down the Wabash and continued on down river to the mouth of the Ohio where they joined the troops of Governor d'Artiguette of Illinois. The assembled force, consisting of 1000 French and Indians, arrived at the enemy stations on the day as planned. The brave d'Artiguette waited in vain for 10 days for the reinforcements from New Orleans. Since his Indians were beginning to lose patience, he ordered the attack. The Chickasaws were attacked and driven out of three stations, but at the fourth the brave d'Artiguette was seriously wounded by a bullet while leading his troops. When the redskins saw their leader fall, panic seized them. They turned and fled leaving de Vincennes and the Jesuit Senat, who were attending to their wounded leader, to fall into the hands of their gruesome enemies. Five days later, de Bienville, the Governor of New Orleans, arrived with his troops, paddling slowly up the Tombechbee. But the Chickasaws were well prepared and, with the help of their English traders, were so well entrenched that all the French attacks were unsuccessful. Now despairing of any success, de Bienville threw his cannon into the river and again turned south. As the depressed French left, they saw the flames from the fire stakes rise above their honored countrymen, Captain de Vincennes and the Jesuit Senat, and they could hear the horrible victory cries of their conquerors dancing around them. The brave d'Artiguette was forced to witness the martyr's death of his companions and, after he had recuperated, was sent back to tell of the deeds of the Chickasaws.

Three years later, a thousand-man French army, a mixed force of whites, Indians, blacks, and half-breeds was encamped at Fort Assumption. It had been dispatched in order to take revenge for the terrible deed of the Chickasaws. However, it waited so long (from the Summer of 1739 to the Spring of 1740) that a fever depleted it ranks, and thus provided a desire for a peace treaty

---

[7] Gordon's *History of Pennsylvania, Vol. I*, p. 326.

with the gruesome enemy. It would be several years later, following a similar act of barbarism carried out against the English, before the fiery death of the French martyrs would be revenged.

Long before that period (1740) German and English traders on packhorses had crisscrossed the Ohio territory trading whiskey, yard goods, powder, toys, and similar items for the Indian pelts. The names of these daring souls are almost all forgotten. Tradition has it that Johann Salling was the first adventurer to travel the entire length of the Ohio. The adventures of that man are too remarkable to ignore. Salling lived in Williamsburg, the capital of Virginia, where he lived the peaceful life of a weaver. One day, a certain trader by the name of Mehrlin entered his shop to buy something. The man sold household goods between the capital city and the German valleys on the Shenandoah. He painted for Salling such a tempting picture of the beauties of the Indian territories, that Salling decided to leave his weaving for a time and accompany the trader on his trading and expeditionary travels to the southwest. While wandering through the unknown wilderness, the two were attacked by Cherokees. The experienced Mehrlin escaped while Salling was captured and led off to the tribal village on the upper Tennessee where he was naturalized as an Indian. After living there three years as a genuine son of the forest, painted, feathered, with rings through his nose and ears, the Cherokees took him along on a buffalo hunt to Salt Lick, Kentucky. There they encountered a group of Illinois Indians and a fight ensued, in which our adventurous weaver again had the misfortune to fall into the hands of the enemy. The Indians took him to Kaskaskia, where he won the favor of an old Indian squaw, who adopted him as her son. Cut off from all contact with Germans or English, he accompanied his new companions to far territories on numerous hunting trips that went even as far as the Gulf of Mexico. After spending two years with the Illinois tribe, one day his gentle Indian mother sold him to a Spanish caravan traveling north which needed a translator. Thus he arrived in Canada where the governor saw to his welfare. He won for him his freedom and sent him to New York, from whence he returned to Williamsburg, where he amazed his friends and neighbors with the amazing stories of his 6-year journey[8].

Like Virginia, so too did Pennsylvania consider the Ohio valley as territory included in its charter. With the occasional distribution of bribes, Pennsylvania sought to maintain a good relationship with the Indians on the Ohio and with the Miamis. The state was reimbursed for its expenses by the traders, who were required to obtain permission from the governor to trade with the Indians. Just before the outbreak of hostilities with the Chickasaws against the French, the governor suddenly recalled all the traders back from the valley, proof that he was aware of the deadly English policy, which would be played out on the lower Mississippi. The events proved that action was proper. The Ohio valley chronicle points out that the French began a deliberate hunt for all traders from the English colonies. In 1752 they captured our own Johann Salling, whose familiarity with the far west would not let him stay within the confines of his weaving establishment. With a certain John Howard he was traveling down the Ohio in a canoe made of buffalo hide. Accompanied by 400 Shawnees, Peter Chartier[9], an influential translator and French trader, attacked the boats of 2 respected Pennsylvania

---

[8] *Coll. History of Virginia*, p. 452. Butler's *History of Kentucky* 2nd edition, Int. 20.

[9] His name remains on one of the tributaries of the Ohio.

merchants, Peter Tiete and Jacob Dimmew, seized them and their entire possessions, and threatened both with death should they ever again travel the river[10].

The restlessness increased even further due to these and similar acts of violence in the frontier areas, in turn caused by the war between England and France, and further caused by the alliances of the Bourbon family. The inhabitants of the frontier areas were relieved to hear of the capture of Cape Breton and the city of Louisburg by colonial troops under Colonel Pepperell. In the same year (1744), and based on the negotiations of Conrad Weiser, the English crown signed a treaty with the Five Nations in Lancaster, PA., which, in addition to guardianship of the western lands, also guaranteed to England unconditional ownership of the territories of the Five Nations. Conrad Weiser was born in Herrenberg in the Black Forest and arrived in New York in June 1710 with his father, Johann Conrad, and seven siblings aboard one of the ten ships, which transported the 5,000 immigrants under the proclamation of Queen Anne. His father was one of the delegates and leaders of those poor people who, after they had founded villages and thriving settlements on the Hudson and Schoharie, were cheated out of all the fruit of their work by greedy and lying landlords. The young Conrad was an honest and adventurous youth. Captain Quagnant, a friend of his father's, had, with his father's permission, once taken him along to the Mohawk villages, where, during his long stay, he won many friends through his sincere and honest behavior and also gained extensive knowledge of the language of the Five Nations, a knowledge which would be of immense value to him later as Indian agent for the governments of Pennsylvania and Virginia. Weiser was one of the first whites who explored the unknown region on the far side of the Alleghenies and, by arranging treaties with the Indians, opened up the territory to European immigration. He later settled in Wommelsdorf in Pennsylvania and earned fame and awards as Justice of the Peace, provincial translator, and later as a colonel in the French war[11]. The Indians called him their "good father," who, during dealings with the authorities looked after their interests and faithfully translated the words of the whites.[12]

In spite of Weiser's honest intentions with his Indian friends, he nevertheless could not prevent the government from cheating them, and the notorious treaty of Lancaster, extremely important in the history of the Ohio valley, is proof of that. In 1744 Lancaster was a village with 300 houses and numerous German taverns, even though a large segment of the neighboring farmers consisted of Mennonites and Dunkers. At that meeting, Pennsylvania, Maryland, and Virginia were represented by business agents. Witham Marshe, secretary for Maryland, left behind a description of the events, which clearly show how, during that time, one played upon the weakness of the Indians in order to cheat them out of their lands.

"The business representatives of Maryland," writes Marshe, "arrived in Lancaster on June 21, ahead of the governor of Pennsylvania, the Virginia representatives, and the Indians. That evening, everyone else arrived with the exception of the Indians. The next forenoon was cloudy, and everyone was genuinely overjoyed when dinner was served in the courthouse, hosted by the Virginians for their friends. Very few let themselves be bothered by the arrival of the 252 Indian warriors mounted on horseback, who arrived with their women, children, weapons, bows and arrows and tomahawks, marched by the courthouse, and in one loud voice invited the whites to renew their earlier treaties with them. The Indians were offered camping places outside of the city limits. There they erected their wigwams and paraded with their friend, Conrad Weiser, while the Virginians drank to the

---

[10] Historical Notes of Pennsylvania in Hazard's Register.

[11] One of his daughters married the venerable preacher Muehlenberg, father of the famous general; and his sons, Philipp and Friedrich, won fame for their bravery in the French and Revolutionary wars.

[12] The fascinating biography of Weiser can be found in Paul A.W. Wallace, *Conrad Weiser, 1696-1760: Friend of Colonist and Mohawk*, (Philadelphia: University of Pennsylvania, 1945). DHT

health of the nobility and ended their party. They then went outside to have a closer look at the dark-skinned allies. Few wore shirts and whatever shirts there were, were dirty and torn. The well-educated and prosperous colonists, had to bite themselves severely in the lip in order to avoid laughing. That afternoon the chiefs and the business representatives met in the courthouse, shook hands, smoked a pipe together and drank "a good quantity of wine and punch." The next day--Saturday--the English retreated to the Dunker cloister, while the Indians drank, danced and yelled. On Monday, to everyone's satisfaction, the talks began and ended with a merry dance with music and a big party. On Tuesday the talks were interspersed with dances, whereby a few very repulsive women appeared who danced even wilder than all the Indians. On that day the trade goods were opened, with which the Maryland people wanted to buy the Indians' claim to the land on which they (the whites) had already settled. Somewhat dubious, the red men examined the goods, in place of which they took 220 pounds of Pennsylvania money and then drank a lot of punch. On Friday, the Five Nations approved the sale of land to the Marylanders, and again a quantity of punch was drunk. On Saturday they gave a feast for the chiefs, who ate well, drank, and became drunk even before they were through eating. Then, after drinking even more, they assembled the Indians in order to sign the bill of sale which had already been prepared and at which time the English had even more to drink. Now well-fortified with a generous quantity of wine and spirits, the Virginians held their conference with the Indians and produced a bill of sale in which the Indians gave up their claim to a large tract of land in that colony. They had convinced the Indians, "to recognize the right of the King to all the land which lay in the colony of Virginia or according to the order of his Majesty should be therein, for that the Indians received 200 pounds in gold and an equivalent amount in goods with the promise, that they would receive more when the settlements increased."

The agents for Virginia were Colonels Thomas Lee and William Beverly. This bill of sale, gained from the Indians while they were drunk on rum, constitutes, in connection with the above noted approval of the Five Nations, the basis of the English claim to the west. Eventually the English crown was able to include the entire Ohio valley within the province of Virginia.

"On July 5," so ended Marshe's description, "all the business with the Indians had been properly completed and the agents were glad to leave the dirty city of Lancaster, where they had suffered mightily from insects and bad drinking water."

One notes that Marshe was an ironic rogue. One can only wonder about his description of the extra thirst for water by the English. However, Marshe forgot to describe one event which deserves mention here, which disproves the contention that all the Indians were so drunk during the transactions that, in regards to the hostile border situation with the French, they were not able to give some good advice to the English colonists, who were horribly jealous of one another.

During the conference on July 4th, the eloquent chief Cannastego arose and said: "We have something else to tell you, and that is: we recommend to you harmony and unity. Our wise forefathers founded an alliance based on friendship among the Five Nations; which made us feared and gained for us respect and influence with the neighboring nations. We now have a mighty federation, and should you follow the example of our wise forefathers, then you will also achieve strength and power. Whatever you do, do not break up." Thus the hated redskin gave the arrogant whites some advice which, when completed 30 years later, would give immortality to those who heeded it and to their people a greatness and power among the nations of the earth.

Chapter 3

The Ohio Company. - Lorenz Washington seeks German settlers for their lands. - French trade. - French and English legal titles to the river area. - Celeron de Bienville formally takes possession of it (the river area) for France. - Pickawillany and its Destruction. - Christopher Gist. - Fortifying the Ohio. - St. Pierre and George Washington.

During subsequent years, when the settlements on the ceded lands were increasing, the Indians began to complain because the grant holders withheld the supplemental payments promised in the original agreements. In order to appease them, the Virginia patricians sent the good friend of the red men, Conrad Weiser, with presents. Weiser was commissioned to research the attitude of the Indians towards the establishment of a trading post in the Ohio valley. The trade for pelts and skins in the Indian territories was already producing extraordinary profits. The forests were teeming with marten, fish and swamp otters, beaver, civet cats, mink, catamounts, bear, and deer. Just how numerous the latter were is reflected in the name of the Scioto, which in the Shawnee language meant "Hair River". When, in the Spring, the countless herds of deer quenched their thirst in the river, they left such masses of fur that the river became full of it. Even though the French sought to maintain their pelt trade monopoly by force of arms, due to the great vastness of the country, they were unable to control a number of competitors, illegal traders of all nations and colors, supported by the Iroquois, who crisscrossed the Indian lands from Canada to Ohio with their packhorses making a fortune with these treasures of the wilderness. The plan of the Virginia speculators was as follows: to use the monopoly of a large trading company to drive out these small traders, and then import items directly from Europe in return for which they would get the pelts and skins from the west. After his return, Weiser's report on the attitude of the Indians favored the plan, and measures were taken to implement it immediately. A group of Virginia merchants and planters formed a company under the name of "The Ohio Company", led by Colonel Thomas Lee, well-known because of the Lancaster Treaty, Lorenz Washington, George Washington's grandfather, and others, who petitioned the English crown for a land charter in the west to start this trading post. The King granted that request, in which he ordered the government of Virginia to assign to the supplicants a half million acres of provincial land on the other side of the mountains. The company was granted the pelt trade monopoly and freed of taxes for ten years under the condition that 100 families would settle within 7 years and a fort would be constructed to protect the settlement. At the same time, several other western settlement companies were formed in Virginia and Pennsylvania and the first steps were taken to carry out the plan.

All of these companies directed their full attention to the recruitment of German colonists. The Ohio Company in particular sought to fulfill the conditions of its contract by settling one hundred German families. However, the situation whereby Virginia imposed a church tax on the German communities to benefit the English bishopric clergy, created a terrible obstacle.[1] There exists today a letter on this topic from Lorenz Washington, who became President of the Ohio Company after Lee's death, to the company's London agent, Handbury. In it he complains that all of his efforts to attract German farmers

---

[1] With regard to the church tax see Klaus Wust, *The Virginia Germans*, (Charlottesville: University of Virginia Pr., 1969). DHT

to the Ohio lands were totally without success. The Germans did not want to pay for English clergy, whose sermons they neither understood nor desired. Such religious oppression was a grotesque measure. "Freedom of religion," wrote the elderly planter, "has been brought to full fruition by England, Holland, Prussia, and our neighboring state Pennsylvania. Our administration has shown its true patriotism by encouraging an expansion of our dominions in America; should this petition be granted, there is no doubt that that which was begun would be completed if the inhabitants of the Ohio and its tributaries could be exempted from those clergy taxes. I have received assurances from Germany that sufficient settlers would come should higher authorities grant this tax exemption. I have promised to work to this end, and request you to do your utmost in this matter. This colony was settled mostly during the late period of Charles the First, during the usurpation, by zealous missionaries; and that spirit, which was then brought in, has continued ever since, so that, except for a few Quakers, we have no dissenters among us. But what has been the consequence? We have increased by slow degrees, except for negroes and convicts, whilst our neighboring colonies, whose natural advantages are greatly inferior to ours, have become populous. P.S. I have recently received reports from several Germans in Pennsylvania that they would take 50,000 acres of the Ohio land and settle them with 200 families, if there were no clergy taxes[2]."

In connection with the affair, Washington also appealed to governor Dinwiddie, who was in England at the time, and received the reply: "It gave me pleasure that the Germans wanted fifty thousand acres of the land granted to the Ohio Company, and I approve completely that you write about appointing their own clergymen, and your endeavor to have the people freed from paying the Church of England. But at present the Parliament and the Ministry are so busy with public affairs that we must wait some time before we can reply. But be assured of my utmost endeavors therein[3]."

In spite of these urgent requests, the oppressive church tax was still not repealed. However the German congregations received the assurance that 600 pounds would be repaid to their own churches.

The French were not unaware of the danger that these projects represented to their holdings and commerce. They knew that the construction of the first English post on the Ohio would result in a conflict with their southern stations. Already in 1744, Governor Vaudreuil of Louisiana had described to his government the dangers which would arise to the colony through the construction of an English trading post among the Creeks. As a result, he feared the loss of Fort Prudhomme on the Mississippi below the Ohio and the resultant interruption of important traffic with the settlements in Illinois and Canada. Lucrative commerce had already developed between New Orleans and these French settlements. Every December, convoys brought to the market in New Orleans flour, corn, pork and bear hams, pickled meat, myrtlewax, cotton, tallow, leather, tobacco, lead, iron, copper, buffalo hides, wildpret, fowl, bear grease, oil, skins, and rough pelts. In 1746 they had delivered 2000 barrels of flour. And the Jesuits had been so successful in producing wine in the hills of the Mississippi and Wabash that the French government, fearing a decline in the export of French wine to the colony and, based on the general notion of the time that the colonies were only there to be exploited by the motherland, ordered the colonial authorities to destroy the grape vines. In exchange for the colonial products, the convoys brought European consumer articles to the settle-

---

[2] *Washington's Writings*, p. 482, Vol. II.

[3] *Washington's Writings*, p. 482, Vol. II.

ments. The above-noted concerns and dangers to the French in New France were suddenly accelerated by the events in Europe.

As Supreme General of the French armies, the great German general, Moritz von Saxony, had, through his glorious Flanders campaign against the Duke of Cumberland, brought about the Peace of Aachen, which forced England to give up all it had won during the war, and, according to the applicable sections of the Peace of Utrecht, restricted England's claim to the Indian lands, specifically the Iroquois' territory. The Americans were not just a little disturbed that they had to evacuate Louisburg, which had gained for them military fame and was the most significant action of the entire war. Furthermore, their bitterness grew when their hated enemy began to connect a chain of fortresses in order the protect their American empire. Just how gigantic that plan was can be measured by looking at the map. According to the discoveries of Champlain, Father Marquette, La Salle, and others, the French claimed all the lands watered by the St. Lawrence and its tributaries, followed by the Great Lakes, and the territory of the Mississippi with all its tributaries, which means then almost the entire United States, with the exception of the Allegheny territories, whose rivers flow to the Atlantic Ocean, and of this latter Kennebec Bay and all of Maine. This right of discovery was reinforced through its occupation for a hundred years with missions, colonies, and military posts. Although the number of the former had been reduced, the trade between the lakes and the Gulf was, as indicated above, still relatively important. In the posts between Detroit and New Orleans there were garrisons of regular troops, who were relieved every 6 years. The English attempted to diminish the strength of the French title through the sovereignty of the Iroquois over the valley of the lakes and all the land east of the Mississippi[4]. The Five Nations, who remained under its (England's) protection, had conquered the land and the Treaty of Utrecht recognized that jurisdiction. It is interesting that men such as Benjamin Franklin, Clinton and others, even most of the history writers of the east, supported these English pretensions. However, in the west, all the famous personalities familiar with the surrender of the Ohio Indians disagreed with the Iroquois title. For example, in 1837 General Harrison supported the French justification in a paper read before the Ohio Historical Society, wherein he praised the fighting capabilities of the Ohio Indians and contended that the Miami Confederation had never been defeated by the Iroquois. He stated that in 1700 the Miamis' military power was considerable, that Captain de Vincennes had noted that they were in possession of the entire valley of the Wabash, that their capital (the area where Fort Wayne now stands) was the key to the entire lower territories, and that, according to his own and the recollections of various other contemporaries, they were able to put 4000 warriors into the field. There is no doubt that the Iroquois, after defeating and driving out all the Ohio Indians who did not belong to the Miami Confederation, did settle colonies of their tribes, namely the Cayugas, Senecas, and Onondagas in the valley; but their sovereignty was always just nominal and, after their humiliation by the French, and after the return of the Ohio tribes, that means for more than 50 years, it was taken from them by the original owners of the land. Therefore, the claims of Great Britain and every purchase contract with the Iroquois in regards to the Ohio territories were illegal and based upon pure fraud.

Upon hearing about the plans of the Virginians for trade on the upper Ohio, the Governor-General of New France, the Marquis de la Gallisoniere, dispatched Captain Celeron de Bienville with 300 soldiers from Detroit to secure those segments of the of the river area which up to that time had been totally ignored by the French. Bienville carried out his tasks in the same manner as had La Salle. At the

---

[4] Even the Cherokees, Catawbas and other southern Indians were, according to England's opinion, subject to the power of the Iroquois.

mouth of every tributary and at the base of every Indian mound near the shore he let the drums be beat and read the "process verbal" of ownership. Then a wooden cross was erected under which a lead plate was buried, whose inscription declared that, based upon the right of initial discovery and formal treaties among the European powers, King Louis XV had taken possession of the land[5].

During that campaign, the Captain sent notice to Governor Hamilton of Pennsylvania (dated August 6, 1749, Champ sur Belle Riviere a une ancienne ville des Chouanons[6] wherein he informed him that, in the future, English traders and trappers were not allowed to travel through the King's territory without permission. This new theatrical crusade did not, however, have its desired effects. The trappers simply continued to swarm across the land, and that very same year, several were seized by French sentry posts on the Maumee, where the French were busy constructing Fort Miami, near today's Fort Wayne. At the same time, renegade Pennsylvania traders among the Piankeshaws, a tribe of Miamis, in present-day Shelby County, Ohio, constructed a fortified trading post named Pickawillany, which was the first known building to be constructed by the English in the state of Ohio. The parish tax continued to hinder the Ohio Company's plans for trade and colonization. Finally, 2 years later, in 1751, the company sent Christopher Gist to the west to seek out its lands. Gist, a young man of German origin, had accompanied Weiser on several of his expeditions to the other side of the mountains and knew the language and customs of the savages. During the course of the year, he had, accompanied by several Delawares, roamed the river area along the Ohio down to approximately 100 miles north of the mouth of the Big Miami; on the return trip he began surveying a stretch of land south of the Ohio and east of the Kanawha, a good area upon which the Ohio Company sought to establish its stations. He was followed by General Andrew Lewis, who, under contract to another Virginia company, was surveying a grant of 100,000 acres in the valley of the Greenbriar[7].

Marquis Duquesne had replaced Gallisoniere, and his first steps were dedicated to fortifying the Ohio valley from Lake Erie to the junction of the Allegheny and Monongahela. A wide and solid barrier was supposed to keep the English traders and settlers out of the west. At Presque Isle, today's Erie, and 15 miles away, at the head of French Creek, two forts arose in the gloom of the forest. At the same time, patrol boats manned with French soldiers and warriors from the Ottawa and Chippewa tribes, traveled down the Allegheny and Ohio in order to keep the river open and drive out the English intruders. They soon became aware of the pelt traders at Pickawillany; therefore they paddled up the river and demanded that the Indians turn them (the English) over. However, the Piankeshaws had smoked a peace pipe with the Pennsylvanians and angrily refused to dishonor the laws of hospitality. Thereupon, the French laid siege to the station; and as the Sachem of the tribe was hurrying to the station's defense with a war party, there was a confrontation, where the Sachem and 14 of his followers fell. The victors then burned the blockhouses to ashes, seized the merchants and led them away to Canada; however, according to other reports, they were also burned on the spot.

This occurred in the beginning of 1752. The tragic end of this first English settlement in the Ohio valley generated the highest alarm in the colonies, no less so than among the owners of the western grants who were desirous of protecting their commercial and property rights. The government of Virginia immediately sent representatives to a conference with the Indians at Logtown and, using the tried and true methods of bribing the chiefs with gifts and rum, persuaded them to

---

[5] Several decades ago, some young boys playing at the mouth of the Muskingum, found just such a plate buried beneath the earth on the shore. A lithographic reproduction of it is in Hildreth's History of the Pioneers. In addition, the young boy, R.P. Hereford also found one in 1846 at the mouth of the Big Kanawha.

[6] Probably the former Shawnee village at the mouth of the Scioto.

[7] For further information on Gist see Hermann Schuricht, *History of the German Element in Virginia*, (Baltimore, Maryland: Kroh, 1898) DHT

approve the Treaty of Lancaster which the tribes had ignored up to that time. Additional and similar treaties were arranged by the representatives of Pennsylvania and Virginia in Winchester and Carlisle with the chiefs of the Iroquois, Delawares, Shawnees, and other tribes. As a further guarantee, Conrad Weiser appeared and, as an agent of Pennsylvania on the upper Ohio, traveled from village to village, in order to exploit the hostile feelings of the redskins against the French. Because of the murderous attack upon the Piankeshaws, the Ohio Indians were quite hostile against the French, and they asked the American colonists to erect a fort at the fork of the Ohio for everyone's protection.

The French scoffed at the treaty efforts of the English as being arrogantly useless. Up to that time it had never occurred to them to take advantage of treaties. They were convinced that, because of their historical sometimes mild, sometimes harsh suppression of the Indians, they would always accomplish more than the English with their swindlous agreements. Therefore, they worried little about the Ohio Indians who were angry because of the attack upon the Piankeshaws, and remained confident in their diplomatic ability to win back their former, grateful subjects to their friendly protection at the first opportunity. In the meantime, they did not let themselves be deterred in their plans for fortifications. At the beginning of 1753, they had already erected a third fort, Fort Machault, near Benango, a former Indian village at the mouth of French Creek. In order to instill respect among the resentful Miamis, they quickly completed the forts of Miami on the Maumee and Junandot (Wyandot) on the eastern bank of the Sandusky river, near the bay, as well as a stockade at the mouth of the Wabash river and a fort on the left bank of the Hocking, in today's Athens county, the location of which is still called "French Margarets". In addition, Legardier de St. Pierre, the commandant of the forts on French Creek, sent a stern warning to the Ohio Indians to remain peaceful. At the slightest act of violence carried out against Frenchmen, he would join with the English, divide the land with them, and wipe out all the redskins from the earth.

Pennsylvania and Virginia diligently sent out scouts to check on the preparations, war materials and movements of the French. Upon returning, their reports were not very reassuring, since fear of the barbaric allies of the French had not permitted them to approach French Creek. As ambassador to the French commanders Governor Dinwiddie selected George Washington, then a young man 21 years old, whose bravery and persistence in adversity had been tested while working as a surveyor for Lord Fairfax in the wilderness, and whose popularity among his neighbors had won for him the rank of Major in the militia at the age of 18. Dinwiddie's letter, which would carry its messenger into world history, demanded, in polite words, that St. Pierre leave the area of French Creek, since, according to the treaties with the Iroquois, it belonged to the English domains.

With an escort of Indians and Christopher Gist as scout, Washington began his difficult and dangerous mission in November 1753, a journey of 750 miles through mostly dark forests. Upon his arrival at the Ohio, he discovered all the Indians formerly friendly to the English, now withdrawn and reserved, a result of the threats of the French. Shingast, the Delaware chief, refused to accept Washington's invitation to a conference, and even the Shawnee chief did not show up. Washington would soon experience the effects of the winning manners of his opponents upon his own escort. The old Louis knight St. Pierre was as much a clever politician as a brave soldier. He received the young, worn-out American with extreme politeness and concern, hosting him in a princely manner. Later, when Washington was about to begin his homeward journey, accompanied by the highest compliments and best wishes, while looking around for his Indian companions, he found that they had disappeared to the last man. Friendly words, the cognac bottle, and new weapons had won them over to the side of the French.

While Washington was in the midst of this wintery mission, the Ohio Company had finally taken steps to erect its forts and trading posts at the confluence of the Allegheny and Monongahela, the site of present-day Pittsburgh. Their European goods for the Ohio trade had arrived. Wagons with some of these goods, loaded with war materials and farming instruments for the families wishing to settle under the protection of the new fort, were making their way slowly up the Monongahela. The return of its representative speeded up the war preparations of the Virginians to protect their stations. St. Pierre's reply, which simply referred Virginia's request to the Governor General, proved that France was far from recognizing even England's smallest claim to the west. Washington also reported that in the Spring a 1,500 man enemy force descend the Allegheny River, erecting new forts on the upper Ohio to carry out Celeron's proclamation. He reported that the old Indian Logtown had already been chosen as a headquarters for the French general. A letter from the Earl of Holderness, England's Secretary of State, called upon all the provincial governors to raise troops in order to repel the intruders with force of arms, should there be a French invasion of the English territory. Virginia offered six companies of volunteers, hurriedly sent to the fort, which was under construction by the Ohio Company, to complete the fortifications and serve as a garrison. In addition to their regular pay, that very same governor's proclamation promised them a gift of two 100,000 acre plots of land on the Ohio. Virginia also swiftly organized the shipment of additional supplies and war materials for the new fort, including 30 cannon and 80 barrels of gunpowder, which had been shipped from England. Virginia then reminded the governors of New York and Pennsylvania of the Secretary of State's request and asked for reinforcements. The assemblies of both provinces did not show themselves to be in a hurry to honor their neighbor's request. Both were envious because Virginia considered the land west of the Allegheny as part of its own domains. The Pennsylvania assembly debated for a long time as to whether the territories of Great Britain's Majesty had indeed been occupied by the French. With a bare majority they finally decided to support the King with a bit of money; however, the declaration had been barely passed, when it was again voted upon and revoked. New York finally authorized the sum of 5,000 pounds Sterling, but sent the money late in the summer, when it could do little good.

Chapter 4

Crevecour seizes the Ohio Company fort. - De Jumonville's death. - Washington's Capitulation. - Benjamin Franklin's Plan for Conquering and Fortifying the Ohio Valley. - Braddock's March and Defeat. - Barbaric Victory Celebration in Fort Duquesne. - Destruction of the German settlements.

It was the beginning of April 1754. From the Alleghenies melting snow along with the rainfall normal for the time of year swelled mightily the feeder rivers of the Ohio. Swarms of birds fluttered through the forests, and already wild bees buzzed around the cherry and dogwood blossoms. Suddenly the sounds of war pierced the woods along the entire length of French Creek. The French forts were completed. In the huts, tents, barks and canoes the French and German languages mixed with those of the natives. Frenchmen, Canadians, people from Alsace and Lorraine, Shawnees, Chippewas, Delawares, Negroes, half bloods from the white, red and black races, moved excitedly about under orders from their officers. Tents, cannon, supplies and munitions were loaded on board ships. Nearby, groups stood about listening to the feathered and gaudily painted scouts, who had brought news of the movements of the English. And while up here there were active preparations for an impending military campaign, downstream, opposite the mouth of the Allegheny, another group, feverish and weakened by hunger, huddled against the earth works of the new fort. Their commander, a veteran indian trader by the name of Frazier, was so unaware of the danger from the north, that he had calmly returned to his small farm at the mouth of Turtle Creek, 10 miles upstream on the Monongahela, leaving behind a totally inexperienced cadet by the name of Ward in charge. The unfortunate young cadet's heart sank, when on April 11 an enemy armada of 60 heavily laden ships and 300 canoes bearing 1000 thousand troops, cannon, and supplies[1] came down the Allegheny and, accompanied by martial music, anchored right in front of the fort. Their commander, Monsieur de Crevecoeur, politely asked Ward to give up the fort, whereupon Ward complied without much hesitation. The next morning as the Virginians gloomily left the fort carrying their shovels and pickaxes, the war began.

When he received word of the surrender of the forks of the Ohio, Washington was a Lieutenant Colonel commanding the Virginia provincials in the area of present-day Cumberland, where his troops were busily hacking a road through the forest for the transport of artillery. Shortly thereafter, his two commanders, Gist and Tanacharison, the demi-king of the south Wyandots, brought him the report that French advance troops were already swarming through the area. Fearing an attack, Washington decided to pre-empt the enemy and, once and for all, end the vacillation between war and peace in his province. He quickly gathered together one of his companies and greeted the next group of Frenchmen who crossed his path with a salvo. Their leader De Jumonville waved a handkerchief to let Washington know that the bearer was carrying a message from his commander. Thereupon the Virginians lowered their muskets and remained still to listen to the message, which a corporal began to read. He had not even finished when the Virginians started to become impatient, probably because they

---

[1] *Washington's Writ.* Sparks pag. 6. Vol. II.

could not understand the Frenchman's English and suddenly opened fire on the enemy. De Jumonville fell mortally wounded along with 9 of his men.

This burst of fire in the far wilderness of western America set the world in flames. It brought about the English-French or Seven Years' War, which cost Europe a million lives and spared no part of the world, devastating and exhausting all the nations which participated.

France declared Washington's act to be a cowardly murder under the justification that De Jumonville was engaged on a mission of peace and also because no declaration of hostilities had been sent from the English side. The French Lieutenant had fallen on May 28, and by July 3 Washington found himself in Fort Necessity, a hastily dug redoubt on the site of an earlier bloodbath, surrounded by 900 of the enemy under the command of Captain de Villiers, De Jumonville's stepbrother. Disregarding severe rainy weather, the French had maintained a constant firing upon the Virginians from 9 in the morning until 8 in the evening, when Washington raised the white flag.

His ammunition was gone and his troops were exhausted from hunger and deprivation. Van Braam, one of his commanders, could speak French and was sent out to receive the conditions of surrender from the victor. In spite of how humiliating they were, they were accepted by Washington. The attack upon De Jumonville was referred to as a cowardly murder. The Virginians would be permitted to leave but had to leave their cannon to the enemy and promise not to work on any more fortifications on that side of the Alleghenies for one year. In order to guarantee the conditions, two of the commanders, Van Braam and Stobo were left in the hands of the French. The Americans maintained that the term "cowardly murder" had been wrongly translated by the "stupid Dutchman". However, since the French word "Assasssinat" was used in the surrender document and is also the equivalent of the English word "assasination", it can hardly be assumed that Van Braam had made a mistake.

Even though the news of the Virginians' expulsion from the forks of the Ohio generated the highest excitement among the people of the colonies, the assemblies were not to be aroused from the sleep of their own provincial problems. In Pennsylvania, initially most effected by the French incursions, with a fiery patriotic fervor Benjamin Franklin now called for a union of the colonies as a common defense against the enemy's incursion. The *Pennsylvania Gazette* from May 9, 1754, had the following article from his pen. After explaining the events on the forks of the Ohio and fervently recommending unification of the colonies, the following appears: "The confidence of the French in the conquest is well founded in the face of the disarray of our British colonies. We have the greatest of difficulty in swiftly convincing the various governments and assemblies to take effective measures for our common defense and safety, while our enemies enjoy the significant advantage of unified leadership in their council and finances." At the end of the article is a woodcut portraying a snake cut up into pieces, their number representing the number of colonies. Each segment bears the initial letter of the colony's name and underneath it all can be seen the motto: "Unite or Die!", a well-known device adopted at the start of the revolution with great effectiveness[2]. In several daily papers of the time, the segmented snake and motto appeared beneath the titles of the papers.

Franklin presented the plan for just such a continuing alliance for protection and safety against internal and external enemies to a congress of the colonies, which had been assembled in Albany that year by the Governor of New York, and had been attended by the chiefs of the Six Nations, whose support would be most important to the provinces in the upcoming battles

---

[2] Spark's *Franklin*, Vol. III, p. 25.

with the French. Even though this congress[3] accepted Franklin's plan, it was approved neither by the Crown nor the American people. To some it was too democratic, while to others it appeared to be too aristocratic, since the president of the union would be appointed by the king. Not discouraged, the tireless Franklin thought up new means. He then suggested the organization and settlement of two independent western colonies based on the establishment of a stock company. One would guard the Niagara border, the other the north side of the Ohio, both protected by forts and armed vessels. As the most fitting base for the latter Franklin suggested the area of the Scioto river. This colony, he remarked, would permit expanded trade with the Miamis and gain access to the natural resources of the Ohio territory. Two small forts, one at the tip of the Hocking and another at the mouth of the Wabash, would suffice to protect this area, for which he predicted future growth in population, power, and wealth. Among the unpleasantries which the founding of these colonies would preclude would be, he continued, that the French, behind their back, could, because of the extensive lands, otherwise increase their population, and that many debtors and homeless English, German servants and slaves could flee there and further increase their (French) power, while at the same time the English would be diminished and weakened. Furthermore, the continued baiting of the Indians by the French against the advanced settlements and the completion of the connection between their settlements in Canada and those in Louisiana would be thwarted. Franklin's suggestions came too early, however, and therefore remained without effect.

In the meantime, the French utilized the rest of the year 1754 to gradually strengthen their power on the Ohio. There arose Fort Duquesne, named to honor the Governor General of New France, on the site of the redoubt captured from the Ohio Company. Through clever diplomatic means, Crevecoeur and St. Pierre were further able to pacify the former enemies of the French, the tribes of the Iroquois Confederation, and negate the treaty they had signed with the English at Albany, so that now, along the entire length of the Ohio and the waters running into it from the north, all the redskins supported the French interests.

In reaction to this unexpected strengthening of the French power on their borders, the governors of the English provinces did not know what else to do except extend desperate cries for help to the motherland. These transatlantic lamentations found George III's ear only after the peace negotiations between Paris and London had broken off completely. As Commander-in-Chief of the armed forces in America, General Braddock, a proud and stiff representative of the English military establishment, departed for Virginia with 1,500 men, where he arrived on February 20, 1755. After a war council held in Alexandria, four targets were chosen for coordinated attacks to destroy French power: Duquesne, Crown Point, Niagara, and the fortified areas of Nova Scotia.

On March 20, (1755) Braddock began the march through the wilderness. Both of his regiments, the 44th and the 48th, the flower of the British army, each counted only 500 men and were commanded by Sir Peter Halkett and Colonel Dunbar. The imposing sight of these veterans departing their headquarters in Alexandria, in their bright red uniforms, their huge, tasseled grenadier caps and shining weapons, with flags flying and ringing music, had awakened among the Americans such a blind sense of confidence in a certain victory, that during the march, subscription lists for fireworks celebrations and illumination were already circulated in Philadelphia and other cities. A wagon train of artillery with ammunition and provisions accompanied the army along with a section of sailors from Admiral Keppler's squadron.

---

[3] The congress took place in June 1774; New Hampshire, Rhode Island, New Jersey, Pennsylvania, and Maryland were represented by delegates.

Unfortunately the enthusiasm and the naive confidence of the colonists in the seizure of Fort Duquesne, did little to support the army's difficult march. The provincial governments left Braddock almost completely in a lurch. The population had to be forced to supply transport and livestock, while the army suppliers and government agents proved themselves to be swindlous thieves and crooks. For that reason, the army's movement through the trackless wilderness was so difficult that only after 4 weeks was the mouth of Will's Creek (today's Cumberland) reached. At that point 1000 provincial troops joined the army, including two independent companies from New York under the command of Captain Gage, later the infamous Major General in the Revolutionary War. Again, a three-week delay became necessary, since there was practically no means of transport. With the help of his son and Conrad Weiser, as well a personal guarantee, Franklin got together 150 wagons, and the army continued its march in two divisions. Excluding the officers, the main army under General Braddock counted 1,200 men with the remainder in reserve under Colonel Dunbar. On a glorious and sunny morning of July 8th, the former reached the confluence of the Youghiogany and Monongahela rivers. At this point, as it crossed the first ford of the Monongahela, George Washington, barely recovered from a severe fever, joined the army, now in a martial spirit, buoyed up with the pleasant thought that in a few hours they would victoriously seize Fort Duquesne. Washington did not share the same confidence, since the friendly offer of help from his companion, the demi-king Tanacharison, whose group was very much needed as scouts and reconnoiterers for points of danger, had been refused in such a brusque manner by Braddock (who, as a European master of war was not about to accept any suggestions from a youthful colonist and who was also quite upset with the Americans for their apparent lack of interest and carelessness) that the redskins withdrew highly insulted. This was an event which would have the most disastrous results for the general and his army.

Beginning with the departure from Will's Creek, de Crevecoeur's French and Indian scouts had kept him informed as to the enemy's every step. For a long time, he remained undecided as to the manner and type of his resistance, since the strength of the enemy had been given as 3,000 men, a force which his own could not match. However, in the meantime, he had approved the suggestions of Captain de Beaujeu, who had offered to advance against the enemy with a weak detachment of French soldiers and Indians and impede the advance with sniping. After crossing the river, the English army's route led through a wooded plateau, which, after extending about a half mile, rose to a thickly forested hill. Two ravines, 8 to 10 feet deep, covered with trees and wild underbrush, snaked along parallel and close to each other from the crest down the hill and ran out about 150 feet from the bed of the river. Into this ambuscade, barely discernible from even a few paces away, de Beaujeu positioned his 500 soldiers and Indians, commanded by, in addition to himself, Captains Dumas and Liquery, four Lieutenants, two subalterns, and two cadets.

Around noon the English force crossed the 2nd ford and was moving in closed ranks through that foreboding valley up the rise. Colonel Gage led the advance party. Then came the general with the artillery and main body, whose rear was formed by Washington's provincials. Barely had the last section crossed the river and the lead columns reached the base of the rise when there was suddenly the horrible war cry of the savages and at the same moment well-aimed musket fire mowed down entire ranks of the advance body. And before the army could even recover from its consternation about the enemy action, a new salvo struck their flanks. The fear now increased, since one could see no enemy, and the shots appeared to come out of the ground. Even though the soldiers emptied their muskets in the direction of the rising cloud of smoke, which naturally had not the least effect, the enemy maintained a continuous and deadly fire from both sides. With the main body, General Braddock then charged forward to assist Gage's hard pressed division; but before he reached the spot, a wild panic had already disintegrated its ranks and these were thrown back onto the artillery and the main body, spreading a similar panic in their ranks. The commands of the officers did little to bring order to the chaos. All semblance of order had been broken. The soldiers wildly used up their ammunition while blindly shooting their own officers. Though several sections maintained their lines in closed ranks according to the insane orders of the general, most of them followed the lead of the Virginians and hid behind the trees. While trying with his sword to stop a fleeing soldier, General Braddock was fatally shot by that same one. For three hours this bloodbath continued, unheard of in the annals of modern warfare. After Sir Peter Halkett, who had assumed command, had fallen and 64 of 86 officers and 714 dead or wounded soldiers covered the battlefield, the wildest flight began under a hale of enemy bullets. All of the artillery along with all the baggage wagons containing the general's correspondence fell into the victor's hands. That anyone escaped at all was due to the fact that the Indians began to plunder and scalp those who had fallen rather than pursue the enemy. Even among Dunbar's reserve force, encamped on the other side of the river, six miles below the bloody site, the remains of the army spread panic. The artillery was destroyed immediately, the heavy baggage, and even the supply wagons were burned, though no one knows on whose order[4]. On the French side, only three officers, including the hero of the day, Captain de Beaujeu, and about 30 soldiers and Indians fell.

A savage cry sounded in Fort Duquesne when the totally unexpected news of this great victory arrived. A remarkable description of the atrocity, to which the celebration led and which burned Crevecoeur's name into history, are given by the memoirs of Jacob Smith, who was a prisoner in the fort at the time. Therein it is written:

"I was full of apprehension about the day's events, since Braddock's arrival would set me free. During the afternoon a loud hue and cry arose in the fort and, even though I did not understand French, I perceived that they were cries of joy and triumph, I feared that bad news for me had arrived. I heard the European soldiers speaking German and since I also spoke German, I asked one of them what was up. The man explained to me that a runner had arrived with the news that Braddock had most certainly been completely defeated. The French and Indians had surrounded him and from behind trees and caves had maintained a constant fire against the English; scores of these had already fallen, and whoever did not make it back over the river, their only refuge, would not be left alive at sundown. Shortly thereafter a group of soldiers and Indians arrived with a wild cry. They carried bundles of bloody scalps, grenadier caps, British field bags, bayonets, and similar items, and brought the news of Braddock's complete defeat. Soon another group arrived, composed only of Indians, about 100 strong, almost every one of them carrying scalps; and then another group with draft horses, and another large number who were carrying scalps. Those arriving and those who already arrived fired their muskets and the heavy cannon in the fort, and a horrible cry sounded from all sides, so that it appeared to me that Hell had released its legions. At sundown a group arrived with about

---

[4] The wagon owners subsequently wanted to hold Franklin personally responsible for their losses; a threat which would have ruined the philosopher. Governor Shirley guaranteed payment and saved Franklin from his dilemma.

a dozen prisoners, their hands tied behind their backs. The poor souls were naked while their faces and parts of their bodies were blackened with powder. They burned these prisoners on the bank of the Allegheny. I stood on the wall of the fort until I saw the fire ignite under one of those unfortunate ones; they had tied him to a post and at first tortured him with torches and red-hot irons; he screamed in a most pitiful manner while the Indians laughed like the devil. The sight was too much for me. Depressed and sick I returned to my quarters. The morning after the battle, Braddock's artillery was brought to the fort and the Indians marched around in the uniforms of the British officers with sashes, half-moons and tasseled caps[5]."

The news of Braddock's defeat spread indescribable horror throughout the English colonies. People streamed into churches to beg the mercy of heaven. In Pennsylvania, the assembly was hurriedly convened in order to hear the "terrible" news. In New York, the sudden fear caused the soldiers and sailors recruited for the campaign against the French post to desert in droves. And when Governor Shirley, Braddock's successor in command, finally reached Lake Ontario after unspeakable endeavors and difficulties, the season had advanced too far and supplies were lacking for a movement towards Niagara. However, General Johnson had somewhat better luck in the north; he defeated Baron Dieskau on the bank of Lake George and wiped out his army, but he could neither attack nor seize Crown Point. In the meantime, Colonel Dunbar had brought the remains of Braddock's army back to Philadelphia and left the frontier settlers to the attacks of the savages. The German settlements, whose long chain of settlements extended the furthest to the west, from the west branch of the Susquehannah up to the Blue Ridge, experienced the first blow of this fury. The annals of that period describe their horrible fates. The fields were destroyed, the herds of animals driven off, while homes and barns went up in flames over the scalped bodies of the settlers, whose wives and children were dragged into captivity. The inflamed frontier was full of wandering refugees. Only in the year 1758 did greater world events finally lessen these atrocities and miseries.

After the war between France and England had actually been in progress for several years, it was finally formally declared on May 17, 1756. With changing fortune, Friedrich the Great, England's sole ally in Europe against France and its allies Austria, Russia and Sweden and most of the German states, crowned his flag with victory in 1758. And at the same time a clever, unknown man accomplished what Braddock's usually victorious regiments could not, a German school teacher among the Indians brought an end to French rule on the Ohio.

That year a third army of 7,500 men under General Forbes was supposed to set out to at last capture Fort Duquesne and subdue the rampaging enemy in the frontier areas of Pennsylvania, Maryland, and Virginia. Already during preparations for this new campaign, serious mistakes had been made--rather than use Braddock's old military road, provincial self interest had caused a new road to be driven across the Pennsylvania wilderness, causing such a long delay that there was general weariness among the population and little success was expected even from the outset. Before the army's departure from Philadelphia, Governor Thomas of Pennsylvania decided to make one last attempt at bringing the Indians of the Ohio Valley over to the English side and thus reduce the force which could oppose Forbes. At Easton in the Fall of 1756, a peace

---

[5] Jacob Smith (Schmidt), the writer of these memoirs, was a Pennsylvania German. After his return from imprisonment he was given (in 1763) the command of a company of sharpshooters, whom he trained in the manner and tactics of the Indians and dressed like the savages. He is the author of a treatise on Indian warfare. He spent the latter part of his life in Kentucky, where he was very respected and several times elected to the legislature.

treaty had been signed with the chiefs of the Delawares in Pennsylvania, but this was barely honored by the tribe's warriors in this province, who explained that the chiefs had no authority to take these steps, and its articles could even less bind the Delawares, who had returned to the Ohio, and even less the Shawnees and Wyandots. Where, under such fluid conditions, could the man be found, whose influence upon the latter, through knowledge of their language, customs, and prejudices, not just through cleverness and persuasiveness, but whose physical strength and moral fortitude in adversity and under constant threat of death complete a mission, such as Thomas sought? The messenger would have to cross the area of devastated border settlements, and penetrate into a distant and hostile wilderness populated by wavering friends, where large bands of declared enemies were encamped. FAced with all of these considerations the Governor was disheartened. He turned to his friend, Bishop Spangenberg, the Moravian bishop in Bethlehem, with the request to choose the man.

In order to understand this confidence, one must look back upon the operation and character of this church society, which the reader will find necessary as well as interesting in light of the coming events. For this German congregation spawned the noblest pioneer heroes of our history, the first settlers of the Ohio Valley, whose cities became the western bulwark of American freedom and union and, through their extraordinarily tragic fate, appear as sacred as the classic sites of antiquity[6].

---

[6] The importance and significance of this early congregation has been a central point emphasized in all histories of the German element in the Ohio Valley since the time of Klauprecht. For references to works on this topic see Don Heinrich Tolzmann, *German-Americana: A Bibliography*, (Metuchen, New Jersey: Scarecrow Pr., 1975), pp. 49-52. DHT

Chapter 5

The Moravians and their Missions. - Persecution and Expulsion of the German Missionaries. - Germans Naturalized as Iroquois. - Schikellimus. - The Burning of Gnadenhütten. - Bethlehem. - German Indian Villages. - Christian Delawares and Mohicans.

The Unity of the Brethren, whose members were called Herrenhuters, Moravian Brethren, Zinsendorfers, and others, was formed from the remains of the Hussite congregations, and held together by a few families in the area around Fulneck in Moravia. Their founder was the carpenter Christian David. When, under the government persecutions in 1722, their members fled to Saxony, Count Nickolaus Ludwig von Zinsendorf offered them refuge on his Berthelsdorf estate in Upper Lausatia. The refugees could not have found a fitting patron more interested in their religious convictions. From his early youth, the Count, under the protection of his pious and educated grandmother, a woman by the name of von Gersdorf, had given himself over to pious meditation, which finally led him to the conviction that the true goal of the Reformation had been led astray by the Protestant scholastics, and that Christianity only in its original form, such as had been preached by Christ and his immediate disciples, could lead to salvation of the soul. Already during his stay at the Pedagogium in Halle, the young mystic had held religious gatherings with his school mates and founded the order of the "Mustard Seed", which sought the realization of his idea, the reintroduction of original Christianity in its entire simplicity and purity. This long cherished dream did not leave him at the University of Wittenberg, where his uncle had sent him to study law and, when the anniversary of the Reformation was celebrated with much pomp in 1717, our young student of both laws did not participate in the celebration, but rather prayed and lamented in his room about the decline of the church. Upon his return, the arrival of the Moravian refugees at his estate gave him the opportunity to carry out his favorite plan. Based upon Christian David's simple church rule, he founded with these people a fraternal community, based on the teaching of love, patience, refusal of all earthly pleasures, and on communal work. Accordingly, the congregation became a club of practical socialists, whose "Platform" was the Augsburg Confession with the Bible and self-inspiration as the source of revelation. They adhered strictly to the original Christian laws. They celebrated Saturday as the Sabbath of the Holy Scripture with pious meditation and total abstinence from work, but also celebrated Sunday to honor the death and resurrection of Christ. They even restored the ancient Christian custom of the washing of the feet and the greeting with a kiss. Their settlement on the "Herrenhut" estate gradually became so strong through constant new arrivals, that Zinsendorf devised the wonderful plan to include the entire world in his activities and construct missionary schools among pagans of all lands. Thus, in 1732 the Moravian apostles journeyed to the palm tree forests of both Indias, under the ice fields of Greenland and Labrador, among the Hottentots on the Cape of Good Hope, among the negro slaves of Berbice and Surinam as well as among the Indians of Georgia and Pennsylvania. In the meantime, the Brethren Synode had developed its current constitution and orders, so successful even today, which differentiates its congregations so totally from the other protestant congregations.

Madame de Stael[1] called the Moravians the "Protestant monks" and, in fact, their bourgeois society is almost purely spiritual: their daily life, even though they forsake oaths and vows, is monastic. Everything they do is based on religion; all social activities are given up to the authority and direction of the church elders. Their business activity is also the result of their religious feelings. Commerce and trade and the fruit thereof are nothing more than the manifestation or realization of the will of God. Therefore, there are no boisterous activities in their villages. Their quiet, orderly work is, as it were, an earnest prayer, in which they all quietly participate. They have forsaken all earthly pleasures, even the true happiness of love. In all questionable cases, particularly in questions of marriage, they appeal to the decision of heaven by drawing lots. Should the decision go against them, the young Moravian will quietly renounce his chosen bride. However, this resignation does cost him much less than the normal suffering; a couple cannot become closely acquainted before marrying, because the unmarried men and women live in separate groups, where absolute equality is the rule and where they see each other only in church. The dress of both sexes is very simple. The men dress in brown in the manner of the Quakers. The women cover their hair and wear a band about their forehead, whose color indicates whether they are virgins, married, or widowed. In church they always appear dressed in white. Even though very simple, a Moravian church service does not preclude a poetic stirring of emotions. Paintings, wreathes, and garlands of white thorns and white roses decorate the walls of the churches. Music is cultivated as an emotional element of the religion, but the Moravians sing only psalms. Their cemeteries are attractive gardens, symbols of the equality of all in death. Next to every gravestone is a shrub. The gravestones, all similar, like white leaves, and no shrub is taller than another. The same inscription is used for everyone. "On this day ____ was born, and on this day ____ returned home." At Easter, the congregation meets in the gardens of death, normally next to the churches, and, in the midst of the gravestones, sermons and choruses proclaim the resurrection. As the inscriptions declare, death represents a return home for young and old, and the happiest return home was a martyr's death in the service of God, which they honor mostly under a picture of the sacrificial lamb.

Thus, it came to be that such a religious community, based upon moderation and renunciation, with a view of death and such a tremendous work ethic, brought a wonderful spirit to the first settlement and culture in the American wilderness. The Moravians possessed all of the virtues and characteristics of the Puritans, but without the latter's desire for power and murderous, impatient anger.

General Oglethorpe, previously the Adjutant to Prince Eugene, entered into an exchange of correspondence with Zinsendorf, and through a generous offer, brought about the resettlement of a Moravian community to Georgia, and became its sponsor. John Wesley, the founder of Methodism, found himself on the same ship with his brother (Oglethorpe's secretary), that was carrying these people to Savannah, and in his writing showed his admiration for their behavior during the trip and settlement. "For a long time," he wrote, "I had observed the solemnity of their behavior. And every day they had proven their humility and brotherly love, in that they performed all the mundane services for the other passengers,

---

[1] The Unity Brotherhood do not provide their bishops any sign of rank or authority. The form of government of their churches is basically representative. The Synode of the entire unity and the source of all their authority, meets at intervals of 10 to 20 years, as determined by a random drawing. Each congregation and provincial conference may send one representative. At the conclusion of the session the body votes for the "Members of the General Conference or the Elders of the Unity" who carry out the directions of the Synode and administer to the matters of the church until the convening of the next Synode, when they will give up their office. These conferences, in turn, named representatives to the various branches of the church, of which there are two in America, whose members meet in Bethlehem, PA. and in Salem, North Carolina. These provincial conferences appoint the pastors of the various congregations as approved by their committees.

which none of the English would do, and for which they neither wanted nor received compensation saying: "This is good for the pride in their hearts and the Redeemer did more for them." Every day they were offered an opportunity to demonstrate the gentleness and charity of their customs, which no insult could disturb. Whenever the rough sailors would bump them, hit them, or knock them down, they would quietly get up and leave without a complaint ever leaving their mouth. And that even the fear of death moved them just as little as anger and revenge, soon showed itself. During one singing of the Psalms, a terrible storm arose. The sea broke over us, ripped the main sail, covered the ship, and rushed seething between the decks, and I believed that the deep had already almost engulfed us. While the English wailed pitifully, the Germans continued to sing calmly. Amazed I asked one of the men, whether they had not felt any fear. "Even our women and children do not fear death" was the answer. About their life in Georgia notes Wesley: "They were always industrious, cheerful, friendly and loving towards each other. The patriarchal simplicity and solemnity of their bishop's elections made the 17 centuries disappear behind me, and it was as if I were standing in one of the original Christian meetings, where there was no church and state, but Paul, the tent maker, and Peter the Fisherman, the leader, led by the power of the Holy Spirit."

Under their elder, Peter Böhler from the University of Jena, their settlement Ebenezer began to bloom and thrive. Silk and indigo, their two staple goods, provided an annual income of 15,000 pounds. In the midst of an environment of greed, thrown together from all the parts of Europe, with their humane teaching that the soul is glorified not in receiving but in giving, their hearts were not impassive to the bitter fate of the black slaves. Their colony presented a picture of the blessings of free work under the burning Georgia sun. In pious writings, they pleaded successfully with the colonial administration for the abolition of slavery and indentured service. In 1734 appeared the decree: "Slavery, the misfortune, if not the shame of the other plantations, is forbidden in Georgia. Regardless of whether greed and selfishness defend it; there is an honorable loathing in the heart of man against the buying and selling of our fellow human beings as goods and chattel." Their agreement with Oglethorpe had released the Brotherhood from taking oaths of allegiance and military service, civil duties which their religion prohibited in the manner of the Dunkers and Quakers. At the outbreak of the Spanish War, however, they were to be forced to serve in the militia. But without any complaint, they left their thriving plantations and moved to Pennsylvania. They purchased property at the forks of the Delaware and founded Bethlehem, the model settlement which would become the Moravia of North America. For from here, this brave and enthusiastic people developed a marvelous missionary zeal among the Indians and at the same time so doggedly and tenaciously supported the British foreign policy, that they outshadowed the efforts of the Jesuits working for the interests of France. While the latter were showered by the government of France with the highest honors, the poor Moravians on the other hand would suffer not only seething distrust, but also horrible persecutions from the Americans. In 1740, their first missionaries Christian Heinrich Rauch, pushed forward to the Mohicans and Wampanos in the provinces of New York and Connecticut. His instructions obliged him to stay strictly away from the efforts of other missionaries or clerics; he was supposed to observe in silence and determine whether the hearts of the Indians were receptive to the Moravian beliefs. Rauch happened upon the natives who were in a depressed state, most of the time they lay in their wigwams drunk from traders' firewater; simultaneously his actions aroused the envy and hostility of the English clergy and their myopic followers. But with quiet perseverance he applied himself to his missionary work in the wilds of the Stissik Mountains with satisfying success. Before the end of the year 1742, in the Indian village Schekomeko on the Connecticut (River) in the province of New York he had a congregation of 28 converts. Soon thereafter, an Indian village on the Kent River was won over for the mission of the Brethren and the bell of a newly constructed chapel announced this second religious victory of the Germans, a hated sound to the Puritans' ears. "What?" asked clergy and laymen, "Are these red skinned Canaanites, whose destruction is the will of God, to be converted by wandering Germans and participate in the glory of the Gospel and become Christians equal to us?" These Moravian conversions were accompanied by their own peculiar material damage. Previously, the Indians would let themselves be led astray with drinking by the rough frontiersmen and while drunk be cheated out of hunting prizes or wages; now the missionaries resisted the introduction of spirits, as well as the association with depraved people and taught their disciples to look after their own welfare. Furthermore, the increased civilizing of the Indians did not permit a transgression of the law within their midst; it now happened that border ruffians were dragged before the judge to be punished for criminal behavior. It was no wonder that soon senseless and false charges were voiced against the brethren. Even though they used the scriptures forbidden by the Catholic church as the main means of spreading their propaganda, they were charged with being secret Papists and remaining in treasonous contact with the French. One zealot released an open letter to the public, in which he demanded that these crazed purveyors of the Indian wars be driven out of the country. Another supposedly knew that the Brethren had already received 1,000 muskets to arm the Indians and, in alliance with the French, use these same weapons to attack Pennsylvania and destroy the settlements. The result was a wild public fanaticism against the Brethren. A formal persecution developed against them. The governors of New York and Connecticut prohibited their meetings. The sheriff seized two missionaries and brought them to the jail in New Milford, while others were dragged by a mob under the most brutal conditions to Poughkeepsie and subjected to a wearisome cross examination before magistrates and clergy. Even though they were in the end honorably acquitted of all charges, the persecution continued. Provincial laws of the time required each inhabitant to take two oaths, one "that King George was the legal prince of the country and that he would in no manner support or encourage a pretender," and another which denounced the "Transformation of Communion, praying to the Virgin Mary, the belief in purgatory and others." Even though the content of these oaths did not conflict with the ideas and religious beliefs of the united Brethren, nevertheless the statutes of their church specifically forbade the taking of oaths. The missionaries' enemies used this opportunity to drive them out; with this goal they secured from the New York legislature two edicts. The one demanded that "all suspicious persons refusing the oath" must leave the province, and the other prohibited the brethren from converting and educating the Indians.

These tyrannical laws finished the missions in New York. The teachers fled back to Bethlehem, since mobs in both the cities and the countryside were carrying out a witch hunt against the outlaws. In Esopus, Martin Mack was saved by Colonel Livingston just in time from a raging mob which threatened to tear him apart. David Zeisberger and Christian Friedrich Post, who had been sent to the villages to learn the languages of the Five Nations, were arrested for treason and, under threats and most brutal mistreatment, dragged to New York and thrown into jail. Only after seven weeks of close arrest and wearisome cross-examinations were they released and banished by law to their home in Bethlehem. The hardship and physical abuse suffered in prison put the oldest missionary, Gottlieb Büttner on his deathbed and he breathed out his spirit in his mission site at Schekomeko accompanied by the wailing of his red apostles.

Even though the government in Pennsylvania was less strict and open minded, the popular sentiment was no less bigoted and adverse to a christianization of the natives. Rather than the Mohicans and Wampanos, here the Delawares, descendants of the friendly tribe, which greeted Penn upon his landing with gifts and wild game, were the hated Canaanites and they were persecuted with the same bitter fury as were their tribal brothers on the Ohio, who up to that time had been allies of the French. The Delaware nation stretched from the west side of the Blue Ridge to the Ohio, but the Five Nations still claimed as their right to all the conquered territory that as well as here on the Susquehannah and Allegheny. When Zinsendorf arrived with his daughter Benigna in 1742 and traveled throughout the province accompanied by Conrad Weiser to direct the missions, one of his first measures was to reconcile the Iroquois with the missions of the Brethren. This was made even more necessary, since the Five Nations still supported the British interests and therefore officially empowered to be openly hostile towards any intruding settlement established on their territory without their permission. With Weiser's assistance, Zinsendorf soon concluded a treaty of friendship with these savages. Spangenberg and Zeisberger, who had been authorized to move the Indian brethren in New York and New England to mission sites in Pennsylvania, were naturalized as Iroquois at the next meeting of the council in Onondaga and given permission to resettle all of their disciples. Spangenberg received the name *Tgirhitontie*, which means a "Row of Trees". They named Zeisberger *Anausseracheri* or "One resting on a Pumpkin"[2]. These Mohicans, assembled by Zeisberger, were settled on the far side of the Blue Ridge in Carbon County, near the mouth of Mahony Creek in the Lehigh valley. The Brethren called their village Gnadenhütten; it was the first village north of the Kittatinny mountains and soon blossomed into a thriving community with gardens, fields, and pastures with large flocks. The bountiful work of the German missionaries in the schools and fields was so greatly praised that Schikellimus, a Cayuga chief, described as the first magistrate and chief of all the Iroquois from the banks of the Susquehanna up to Onondago, became their truest friend, which increased their stature within the Iroquois Confederation and assisted their missionary efforts extremely well. Schikellimus, the official representative of the Iroquois Confederation to the government of Pennsylvania, who resided in the mission of Schamockin, today called Sunbury in Northumbria County, had been converted by Roman Catholic priests in Canada, but it appeared that his conversion was not very deep, because it took Zeisberger, who was active here, a long time to convince him to destroy a heathen image which he wore around his neck[3]. Nevertheless, he gladly permitted Zeisberger to raise his son, Logan, who would later play a magnificently tragic role in the Ohio Valley; and when he approached his end in 1749, he called in his German friend and died in his arms in the faith of the Brethren. The venerable fruits of spiritual and material culture, which the tireless activities of the Brethren slowly brought to fruition among the savages of Pennsylvania, were not won at a small price, but rather with hard work, deprivation, suffering, hunger and sickness. The missionaries did not show their disciples any superiority. They appeared both as teachers and servants, participating in the field work and, recognizing the Indians' own physical limitations for physical exertion, did the hardest work themselves. Their weak constitutions suffered from this task, often exacerbated by weeks of journeying through the wilderness, and soon, within a few years, the grass of the forest covered the mortal remains of the missionaries Cammerhof and Hagen.

And they had to be considered happy. For the darkest of times would begin for their brothers, when the Six Nations[4], pursuaded by St. Pierre's diplomacy to fight

---

[2] Heckewelder's Narrative of the Mission of the United Brethren Philadelphia. pag. 34.

[3] Loskiel's N.A. Missions, part II, pag. 120.

[4] In the meantime the Confederation had been strengthened by the addition of the Tuscaroras who had been driven out of the south.

against England. The Iroquois Confederation then issued a call to arms to all Indians, and, because of their presumed sovereignty, they included therein the Delawares and Mohicans within the settlements of the Brethren, with the threat to visit fire and tomahawk on the settlements should they refuse.

The poor Brethren communities suddenly found themselves between two fires. Everywhere could be heard the renewed and frantic cries of the fanatics about the "secret Papists and lackeys of the French." The missionaries had their missions among the Indians, who were now all hostile to the English; their unique religion accused of being a fraudulent pretense to conceal their treason. Lies and deception were voiced against them. The newspapers published a letter, allegedly written by a French officer, captured while en route from Quebec to Bethlehem, in which it was joyfully exclaimed that, now that the German teachers of the Indians had gone over to their side, the French would soon put their feet on the back of the English necks. In Virginia, scoundrels swore before court, that during their stay in Canada, reports from Bethlehem arrived every 14 days. In the cities of New Jersey, demagogues, who were preceded by a drummer, posted signs on the corners demanding of "all patriots" that Bethlehem be destroyed and all Moravians be massacred[5]. In this manner, aroused from all sides to acts of violence, the stupid mob considered it their civic duty to murder the missionaries and their pupils. During one trip, Bishop Spangenberg was attacked while entering an inn, cursed and mistreated. Scores of murderous bullies gathered together to carry out New Jersey's threats against Bethlehem. Even though the loving, hospitable behavior of the elders calmed the beastly sentiments upon their arrival, it merely postponed them. Waiting for an opportune moment for a deadly fire, the crazed mob was moving about the neighborhood, when a horrible event saved the population of Bethlehem from their fears. On the evening of November 24 (1755), the horizon over the Blue Ridge mountains glowed from the light of a massive fire. Horror seized the Brethren, for based on the direction and extent of the fire, it could be assumed that Gnadenhütten was already a victim of the firebrands[6]! The families had just gathered for dinner, when the Indians surrounded a dairy house, which lay across from Gnadenhütten. When the dogs began to bark and one of the men opened the door, the savages fired into the corridor and killed Fabricius and Nitchman. Those remaining swiftly barred the door and fled to the attic. Then the Indians set fire to the house, and 11 persons, including a 15-month old child, perished in misery. Aflame all over her body, Sister Sensemann threw open the window and died with the cry: "Welcome death! I happily return home." With his wife and son, one Moravian sprang from the burning roof of a rear building and escaped. In addition, Sister Parsch and one poor sick man escaped through a window. One of the Brethren who helped them escape and was attempting to follow them, was seized and scalped. All of the communities, homes, barns, and stalls went up in flames and heartrending were the screams of the horses and cattle trapped inside.

Though this event was horrible, it saved Bethlehem and its people from a similar fate. For the bloody mob, which had called the Moravians "snakes in the grass" and accused them of being secret Papists and allies of the French, and had brooded over their demise, stood ashamed before the smoking remains of the unfortunate victims, the proof that exposed and destroyed their vicious accusations. The missionary Johann Schebosch gathered from the forests those who had fled Gnadenhütten and brought the remainder to safety in Bethlehem.

---

[5] Loskiel's *History of the Moravian Miss.* Chapter 12, pag. 7.

[6] Gnadenhütten lay barely 30 miles away from Bethlehem.

The governor sent troops to protect various undamaged mills and barns; but, on the following new year's day, while a group of them were enjoying themselves ice skating on the frozen Lehigh, the savages again broke in, killed all those remaining, and set the communities' remaining possessions in flames. And this was merely the signal for renewed murderous deeds and devastations. The war parties of the savages now inundated the far border territories and pushed the settlers back to the sea coast. From the Blue Ridge Mountains to Philadelphia, Bethlehem offered the only safe haven to the refugees. The Moravians had fortified all of the public areas with stockades, erected watchtowers, and had sentries watching in every direction. Now many of their former enemies joined in this military duty and found in the once hated city hospitable shelter for their families and care for their wounded. Tedeuskung, chief of the Pennsylvania Delawares, admitted after the peace treaty, that the Moravian settlements represented the only major obstacle to the savages' campaign. Without them the entire territory all the way to the sea coast would have become a desert. The alertness of the Brethren and the thought of their own relatives and friends living among them (the converted Delawares) hindered the completion of their original destructive plans. For, under the law of retribution, in case of an attack, the latter would have had to take up arms against their own tribe or be subjected to being exterminated by the English. And, for other reasons, the situation of these christian Delawares had become extremely bad. At the outbreak of hostilities, the governor had issued a proclamation, declaring war against all the Indians nations, offering a price of 38 pounds for the capture of each enemy Delaware and 32 pounds for each scalp. Even though the proclamation included an exception to the benefit of the Delawares and Mohicans from Bethlehem, Nazareth, Gnadenthal and Christiansbrunn, nevertheless, in a private letter to Spangenberg, the governor had good cause to warn them away from the white settlements, in order to avoid falling into the hands of some assassin wanting to swindle his way to the reward in the proclamation. On the other hand, they were often sent as peace messengers by the government to the hostile Delawares, a service which no white could be entrusted to perform, since several members of their own blood had been murdered by the mistrustful Iroquois who did not tolerate any contact with their red allies. As a result of various invitations from the governor, the eastern Delawares finally showed themselves prepared to conclude a peace treaty; as one condition they demanded that the parley site had to be in Bethlehem. Aware of the significant influence of the German teachers on the Delawares, the government representatives agreed, but since Bishop Spangenberg wisely protested, Easton was selected. The forced nature of the relationship of the Delawares to the Iroquois came to light during the following event. En route to Easton, Tedeuskung, Chief of the Delawares, encountered the leader of the band, which had reduced Gnadenhütten to ashes, and because of the latter's arrogant, insulting speech, got into a fight and killed him[7].

The failure of the peace treaty has been mentioned above. The campaigns and devastations of the savages continued until 1757. At the urging of Tedeuskung, the Delawares finally buried the hatchet and made peace with the English. In order to convince their western tribal brothers to accept the same treaty, the governor, upon Spangenberg's suggestion, sent Christian Friedrich Post to the Ohio.

---

[7] Several years later, the Iroquois avenged this deed by setting Tedeuskung's house on fire during the night. This true friend of the Germans died in the flames.

Chapter 6

Post convinces the Indians of the upper Ohio to desert France. - The French destroy Fort Duquesne. - The decisive Battle at Upper Piqua. - Defeat of the French Indians. - The Miamis depart the Ohio Valley. - The English occupy the Fork of the Ohio with German Troops.

The Moravian annals first refer to Post in 1743 as one of Rauch's helpers at Schekomeko, an Indian village at present-day Poughkeepsie in eastern New York. After his release from apprenticeship, the young man continued his work among the Connecticut Indians and then moved to Pennsylvania where he soon achieved great influence among the chiefs of the Delawares. From his external appearance, Post was a worthy son of the mighty, warlike Hussites, a giant figure, tempered by adversity and weather. But the herculean breast hid a soft heart filled with a charitable love for his neighbors. It was not the myopic missionary zeal of the Zealot that drove him to the sons of the wilderness, but rather the need to spread culture. With text books and Bible in his pack, an ax in his arm and a musket on his shoulder, he often dared to visit the most feared tribes, there to build a schoolhouse and convince the suspicious natives to send him their children to receive the Moravian teachings. For 17 years he worked successfully among the savages, and his reputation as a true friend of the red race extended to the Ohio, a reputation which was helped by his marriage to a Delaware woman. By the way, because this marriage was against the wish and recommendation of the Bethlehem Directorate, he thus fell into disfavor and from then on was only recognized as an assistant and teacher in their missionary service, and not as an ordained missionary[1].

Post's diary, printed in London[2], testifies as to the unheard-of dangers and deprivations of this mission, even though the missionary Johann Heckewelder, who read the original manuscript, explained in his own memoirs, which were published in Germany, that our hero, in Christian humility and charity, had purged everything which could have in the least manner reflected glory on himself. Post departed Philadelphia on July 15, 1758. Disregarding Tedeuskung's warnings, which described the insanity of his daring in the most vivid pictures, the adventurer, accompanied by two Delawares, went up the Susquehannah, on whose banks all the settlements lay devastated. On August 7 he reached the Allegheny in the vicinity of French Creek. His path took him very near the Fort at Benango, where the hostile looks of the French sentries followed him for a while. But the officer of the watch permitted him to pass unchallenged. At "Kuschkuschky," a Delaware village near the Big Beaver, he found two hundred warriors assembled; even though they gave his eloquent pleas for peace a sympathetic ear, nevertheless they were afraid of the French soldiers and their Indian allies, the North Wyandots, Ottawas, Miamis and others. Therefore, they invited Post to a great council, which was to be held right across from Fort Duquesne, on a forested hill, where hordes of Indians from eight tribes, including several from the south, were encamped. In spite

---

[1] Loskiel's *History*, pag. 118.

[2] Ch. F. Post's *Diary of a Trip from Philadelphia to the Ohio*. London, 1750. It was also partially reprinted in Craig's *Olden Times*.

of all his bravery, our messenger was at first unwilling to bait the lion in front of his own lair; however, the savages promised him a safe escort and kept their word. On August 25, the same day that England's great ally in Europe, King Friedrich II, won his bloody victory in a terrible battle at Zorndorf, England's unpretentious American champion, the Moravian Post stood at the crossroads, within range of the enemy cannon, surrounded by the Indian warriors of the French and, within sight of the flag of Lillies fluttering in the fort, convinced them in a long, fiery speech to break with their allies.

The first to react to his speech and waver in their dependence on the French were the Delawares, with whom he had been friendly from the beginning. And when an old, deaf Onondago grumbler reminded Post in a rough manner, that the very land on which they were standing belonged to the Iroquois Confederation, a Delaware ordered him to be silent with the words:" This one does not speak like a man; he just wants to frighten us into believing that this land belongs to him; he is dreaming; both he and his father (the French) have become drunk on rum, and the best thing to do is quiet them down so that they can again become sober. He does not even know what his own nation does at home, even less, what the Confederation has to say to the English. Sleep it off, you old whiskey barrel, we will talk to you only when you again become sober."

This lapidary style of speech had its effect on those wavering, and when Post finally threatened the imminent arrival of the English army on the Ohio, everyone was won over. At the same time they all bitterly complained about the voracity and greed with which the whites were falling upon their land.

"Why did not the English and the French fight their battles in their own country or on the sea?" they asked Post. "Your heart is good, Father, you speak the truth. But we know that among your people there are always those who wish to become rich. We let others have what is theirs. The whites believe that we have no brains in our skulls, that they are mighty and we are a handful. But they should consider, when one hunts rattlesnakes, they often cannot be found and they might even strike before one sees them." Post was successful in moving the assembled tribes to conclude a peace treaty and after suffering horrible deprivations and under constant danger from roving French and Indians, he safely returned to his home settlement.

For Captain de Lignery, the commander of the French forces on the Ohio, the desertion of so many allies came like a bolt out of the blue sky. Crevecoeur had led a large segment of the Fort Duquesne garrison back to Canada, in preparation for the decisive battle with England. With the 500 soldiers and faithful Indians remaining to him, de Lignery could do little against Forbe's army, when more bad news arrived. The English Colonel Bradstreet had conquered the fortress Frontenac, today's Kingston (ON), and along with it all of the provisions and military supplies destined for the French troops on the Ohio. With that they had lost all hold in the valley. But the brave garrison of Fort Duquesne wanted to show what awaited the English army had it not been for Post's success. Informed by their scouts about their approach, they bravely advanced against them, defeated the advance party under Majors Grant and Lewis, and took the former prisoner along with 18 officers. De Lignery then had the fortress buildings and stockade burned and pulled back to the lower Ohio stations. On Colonel Johnson's farmstead near Upper Piqua in Ohio's Miami county, the remaining faithful Indian tribes fought their final battle under the Flag of Lillies. The Miamis, Wyandots, Ottawas, Chippewas and other northern tribes had fortified themselves with the help of French officers and Canadian traders. Led and directed by English traders, the war parties of the Delawares, Shawnees, Senecas, Cherokeess and Catawbas attacked. The siege lasted over a week. In spite of repeated fierce attacks, the fort held. Many fell on both sides, but the attackers suffered the most. Black Hoof, chief of the Shawnees, later told Colonel Johnson of the unbelievable ferocity of this battle. The ground was so covered with bullets, that one could have picked them up by the basketful[3]. Of the besieged, the Miamis lost such a large segment of their warriors, that the remainder sadly transferred their former hunting grounds on the Big Miami and Wabash to the Shawnees, and moved to the Maumee near today's Fort Wayne, never to return.

The French war with the English in the Ohio valley ended with the battle at Upper Piqua. Its theater then moved to Canada. On the site of Fort Duquesne arose Fort Pitt, the cradle of Pittsburg. Its new fortifications arose to the tune of German military songs; for the occupying troops were to a large part Germans; namely 850 men from the German-American Royal Americans under Colonel Stanwix and 4,300 Pennsylvania and Virginia provincials, including many Germans. In his "History of the Germans in America," Franz Löher reaffirmed the story of a Pennsylvania German that Colonel Heinrich Bouquet, a Swiss officer in the English service, who assumed command of Fort Pitt and the surrounding area, commanded his troops in German. In October, the English concluded a definitive peace treaty at Easton with the Iroquois and their allies, the Delawares and Shawnees, and again it was Post who bore the news and articles of the treaty to the Ohio. Perkins and Taylor, the Anglo-American historians of the Ohio Valley, recognize Post's valuable service in the surrender of Fort Duquesne; they admit that the unpretentious German had given his British majesty the key to the west, which "without his mission, surely a large force of western Indians would have opposed Forbe's army or would have hurried to the defense of the fortress, in which case, due to the poor condition of the roads and unfavorable season of the year, along with the incompetent leadership of the campaign, Forbes' army could have expected a "second Braddock's field".

---

[3] Col. Johnson's Narrative in Howe's hist. Coll. of Ohio, pag. 303.

The English Sovereignty

Chapter 7

Advance of the Anglo-Americans to the West. - Ohio one hundred years ago. - Post and Heckewelder, the only settlers. Their adventures and tribulations. - Pontiac's Conspiracy. - Captain Schlosser. - Ensign Pauly.

Due to the devastation of the French war, the Blue Ridge mountains became the boundary of the American settlements. However, barely had the forks of the Ohio received an English garrison, when the border settlers returned from all sides to their destroyed homesteads on the other side (of the Blue Ridge.) In addition, droves of land speculators, traders, and adventurers began to explore the Ohio valley. Braddock's and Forbes' soldiers had seen the "beautiful river", and the memory of these splendid, game-rich forests; its fertile valleys and picturesque heights made them and many others who had heard these seductive descriptions dissatisfied with their former, desolate homesteads. But there was an additional reason why the eyes of so many turned towards the river valley. The Virginia government had not only turned to extensive gifts of land grants for its volunteer soldiers, but furthermore, the back pay and the constant land grants had demolished the state currency. Also, using a provincial prerogative, the state legislature had granted to the settlers "free homesteads", which they could claim at will in the apparently limitless Ohio valley. It was no wonder that the Virginians soon traversed the entire length of the Blue Ridge and the Alleghenies with their surveying chains and rifles on their shoulders, seizing the rich valleys of both Kanawhas, that glorious contrast to their exhausted tobacco fields on the James river. A report of the provincial secretary notes that in 1757, the Virginia government had already granted 3 million acres of land west of the mountains, at times granting the same tracts to different companies and individuals, a fact which later spawned ill-will and expensive trials. Naturally, the Ohio Indians soon began to protest these intrusions into their hunting grounds, whereupon Colonel Bouquet found it necessary already in 1762 to publish a proclamation, in which he, in the name of the British government, pointed out that the 1758 Treaty of Easton unconditionally guaranteed to the red man all the lands west of the Allegheny mountains as hunting grounds, whereupon he forbade all settlements on said land and ordered the arrest of all traders and settlers, which in itself aroused the mistrust of the Ohio Indians. This action on the part of the British was of little help to the natives, since the border populations laughed at the empty threat. And when the 1763 Peace of Paris ceded to England the entire North American French territory east of the Mississippi[1], the Ohio valley became a special target of the speculators. The former land companies received new life, and new clubs

---

[1] During the previous year, in November 1762, France had ceded Louisiana to Spain in a secret treaty.

were formed. Numerous pamphlets were published, which depicted the Ohio homesteads in the most seductive colors. While in this manner the sights and exploratory steps of the speculators and pioneers turned toward the uninhabited hunting grounds south of the Ohio, that is, today's West Virginia and Kentucky, already in 1761 the adventurous Post, explorer of the Ohio Valley, built a blockhouse right in the midst of the aboriginal owners of these lands, on the north side of the Muskingum at the fork of the Sandy and Tuscaroras (in the present day community of Bethlehem, in Stark County).

If one excludes the Jesuit or trader stations[2], then this was the first dwelling to be constructed by a white man in Ohio. After inquiring among his in-laws, the Delawares, and finding them receptive to his teachings, he returned to Bethlehem to find a fitting companion to teach reading and writing to the Indian children, while he would preach to their parents. He found this companion in Johann Heckewelder, an alert 19 year old youth, whom the Directorate had released from his apprenticeship with a cooperage, and who happily followed Post to his hut in the far wilderness. In March 1762, their packs stuffed with instructional and prayer books, the two began their dangerous journey. Having crossed the snowy fields of the Alleghenies and the swollen rivers, they barely made it to Pittsburg, where they recovered from their adversities and enjoyed the hospitality of Colonel Bouquet, who provided them with ample supplies and munitions to continue their journey. Some Delawares brought the adventurers across the Beaver and gave them game and bear grease for the journey. Even Chief White Eye, out of exceptional generosity, presented them with several chickens. Four days later, on April 11, after a journey of 33 days, the two reached their isolated house. Wild birds and squirrels had, in the meantime, built nests inside, but fled to the nearby budding oak branches, as the two, "singing a hymn", entered the blockhouse.

The next day our heroes sprang to work to clear a field of 3 acres for corn and garden vegetables. But with jealous eyes the redskins already protected the sanctity of their forests as a Palladium against the white land thieves. Their axes had barely felled the first trees, when a Delaware runner from the village of Tuscarora[3] demanded that the two appear the next day in the conference hall and immediately cease their clearing work. The adventurers obeyed the summons. Upon their entrance into the council wigwam, the speaker arose and in a ceremonious speech reminded them of the basis of their right of settlement, namely that they had only requested to live among them and teach the children; however, rather than open a school, they had marked out a large tract of land for planting and felled trees, as the whites did everywhere; were the council to permit this, then other whites would come and do the same, then build a fort to protect the intruders, and in the end seize the land, as it had always been done. Post informed the assembly that they intended only to grow enough for support themselves to avoid becoming a burden on their red brothers for their food, and for that, these three acres would be barely sufficient. The planting of a bit of corn and vegetables did not give them nor anyone else the slightest claim to the land; they were seeking no gain for themselves. Thereupon the speaker replied: "As you say, you have come at the behest of the Great Spirit, in order to teach and preach to us. The French priests from Detroit, whom the Great Spirit sends to his Indian children, say the same. However, these men do not cut down trees, do absolutely no hard work, and still appear to be well fed.

---

[2] The foundation of Post's residence can be seen to this day. A pile of stones, the backside of his chimney, still lies on the same spot. The garden site can only be differentiated from the surrounding woods due to the underbrush which sprang up in the meantime.

[3] It counted 40 wigwams and stood near today's Bolivar (OH).

If you are his true servants, then the Great Spirit will care for you in a similar manner. Therefore, we will allow you a plot of ground of 50 paces square, larger than the flower and vegetable gardens of the French priests in Detroit. Are you satisfied with that?" Post gave his assent and the next day, Chief Pipe himself measured the plot with his own steps.

This conference shows that already in 1762 the Indians on the north side of th Ohio were well aware of the dangers, which the constantly changing government policies and the hordes of white intruders upon their lands south of the Ohio represented and declared their participation against the English in the impending battles of destruction.

During the summer of that year, Post and Heckewelder built their garden, taught the little Delawares, and preached the Bible to the adults. But their situation soon became full of tribulations and dangers. The Indians treated them with suspicion. Numerous councils of the chiefs of the northern tribes took place there, where war against the whites was suggested, and in which the two were accused of being alleged spies for the English. In addition, starvation threatened them. No more flour could be obtained from Fort Pitt, since the supplies there had been destroyed by a flood. Even among the Indians there was a certain scarcity. Their sparse supply of corn had been used up for planting, and even potatoes were scarce. There was surplus of wild ducks, but the two did not have a canoe with which to hunt them; the wild geese stayed in the middle of the river and the pheasants and squirrels could not be eaten in the summer. Their main nourishment consisted of fish and forest herbs which grew particularly well in the lowlands. Due to a lack of nourishment, the hard work of clearing and loosening the thickly rooted soil weakened them physically. "One day," writes Heckewelder in his memoirs, "several chiefs came and requested my presence for a few days to help them enclose their land. I happily accepted their invitation, since I wished to gain their confidence, and therefore worked as best as I could. At the same time I was able to regain my health and earlier strength, since, as long as I remained with them, I had enough to satisfy my hunger. Thus, I suddenly found myself in the land of plenty, where I had the opportunity to make the acquaintance of the Indian youth and at the same time use my coopering abilities for the benefit of the tribe. During my stay in the village I received the name 'Piselatulpe' (Turtle), by which I was later known to the Delawares."

In late summer a conference with the Delawares took place in Lancaster. Post was sent there by the governor of Pennsylvania and instructed to bring as many chiefs from the west as possible, particularly King Beaver and the great war chief Schingask. Beaver and White Eye accompanied Post back to Lancaster, but Schingask refused to go since the governor had earlier put a price on his scalp. The community elders in Bethlehem decided that, should Post return to Lancaster, Heckewelder should not remain alone in the wilderness, but the brave young man did not want to give up this great undertaking and therefore decided not to leave the lonely blockhouse on the Muskingum. He built a canoe to carry cedar wood in order to make buckets, barrels, and other items for the Indians and thus trade for wild game. Post had left him the remains of old sermons and religious books, which he faithfully studied on rainy days, but did not ignore the advice of his experienced friend, never to read or write in the presence of the Indians, since they suspected that the writing concerned them or their lands. After Post's departure, Heckewelder did not lack food; there were such great swarms of ducks, that he would sometimes bag 5 to 6 with one shot. In regards to his own spiritual nourishment, the hermit writes: "I kept my books and papers carefully hidden in the attic, from where, through the windows, I could see when anyone approached the blockhouse. Here I passed many hours, far from civilization, alone with my books and with my God." Several days later, his canoe was lost due to the carelessness of the Indians who had often borrowed it to catch fish or hunt deer on the river by torchlight. Again the former problem of lack of food arose. The nettles were too hard and therefore could not be eaten. The Indians stole the vegetables in the garden, and in addition to all the other problems, the cold fever reappeared, which he had caught while wading across the river visiting an Indian trader by the name of Calhoun, who had settled on the other side and, as a god-fearing man, had come to like our young, earnest hermit. Soon after, he was a witness to a special occasion. In the still of the night he suddenly heard the most miserable wailings; the wife of Schingask had died and, as was their custom, the Indians believed it was the result of black magic, which an evil shaman had cast over her. Her death was announced by the nightly wailings of the crying women. According to local custom, Heckewelder joined the mourners at the bier the next day and, in recognition for his participation, he received a black silk shawl and a pair of leggings as a gift. However, the mourning women received the best reward. Every evening for three weeks after the burial, a cooking pot of delicacies was brought to the grave, in order to comfort the departed spirit on its way to a new land. During this period the monotone wailing of these women put the settler to sleep every night. The paroxysm of the fever stricken (Heckewelder) at last became greater, and the resultant weakness prevented him finally from even fording the river. He was now alone in his blockhouse, poor and in deprivation. He had to refuse Calhoun's friendly invitation to stay at his house, "because he had promised Post to remain in the blockhouse, and, had he left, the Indians would have stolen all his possessions anyhow." In this desperate condition, he traded an Indian visitor his pocket knife for a small bark canoe and paddled to Calhoun, who barely recognized the scrawny sufferer. His misery finally forced him to admit the failure of the undertaking. Furthermore, after Post's departure, the absurd suspicion was again raised, that he intended to deliver the Indian lands into the hands of the whites. When our adventurer finally realized that permission for him to stay in the wilderness would soon be revoked, he wrote to Post and described his sad situation. In his reply, (Post) told him to return immediately, the only sensible recommendation, since war threatened to break out between Great Britain and the Indians. Unfortunately, the poor youth's horse was stolen; he was too weak to travel on foot, but too impatient to wait for another opportunity. A fever had suddenly gripped Calhoun's servants, who were supposed to take pack horses laden with furs to Pittsburg. The danger increased. Snakelike eyes of strange Indians followed his every step in Tuscarora. An old Indian woman finally told Calhoun, that these were looking for an opportunity some night to attack his young friend in his blockhouse and kill him. For that reason, Heckewelder remained that night under Calhoun's roof. The next day, he wanted to return to see whether any thing had been taken from his hut and collect several necessary items, which he had forgotten in his haste to leave. However, Calhoun prevented him from doing this and instead sent a giant servant, strong as an ox, whom the Indians feared as a "Manitto" (forest spirit). On his return, he reported that the hut had been broken into and that apparently two persons had spent the night there. Hot coals were still glowing in the fireplace. Assassins had apparently waited for the young man.

To remain in the hut or even in the territory was now out of the question. Any delay was insane. "I did not see my lonely forest paths any more," writes Heckewelder, "but rather remained under the hospitable roof of the trader. Emissaries from the Senecas and other tribes from the north inflamed the Delawares against the English. Shortly after my departure, the war broke out and more than 30 of my acquaintances lost their lives."

Under the protection of Calhoun's servants, our hero traveled to Pittsburg. On the third day, he met Post, accompanied by the Indian agent McKee, who was traveling back to his station. The latter did not think the danger too great and would not be kept back. However, just as he arrived, he had to flee in order to save his life; he safely returned to Lancaster via hidden forest paths. Even Calhoun had to leave the territory at the behest of the Delawares; a group of warriors attacked him at the Beaver, but the swiftness of his horse saved him. His servant Jacob Smith, the "Forest Spirit", escaped with his skin intact; he put his gigantic hands around the throat of his attacker and strangled him to death.

Heckewelder writes, "After taking my departure from Post, I galloped after my companions, who, during our conversation, had continued onward with the pack horses. Within a distance of 5 miles I thought I had found their tents. A column of smoke between the trees indicated to me how near they were and I rode there without hesitation. Who could describe my surprise, when I found myself in the middle of a war party's camp. The sight of bound captives, lying around the scalping post with its barbaric decorations, was not very encouraging to me. I thank God, that they let me continue, and after another five miles I happily greeted my companions again[4].

Heckewelder arrived in Pittsburg in the third week of October. When he finally reached Bethlehem, sickness and tribulation had so changed his appearance, that none of his brethren at first recognized him. Our adventurer had barely reached safety, when the storm of united Indians from Lake Michigan south to the borders of North Carolina burst upon the English frontier settlements. In order to destroy them, Iroquois, Wyandots, Delawares, Miamis, Shawnees, Ottawas, Chippewas under Pontiac's leadership, had buried their former divisive tribal rivalries in oaths of unity. If the Ohio Indians stood against the English intruders, bitter about the continual robbing of their lands, the ownership of which had been ceremoniously guaranteed to them by the British government, so, too, were the lake tribes incited by Canadian priests and traders, for whom it was painful that the Catholic territories, won with the blood of so many heroes and religious martyrs, should fall into the possession of a Protestant government and become the property of that same people that mocked and hated their religion and whose fanatics had murdered the Jesuit priest Rasles at Norridgewock under the most horrible of tortures. Just about the time of the surrender of Canada when Governor Vaudreuil was supposed to hand over the western forts to Major Robert Rogers, who was sent by the British government, the simmering hostility against the English arose anew. Rogers appeared before Detroit with two hundred mounted marksmen, whom he, as a compliment to the Indians, had armed with tomahawks and scalping knives. The emissary whom he sent to inform the Commandant Beleter as to the reason for his arrival was thrown into prison, and in a mocking greeting he saw before his eyes the erection of a flag pole, with a wooden caricature of England, from which a raven was biting out the eyes. Without Pontiac's protection, the major and all of his people would have been massacred[5] on the spot.

But that same Pontiac, at one time the friend of the whites, was now inflamed against the lying, murderous, land thieves on this side of the Alleghenies, as Philipp of Pokanoket had done once before, rose against the Puritan enemy on the other side (of the Alleghenies). As with the noble warrior among the New England Indians, so did Pontiac embody

---

[4] *Life of Heckewelder* by Rev. Edw. Rundthaler 45-58. Post's Journal in Craig's *Olden Time*, Vol. I, pag. 98-145.

[5] This generally popular hostility against England in the French territory, also slowly infected Rogers himself. For several years later, he was taken before a court martial for alleged sedition, the surrender of Fort Michillimacinac to the Spanish, who then occupied Upper Louisiana. Shortly thereafter he entered into the service of the Bey of Algiers and fought two battles in the cavalry. At the beginning of the War of Independence he returned to America, and since Washington refused him a position because he considered him a spy, he went over to the British who made him a Colonel.

the collective hatred of all the western tribes, whose burning revenge inflamed all hearts and caused the most respected and proud (among them) to disregard the lowly extraction of the new leader. Pontiac was an Ottawa; his tribe a pariah among the others, which, instead of warriors and hunters, produced only trappers, fishers, and traders[6] Along with the Wyandots, the tribe was forced from its former homeland by the Iroquois and found a refuge on the west bank of Lake Huron and the northern Michigan peninsula among the Pottowatamies and Ojibwas, and the alliance with these famous warriors formed the basis for Pontiac's conspiracy. It was set into motion, not as a helpless, bloodthirsty giant, but rather with deliberate self-confidence and enlightened cunning. During a festive ballgame, which the Chippewas ostensibly gave to honor the Commandant, Mackinaw was taken and, in a similar manner, nine additional British forts, including the important Fort Michillimacinac. Many officers, including several Germans, fell into the hands of the savages and were killed. One stockade at the mouth of the St. Joseph, on the eastern shore of Lake Michigan, was commanded by Captain Schlosser; a band of pelt-laden Pottowatamies, ostensibly having come to trade, attacked him in his own quarters, took him prisoner, and cut down the garrison. In a similar manner Sandusky came under the power of the savages. The troops were cut down. Bound hand and foot, their commander, Ensign Pauly, was led to Detroit, and along the way was given the comforting news that he would there be burned alive. Upon his arrival in Pontiac's camp, he was received by a mass of Indians, mostly women and children; accompanied with enraged curses, (he was) was stoned, beaten with rods, and made to dance. Even worse things awaited him when luckily an old woman, whose husband had died shortly before, approached him and adopted him as a replacement for her recently perished warrior. Pauly accepted this life-saving offer, since the only other alternative was being burnt at the stake. With a ceremonious gesture, an icy gray warrior approached him, a piece of bark covered with ash in his hand. After sticking thumb and index finger into it, he carefully pulled out every hair from the unhappy ensign's head, with the exception of a patch on his crown, in which he entwined feathers and other decorations. After this beauty operation was completed, a flock of Indian girls fell upon him and, laughing and joking, pulled him to the river and dunked him under several times in order to wash the white blood from his veins. Thereupon this naturalized Indian was, in the customary manner, accompanied to the wigwam of the elderly bride decorated for the wedding, and from then on was treated with all the respect which was due to a warrior of the tribe. The forced marriage took place on May 20 and the divorce the following July.

On a beautiful evening that month, the sentries on Detroit's walls suddenly saw a man, chased by Indians, running towards the fort with the swiftness of a deer. When they came into gunshot range, the Indians gave up the chase and the heavily sweating refugee made it to the wall, where a door was opened to receive the exhausted man. It was the youthful Commandant of Sandusky, who had used the first opportunity to flee from the arms of the elderly Ottawa widow.

At the same time as the seizure of the British forts, the Indians seized many traders on their territory along with their goods and murdered over one hundred of them. The frontier settlements were again devastated, and the streams of western Virginia and Pennsylvania ran red with the blood of the murdered pioneers. In the first instance alone, 20,000 persons were driven from their homesteads. Only the fortresses of Detroit, Niagara, and Pitt were able to withstand the determined sieges of the Indians. In the latter, starvation arose; but Bouquet defeated the besiegers in a two-day

---

[6] According to Bancroft, "ottawa" means "huckster".

battle at Turtle Creek and successfully brought a packtrain of 340 horses loaded with flour to Fort Pitt.

In order to pacify the redskins, the British government issued a new proclamation in the Fall of 1763, in which the Indians were guaranteed their lands absolutely and without conditions. All settlers on those lands were ordered to depart and the governors enjoined from issuing additional patents or even surveying permits for lands on the other side of the Alleghenies. No one would be permitted to make private land purchases from the Indians, since, additionally, this privilege was reserved for the Crown. Generals Bradstreet and Bouquet were sent at the head of an expeditionary corps to be present at the reading of the proclamation to the tribes and lend it further credence with the sight of their armed force. The former rivalry between the Iroquois and the Ohio Indians had again come to light and seriously weakened the alliance against the whites and, since the fortunes of war had become somewhat fickle, the missions of the two generals had the most effect. Bouquet's expeditionary column consisted of the remains of the 42nd and 77th Highland regiments, which had returned from the seizure of Savannah. From Fort Pitt he marched to the upper Muskingum, established a camp at the mouth of the White Woman, and had made peace with the chiefs of the Delawares and Shawnees. The remarkable scene which occurred at the return of the white captives was described by one who witnessed it, the engineer Hutchins, in an interesting paper about the expedition which was also depicted by the brush of Benjamin West in a powerful painting. "Fathers and mothers" writes Hutchins, "recognized and clasped their lost children in their arms, men their stolen wives; siblings, barely in a position to speak the same language and, because of the long separation, doubting whether they were of the same parents, extended to each other their hands. The mental state of the Indians was a unique contrast to their normal fierce hatred and increased the effect of the touching scene. They unwillingly delivered their beloved captives and with moving gestures they committed them to the care of the commanding generals. As long as the camp was there they brought corn, skins, horses and other gifts. The tenderest of bonds had been woven between the hostile races. In spite of a constant danger of death from the hostile pioneers, one Iroquois accompanied his beloved, a young Virginia woman, to the border. The Shawnees had to bring a few of the female captives tied up to the camp. Girls and women would flee at night back to the wigwams they had left; others, who had been forcefully torn from the arms of their copper-colored lovers, cried miserably during the journey and refused all nourishment[7]."

For his successful campaign, Bouquet received the gratitude from the legislatures of Pennsylvania and Virginia. During the war he was promoted to divisional commander; however he died next year at the seat of his new command in Mobile. On August 21 in a great council with 20 tribes in Detroit, General Johnson, Commissioner for Indian Affairs, concluded a definitive peace treaty, in which all the lost military posts and forts were returned and permission given to the English, to maintain fortified stations in the Indian territory in order to protect their traders. Around each of these they were given all the land over which a cannon ball would fly.

For the protection of the Indians there was an agreement reached, that in the case of the murder of an Englishman by an Indian, though the murderer would be treated according to English law, half of the jury would consist of Indians. In April of the following year, Johnson concluded a general peace treaty

---

[7] *A historical Account of the Expedition against the Ohio Indians in the year 1764 under the command of Henry Bouquet, Esquire, by a Lover of his Country.* London 1766.

with the western Indians in the German sections of New York. The latter had stipulated that the Susquehannah, Allegheny, or at most the Ohio should be the western boundary for the Europeans; the scheming Johnson, however, got around this article of the treaty and secured a rich compensation of land in the west for all the traders who had lost their goods in the war of 1763. In order to ensure for the future the peace and good relations with the French settlers, who were considered the secret instigators of the previous wars against the English, Johnson sent George Croghan as his Deputy Commissioner to the west. This mission, however, had no success. In his published report, Croghan describes the French population of Vincennes, Detroit, and other communities as a lazy, dirty, faithless rabble turned wild Indian, far worse than the Indians themselves and doing everything possible to make the English as repulsive and hated as possible to their copper-colored blood relatives. Therefore, he suggested that, to have peace in the future, this irreconcilable arch enemy must be driven out of the land.

After his marvelous plan to destroy the whites failed due to the disunity of his tribal brothers, the Indian Hannibal returned to the far west. Of his end, his biographer Parkman reports: "Near the end of 1769, in the dress uniform of a French officer, a gift from the Marquis de Montcalm, Pontiac arrived at the site of present-day St. Louis, where his friend St. Ange, whom he highly regarded, was commanding officer. After remaining two days in St. Louis, it came to his ears, that Indians in Cahokia were assembling for a drinking party, and he went there against the advice of St. Ange. During the festive reception given him, he became drunk and stumbled out of the village into the forest, singing the medicine chant, to whose melody he ascribed a magical effect for all occasions. In the meantime, an English trader by the name of Williamson bribed a Kaskaskia Indian with a barrel of rum to kill him. This assassin followed him, waited for an opportune moment, and buried his tomahawk in Pontiac's brain. This shameful murder awakened the feeling of revenge of all the nations friendly to him, and in the destructive wars against them, the Illinois tribes were almost annihilated. The French officers buried Pontiac with military honors near the Fort in St. Louis. In the meantime a city has arisen as a mausoleum over the ashes of the forest hero. The race which he had so bitterly hated treads with a tireless business energy over his forgotten grave."

Chapter 8

The Treaty of Fort Stanwix. - George Washington seeks German Farmers for the Ohio Valley. - Boone's German Companions. - George Jäger, Kenton's Mentor. - The German Long Hunters. - Michael Schuck. - David Zeisberger Establishes Friedensdorf. - the First Community. - Johann Herrmann Plants the First Corn in Kentucky. - Glikhican's Vision. - A German-Indian National Church in the Ohio Valley.

What the British government promised in its proclaimation to the rebellious Indians of the west was honored neither by the settlers nor by the government itself. Based on their Virginia land grants, the settlers not only ignored the orders which General Gage had issued for their removal and remained where they were, but also inched unnoticed even further than the agreed upon boundary on the Monongahela and Allegheny. Even the land speculators were not dissuaded. General Johnson himself, Benjamin Franklin, Johann Sargent, the London banker Walpole and others badgered the ministry for permission to grab the land of the Six Nations south of the Ohio and from that establish an independent colony. The cabinet hesitated for a long time, but finally approved the faithless step. The governors of the various provinces called together representatives of the Six Nations[1], the Delawares and the Shawnees, to a congress which took place in October 1768 in Fort Stanwix. The invited tribes were all represented, and, with the exception of the latter two, the representatives signed a treaty which transferred the title of the entire territory south of the Ohio from the Six Nations to the English. The stretch between the Little Kanawha and the Monongahela was received by William Trent, an attorney for 22 traders, whose goods had been destroyed by the Indians, while the King received the rest.

The majority of the Kentucky, western Virginia and Pennsylvania land titles[2] are based upon this Treaty of Fort Stanwix. Its conclusion was an intentional fraud, for the English crown was certainly aware of the former claims of the Ohio Indians; just two years later, a treaty signed at Lochaber recognized the right of the Cherokees to a southern section of this territory. Companies of land speculators shot up like mushrooms. The Ohio Company renewed its former claims. Through its eloquent speaker, Benjamin Franklin, the Walpole Company presented to the King a request for the formation of an "Ohio province" from the Kanawha territories. At the head of a "Mississippi Company", which requested from the King a grant of 2 1/2 million acres of Ohio land, appeared George Washington, whose interest had already been directed at this land through a royal gift of 10,000 acres, presented for services rendered during the French war. In 1770, accompanied by his agent, William Crawford, he traveled down the Ohio, exploring and surveying a large tract between the two Kanawhas. Upon his return, he complained in a letter that the English considered the Indian lands as free booty, and that therefore the Delawares and Shawnees were watching their progress with hostile eyes; he prophesied, that the usurporious greed of the Virginians would soon grab all the valuable land not just on the Redstone and other tributaries of the Monongahela, but even down to the Big Kanawha. This complaint and prophecy appear somewhat sanctimonious. For through his own example Washington had given to the

---

[1] The Iroquois Federation was strengthened by the Tuscaroras.

[2] *Western Annals* by Perkins pag. 168.

Indians a valid reason for complaint as well as giving to his countrymen such a shining challenge for a relentless seizure of the western lands. The stretch which the cuts of his own ax marked, include no less than 32,337 acres between both Kanawhas with 13 1/2 miles fronting on the Ohio; 23,216 acres on the Big Kanawha with a river front of 40 miles. Fifteen miles south of Wheeling he acquired 587 acres with a river front of 2 1/2 miles. Like his grandfather Lawrence, the young land speculator was busy trying to win German settlers for his Ohio land. In a letter from Mount Vernon from February 1774, which he directed to James Tilghman in Philadelphia, he wrote: "Politics and general interest, necessitate the settlement of these homesteads on the Ohio in the fastest, most effective, and most efficient manner. Numerous suggestions on this topic have already been made to me, among which, in my opinion, none has a better chance for success than the importation of Germans, Palatines." Washington directs the question to Tilghman, how he might in best manner be able to send an intelligent German to Germany, in order to there arrange for the immigration, the embarkation in Holland, and similar items. At the same time (February 22, 1774), he turned to the shipper Henry Riddle in Philadelphia in regards to the same topic. In this letter he promises to the German settlers free passage to the Potomac and Ohio and supplies up to the first harvest. They would live rent-free for four years on lands where there was no house and for two years where there was a house and a clearing of five acres or something similar.

The outbreak of the Revolutionary War ruined all of the plans of companies and individuals for the settlement of the Ohio valley. The Ohio, Walpole, and Mississippi companies went under in its storms; Washington and Franklin were called away from the founding of English provinces on the Ohio to another arena, the establishment of the great American republic.

What the capital and prestige of companies and individuals in the east had not been able to achieve, the settlement of the Fort Stanwix section was undertaken, in the meantime, by unknown and poor adventurers from another direction. For the first explorers of the western parts (Kentucky) did not come down the Ohio from Pennsylvania and Virginia, but rather forced their way through the Cumberland Gap from North Carolina. It was daring hunters or traders with the Cherokees, of whom a certain McBride left behind the oldest trace from 1754 when he cut his name with that date into a beech tree at the mouth of the Kentucky river. At that time, an Indian warpath led from the Cumberland ford, along the highlands on the east fork of the Kentucky river, and across the Licking river to the mouth of the Scioto. It was the connection between the Indians of the south and those of the Ohio valley, and along its path the Virginia and North Carolina traders dealt for the hides and skins taken on the hunting grounds of the latter. The Virginian Walker, who pushed along this trail to the Ohio in 1758, is considered the discoverer of the Cumberland mountains; he gave them the name of the brave English count. In 1767, John Finley, with a group of companions on a hunting expedition, entered Kentucky, which at the time was still unknown even in Virginia.

Among the bravest and most daring of these adventurers, there appeared in the earliest times Germans from the predominately German-populated northern and western North Carolina counties of Granville, Stokes, Mecklenburg, and Lincoln. George Jäger, one of the best marksmen and trappers, was the teacher of the famous Simon Kenton, when the future hero of the Ohio valley had fled from Virginia for an alleged murder. For Kenton had, on a deserted forest path, actually attacked a certain William Beach, who had stolen his fiancee, used Beach's own long pigtail to tie him to a tree and so mistreated him, that he left him for dead on the ground. Afraid of a trial, he fled to the west, the goal of so many fleeing provincial law. Under the assumed name of Simon Butler, he joined Jäger on the Big Kanawha in 1771. The latter told about the "Cane-land" called "Kentucky" by the Ohio Indians, and, through his descriptions of the new, fertile lands and their abundance of game, inflamed his youthful fantasy[3]." Jäger was Kenton's inseparable companion on all his hunting trips in the years of 1771-72, and was killed at his side by Indians the next year at a camp on the Big Kanawha.

Another similar son of the forest was Michael Schuck, who, at the same time, accompanied the renowned bear hunter Boone into Kentucky. His parents had immigrated from Germany and they and all of this brothers and siblings had been killed by Indians in the frontier area of North Carolina. He remained in the woods as an 8 year old orphan, alone in the lonely blockhouses, depending on himself to stay alive, growing up with the instinct of a panther and the vision of an eagle. Snow-white hair and a huge frame marked this German Indian, whose hunting expeditions and battles with the redskins appear to be the fictional imaginings of some writer[4]. No less known in this forest life were the German pioneers Kaspar Mansco, David Link, Christopher Stopf, George Hofacker. The latter became particularly famous in a meeting with the Cherokees at Heaton's Station (July 20, 1776)[5]. Already in 1770, the people in New River, Holstein, and Clinch, had sent an expedition to explore the Ohio territory. It consisted of 40 brave woodsmen under the leadership of Colonel James Knox. Dressed in deerskin shirts, leggings, and moccasins, their muskets on their shoulders, the adventurers followed the path of the Cumberland, where the forests were full of buffalo and deer; at the site of today's Nashville, they discovered French Lick. Due to their absence from home over several years these 40 Nimrods were called the Long Hunters. On the north side of the Big Barren, three miles from Bowling Green, now made famous because of the fortifications of the Secessionists, in Warren County, Kentucky, stands a group of ancient beech trees, which marks the camp of a group of these adventurers. Thirteen names were cut into the thickest of these trees with the date June 13, 1775. Among them are the following: Johann Jackmann, Valentin Herrmann, C. Bulge, Nic. Nall.

At first the Indians of the Ohio valley calmly observed the wanderings of the whites through their southern hunting grounds, but they permitted no settlements. In spite of the fraudulent Treaty of Fort Stanwix, the English adventurers generally recognized the Indians' title. The famous Thomas Bullitt, who traveled down the Ohio in 1773, first stopped at the mouth of the Scioto, to seek permission to hunt from the Shawnees, even though the government of Virginia had already annexed this territory to the province under the name of Fincastle County. Under the pretense of a hunting trip that same year, Bullit's companions surveyed the magnificent valley, where today Frankfort stands and drew up the plan for Louisville for John Campbell and John Conolly. And General Thompson of Pennsylvania secretly stole down the Ohio, slipped into the wilderness of the Licking and, with the permission of the government of Virginia, laid out on its north fork the land grants for the provincial soldiers, who had served in the French war.

While West Virginia and Kentucky became better known to the eastern provinces through the descriptions of these white intruders, the German Moravians already had permanent settlements among the owners of these huge hunting grounds, among the Indians north of the Ohio. Should Boone and his companions be honored as heros and as the founders of a state, because they risked the dangers of

---

[3] *Historical Sketches of Kentucky* by Lewis Collins. Cin. 1847, pag. 383.

[4] His biography appears in the *Western Monthly Review* of 1829, and was taken from the *Missouri Intelligencer* of November of the same year. Schuck followed Boone to Missouri, where he passed away in its wilderness.

[5] *Annals of Tennessee* by Ramsay, pag. 105, 154.

undertaking the exploration of a lonely, uninhabited wilderness, then what glory is due these German knights of the gospel, who even earlier had founded their outposts of culture in the midst of the bitterest enemies of all whites? The storms of the previous war had barely settled and the autumn of the year 1767 arrived (the same year, in which John Finley, Boone's guide, first undertook his adventurous wanderings through Kentucky) when David Zeisberger, accompanied by the national helper Anton[6], following Post's footsteps, appeared on the Allegheny at the request of the natives in order to open a school amongst them. Upon his arrival, our religious hero found such a fertile ground for his work, that he immediately decided to establish a Moravian advanced settlement. As a result, the next spring he settled with his companion Gottlob Sensemann in the Indian village of Goschgosching[7]. But his "House of the Lord" had barely filled with eager students, when, as with his predecessor Post, the former suspicion of the chiefs and priests was raised against him with hostile cunning. Allegations of every sort were soon voiced against him. It was charged that he was only teaching the Indians in order to steal their confidence and then sell them to the English like Negro slaves. The old women of the village soon ran wailing from hut to hut with the complaint that, since the Germans began living amongst them, corn worms were ruining the cornmeal, chestnuts and bilberries would not ripen, and the game had fled the hunting grounds. The mighty priest and visionary Wengomend cast heinous curses upon the disciples of the German teachers; he informed his followers that only the ancient offerings and celebrations of atonement would please the Great Spirit and that the burning of Zeisberger and Sensemann at the stake would be a deserving act. His magicians brought whiskey to the wigwams in order to use this means of intoxication to further their murderous plan. In order to face all of these hardships and dangers, this situation required the apostles of a religion which considered death to be an act of salvation, greeted as a return to the fatherland of eternal glory. Death at the stake or the horrible agony of a death by dismemberment meant nothing to these brave followers of the martyred Savior. Nevertheless, after the end of that year, Zeisberger, recognizing the dangers, and that a continuation of his holy work would not be useful, departed from his enemies and moved to Lawunakhannock[8], a village which lay 15 miles southwest of Pig Place (40 miles from Pittsburg, in todays Butler County, PA.) Among the first who came to hear him was Glikhican[9], a well-known speaker and warrior of the Delawares, first counsel of Chief Palanko from the "Wolves", who lived in Kuschkuschky, a village on the Big Beaver. Confident in his powers of debate, he wished to listen to Zeisberger's teachings, in order to destroy them in the presence of his listeners. But instead the external appearance of the German preacher no less than the unique flow of Indian oratory which flowed from his lips exercised a wondrous magic upon (Glikhican's) disposition and totally erased all of his arrogance. He saw a vision fulfilled, which he had seen one year before. Then he had dreamt he was walking into a hut where many Indians were assembled. They wore their hair plain and no rings in their noses; in their midst stood a white man of small stature, but with an honest appearance. At the invitation of the Indians he stepped into the circle; the white man handed him a book and asked him to read. But when he answered that he did not understand it, the white man said with a tender smile: "After you have spent some time with us, then even you will be able to read." Zeisberger and his apostles completely fulfilled this vision. But more than this, Glikhican had perceived that Zeisberger's teachings contained divine truths, and wherever he went and on

---

[6] The Moravians so named those of their Indian students who could speak the German language and worked among the savages, helping with the church service, in the school and as translators.

[7] In English: Pig Place.

[8] In English: Middle Stream.

[9] In English: the Sight on the Musket Barrel.

his entire trip home praised the white man with the fiery tongue as a messenger of the Great Spirit. This recommendation of such a widely-known person caused a sudden change of spirit among the leaders and council of "Pig Place;" the leaders now considered Zeisberger's work to be very praiseworthy and urged their people to listen to him. Accordingly everyone streamed to hear his sermons and, to go along with the will of the majority, even the crafty Wangomend felt it necessary to ensure the welfare of the German teachers. Now the mission happily thrived; a spacious school and house of the Lord arose shortly thereafter. In effect, while the first buds of a Christian community were beautifully developing among the children of the woods, the territorial conflicts of the Senecas, one of the most belligerent of the Six Nations, with the English and the Cherokees, raised a sudden obstacle. Because the area around the missions threatened to become a battleground with no end in sight, Zeisberger accepted a request from the chiefs of Kuschkuschky. On April 17, 1777, the quiet community of peace traveled under his protection in 16 canoes down the Allegheny to Fort Pitt and down the Ohio to the Big Beaver, and then paddled from the mouth of the Big Beaver upstream for about 20 miles. When they landed, Chief Palanko, accompanied by Glikhican walked down to the bank and ceremoniously welcomed those arriving. Soon there arose on the new site a properly laid out village, surrounded by fields and plowed pastures, to which Zeisberger gave the name "Friedensdorf."

This was the first village in Ohio founded by whites. Four years later, in 1774, James Harrod built the first blockhouse in the state of Kentucky and therewith laid the foundation for today's Harrodsburg. And as Post and Zeisberger were the first whites to plant corn in the earth on the north side of the river valley, so to on the other side it was the German Johann Herrmann who turned the first furrow of corn on the east side of Harrodsburg[10]. Thus, our countrymen can well boast of being the founders of agriculture in the Mississippi as well as in the Ohio Valley.

The support of the venerable Glikhican had a significant influence on the growth of the Brethren community. And a no less favorable occurrence followed him. While Palanko was still mourning the loss of his wise counsel, he received a black wampum belt from the great council of his people at Gekelemukpechink (capital of the Delawares) with the message that "evil magic" had cast a pestilence upon the Delawares, and had already carried off many warriors. Several councils had expressed their belief that acceptance of the German teachers would exorcise the evil; the great council had unanimously agreed to this remedy and declared anyone who resisted this realignment to be an enemy of the nation.

This happy news caused Zeisberger's heart to sing with joy. A favorable star would now shine upon his missionary work. All those resisting him were commanded to silence, and a glorious hope opened to him, to see his church as the national religion of a mighty people in the heart of the North American continent and its branches with all of the seeds of culture spread to the related tribes. The great council of the Delawares then formally adopted the German teachers as sons of the nation and at the same time issued a request to their communities of Friedenshütten (Wyalusing) and Gnadenborn (Scheschequon) on the Susquehannah, to move away from the vicinity of their enemies to the Ohio and the peaceful homes of their tribal and religious brethren. The prospect was also held up for unlimited ownership of their own homesteads, fields and hunting grounds. The Wyandots, the "Uncles of the Delawares" ended this invitation with the assurance that the ceded land would never be pulled out from under their feet and sold to the whites, as the Six Nations had done with their homesteads on the Susquehannah.

---

[10] *Historical Sketches of Kentucky* by Lewis Collins, Cincinnati 1847, pag. 452.

Chapter 9

The 3rd of May 1772. - David Zeisberger founds Schönbrunn, the First City in Ohio. - Terrible Fate of its Inhabitants. - The Evacuation of Friedenshütten and Friedensdorf. - An Ancient Indian Saga. - The First Municipal Regulations of Ohio. - Founding of Gnadenhütten, Ohio's Second City by Johann Jacob Schmick.

Zeisberger returned to Bethlehem with this good news. There he met Bishop Nathaniel Seidel and two of the society's directors, Gregor and Loretz, who had arrived from Europe. Delighted at the wonderful prospects made possible by Zeisberger's successful efforts for the church in the west, they gave their permission to move both communities from the Susquehannah to the Ohio. The prior history of both of these Moravian Indian communities had been, much more so than all the others, a series of tribulation and suffering. In persecuting them, the whites had used all the atrocities of the barbarians. Since these poor souls had been called to constitute the hard working and civilized population of the German villages, the first Christian settlements in the contemporary state of Ohio, so even to this day there is a two-fold interest in their painful martyrdom.

It was 1763, the time of the Pontiac wars, when the recruiters' drums were sounding throughout Pennsylvania, that a group of recruits under the leadership of Captain Wetterhold, encountered a group of Moravian Indians, who were proceeding peacefully on their way. Without the slightest provocation, and under the very eyes of their commander, the boys started a fight and murdered Zacharias along with his wife, child and relatives. According to the code of honor, the revenge for this bloody deed was the responsibility of the Delaware nation, where four of Zacharias' brothers still lived. Several months later, the inn of the Irishman John Stinton, which was in the area of Bethleham, was attacked in the early morning hours. The innkeeper, Captain Wetterhold, his second in command and several soldiers who at the time were lodged there were either killed or mortally wounded. As usual the Moravian Indians were blamed since they were nearest to the scene of the crime. And, unfortunately, just about that time, savages from the north forced their way into the province and destroyed the settlements of the New Englanders in the Wyoming valley. Thus a mob arose throughout the entire vicinity with the avowed purpose of driving all the Indians from the face of the earth. The provincial leader, Penn, was fully aware of the spurious nature of the spreading rumors so he quickly ordered the local sheriff to bring the Christian Indians to safety in Philadelphia and house them in a local military barracks. But the garrison, Royal Scots, refused entry to the red Canaanites, who were pursued and surrounded by a mob armed with clubs and knives. Only with the greatest of effort were the authorities able to save the poor souls. With the help of the faithful Quakers, the loyal friends of the Indians, the refugees were taken to safety on Province Island, 6 miles distant from the City of Brotherly Love.

Even before reaching Philadelphia, their villages of Wequetank[1], Nain, and others went up in flames. Bethlehem was supposed to share their fate. The murderous thugs threw firebrands into the village; the big oil mill burned down, and only with the utmost efforts were the Brethren able to put out the fire which had already attacked the costly water works, which was to become the model for the Philadelphians.

---

[1] Friedenshütten lay in today's Bradford County near the southern border of New York.

But this was to be merely the first in a chain of persecutions. One hundred and twenty armed murderers rode from Donnegal and Paxton in York County to Canestoga near Lancaster, a small settlement of Delaware Moravians. Upon their arrival, the men and women who were busy in the fields fled to Lancaster, where they were kept in jail for their own protection. The monsters then killed every old person, woman, and child they could find, including an old chief by the name of Schahacs, famous for his charitable friendship towards the whites. Even though the governor condemned this shameful bloody act in a proclamation, put a reward for the seizure of the barbarians, and forbade anyone from touching a hair of the peaceful Indians, nevertheless, his threats merely provoked the beasts to new murderous acts. They threw themselves on horses, rode to Lancaster, broke into the jail during the light of day, and, unhindered by the very regiment of Highlanders ordered there for the Indians' protection, murdered every man, woman, and child, even though they pleaded on their knees for their lives. And this atrocity did not quench their thirst for blood. The monsters then made a deal with their co-monsters in Philadelphia, for the purpose of murdering every Indian on Province Island. Informed as to these murderous plans, the governor had the poor souls secretly transported to Amboy, where two sloops lay prepared to bring them to New York and the protection of the British army. But, after a truly tortuous trip through New Jersey, where they were subjected to mistreatment and curses of the mob, a courier from the Governor of New York arrived with an edict that forbad the refugees from entering the province. Even the English general Gage ordered a captain to the dock to prevent their landing in case they disregarded the order. In addition the ferrymen were prohibited, under threat of a heavy fine, from bringing the refugees across the river. Even the Governor of New Jersey issued a proclamation ordering them to leave the state. Guarded by royal troops, the weary refugees were returned to the extremely hostile Philadelphia. There they languished in the barracks for 8 months, guarded day and night against the fury of the mob; for after their return the hyenas from the surrounding countryside had attempted to force their way into the barracks in order to repeat the atrocity of Lancaster. The alarm bells sounded several times. Barricades were erected in the streets and cannon trained on the mob. Among the citizenry even the young Quakers took up arms against the bloodhounds. Only the signing of a peace treaty with the hostile tribes freed those remaining from their unhappy suffering. The constant fear of death, inactivity, foul prison air, and particularly the fever and measles which had broken out in the barracks during the summer had put most of them into the sick ward; death had released 56 of them from their suffering. And now that they were finally free, everyone around them shunned them as if they had the plague; even Bethleham did not dare to permit their settlement in the area without fear of a repetition of the earlier horrors, since the revenge of the Paxton mob still hung over them for the murder of Wetterhold and his companions.

There remained no safe refuge for them among the whites and Christians. At that point David Zeisberger approached the refugees and raised their hopes with words of heavenly consolation. He suggested that they seek refuge in the forests of the Susquehannah, far from the border settlements of the white barbarians. At the same time he offered to accompany them, there to obtain a fitting piece of land from the Six Nations, and live among them as teacher and friend. For those poor souls, Zeisberger's suggestion was a message from heaven. Thus, these persecuted Christian wanderers shook the dust from the Christian cities and accompanied Zeisberger and his missionary companion Schmick through the wilderness on the east branch of the Susquehannah, to where the Wyalusing empties into it. The Cayugas claimed this land as their own from their own masters, the Six Nations. Zeisberger, who years before had been adopted as a son by one of the Onondago chiefs, enjoyed a greater influence on the Iroquois Confederation than the Delawares themselves and it was easy for him to secure permission from the grand council for a settlement in this wilderness. Happily the work began, and soon, through the work of many industrious hands, arose a friendly village which received the name of "Friedenshütten" as a remembrance of the suffered tribulations. Charles Minor, the historian of the Wyoming Valley, describes the daily activities of this banished people: "Order, industry and cleanliness found here a thriving environment. Land was cleared and plowed, corn, cattle, horses, poultry, in short, every sort of useful fruit of the land and animals introduced, schools opened for the education of the children. This settlement blossomed like a rose in the wilderness. For the first time in the Kittatinny mountains, a bell rang from the tower of the spacious church, built and gaily decorated with the trunks of white pine; it called the Christian Indians to the church service. And when its deep, ceremonious tones flew through the air, the wandering nearby Indians were shocked, for to them it was a voice announcing the death of their race."

Indeed the barbarism of the English had gone so far, that the bell of a Christian church appeared to the Indians as the death knoll of their race. Only among the German Brethren Unity and the French Jesuits did "Peace of the Bells" mean the saving of the Indian race under the protection of Christian culture.

Because of newly converted Delawares, Friedenshütten increased its population so swiftly that in the Spring of 1769, another branch mission could be laid out at Scheschequon, 30 miles away. But barely had its protector Zeisberger left for the Ohio, when the hostile trickery of the Iroquois again came to light against the praying Delawares. And it soon increased to open betrayal. At Fort Stanwix, the Confederation sold the community's land to the Indian agent Johnson, even though the land had been formally deeded to Zeisberger's followers in the year 1765. When the land speculators began overrunning the land with surveyors, Friedenshütten's peace came to an end. For along with them came the former archenemies, the whiskey dealers from Paxton, tempting the weak to drink, destroying the order and customs, even though they had often having been run out of the villages and having their barrels smashed. Upon Zeisberger's return, the uneasy communities declared themselves more than ready to follow their former teacher to the Ohio. In order to make preparations to receive his former charges, Zeisberger returned to Friedensdorf in the summer of 1771 accompanied by Heckewelder. But additional bad news awaited him. During his absence, the peace here had also disappeared. War cries sounded through the woods. On the south side of the Ohio some white scoundrels had again murdered several harmless natives, and the tribe to which they belonged was preparing itself for a campaign of retribution. All the Indians who had formerly lived near the river fled to the villages in the interior. Columns of these refugees threatened the missionaries because they had the same color of skin as the murderers. Horrified, the women of the communities fled into the woods. The men formed up around their teachers and guarded their lives day and night with the utmost of concern. The storm clouds went on by without bursting, but Zeisberger realized that the nearness of the Ohio, and the hereditary lust for murder by the approaching border ruffians from the settlements would constantly bring new dangers. Thus when the chiefs at Gekelemukpechink renewed their invitation to their land in the Spring of 1772, he decided to accept it.

On April 14, the patriarch departed Friedensdorf with five Indian families, a total of 28 persons, and arrived at the land selected for them on May 3, a charming, fruitful area on the Tuscarora, the eastern arm of the Muskingum. Here the woods were rich in excellent timber. A crystal clear stream flowed to the river through nutritious grass and fields of edible herbs. "We can build good huts here!" exclaimed Zeisberger, "Let us settle here and call it Schönbrunn.'" With restless enthusiasm began the erection of temporary blockhouses, the clearing and planting of the land.

While everyone here was preparing for their reception, the inhabitants of Friedenshütten tearfully took leave of the graves of their loved ones and their former most beloved sanctuary. They departed it as poor as they had arrived, with gratitude towards their only remaining friends, the Quakers, who had sent them 100 dollars as a remembrance. As the hour of departure approached, they came together in the chapel for the last time for a pious prayer of thanksgiving for God's protection which they had enjoyed, and then, in hushed sadness, with their pastor Johann Ettwein and their preacher Rothe, his wife and child in their midst, they departed on their difficult journey to the Ohio. During the trip the group of 241 persons split up. One segment led the wagons with the sick and the baggage or drove the herd of cattle (70 animals) ahead of them, while the others, as far as possible, used the waterways and transported in boats the heavy farming utensils, plows, harrows, large brass kettles for boiling maple sugar, and other similar items. Those taking the land route had to overcome the greatest exertions. Very often they had to force their way through almost impenetrable underbrush or wade through swamps and rivers; terrible thunderstorms made their journey difficult; they often camped near areas infested with rattlesnakes, from whose bites several horses were lost, but most of all they were plagued by swarms of sand flies, which in several areas darkened the air like a cloud of fog; this happened at one location which the Indians called "Ponks Uteney," which means abode of the sandflies[2]. Only upon lighting a large fire and remaining in the middle of the smoke could one even somewhat keep the tortuous pests away from one's body. In addition to all of these tribulations, measles broke out and took several children. However, the refugees did not lack for food; during the 8 week journey they killed about 100 deer.

On August 5, the first group under the leadership of Johann Ettwein arrived in Friedensdorf; several days later the missionary Rothe arrived with the remainder. Zeisberger and Heckewelder came to welcome them, and thus the former communities again accompanied their former, beloved teacher to their new homesteads with the greatest of expectations for the future. Zeisberger's preliminary settlement counted 28 persons, the communities from the Susquehannah 241, and that from Friedensdorf 100, so that upon their arrival in 1772, 369 souls were already assembled in Schöbrunn.

Shortly after their arrival, the elders Zeisberger, Ettwein, and Heckewelder, after consulting with the native assistants, drew up the laws, which were to guide the new settlement. This memorable municipal code from the first pioneer community of Ohio says:

Municipal Regulations of Schönbrunn

Para. 1. We recognize and honor no other God than He who created us and saved us with His precious blood. Para. 2. After the work and church service, Sunday is dedicated to rest. Para. 3. We desire to honor father and mother and support them in old age and adversity. Para. 4. No one will be permitted to join our settlement without the permission of our teachers . Para. 5. Thieves, murderers, drunks, adulterers and debauchees will not be permitted among us. Para. 6. Whoever participates in dances, pagan offerings and festivals, will be ex-

---

[2] According to Indian superstition, the woods of the Ohio were at that time the home of numerous gnomes, magicians, and witches, who practiced their evil in different forms to the detriment of the red inhabitants. Thus, the following story surrounded this abode of the sandflies in 1772: 30 years ago a hermit, who was a magician, built a cave here and plagued hunters and travelers by assuming various terrifying forms, even killing several of them. Finally, a brave chief attacked and killed him. In order to totally destroy his magic, he cremated the body and scattered the ashes in the air. But wait! Rather than being scattered by the wind, the ashes became "Ponksal" or sandflies.

pelled. Para. 7. The same for anyone who uses Thrapics (pagan magic spells) while hunting. Para. 8. All games of chance, lies, and tricks of Satan are banned from our midst. Para. 9. We desire to show obedience to our teachers as well as to the national helpers, who have been named to maintain order both within and outside of the settlement. Para. 10. Laziness, slander, and acts of violence are banned from our midst. We wish to live in peace and harmony. Para. 11. Whoever damages another's herds, goods, or effects shall make restitution. Para. 12. A man may have only one wife, love her, and care for her and her children. Similarly, a woman may have only one husband whom she shall obey and be cleanly in all matters. Para. 13. Rum or spiritous drinks may not be brought into our city. Should strangers or traders bring same, then the national helpers will take it into their possession, carefully store it, and return it to them only upon their departure. Para. 14. No inhabitant may incur debts with traders or accept goods on commission from traders without permission of the national helpers. Para. 15. No one may embark on journeys or long hunts without permission of the church authorities or city administrator. Para. 16. Young persons may not marry without the permission and advice of their parents. Para. 17. Should the municipal administrators or helpers request assistance from the inhabitants for public buildings and works, for example to construct assembly places or schools or for clearing or fencing in land and similar items, they should find obedience. Para. 18. All the requirements for the public welfare should be willingly accepted.

The above ordinances were drawn up during peacetime. But, during the Revolutionary War, since individual warriors of the Delaware nation joined campaigns against the American colonists, the following laws were added:

"Para. 19. Whoever desires to participate in war, that is spill human blood, may no longer live among us. Para. 20. Whoever buys war booty from warriors, with the knowledge that they were stolen or plundered, must leave us. For such is nothing more than an encouragement to murder and thievery[3]."

With the beginning of the new year these laws were read in a public meeting, and no additional members were admitted without formally declaring their obedience to them. The initial transgression against them would be met with a friendly word from the helpers; however, should this prove fruitless, then the church elders, after thorough investigation, could ban the affected member either from the meetings or from the city itself. In addition to these general regulations, there were other regulations pertaining to the selection and duties of the church elders and school principal, nurses for the poor and sick, taxation for the common welfare, burial of paupers, and similar items.

Thereafter, all the vigorous energy was directed at the construction of houses and cultivation of the fields. Ten miles below Schönbrunn, the Mohicans of the Friedenshütten community built their own settlement, which received the name of Gnadenhütten and Johann Jacob Schmick as Elder and preacher.

---

[3] Heckewelder's Narrative.

Chapter 10

Connolly captures Pittsburg for Virginia. - His Blood Letter to the Inhabitants of the Ohio Valley. - The Murder of Logan's Family. - The Battle of Point Pleasant. - Captain Johann Nieswanger. - German Marksmen from Tennessee. - Colonel Christian. - Cornstalk and Zeisberger. - The German Cities during Dunmore's Campaign.

As the followers of Jäger, Boone, and Schuck slowly began to settle in West Virginia and Kentucky, the rising anger of the Ohio Indians, especially the Shawnees, Cayugas, and Senecas became a bitter hatred against the English. French traders from Canada visiting their former, red skinned customers, blood relatives and friends, nurtured that hatred so that all that was needed was an occasion for a renewed outbreak of bloodletting. Ever since the signing of the Treaty of Fort Stanwix, the Indians could not mistake the intentions of the English. Vast stretches of their southern hunting grounds were taken away before their very eyes, and the time was approaching, when not only the terms of the swindlous treaty would be carried out, but also the prophecies of the Iroquois would come to pass in the west as well as north of the Ohio. The enemies' greed and their murderous hatred demonstrated itself in the bloody battles of the English for their land. Based upon its charter, the Treaty of Lancaster, and the fact that it had been the leading province in the French wars, Virginia claimed Pittsburg along with the the areas of the Allegheny and Monongahela. The governor, Lord Dunmore, sent his nephew Connolly, a brutal good-for-nothing, to claim that stretch of land in his name. Upon his arrival in Pittsburg, and after a short street battle at which the population was on his side, Connolly was arrested by the Pennsylvania militia led by Arthur St. Clair. However, on the evening following his arrest, the crazed mob used this opportunity to again show its hatred against the Indians by using the weapons which Connolly had brought against a peaceful Indian village, that lay opposite Pittsburg. After his release, Connolly collected brutal border settlers, ne'er-do-wells, and refugees from the eastern provinces and seized Fort Pitt, which he tore down and subsequently rebuilt as Fort Dunmore. The monster then began a reign of terror in the Ohio valley. Any magistrate or citizen opposing him was thrown into jail. In order to maintain his own influence and that of the Virginia interests with the mob, he inflamed their murderous desire for killing the redskins. In a proclamation to the settlers of the Ohio valley, he proclaimed that the Shawnees were henceforth not to be trusted and they (the whites) should be prepared to take prompt revenge for any act against them.

Knowing full well that the Virginia legislature would never agree to reimburse his expenses unless they were the result of a war, Connolly welcomed the outbreak of a new Indian war in order to justify his own wasteful spending and to increase his own power and that of his uncle. In Wheeling[1] Connolly's blood letter found a ready reception among the various murderous thugs in the area. Unfortunately, just a few days before, a band of roving Cherokees had attacked a trading boat

---

[1] The area had been settled in 1770 by the brothers Ebenezer, Silas, and Jonathan Zane. The name comes from a reference of a Catholic missionary, Whelan, who had camped here, to a certain Indian war ceremony, a Wieling, in which a bloody skull was impaled. (Bowan's Wheeling Directory of 1839.)

on the Ohio, robbed it and on that occasion killed a white. Using this as a pretense, two monsters by the name of Cressap and Greathouse led a group of similar-minded beasts, to carry out Connolly's challenge. Two Indian rowers, in the company of and working for whites traveling down the Ohio seeking pelts and skins in the Shawnee lands, were their first victims. They were beaten to death and their bodies tossed into the river. That same evening, the murderers went downstream to the mouth of the Captina Creek, where a group of Cayugas, worn out from a long hunting trip, was camped with their women and children. Along their way, they encountered George Rogers Clark, who was later to become famous as a hero of the west and a founder of Kentucky, and who, at the mouth of the little Kanawha, had assembled a society of pioneers to settle the "Dark and Bloody Ground." In vain did the sensible Clark attempt to dissuade them from an undertaking that was made even more sinister, since it was against the tribe of Logan, the 2nd son of Schikellimus, a protegé of Zeisberger, and the truest friend of the whites. During the French and Pontiac wars, Logan had stubbornly refused to participate against the English and was then carrying out Christian deeds. Wounded from both sides had been carefully cared for in his huts, and white travelers had found there a hospitable refuge. After the war, Logan had settled with his tribe at the mouth of Indian Creek, where his house was open to every stranger. When Heckewelder was leading the refugees from Friedensdorf to the Muskingum, he enjoyed the hospitality of Logan's family, which showed a particular cordiality towards the Germans. Thus, Cressap's crazed mob marched against the family of that venerable person, after having scoffed at Clark's warning, who had specifically warned them that that savage plan would ignite an Indian war against the settlers. After their arrival in the Cayuga camp, they fooled the Cayugas with friendly words, the help of a whiskey bottle and their trust, they then slaughtered them in the dark of the night. Among the victims were several members of Logan's family. Several days later a similar tragedy would be repeated above Wheeling, where a second group of Logan's family were tricked and murdered. Greathouse had hidden his thugs in the tavern of a certain Baker and had invited the Cayugas to a friendly drinking session. Everyone who accepted his invitation paid with his life. Those murdered included the rest of Logan's family, his brother, and his very pregnant sister. The news of these bloody deeds burst upon those whites scattered about in Indian territories like the thunder of an approaching hurricane. Whoever could escape, fled swiftly to the forts and stations in order to avoid the revenge of the Indians. Boone and Michael Stoner barely managed to bring to safety the surveyors and pioneer families from the Elkhorn and Kentucky rivers. Not so lucky were the traders, who, unaware of the danger, remained in the wilderness. Their mutilated bodies decorated the trees in the woods. Initially the Shawnees and the war faction of the Delawares, the Wolves (Munseys), were not about to participate in the revenge campaigns of the neighboring Iroquois. Cornstalk, the Shawnee chief, even sent all the traders in his area with an escort to Pittsburg. But this act of good faith worked against Connolly's devilish plan. And in order to inflame the peaceful Shawnees to rage and revenge, he had the escort murdered. Logan, a former true friend of the whites who was now their sworn enemy, had in the meantime assembled his braves and moved with the war party of his tribe, the Senecas, the Wyandots, Shawnees, and the Wolves under Cornstalk, Red Falcon, and other mighty chiefs, to the mouth of the big Kanawha. There they erected their palisades and impatiently awaited the enemy, whose left flank was 1,100 men strong under General Andreas Lewis. Never before had the Indians fought a battle with more cunning and bravery. They controlled the battlefield from sun up to sun down. The Virginians demonstrated the same sort of bravery, and, rather than tiring, their thirst for battle rose with the sun. Their well-aimed musket fire was returned with equal effectiveness and duration by the Indians. Though half of their officers had already fallen, including Colonel Karl Lewis, the general's brother, the determined provincials stormed the Indian palisades with bayonets. But like a raging lion, Cornstalk threw himself against them and shattered their lines. Whenever his lines would waver under attack, his battle cry "Be strong, warriors!" would echo through the cloud of powder and confusion. His tomahawk struck those retreating. While night was falling, Lewis went around the enemy's left flank by crossing Crooked Creek, a tributary of the Kanawha. Thus, the next morning, the Indians, after bravely resisting the enemy, were forced to leave the field of battle to the enemy and retreat across the Ohio.

Among the victors of Point Pleasant, a German, Captain Johann Nieswanger, was named one of the bravest. He was one of the most famous Indian fighters of his time and had come across the mountains with his younger brother, Peter, who soon enjoyed the same fame. His daughter Susanna did not dishonor her father's blood; she spoke fluent German and English and married a worthy son of the forest, Hamilton Kerr, one of the bravest pioneers of Ohio[2]. Many other Germans fought in the lines of Virginians, even in the auxiliary sharpshooter company of Captain Evan Shelby (father of Isaac Shelby, later governor of Kentucky); from Tennessee were the Germans Heinrich Span, Friedrich Munkel, Johann Fein, and others[3].

The costly victory was of little benefit to the Virginians. Shortly after the battle, Colonel Wilhelm Christian[4] arrived with 300 reinforcements from Fincastle County. The Virginians, burning to revenge their fallen comrades, followed the enemy across the Ohio. But, in the meantime, Lord Dunmore pushed the right flank of the army across the Scioto and, contrary to all expectations, signed a peace treaty at Fort Charlotte[5], in which the Shawnee chiefs agreed to cease their hunting trips south of the Ohio. Lewis, who wanted to revenge the death of his brother by massacring the Shawnees and burning their villages, refused to quit. In response to his insults, Dunmore pulled a dagger and had him seized as a rebel.

The famous battle at the mouth of the big Kanawha, on whose bloody field a village was named Point Pleasant in honor of the victory, took place on October 10, 1774. Since the revolution in the east was already sending up mighty flames, Dunmore's hasty peace treaty was politically motivated, an obvious attempt by the crown to gain support of the Ohio Indians in the battle against the colonies.

Because of the war and the terrible danger for their settlements, the activities of the leaders of Schönbrunn and Gnadenhütten were interrupted. Even before 1773, the tireless Zeisberger, accompanied by Glickhican, had often visited the Shawnee villages and signed a friendship treaty with Cornstalk. The outbreak of the war stopped a settlement in their territory, which had already been arranged with the Shawnee chief and which was to be led by Schmick. The cry for revenge from Logan's relatives now sounded in the German cities. War parties of raging Iroquois and Shawnees came through, threatening every white with death. One of the Shawnees, wounded by Connolly's murderers, was brought to Schönbrunn, in order to inflame the Delawares' desire for war.

---

[2] An extensive biography of Kerr is found in Hildreth's History of the Pioneers, pag. 473.

[3] Ramsay's *Annals of Tennessee*, pag. 116

[4] Christian, of German descent, grew up in Staunton. He married a sister of Patrick Henry and, as a Kentucky pioneer, fell in battle with the Indians. A county in Kentucky bears his name.

[5] It lay near today's Westfall.

The missionaries had to conceal themselves and had their hands full just keeping their people out of the war to which the neighboring tribes were urging them. Every trader who arrived in their town, not knowing the situation, was looked upon with deathly fear, for, if he were murdered, then the suspicion of his murder would fall upon their young men, and the wrath of the whites would fall upon their cities. Near Schönbrunn, the servant of a trader fell into the hands of Shawnees roaming between the two Miamis. They murdered him, cut up his body, and planted the parts atop bushes, in hopes of directing suspicion of the deed onto the Delawares. But at Zeisberger's urging, White Eye, the chief of the Delaware peace party, collected the parts and buried them. The Wolves, the tribe's war party, discovered the grave, cut up the body parts and spread them on paths over a wide area, as a sign of approval for murdering all whites. But White Eye came through again, collected the scattered parts and carefully buried them in a hidden place. Since he had led several traders safely through the wilderness, there were hostile threats against the Delaware peace party. They promised to take revenge on the German cities as soon as the Virginians were defeated, whom they were confidently expecting. Thus, the missionary Roth and his family were brought in safety to Bethleham, while Zeisberger and Heckewelder remained prepared, in case of Dunmore's defeat, to flee up the Cayuga. But as the news of the peace treaty reached Schönbrunn, there was great happiness, and November 6 (1774) was selected as a day of thanks and festive prayer.

Chapter 11

The German Pioneers and Stations in Kentucky. - Meyers, the Land Agent. - German Village Life in Schönbrunn. - The Beginning of the Revolutionary War inthe Ohio Valley. - Zeisberger Prevents a General Alliance of the Indian Tribes Against the American Colonists. - The Founding of Lichtenau. - The Murder of Cornstalk. - Dangers to the German Cities.

After peace had returned, most of those pioneers who had fled Kentucky, including Daniel Boone, James Harrod, and others who had fought in the great battle on the Big Kanawha, returned to the dangerous solitude of the lonely wilderness. Boone entered into the service of a newly formed North Carolina land company headed by an ambitious land speculator, Judge Henderson. The company had purchased from the Cherokees two provinces supposedly for the sum of 10,000 pounds Sterling. The one included the area between the Kentucky and the Cumberland rivers with its northern boundary, the Ohio. The other one was of a similar size on the Holstein River. The undertaking earned the highest displeasure of Governor Dunmore. He made a proclamation to the people of the Ohio Valley, in which he not only condemned this purchase of Indian land by a private individual, but he also declared that the Cherokees had no rights to the land in question, and furthermore, the land, according to the Treaty of Fort Stanwix (NY), was now a dominion of Virginia and was already within its boundaries. Simultaneously he warned the people against the false promises of Henderson and of "other unlawful persons whose true purpose, was to establish on these royal lands a refuge for people fleeing their creditors." Caught between the two fires, the bann of the Virginia legislature and the murderous hostility of the Ohio Indians, Henderson and his companions did not let themselves be dissuaded from their great plan of establishing a new western province. On behalf of the Transylvania settlers, Boone's ax had already hewn a path for pack horses from the valleys of the Holstein through the forests. Shortly thereafter arose the stations of Boonesborough, Harrodsburg, the High Springs settlement and St. Asaph. Impatient to form their own community, the colonists elected a legislative assembly, which was opened by Henderson with a "speech" that was more like a present-day governor's acceptance speech. The assembly, which ran for three days on the banks of the Kentucky river under the branches of a huge elm tree, set up various courts and issued laws for the protection of the province. One year later, in 1776, revolutionary Virginia nullified the bann of its governor against the colony, and recognized Transylvania under the county name of "Kentucky" as an organized part of Virginia. In the meantime the inhabitants of the area had become disenchanted with the greedy measures of Henderson and his co-monopolists of the Transylvania Company and elected Major George Rogers Clark and Gabriel Jones as representatives to the Virginia Assembly to bear a request for their inclusion in the area of the mother province. Among these names of those Kentucky pioneers signing this monumental document were the following Germans: George Uhland, Hermann Consoly, Johann Maxfeld, Bernhard and Conrad Walther, Peter Paul, Johann and Andreas Haus, Wilhelm Myers, and others. The latter soon became one "of the most enterprising Germans of the West," who explored all of the best land areas of the Ohio Valley and secured more of them than any other of the pioneers. He was the first Land Agent and "General Locator" in the valley and also owned an interest in the salt works at Bullit Lick. There was produced the first salt on a large scale in the west. Five to six hundred persons were employed here in the various branches of this factory when Louisville and Lexington counted barely a few blockhouses and the buffalo still roamed the capitaline hills of Kentucky. Among the German workers in the above-mentioned factory, Christian Krebs was singled out as a "lion-hearted Indian hunter[1]." From the earliest of times, German settlers had established stations against the Indians in the Dark and Bloody Ground, such as Strode's Station in Mason County and, 6 miles from Harrodsburg the "German Station" (Dutch Station). The first session of the District Court in the "District of Kentucky" took place in the meeting house of the latter[2]. Even the Anglo-American pioneers became so used to the sounds of the German language, that it came to be known as a warning of an Indian attack, if one heard anything besides German in the forest[3]. In general, the Ohio Indians called the Germans "Schoharies," a name which denoted exactness and thriftiness and probably originated among the Mohicans, who so named the Germans after their settling on the river and in the county of the same name in New York[4].

During the year 1775, Britain attempted to use its agents and traders to recruit the Indian tribes of the west against the rebellious colonies, a fact which, based on its (England's) material advantage, should have presented no difficulties. The natives could get their clothing, firearms and similar articles only from the British, while the Americans could give them nothing for their pelts. In addition there were the constant land grabs and brutal atrocities of the frontier settlers. With the exception of the Oneidas and the Tuscaroras, the Six Nations all immediately joined the British cause; of the Ohio Indians, the Wyandots, Miamis, Shawnees as well as the war clan of the Delawares, the Wolves, under their chief Pipe, openly favored the British. In order to lure the Ohio tribes to their side or at least keep them neutral, the Congress called a meeting of their chiefs to a meeting in Pittsburg in October of that year. But only representatives of the Delawares, Senecas and Shawnees appeared. Furthermore, the intrigues of Iroquois messengers prevented an agreement, even though the American commissioners did their best and among other things, guaranteed to the Delawares, as the leading connection in the chain between the northern and southern Indians, equality with the whites and the inclusion of their territory as a state in the new Union. When White Eye, the chief of the Turtles, (the peace clan of the Delawares) finally exposed the intrigues of the Iroquois in an open meeting and mightily protested their representation of the Ohio Indians, the meeting ended in noise and disorder and Chief Pipe used the opportunity to effect a formal break between the Wolves and the Turtles. After his return, he moved his people from the Muskingum to Lake Erie in the immediate neighborhood of his allies, the Wyandots and the British. Even though Schönbrunn lost several citizens because of this split, the mission suffered no blow. In spite of the warlike conditions during the year, peace and tranquillity reigned. The high council of the Delawares happily observed the growth of the German cities and increased the stretch of land granted to them along the Muskingum by more than 30 miles. On Sundays, large numbers of visitors streamed out of the neighborhood to Schönbrunn in order to hear Zeisberger, and the chapel soon was not large enough to hold their number. At the end of the year, the city counted 414 souls. "Young and old," writes Loskiel, "enjoyed during this year the comfortable luxury of a civilized life, and

---

[1] *Hist. Sketches of Kentucky* by Lewis Collins, pag. 217

[2] Butler's *Kentucky*, pag. 142.

[3] *Pioneer Women of the West* by Mrs. Ellet pag. 58.

[4] Smith's Narrative.

the life of the inhabitants was as exemplary as their death." Zeisberger was a loving as well as an effective teacher; he had composed a spelling book for the children and a well-organized grammar of the Delaware language, taught not only their mother tongue, but also taught them to read and write German and English. Whereas in the west the English language had not yet achieved a firm foundation, here in the depths of the Ohio wilderness, German hymns sounded from the mouths of the Delaware children. In addition to farming and animal husbandry, almost every craft was represented in Schönbrunn. Even artists, instrument makers and musicians were not lacking[5]. If one reads the diaries which Zeisberger so carefully kept in an ornate German script during his stay on the Muskingum, one would appear to have been transported into a genuine German community. The wild Indian hunters and warriors appear as Auerbasque figures, true Germans, under the newly baptized names as Konrad, Anton, Christian, Johannes, with their squaws named Erdmuthe, Creszenz, Anna Charitas, et al. All daily occurrences, marriages, births and deaths were carefully noted; a judicious spirit kept an eye over the personal and municipal occurrences as well as over the dangerous, shifting relations of the neighboring tribes with the British and Americans. After the Great Council of the Delawares had moved its residence from Gekelemukpechink to Goschocking[6], Zeisberger was asked to establish a new settlement in the area so that the young and old residing here could take advantage of attending the German school and church. Zeisberger granted this wish. In April 1776, at the forks of the Muskingum, two miles from Goschocking, he founded the third city Lichtenau, with eight families, totaling 35 persons, and moved there with Heckewelder. Here he daily won new converts. Netawetwie, the chief of Goschocking, joined the community with his family as well as the chief from Ahsimik (Solid Rock) with his family, who previously had resided at Hockhocking (Pumpkin Gourd Plantation). Colonel George Morgan, American commissioner for the western Indians, visited the German cities often during this period and each time expressed his amazement about the orderliness, cleanliness, and civilization, with the desire that all Indians would, in this manner, embrace the peaceful life of civilized society. Countering all the intrigues of the neighboring tribes against the Americans, Zeisberger was continuously busy maintaining the friendship of the Delawares and Shawnees. For that reason, Taylor, the historian of Ohio, dedicates to him the the following well-deserved recognition: "Through his early colonization on the Muskingum in 1772, as well through his direct influence three years later, the missionary Zeisberger prevented the establishment of a hostile alliance of all the tribes, from the Cherokees to the Chippewas, against the embattled colonies. Thanks to his patriotic efforts, the savages were not able to accomplish this until the year 1780, when the French alliance and an increase in population on the south shore of the river hindered its most fearsome effects. Had God not sent this enlightened messenger of the Gospel in the mid Ohio Valley into the most uncertain circumstances, then surely undefeatable war parties of Indian warriors would have pushed into the heart of the Atlantic states at a period of time when the American army was totally prostrate in defeat. Therefore, Zeisberger's grave should be declared for us a patriotic monument. Among those who bore weapons, few made more progress to the successful conclusion of the Revolutionary War than he[7]."

When the Shawnees, embittered by the additional murders of their people by the whites in 1777, listened to the rumors whispered into their willing ears by British agents, Zeisberger sent Chief Cornstalk, accompanied by Red Hawk, a brave of that tribe, to the newly constructed fort at Point Pleasant, in order to discuss with the commandant, Captain Arbuckle, with whom he was personally acquainted, the diffic-

---

[5] Heckewelder's Narrative, pag. 490.

[6] Goschocking or Place of Owls is now known as Coshockton.

[7] *History of the State of Ohio* by James W. Taylor, pag. 268 and 339.

ulty of his situation. Trust in the honor of this officer led them both into a trap. Arbuckle had the chiefs seized, as the best insurance for peace with their tribe. The next day an Indian yell sounded across the Ohio. It was Ellinipsico, Cornstalk's son, worried about his father's fate, whose trail he had followed. Upon his entrance into the fort he was also seized as a hostage. Unfortunately, several days later, unknown savages shot a soldier from the garrison on the Kanawha. In order to avenge this bloody deed, many of his friends rushed into the fort with the shout: "Down with the red dogs!" In vain did Arbuckle throw himself into their path. With a classic composure and honor, the venerable Cornstalk fell under the bullets and knives of the murderers, as did his son, protesting and after a painful battle, along with Red Falcon.

From that moment, not just the Shawnees, but also the Wyandots, Ottawas, and Wolves in Sandusky raised the war club in a war of annihilation against the Americans, only to bury it forever sixteen years later at the peace treaty of Greenville. Only the chiefs of the Senecas and Delawares kept their intentions of not permitting themselves to be drawn into the war between Great Britain and its colonies. The hostile tribes correctly attributed this intransigence to the influence of the German missionaries. Furthermore, an ancient custom of the Delawares reinforced this opinion. The chiefs had in their possession all of the documents, deeds, wampum buckles and belts, which their forefathers had received from the government of Pennsylvania since the time of William Penn. Each year, one day was selected for a conference, on which all of the documents were read aloud by the missionaries and translated, so that the young men and boys could become familiar with the history of their nation. Since, these conferences were held in deserted areas of the woods in order to avoid disruptions, the hostile tribes spread the rumor that during those conferences the missionaries used the opportunity to distribute written communications from the American Congress in order to win over the Delaware nation. Zeisberger's enemies presented these rumors to the ear of the English governor Hamilton in Detroit as being factual, and thus it did not take long that, as a result, movements started from there which developed the plan to seize the missionaries and bring them into British custody. To this end, in early August of that year, Pomoacan, the half-king of the Wyandots, came to Goschocking with two hundred of his warriors. In the face of this danger, Zeisberger acted with cleverness, civility and firmness. He sent Isaac Glickhican with the women and children bearing food and refreshments to Pomoacan's camp and informed him that the word of God ruled that the Moravian cities should live in peace with the entire world; the emissary requested protection and peace for his people and their white teachers, the missionaries. Moved, the red chief replied to him, that he was indeed on a mission of war, where his heart was hostile, and blood was his goal, but that the words of his brother had opened his eyes. "Return home in peace," he continued, "we will do you no harm. Respect your teachers, who instill such wise teachings in your hearts; honor your God and do not be afraid. Not a hair will be touched." Great happiness reigned upon Glickhican's return with this joyful news, for most of them had already prepared to flee Lichtenau. Schmick had already fled Gnadenhütten with his family for Pittsburg. On that very same day the half-king arrived in the city. Zeisberger received him in the schoolhouse. They shook hands and the chief spoke: "From this day forward we Wyandots consider you as our father and you should consider us as your own children. Let nothing disturb the friendship between us and this covenant should stand forever. Furthermore, the other nations should know of this bond of friendship, and they will undoubtedly rejoice as do we." Zeisberger responded to this friendly speech with fitting words. After this agreement there was a large festive meal for the half-king and his officers in grass huts out in the open, during which the school children sang happy songs to honor the guests. They enjoyed themselves so much that it took 14 days before the people from Lichtenau could get rid of them. Upon departure the half-king informed Zeisberger that he had already sent a messenger to Governor Hamilton and the chiefs of his tribe in order to inform them of the completion of this agreement.

This danger had barely passed when new storms visited the German cities. Since the hostile attitude of the savages against the Americans was being constantly nourished through the continuous barbarous acts of the border ruffians, the zealous efforts of the Congress against the British intrigues on the Ohio were thwarted. In this regard, representatives of the Senecas were called to Pittsburg at the end of July of this year to conclude a peace treaty. But while en route, they were attacked by white bushwackers firing muskets and driven back. The result was a unified cry for revenge from the nation. Again Zeisberger had the greatest difficulty in maintaining the peaceful intentions of the council at Goschocking. But the gang of white murderers decided at the beginning of October to destroy and plunder even the German cities. With this intent in mind, an armed group had already crossed the Ohio; but a group of Wyandots with the half-king at its head struck at them soundly and drove them back across the Ohio. Just shortly before, the best guarantees for peace had arrived from Pittsburg, and the distrust against the whites now grew, while Chief Pipe's party gained in respect. The Wolves gained in numbers and influence. Only Zeisberger's definitive declaration to the council of the Delawares that the Christian communities would leave the territory, should the nation take the field as allies of British, maintained the peace. In a later session of all the chiefs, which occurred on October 31, Zeisberger pushed through the solid declaration which included that peace and neutrality with the Americans must be maintained in the face of any danger.

A great loss for the German cities was the death of their true friend White Eye who died of measles in the fall of 1778. The secret plans of Chief Pipe to involve the Delawares in the war against the American colonists and thus end the influence of the missionaries among his nation, so ruinous to him, was given free rein to be carried out by the removal of his competitor. Soon his intrigues won over to his view even some of the Delawares who were inclined to war, so that now joining his party was considered as proper. All the Wolves from Sandusky were his followers, and these thirsted for a war with the Americans. Slowly hostilities against them were demonstrated in the immediate area of Goschocking. When Commissioner Sample from Fort Laurens appeared with several people on the forks of the Muskingum to bargain for corn and other supplies, the guard of his camp was attacked and scalped. Fearing the results, the Shawnee tribe which had joined the peaceful Delawares two years previously, departed their homes in Lichtenau and returned to the Scioto. With the evacuation of Fort Laurens by the Americans, the peace chiefs of the Delawares lost all their support, while the British party grabbed their remaining supporters. The leaders had to return to the area of Pittsburg, and thus, in the summer of 1779, the German Indians in the Ohio Valley stood alone in their determination to observe unshakeable neutrality between the warring whites, an untenable position in that wild tumult of war in their immediate neighborhood, which would lead to destruction for them and their settlements.

Chapter 12

The First Settlement in the Ohio Valley. - Character of the Pioneers. - Belief in Witches and Magic. - Professional Sorcerers. - Old and Young in German Homesteads. - The German Immigrants. - Indian Attacks. - Colonel Peter Nieswanger. - Six German Spartans. - The Intrigues of British Agents in the German Cities.

At the outbreak of the Revolutionary War, the stream of immigrants from the eastern provinces had reached the Ohio. In 1771 settlements were started on this side of the mountains along the Monongahela River and the Chestnut and Laurel mountains. The very next year they reached the Ohio. The largest group of settlers came over the mountains along Braddock's old military road from the regions of upper Maryland and Virginia. A smaller number from Pennsylvania came along the route from Bradford and Fort Ligonier, the military road which Bouquet had laid into Pittsburg. Horses with pack saddles were the mode of transportation. Among the natives from the eastern provinces were already the sons of German immigrants, competing with Boone's followers from North Carolina in trying to grab the best land in the valley that was so easy to get. The erection of a crude blockhouse and the planting of a small field of corn gave title to 400 acres and the right to buy another 1000 acres. Even earlier the Tomahawk Law had been in force. Whoever cut the first letters of his name into the trunk of a tree near a creek or just circled the trunk had claim to a farmstead. A unique mixture of diverse elements made up the pioneer population. As in our times when Texas and California are an asylum for the dregs of the colorful mixed American society, so too was the Ohio valley during the time of its first settlements. Here one had a free hand for new dirty tricks. Murder, robbery, and beating to death were the rule. The laws of Virginia did not extend this far. According (to that law) every criminal had to be brought for sentencing to the capital city of Williamsburg where there was the royal court of justice and the provincial tribunal. The province had neither the law enforcement officials in the far border lands nor the money to transport the accused or transport or accommodate witnesses, who would have to travel 800 miles to get to Williamsburg and then return home another 800 miles. Among other reasons, Commissioner Wright's protests to the British government against opening the Ohio valley, argued that the region would become the playground for all the murderers and outcasts of the country. The accuracy of this prophesy was further supported by Benjamin Franklin in his outstanding request to the Cabinet for the establishment of his "Ohio province". He states: "More than 5,000 families, who have already settled on the south side of the mountains near the Pennsylvania border, are living without governance, law and order, in constant hatred and strife with each other. They are murdering the natives and robbing them of their land on the Ohio. If we do not hurry up and install some lawful order, then this whole mess will increase to such an extent so as to endanger the old colonies as much as the Indians." The best segment of the population consisted of the farmers from the old provinces. They were hardworking, devout, hospitable, but also deeply entangled in uncertainty and pure superstition. The belief in magicians and witches was common among them.

One settler of this period, the clergyman Joseph Doddridge, reports[1]: "The people believe that witches have the power to afflict children with uniquely horrible diseases; that they can harm cattle by shooting them with balls of hair; put curses onto hunting rifles and other items; that they can turn people into horses, and after saddling and bridling them, the witches could ride them at a gallop wherever they desired, over mountains and valleys, until they drop." Therefore, there arose a group of professional magicians in the Ohio valley, who had offices much in the manner of doctors, gruesomely decorated with magical symbols and means against the evil effects of devils and witchcraft. One common cure for curses involved the following: a picture of the witch would be hung against a tree trunk or a piece of wood, it would then be shot at with a ball which included a bit of silver. Wherever the bullet struck the picture, that area would hurt the witch. Another method involved hanging a bottle of child's urine in a chimney. As long as the bottle would hang there, the witch would have difficulty passing urine. The witch could be rid of that affliction only by borrowing something from the family. This caused problems for old women wishing to borrow things. Children and dogs under the influence of witches were burned on the forehead with a red hot iron, or, if dead, burned to ashes. Then it would be necessary for the witch to borrow something anew and thus be discovered. These thieving magicians, from their own houses, could also rob their neighbors of the milk from their cows by wrapping needles, one for each cow, in a new towel. The towel was then hung on the door and, using a magical spell, the milk was drawn from the folds (of the towel). The first glassmakers on the Ohio (they were Germans) drove the witches from their ovens by tossing young, live dogs into their ovens[2]. The German farmers from Maryland, Virginia, and Pennsylvania with their large families were the first in the valley. Their farms were the most admired. But their silos and animal stalls were normally in better condition than their own living quarters. And oh what toils and obstacles did the German immigrants have to endure the first years after their arrival! In 1750 the schoolteacher Gottlieb Mittelberger wrote[3]: "The greatest number of immigrants in Pennsylvania, Virginia and Maryland consisted of Palatines, Franks, and Swiss. Alone in the colony of Pennsylvania there were over 100,000. Of that number around 20,000 were Reformed, with just about as many Lutherans, and around 1700 Roman Catholics. The rest were Reborn, Moravians, Brothers of Zion, Randorfers and other Separatists. In Autumn 1754 another 22,000 souls arrived in Philadelphia, further overburdening the land. Most of those were from Württemberg, the Palatinate, Durlach and Switzerland. Most were so miserable and sick that, because of their poverty, they were forced to sell their children. Late in the year, for as long as I can remember, 20 to 24 ships loaded with people would arrive in Philadelphia. They had barely landed when, in pairs they were led to the courthouse to swear allegiance to the British crown, and then sold to the highest bidder. There were a lot of fugitives from the gallows among them. For prisoners and criminals Pennsylvania is the promised land. The Americans ship them out to the west to serve as the first line of defense against their enemies. In the Blue Mountains there are several congregations, Protestant and Reformed. The pastors there are Schärtel, Schulz, Wiegand and Schreck. Kercheval says[4]: "It was this German breed that had to face the various Indian wars in the west, somewhat akin to the waves of the Revolution. Many of them were giants. They grimly clung to the language and culture of their fatherland. Generally cut off from the misery of the Revolutionary War, they shaved their heads and wore wigs or white

---

[1] *Notes on the Settlements and Indians Wars of the Western part of Virginia and Pennsylvania, from the year 1763 until the year 1783 inclusive*, by Rev. Dr. Joseph Doddridge, Wellsbury, VA., page 162.

[2] One must realize that belief in witches existed both in America and in Germany. In Bavaria from 1754-56, and even later in Switzerland, several witches were burned, including one 14-year-old girl.

[3] Gottlieb Mittelberger's ***Journey to Pennsylvania in 1750***. Stuttgart, F. Jenisch 1756.

[4] Kercheval, ***History of the Valley of Virginia***. Winchester, 1833, page 486.

tasseled caps, which had to come from Germany. Their vests, with wide pocketflaps, reached down to their knees. Among the rich, the buckles of the short trousers and shoes had to be decorated with gold or silver ornamented with precious stones. The women wore simple short skirts with calico bonnets and helped in the fields and with the animals." Their sons became the best soldiers, hunters, and boatsmen, and, in the wars against the British as well as against the Indians, became famous for the most desperate and wildest deeds. Among others they formed the 8th Virginia regiment, which under Mühlenberg won eternal laurels at Brandywine, Monmouth, and Germantown. Peter Helfenstein, the brave major, lived in Winchester and is buried there in the Lutheran cemetery. Due to the continuous Indian attacks, the boys drank in hatred of the Indians along with their mothers' milk. The valley chronicles lift them to the same level as their sworn and most gruesomely bitter enemies. Furthermore, the life in the woods with its dread and dangers turned their mothers into true amazons. In 1766, two farmers, one of them named Schütz, attempted to bring their wives and children to the safety of Fort Woodstock in a wagon. Three miles from the fort, five Indians attacked them and killed the men outright. Rather than fall down in a faint from the sight of their husbands bleeding to death, the women grabbed axes and, with a supreme effort, defended their own lives and their children. When an Indian attempted to drag a child out of the wagon, one of the women caught the child with one hand and with the other hand crushed the Indian's head. The Indians had to flee from the furious women. The Indian attacks against the settlements increased when the barbarian Hamilton in Detroit put a price on the scalp of any American colonist in the Ohio valley, including women and children. There arose among the Indians a lively hunting and trading of scalps. Near Point Pleasant lived the brothers Mathias and Jacob Bebber. Rhoda, the daughter of the former, was attacked in the forest and killed. They cut her scalp into two pieces and sold it to the British scalp dealers in Detroit for 30 dollars. The high price was intended to lead to further bloody acts. In the Spring and Summer of 1777, the Indians had continually attacked the new settlements near Wheeling, but without taking a large booty of scalps. For each time the settlers sought refuge in their stockade which had been built in 1774. Originally called Fort Fincastle after the county, it was later renamed Fort Henry in honor of the governor of Virginia, Patrick Henry. In order to destroy this station once and for all, 400 Indians led by the renegade Irishman, Simon Girty, surrounded the fort. Hamilton had named Girty Indian agent in order to win a segment of the American borders for Great Britain. Twelve men and boys defended the fort from morning to evening against the much larger force. In case of a break (in the palisade), the commander, Colonel Peter Nieswanger, the brother of the hero of Point Pleasant, braved the hail of bullets to raise the palisade, while it was reinforced with a chain from inside. Peter was over 6 feet tall and with a muscular build. His face was terrible. He had deepset, coal black eyes, a wide mouth, and a massive nose, which had been knocked to one side in an earlier battle with Indians. He painted himself with the brightest of Indian colors and otherwise acted like a chief. Though rough and uncultured, this giant had a good and friendly heart[5].

In order to get even for their repulsed attack, a segment of the attackers, 100 men strong, started out the next morning for the German settlement on

---

[5] Hildreths *Pioneer History*, page 830.

Buffalo Creek, at the tip of which stood Fort Reis, about 12 to 15 miles from the mouth of that stream which empties into the Ohio. It consisted of several small and one large blockhouse, which offered refuge for 12 neighboring families. The Indians did not expect much resistance there and hoped to engage in a general bloodbath without much trouble. However, Jacob Miller had sent the settlement news of the impending attack. A group of spartans consisting of six men formed up to defend the fort and their families. The members of this group were George Fellebaum, Gerhard Löffler, Peter Follenweider, Daniel Reis, Jacob Löffler Jr., and Jacob Müller. In the first volley Fellebaum received a ball in the forehead and died instantly. The remaining five revenged his death 20 times over with their well-placed shots and here, too, the barbaric enemy was forced to withdraw exhausted[6].

At the beginning of 1778, one of Hamilton's threatening letters arrived at Schönbrunn, whose effect could have been the end of the German cities. For in this letter the British governor ordered all Indians of every tribe in northern Ohio to join the war against the Americans. Anyone refusing would have their cities laid waste with fire and sword. Totally shocked, Zeisberger threw the letter into the fireplace[7] and prayed to God to turn these terrible dangers away from his beloved mission fields. To his dismay three British agents arrived in Coschocking, the Indian agent McKee, Captain Matthew Elliot, and the above-noted Simon Girty. The Shamrock (meaning the three Irishmen) had been unwisely released on parole from Pittsburg, and on their own initiative had sought out the residence of the great council in order to involve the Delawares in the war against the Americans, using any possible trickery or lies. The Irish told the Indians that the Americans intended to wipe out all the Indians, both friend and foe alike, and take over their lands. All guarantees of friendship and promises of the Congress were merely a pretense to further enable the people on the borders to attack the unprepared tribes and destroy them. Now was the time for a general uprising of the western nations against the false-tongued brood. The American troops had been defeated by the British, Washington shot, and the members of the rebel Congress either captured, flown, or worse. These terrible lies caused quite a bit of confusion and dismay among the Delawares. Only with great difficulty was White Eye able to counter the urgings of his opponent Pipe and convince the great council to wait 10 days in order to confirm among friends in Pittsburg the veracity of the British allegations. Luckily, Heckewelder was just returning from Bethleham. From the President of the Congress, Henry Laurens, and from the Secretary of War, Horatio Gates, (Heckewelder) extended their best guarantees about the friendly attitude of the American statesmen towards the Indians of the west and particularly about the continued protection of the German cities by the government. His rebuttal, supported by a newspaper which he had in his baggage and which reported Burgoyne's capitulation, not only countered the terrible impression created by the British intrigues, but simultaneously aroused a hatred among the Delawares against the party which might have offered them up to a dangerous lie. Even the renegade Wolves participated in this change of opinion. Many of the young people who had been alienated from the missions by Chief Pipe returned to Lichtenau. Even a tribe of Shawnees which did not support the war settled in the vicinity of that community.

---

[6] Doddridge's Notes.

[7] Loskiel, Part III, Chapter VII. Heckewelder's Narrative, page 169.

Chapter 13

Clark's Victories in the West. - Leonard Helm. - The Capture of Hamilton. - Girty's Murder Attempt against Zeisberger. - The Battle on the Licking. - The Claims of Spain on the Ohio Valley. - Fort Jefferson. - The Wars of Destruction on both Sides of the Ohio. - Destruction of Loramy's Store.

As long as Great Britain remained in possession of Detroit, Vincennes, and other western posts, there was no end in sight to the murderous incursions of the Indians into the area of the settlements south of the Ohio. From these posts, Britain maintained a contact with the red skins, stirred them up and equipped them for new campaigns. Even though Congress, pressured by the increasing dissatisfaction of the affected border settlers, early on (in April 1776) considered the seizure of these forts, the implementation of this project was only half carried out with the initiation of two operations, the construction of Fort McIntosh by the general of the same name below Pittsburg, and Fort Laurens[1] on the Tuscarowas near Schönbrunn. George Rogers Clark, in the meantime promoted to Lieutenant Colonel, then undertook the great task of saving the Ohio valley settlements, after securing the reluctant approval of Governor Patrick Henry. With four militia companies and a few courageous trappers and hunters, including Michael Schuck, Leonard Helm, and others, Kentucky's hero started downstream in a few boats on June 24, 1778, to seize Kaskaskia. His belief in success was further significantly increased with the arrival of unexpected good news. It was the news of the alliance of France with the colonies, an event which would, to the advantage of the Americans, win the support of the French and Indians in the Illinois and Wabash territories, who had remained loyal to their former empire, and simultaneously alienate the British, who had never been accepted there. At Fort Massac, Clark disembarked his small band of ragtag frontiersmen and slowly stole along an old, practically extinct Indian hunting trail through the Illinois wilderness towards the British outposts on the Mississippi. On the evening of July 4, they arrived undiscovered at the city. During the night, part of his command occupied the fort, whose unguarded gate had been left open, while the remainder, with savage yells, stormed into the city, terrified the inhabitants, threatened to shoot anyone appearing in the streets, and captured the British commandant, Rocheblave, in his bed. In spite of his rough outward appearance, Clark was an accomplished diplomat. During the next few days, continuing to act in a respectful and honorable manner towards their practices and customs, he easily won the begrudging respect of the colorful population, so that soon both young and old were ready to accompany him to seize Cahokia. Clark was only too happy to let them, and by July 6, both of the important Illinois posts had been seized without bloodshed from Britain and occupied by Virginia[2]. And several weeks later, Vincennes, after Detroit the most important British post, came under the flag of Virginia through the influence and persuasion of Clark's secret ambassador

---

[1] Named for the then current President of Congress.

[2] At the time, about 70 families lived in Kaskaskia, mixed bloods of French, Indians, and Negroes. Cahokia had only 45 houses.

(Pierre) Gibault, the Catholic priest from Kaskaskia. The province incorporated the swiftly conquered territory into its territories under the name of "District of Illinois", established courts, occupied the central points with troops, and appointed John Todd to be the military and civil commander of the district.

When this unexpectedly bad news reached Detroit, Governor Hamilton did not remain inactive. After assembling a considerable force of Canadians and Indians, toward the end of the year he set out to recapture the lost posts. His movements were so well concealed that he arrived unexpectedly at Vincennes, whose entire garrison at the time consisted of two men, Captain Leonhard Helm and one soldier by the name of Willing. Helm was indeed a daring soul and was determined not to surrender the newly won victories of the Virginia frontiersmen. Standing at the fort's only cannon with a burning fuse, he loudly demanded their conditions for surrender. Bluffed by this audaciousness, Hamilton believed that the fort had been reinforced since the last report of his scouts, and, not willing to engage in a long siege, he gladly granted the normal honors. Amazed when he saw only two men march out and angered at this insult to his honor, he broke his given word and retained Helm as a prisoner.

In the meantime, through energetic and clever actions, Clark had persuaded the Illinois Indians to form an alliance, which, at the news of the fall of Vincennes, would cover the rear of the next campaign. He then realized that the great moment for the Ohio Valley had come and that either Hamilton would capture him or he the great scalp dealer. There was not a moment to lose. With 170 men, Creoles and Kentuckians, he departed Kaskaskia on February 5 to capture Vincennes. It was terrible weather for a campaign. For weeks without end snow and rain had fallen; the prairies and forested flatlands of Illinois and Indiana along the route lay were flooded, impassable, and turned into knee-deep swamps; at the same time it rained constantly. Undaunted, the little band continued onward, often under unspeakable conditions, half of them being in watery swamps up to their necks; Clark, his face covered Indian style with black powder, continued to lead his troops to exhaustion, while the little drummer floated along on his drum, and in spite of all the adversity, every day would sing Yankee Doodle Dandy with youthful enthusiasm. Randolph, the famed Speaker of the Virginia House, compared this march of Clark with the march of Hannibal through the swamps of Elysum, which opened up the way to Rome to the Carthaginian hero. But that one had lasted only 4 days, whereas Clark spent 16 days, before his exhausted and hungry troops, from their first dry spot, saw the church tower of Vincennes. In the meantime, Hamilton had sent his Indians to the Ohio, in order to cut off the retreat of the American troops and harass the settlements in Kentucky. In the middle of winter, and certainly not expecting an attack during such terrible weather, the Governor and Helm were sitting comfortably in the quarters of the fort's commandant playing cards, while a bowl of apple punch boiled on the fire in the fireplace. At the first shot from a Kentucky rifle some mortar from the fireplace wall fell into the fragrant drink. "That is Clark," yelled Helm with a foreboding look. Ghostly white, the governor jumped up: "Clark?! Will he have mercy on us?" Even though the garrison counted 600 men, Clark, with a threatening proclamation and by cleverly marching his troops behind the rolling hills in front of the city, so that his force appeared to be 10 times larger, so confused the scalp dealer that he surrendered several hours later. Clark sent him as a prisoner to Virginia, where the provincial council, against the conditions of surrender, kept him constantly in irons. With those troops, who remained inactive under the incompetent McIntosh in the fortresses of McIntosh and Laurens, Clark could have crowned his great work and taken Detroit, but he, like they, lacked the provisions and transport. The garrison of the latter fort had suffered mightily from hunger during the winter, and when a train of packhorses with provisions finally arrived from Pittsburg, the ecstatic troops unfortunately greeted their arrival with cannon shot from the fort. Thereupon the freightened horses bolted loose losing most of the provision in the woods. Luckily for the troops, the German cities were near, and the missionaries, as they had done earlier, again helped out the commandant, Colonel Gibson.

When the news of Hamilton's capture reached the Muskingum, a stone fell from Zeisberger's heart. He assumed that the threatened danger was over. But he was mistaken; for a new danger for him personally grew out of it. In Sandusky, Simon Girty had hatched the plan to fall upon the tireless opponent against an alliance of the Delawares and Shawnees with the British and bring him to Detroit, or should this fail, at least bring his scalp. Luckily, the trader Alexander McCormick, a friend and admirerer of the missionaries, heard of the plot and sent Heckewelder news of the plot to Lichtenau. When the news arrived, Zeisberger was just preparing to travel to Schönbrunn. Girty had found out about the departure and had set up an ambush along the way. Two brave Indians, one of whom was Isaac Glickhican, accompanied Zeisberger on the detour to Gnadenhütten, where a stronger guard was to be picked up, should that appear necessary; but barely had they put a mile from Lichtenau behind them, when the hostile group, eight Senecas with Girty at their head, barred their way. "That is the man!' cried the assassin, "after him as you have promised!" By accident, at that very same moment, two young Delawares out hunting, suddenly appeared from the bush. They immediately recognized the danger to the old father and, along with his guard, pointed their muskets at the boys. Girty, in spite of his advantage, a coward, waved off the attack with his hands and, cursing between his teeth, disappeared like lightning with his men into the darkness of the forest.

While Clark was winning his victories in the west against the British and Indians with sword and cunning, the pioneers remaining in Kentucky suffered a grievous loss. While busily collecting salt to cook for the settlements, their brave leaders, Daniel Boone and Simon Kenton along with 28 companions were seized by Shawnees at Blue Lick and brought as prisoners to the village of Old Chillicothe on the Little Miami. During his half-year imprisonment, the wily Boone, through energetic participation in their work and hunting trips, as well as making jokes for their women and children, knew how to win their confidence, and after winning their trust, escaped with his comrade of the woods, Simon Kenton, to their home at Boonesborough. Fortunately, they both arrived just in time to help repel an attack from a group of French-Canadians and savages under Captain Duquesne, who had subjected the fort to a ten-day siege. The enemy was forced to abandon 37 dead and a huge amount of powder and shot on the battlefield.

During the next few years, this mutual war of destruction continued on both sides of the Ohio; as soon the settlements of West Virginia and Kentucky were visited by the Indians, shortly thereafter their own villages north of the river were visited with murder and fire from the republican militia. Thus in 1775, Colonel Brodhead laid the villages of the Iroquois on the Allegheny to ashes while Colonel Bowman destroyed those of the Shawnees on the little Miami to ashes and drove away the cattle and horses. In contrast, one expeditionary corps, returning from the area of Lexington, whose first municipal surveying by the founder Robert Patterson occurred that year, suffered a bloody defeat at the mouth of the Licking where Colonel Rogers and Captain Benham were proceeding up the Ohio in boats with a number of frontiersmen, returning from a fruitless patrol against marauding Indians in Kentucky. While passing the site where West Covington stands today, Rogers saw the feather-bedecked heads of several Indian warriors peering out of the bush. Believing that he outnumbered the enemy, and acting in coordination with those from Lexington, he put 70 of his people under Captain Benham ashore at the mouth of the Licking to surround and wipe out the redskins. But Rogers had made a bad miscalculation. His people had barely reached the shore, when they found themselves surrounded by a superior force of Indians. A desperate battle began. Immediately 50 militia soldiers fell after the first volley, while the rest barely made it back to the boats, where everyone grabbed paddles to effect a swift retreat. Among the seriously wounded was Captain Benham. His legs shattered, he dragged himself with his musket into the bush and hid there among fallen tree trunks until the Indians left the field of battle with the scalps of his unfortunate comrades. He was truly in a hopeless situation, alone in the dangerous wilderness, without food, and, because of his wounds, unable to make it safely to the next settlement. Driven by hunger and alone on the evening of the next day, he spotted a partridge on a nearby branch and shot it. The sound of the report had not even died away, when Benham heard a human voice very close by. Thinking he was in the proximity of an Indian, he swiftly reloaded his musket. But he was mistaken; the voice was from a soldier who had remained lying on the battlefield shot in the arms. One can only surmise how the two invalids greeted each other. Immediately the two healthy arms formed an alliance with the two healthy legs for mutual support and protection. Benham would shoot the game, driven to him by his companion; the healthy legs would push it to the spot where the healthy arms could prepare the meal. With a hat between his teeth, one would carry drinking water from the Licking, while the other was ready to give a signal should a boat suddenly appear. But that occurence would not happen for a long time. They would have to spend six weeks in the wilds, before a passing barge would finally save them[3].

Intending to extend the battles and difficulties of the settlers of the Ohio Valley for many years, Spain now began a new, serious disagreement with the young union of states. As indicated above (page 43), shortly before the conclusion of peace with England in 1762, France had given to Spain the Louisiana territory, containing the huge stretch of land west of the Mississippi, in return for services rendered during the war.

Following the example of the former, Spain had evidently taken the side of its neighbors in the eastern United States and declared war against Great Britain. So when the American ambassador Jay arrived in Madrid in 1780, he soon found out why this assistance had been tendered. For it was explained to him (as the French ambassador had already explained to the Congress in the name of Spain), that the territory of the United States extended no further west than that declared in the proclamation of the British government of October 7, 1763[4] which permittd the settlers no further settlement beyond the Alleghenies. The huge land mass between these mountains and the east side of the Mississippi belonged to the British crown and were therefore a fitting target for Spanish arms and long term seizure. The United States were urged to consider any settlement or seiz-

---

[3] Benham later moved to Ohio and was one of the first settlers of Warren County. There he served under generals Harmar, St. Clair and Wilkinson. In 1797 he was the commissioner and assessor for Hamilton County. His companion in suffering, Butler, still lived several years ago in Brownsville, PA.

[4] See page 49.

ure in this territory as illegal, based on the fact that no American state had raised a legal claim before the war, and could not now base anything on England's right, whose sovereignty all the states had denied. Therefore, since the United States did not possess any land on the Mississippi, the cabinet in Madrid assumed for Spain the sole right to navigation on the Mississippi.

Against this extraordinary Spanish claim, Virginia arose as the state whose claims and goals were most affected. It claimed the land in northwest Ohio to the Mississippi based on the rights of conquest by General Clark. Its souvereign flag was already flying there, and its governor Todd resided there. Its right to the stretch of land south of the Ohio, based on its original British charter, included all the previous royal grants and gifts to companies, soldiers, privates, end encompassed the purchases from the Indians -the large stretch of land which Henderson had brought from the Cherokees, whose ownership the revolution had sanctioned. Virginia had already reserved the entire region between the Green River, the Cumberland Mountains, the Tennessee River and the Ohio for military claims. All the homesteads owned by Tories in Kentucky County were declared by the legislature to be property of the state, eight thousand of which had been reserved for the establishment of a university in this wilderness[5]. The year before, four of its commissioners had opened the first court in St. Asaph, KY., and settled no less than three thousand claims. Indeed, Virginia's land agent, George May, was already busily dividing up Kentucky with the surveyors chain. For during the previous few years, settlers from north and south had forced their way in droves into the new area, lured there by the generous property laws. Even though the winter of 1779-80 was among the most severe - domestic and wild animals froze in the woods and birds froze in flight - with the beginning of the new year, no less than 300 large houseboats had landed at the falls of the Ohio alone. In that same year, the legislature had declared Louisville a town and Kentucky County divided into three new counties, Lincoln, Fayette, and Jefferson.

To defend Virginia's sovereignty in the areas south of the Ohio and the right of ship navigation on the Mississippi against Spanish claims, Governor Jefferson ordered the construction of a fortress on that river below the mouth of the Ohio. The brave Clark led and completed the construction in the Spring of 1780. It was called Fort Jefferson after its sponsor, but brought only misfortune to the American cause. For at first, the population of Kentucky was dissatisfied with this measure, since garrisoning the fort required a number of armed individuals, whose services it was felt could better be used at home against the constant attacks by the Shawnees and Wyandots, and secondly the Chickasaw, formerly a tribe friendly to the Americans, had become hostile, since the fort had been erected upon their land without their permission. When the garrison was severely weakened with hunger and sickness, they surrounded it, and when their chief, Colbert, born a Scotsman, appeared before the ramparts under a flag of truce in order to treaty with the commandant, some hotheads fired at him. This shortsightedness inflamed the savages into such a rage, that they threatened to scalp the entire garrison. Only Clark's timely arrival with reinforcements saved them from a horrible death. Soon thereafter the fortress was abandoned as being too distant from the settlements and therefore useless.

During the summer of 1780 occurred the most terrible and at the same time most noteworthy invasion

---

[5] The justification for this decision reads: "Since it rests in the interest of the Virginia republic to cultivate everything that enriches the soul and spreads practical knowledge, even among the citizens far away, whose remoteness in a barbaric region and whose contact with the savages would otherwise tend to alienate them from the sciences."

in the annals of Kentucky. Well equipped with artillery, an army of 600 Canadians and savages under the leadership of Colonel Byrd crossed the Ohio at the site of present-day Cincinnati, marched rapidly up the warpath along the Licking and, with one blow, captured the remote stations of Martin and Riddle, whose palisades could not withstand the artillery. For some unexplained reason Byrd suddenly turned from his victorious march and departed the territory even faster than he had arrived. Since his force was stronger than the entire complement of Kentucky, the depopulating of the area to the east of the river of the same name would have been an easy task for him. It can only be assumed that the horror brought about by the atrocities of his red soldiers caused the sympathetic warrior to retreat before the completion of his mission.

After his return from Fort Jefferson, the brave Clark had heard about the latest incursions of the British into his beloved Kentucky. Like a bolt of lightning, he appeared in Harrodsburg, thirsting for revenge, where droves of new settlers and speculators had assembled, since the surveyor May had opened his land office under contract to Virginia. He closed May's shop, raised a thousand of the perspective buyers and marched with them to the mouth of the Licking. There he crossed the Ohio, and continued secretly through the area of the Little Miami and Mad Rivers and everywhere set ablaze the villages and fields of the Indians. On the site of the former Pickawillany, established by Pennsylvania traders and destroyed by the French in 1752, (see page 23) a French Canadian by the name of Loramie, who had a Shawnee wife, had lived ever since the initial settling of Kentucky. He was known as a genuine enemy of the Americans and his trading post, called Loramie's Store, had long been identified as the headquarters for the British marauders in the Valley. Clark burned his storehouses along with the vast supplies of goods and furs and drove Loramie himself along with the colony of Shawnees, who lived around him, towards the Spanish area, where they settled at the fork of the Kansas and Missouri (rivers)[6].

The successful completion of this campaign aimed at the heart of the enemy, gave the settlements in Kentucky the respite needed for their thriving development. It persuaded Virginia to decide to crown its victorious northwestern campaign with the capture of Detroit. Jefferson turned to Washington for weapons and other war materials and he issued an order for their delivery to Colonel Brodhead, the commandant in Pittsburg. This operation failed, however, first because Fort Pitt itself was threatened by a force of the Tory bloodhound Connolly, embittered about the confiscation of his lands in Kentucky, who from then on defended the British side with even greater determination and energy, and secondly because (Congress) was without any resources and credit. The continental currency which it had created had become almost worthless during the past three years. In January 1777, the cash value of one paper dollar was still 95 percent. In April 1778 four paper dollars were worth one silver dollar. In September this same was five dollars and by the end of the year 6 and one half dollars. In 1779 the value of paper money decreased even faster. In February eight and one half dollars were equal to one silver dollar, in May it stood at twelve, in September at eighteen paper dollars, and before the end of the year one paper dollar was worth only 4 cents. In March 1780, one could have a paper dollar for three cents, in May for two cents, and by December seventy-four paper dollars were worth one dollar in silver[7].

---

[6] Loramie's name has been retained in the creek, whose mouth is in Shelby County 0., 16 miles northwest of Sidney.

[7] Lessing's *Fieldbook of the Revolution*. Translator's Note: Klauprecht made a mistake here. The author is Lossing.

Chapter 14

Founding of Salem. - King Schingask's Warning. - Birth of Marie Heckewelder and Christian David Sensemann, the First White Children in the State of Ohio. - Plundering of the German Cities. - Capture and Deportation of their Inhabitants.

As long as the chiefs of the Delaware tribes in Goschocking maintained neutrality in the battles swirling about them between the American colonists and the British and their Indian allies, Lichtenau, only two miles away, remained the headquarters of the German missions. The raids of the frontiersmen caused Zeisberger to evacuate Gnadenhütten and Schönbrunn in April 1778 and concentrate the communities in the new city. But in 1779, the area around Goschocking threatened the safety of the settlement. Drunkenness, robbery, and every act of violence became prevalent. Bands of drunken Sandusky Indians frequently stopped in the settlement of the crafty Pipe, and it soon became the collection point for all the waring tribes fighting against the Americans. With a bleeding heart, Zeisberger saw himself forced to desert the thriving Lichtenau and move the community to a safer location. On May 3, 1780, after completing a church service, the chapel was torn down so that it could not be used for pagan purposes. The population, counting 440 souls, then moved with its herds and implements 20 miles up the Muskingum and built the new town of Salem, 6 miles from Gnadenhütten. All the homes and a splendid church, 40 feet deep and 36 feet wide, with an ornate bell tower of hewn tree trunks, were completed by the beginning of winter. New arrivals from Pennsylvania soon enlarged the settlement.

Leonard Adam Grube came from Lititz as an assistant serving the Muskingum missions, later to be joined by Michael Jung, Johann Schebosch, who was married to an Indian woman, Johann George Jungmann and several sisters, including Sarah Ohneberg, Heckewelder's bride. During their dangerous trip from Pittsburg through the wilderness, the pilgrims had experienced the friendliest treatment from the Indians; in contrast, white frontier thugs fired murderously into their camp from ambush, and from then on it appeared that they would have to protect themselves more from the white barbarians than from the so-called savages.

Shortly after the evacuation of Lichtenau, at the council in Goschocking Chief Pipe threw away his mask completely and poured out such wild curses and threats of death against everyone who was for neutrality in the war, that the council broke up in a tumult and those remaining of the peace party fled to their leaders in Pittsburg. Pipe was himself taken aback by what he had done, in effect the destruction of the national council. Fearful of the results, he moved with his followers to the Wyandots in Upper Sandusky, near the settlement of his like-minded comrade, Pomoacan, who, as he, was looking forward to the moment to take the field against the Americans.

Several clouds, which had already appeared darkly on the horizon, warned of the storm, which would soon break loose from all sides and overwhelm the peaceful settlements. South of the Ohio, gangs of frontiersmen were gathering, in order to visit fire and sword upon the German cities, which, according to their own superstition, were the "halfway-house," the resting station for the enemy warriors from the lake on their murder and robbery raids against the white settlements. Fortunately, Colonels Brodhead and Shepherd blocked them with a militia corps and convinced them to give up their plan. Loskiel describes the situation of the mission, made so dangerous by the national political situation, as follows: "It was particularly unfortunate that every act of charity and humanity of the Brethren caused distrust and hostility from the opposite side. Should a war party stop in the city and, according to Indian custom, enjoy their hospitality, take their food or trade prisoners, then the American frontiersmen considered this as proof of the complicity of the missionaries with their savage enemies. From the other side, the British representatives, McKee, Elliot and Girty, reported to the Governor in Detroit, that Zeisberger and his companions were American spies, and that they had passed on information to their commanders in Pittsburg each time a war party of British and Indians were en route to the Virginia border. This was certainly the case on numerous occasions. But these demonstrations of friendship to the Americans were in the form of confidential reports to the commanders Morgan, McIntosh, or Brodhead. They had to remain concealed from the frontier population, whereas the contact of the Moravians with the savage warriors was public knowledge."

But barely had the above-noted danger from the frontiersmen of the Kanawha valley subsided, when King Schingask, the supreme war chief of the Delawares, surrounded Gnadenhütten with a war party and demanded that the inhabitants deliver to him all of the Delaware peace chiefs, particularly "Killbuck," who, the king believed, was hiding in the city. The ensuing reply, that those sought had gone to Pittsburg, was not believed by the king, who had every house, celler and barn searched. After being convinced as to the truth of the reply, he called together all the national helpers from the three cities. They came and entered into a semi-circle formed by his warriors, whereupon, leaning upon his war lance, he gave them the following speech:

"Friends and brethren! Hear my words! You see a great and mighty nation torn asunder. You see father fighting against son, and son fighting against father. The father has called his Indian children to help him control his rebellious children, the Americans. I thought carefully about what I should do, whether to take the war club from the hand of my father in order to help him or not. At first it appeared to me to be a family matter, in which I had no interest. But now it appears to me that the father is right, and that his children deserve to be punished. Have they not time after time carried out the most horrible deeds against his Indian children, robbed them of their lands, stolen their property, and without the slightest provocation, shot and murdered their women and children? Even those who were always friendly to them and for their protection had been taken under the roof of their father's house[1].

"Friends and brethren! Often the father had to demand an explanation for the bad deeds and crimes of his rebellious children, in order to somewhat rectify them, but they did not improve. No, they remained the same and will not change as long as we still have one clump of land. Remember the murderous deeds, which the Long Knives carried out against our relatives, who were their peaceful neighbors. Did they not murder them without the slightest provocation? Are they better now than they ever were? Truly not, for how many days have passed, when a number of these same people, thirsting for your blood, appeared before your threshhold, but fortunately they were hindered in their murderous plans by Great Sun[2], whom the Great Spirit sent for your protection.

---

[1] Reference to the Conestoga Indians, who had been kept in jail for their own protection.

[2] Great Sun was the name which the Indians gave to Colonel Daniel Brodhead.

"Friends and brethren! You love that which is good. You wish to live in peace with humanity and in a place where you are not disturbed while praying. You do that, and I find no fault with you for that. But friends and brethren! Does the location of your settlement serve this purpose? Do you not live on the main road between the warring parties? Have you not seen the tracks of the Long Knives before your city and seen the smoke rising from their camp? Should not this be sufficient warning and move you to prepare for your safety? For a long time we turned our gaze towards your homes, with the hope to see you come to our land, where every danger would be lifted from you, but you are so engrossed in praying, that you have not noticed our concern for you."

"Friends and brethren! Listen to what I have to say to you. Arise and follow me to a place of safety. Leave your homes and fields. I will lead you to the Miami land, which will give you harvests in abundance and thick pastures for your cattle. There there will be game in abundance, and no Long Knives will injure you, your women, or children. No. I will live between you and them and not permit them to put you into fear. There you will honor your God without fear! -- Here you cannot do that. Listen to and believe my words. If you remain here, then one day the Long Knives will speak kind words to you in their normal manner and at the same time murder you."

Just how true were Schingask's concerns, will be borne out by the following. The German Indians did not accept the wise suggestions. After discussing it for an hour, they sent the king their thanks for his well intended and caring attitude. They still had no reason to doubt the sincerity of their American brothers, they said, and if their friends really loved them, then they should completely avoid their settlements while on the warpath, then nothing would draw the enemy to them for marching through their settlement, as had occurred at Lichtenau.

Thereupon, Schingask discussed this reply with his chiefs and informed the German Indians as follows:

"My friends! You the praying Indians! I have well weighed your words, they come from a good heart, from a heart that cannot think evil of others. But my belief is different that yours. The Long Knives will always be against us, until they have robbed all the land, until we have been ruined or driven by them into the great salt sea. Listen to my warning not to be tricked by the kind words of the whites. You rejected my first suggestion. Therefore I say: Let everyone among you have a choice to go or to remain. Prevent no one from freely moving to a safe place, and I will be satisfied."

This suggestion was accepted on the spot; the council broke up, and the national helpers returned to their homes. Only a few elderly people, who had belonged to the original communities in the east and in whose memory the former atrocities of the whites lay, took the suggestion to heart and followed the king. From Gnadenhütten, Schingask rode with his party to Salem, where again a large celebration was held in his honor. "With solemn dignity," explains Loskiel, "the warriors assembled. The king ordered a halt in the middle of the city, opposite the chapel and Heckewelder's house and gave a compliment to the assembled population. In a nearby grove of maples, the tables were set with the best that the settlement offered. Together with the senior war chiefs, Schingask ate in Heckewelder's house, whom to his surprise he recognized as the youthful mourner, who had attended the funeral of his wife nineteen years ago on the Tuscarawas. Upon departure he heartily shook the missionary's hand." "Remember," he said, "that Schingask is the unshakable friend of the Germans, should you hear otherwise, then it is a lie."

On April 16 of the same year (1781) a daughter was born to Heckewelder in his mission at Salem, which at baptism received the name Johanna Marie and is acknowledged to be the first white child born in the state of Ohio. She remained unmarried and still lives in robust health in Bethleham, PA. Her letter to the president of the "Western Reserve Fair", accompanied by a photographic likeness, was well noted at the large exhibition and fair held last December for the benefit of wounded soldiers. The letter ended: "I am called the first white person to be born in your state, which has become so large and, even though I am 83 years old, I am still able to send greetings to my sisters in the west and wish them success in their honorable endeavor."

The enemies of the missionaries, namely McKee, Elliot, Pipe, and the Wolves attributed the failure of the latest peaceful attempt by King Schingask to remove the settlements on the Muskingum, not to the devotion of the German Indians to their land, but rather to the continued influential status of Zeisberger and his companions. Therefore, they took extreme measures and sent assassins to get the patriarchs out of the way. But the attempted murders failed in all three cities. In Schönbrunn, Sensemann was attacked by an enraged Wyandot while working in the field and was saved only by the chance appearance of two brethren. Near Gnadenhütten, a wild white man, who had joined a war party of savages, shot at Jung and Edwards but luckily missed each time. Even Heckewelder was shot at several times from ambush on the paths near Salem; his strong arms overpowered one assassin, who had forced his way into his house and tore the murder weapon from him. These attempted murders constituted the second to the last act for the unspeakable horror, whose location would be in the venerable Zeisberger's domain.

Colonel Arent Schyller von Peyster assumed the governorship of the Indian territories in Detroit, replacing the captured Hamilton. As with his predessesor, he was deceived by the Indian agent McKee and Captain Elliot, who had visions of taking rich booty in the German cities, into the opinion that the missionaries were supported by the American Congress as spies among the Indian tribes on the territory of the Delawares and maintained with that body a correspondence contrary to the British interests. They had convinced Pipe and Pomoacan to support them in these allegations before the governor. But that was not enough for McKee. Since his repeated murder attempts had failed, he went to Niagara, where a great council of the Iroquois Confederation was convening and, under the pretense that he had come upon instructions of the governor, demanded the destruction of the German cities and the murder of the missionaries and their disciples. Even though the Six Nations were fighting with murderous fury for the British side, they were, however, reluctant to carry out the bloody deed suggested to them against their tribal brethren because of political reasons. Therefore, their council sent instructions to the Chippewas and Ottawas: "We present to you the Christian communities. Make soup of them!" which meant in other words: "You are ordered to kill these people!"

But these two nations, branches of the Delaware family, were, according to Indian geneology, their grandchildren, and they refused the demand with the abrupt words, "that their grandfather had done them no harm." Even Pomoacan, bound by the same instructions, refused to act in such a gruesome manner against the "relatives", whose guardian and protector he supposedly was, since a large segment of his tribe also consisted of "Christian communities." We have already explained above (Page 7), how, in the earliest times, the Jesuit fathers had successfully established missions among the Wyandots. Boys and girls from this tribe were brought by the "Black Robes" to Europe and educated in schools there[3]. Thus, for example, a letter from Father Cholmac, of the "Society of Jesuit Missionaries" in New France, in America, to Father Augustin Le Blanc, the Procurator of the aforementioned society in Canada, written on August 27, 1715, reports of the successful medical practice of a Genovesa from this tribe, "whose mother had received her baptism in the city of Dreybach, and who herself had been raised among the French." According to her Indian name she was called Tegah Kuita, and Mr von Luth, commander of a combat group on the lake and commandant of the fortress Frontenac, testifies about her, "that she had cured him from Zipperlein or painful gout, which had severely plagued him for 23 years[4].

French priests continually held masses in the villages of the Wyandots, and the rosaries of the church decorated the necks of the warriors along with strings of glass beads. Pomoacan would have been able to move these people to a murder attempt against their co-Christians on the Muskingum, had the latter not been their "nephews." However, McKee's threats soon shook his determination, and he finally promised, to journey to the German cities, together with Pipe and under the command of the English captain, to carry out the orders of Governor von Peyster.

In July 1781, a new municipal organization came into effect in the cities on the Muskingum. Zeisberger, elected to the senior council, resided in Schönbrunn with Johann Georg Jungmann as his deputy. Johann Heckewelder and Michael Jung were in charge of Salem, while Gottlob Sensemann and W. Edwards were the elders in Gnadenhütten.

On the afternoon of August 16, Captain Elliot along with Pomoacan and a party of Wyandot warriors arrived before Salem. After resting a while in the woods, he set up a great camp of tents, in the middle of which he planted a flagpole with the British flag and established his headquarters. While these preparations were in progress, the half-king went to Heckewelder's house and, in hypocritical friendliness, asked him to select a spot where the "relatives" from all three cities could assemble, in order to hear news of importance to their interest. Heckewelder replied to him, that, since Gnadenhütten lay in the middle, it would be the best place. As a result of this decision, the warriors broke camp the next day and marched there. Poor Gnadenhütten then became the collection for enemy parties. There were camped, one after another, the Wyandots from Upper Sandusky under Pomoacan, Chiefs Pipe and Wagemun with their people, Shawnees, Chippewas, Iowas, Mohicans, Ottawas and, surrounded by French Canadians and English, and the plotter Elliot. Their pretense was that they intended an operation against Wheeling, Forts McIntosh and Pitt. After a week long, during which the parties had stuffed themselves at the cost of the three cities, and during which time their chiefs had put their heads together in daily conferences, the half-king ordered the national helpers and most prominent people of the three cities before him and described to them in the gruesome Indian metaphors all the dangers to their situation, which King Schingask had already so clearly described. He asked them to move, under British protection, to an area where there would be sufficient supplies for them. As a reply he received the same refusal for the same reason, which had been given to the war chiefs of the Delawares. Evidently the half-king and his warriors were convinced of their validity. They saw that, in spite of all of Elliot's pious promises, the German Indians would fall into extreme misfortune, were they, before the winter came, to be driven from their comfortable houses and from their full barns and extensive

---

[3] The Jesuits were honored with the name "Black Robes" by the Wyandots and Iroquois. Father R. P. Sebastian Rasle's Letter in the collection of the writings of the fathers of the Society of Jesus. No. 567, page 81.

[4] Instructional as well as learned letters, writings and travel descriptions, sent by the missionaries of the Society of Jesus from countries overseas from the years 1642 to 1726, collected from written sources by Joseph Stöcklein, of the aforementioned Society of Jesuit Priests.

cornfields, which promised them a rich harvest, were they to be driven out into the inhospitable bush. After their eyes were opened, the Wyandots were so outraged at the cruel action planned against their relatives that they marched before Elliot's tent, muskets on their arms, shot the British flag from the flagpole and threw it into the fire.

The clever Elliot permitted the anger of the Wyandot's to subside. For a week he kept to himself in the camp, but in constant consultation with Pipe and the chiefs of the Wolves. Then he asked the Wyandots to come before him, and reminded them that they had already fought against the Americans and that they had been declared their enemies. Should they now not carry out the orders of the British governor against the German cities, then they would have a new, powerful enemy in the British and condemn themselves, their women, and children to destruction. Therefore, for the last time, he ordered the seizure and deportation of the inhabitants of the three cities. Should they not obey, then he would mount his horse and return to Detroit. They must then consider their ties with the British as broken; from that moment on they would be considered as enemies.

Taken aback at this declaration, the half-king requested a delay of several days, in order to consider the situation. In his simple language, Zeisberger thus recounts the succeeding events in his Muskingum diary[5] as follows:

"Pipe and Elliot allowed Pomoacan no respite. They insisted upon our immediate deportation from our cities. We repeated that it was impossible. We had to first harvest our fields in order to provide for the women and children. Should we blindly and without forethought leave our towns, where we had enough to live, to go into the bush, where nothing could be found, then we would be cast into extreme deprivation and misery. We pleaded for just enough time to prepare us for the departure."

"Several helpers and Indians were for an immediate departure, while others would rather die right here, since they would die anyway in the bush. At the same time there was much confusion in Gnadenhütten; the town was full of warriors; our people were being ruined and openly sinning on the streets. For several days now, several began anew the former heathen ways and customs, and when they were reminded of this, they became angry and stubborn and reminded us that we had better remain silent, since, during these times of war, our lives depended upon them. Gambling, dancing, and all sorts of mischief became the order of the day. In Schönbrunn and Salem, the brothers and sisters were somewhat peaceful, and even when the warriors visited there, there was no disturbance. At both places we provided food, slaughtered pigs and cattle for them, as long as they were there, and we would still have done it, were they to leave us in peace. In the meantime, war parties went throughout the area and brought prisoners to Gnadenhütten, and the area became a theater of war."

During this time of war, so wrought with disaster and grief for the German villages, was born the first white male child within the borders of the present-day state of Ohio. Zeisberger continues:

"On August 30, Sister Anna Sensemann was delivered of a son. On September 1 in Schönbrunn he was baptized in the death of Jesus with the name Christian David. She had been brought from Gnadenhütten eight days previously, since the warriors were committing many excesses there and here it was still bearable. For the warriors did not come here in such great number.

The English finally decided to lead us away by force and the half-king and Pipe agreed. Their warriors found out that our Indians

---

[5] This valuable diary of the first settlers of Ohio, so interesting for the historian, is in the library of the Cincinnati Historical Society, a gift from Judge G. Lane of Sandusky.

were not in agreement; had they remained united and supported each other, then they would not have collaborated. But there were unfaithful, evil people among us who helped (the English), giving them suggestions on how to achieve their goals. They clearly pointed out that should the white brethren be seized and led away, then all the Indians would follow."

"On September 1, we received instructions that all the white brethren and helpers from Schönbrunn and Salem were to come to Gnadenhütten. We obeyed the instructions. "After enjoying themselves in Gnadenhütten, the warriors became mischievous; each acted according his own inclination and savagery; in spite of the fact that we had denied them nothing, out of pure maliciousness they shot our cattle and pigs to death. The dead animals lay around in such great numbers, that the area stank."

"In Schönbrunn a Munjay leader had promised help to Brother Lucas. The Munjay nation had adopted Brother David and looked upon him as their own flesh and blood. Had Brother Lucas acknowledged and desired to take advantage of this, then no one would lay a hand on him; they, the Munjays, desired to think of him as one of their nation, but he would have to move to their village."

This well-intended suggestion was rejected by Zeisberger for the reason that only he (Lucas) and the Jungmann family would benefit, while the other "brothers and sisters" in Gnadenhütten and Salem would be excluded.

"While we were discussing the matter," continues Zeisberger, "the Wyandots came to us, seized David, Heckewelder and Sensemann and led them as prisoners to the Delaware camp. There they yelled the Death Yell over us. They stripped us naked and took away all our clothes as well as our watches and belts. But at the same time they swiftly loaded their rifles, for they were mostly afraid that they would encounter resistance from our Indians. While this was taking place, the entire party of remaining warriors went and plundered the mission house. Each took what he could find. Even though several of our young people had placed themselves with tomahawks before the doors of the house, they had to yield to the stronger party."

"During this episode, the Delaware chiefs and Captain Elliot had convinced everyone, probably out of fear that it might not succeed; that they were the very ones they needed to take us prisoner, since the Wyandots would never have done it alone. The English regretted the situation, but they had express orders from the commander in Detroit to lead us away. Since we had been brought totally naked into their tent, Elliot returned some old clothes to us, so that we were not completely naked. Brother David received an old night gown that had belonged to Sister Sensemann to wear, while we were to be taken as prisoners to the huts of the Wyandots. But we were not bound as were other prisoners. We would have had nothing, not even a blanket to lay down upon the bare ground, had not the Indian sisters brought us blankets that evening."

"Then one party of warriors went to Salem and another to Schönbrunn. About thirty warriors went to the former place; they arrived during the night, seized Brother Michael Jung along with Sister Heckewelder and her child, led them out of the house and set them onto the street; they plundered the house, taking everything they found, did the same thing with Brother Michael Jung, and returned during the night to Gnadenhütten yelling the Death Yell. But Sister Heckewelder and her child received permission to remain (at her home in Salem) to be brought there the next day by the Indian sisters. In Schönbrunn, where only 2 Wyandots arrived with several squaws, they took the Jungmanns, Sisters Susanna Zeisberger and Sensemann captive. Then they said, they wanted to bring them with all of their possessions to Gnadenhütten, where everything would then be returned. The sisters helped with the packing until they saw that the bedding was being cut open and the feathers spilled onto the street, and they knew that they had been tricked, as had been the case in Gnadenhütten and Salem. The Indian sisters were totally taken aback, weeped loudly and did not know what they were to do; some wanted to take up arms; but others felt that this was not wise and kept them from it. They stole the communion articles, the candleholders and bells. Sister Anna Sensemann, who had given birth just three days previously, had to depart with her baby at night in the rain, it would have been no surprise had mother and child perished. But the Lord, who makes all things possible, saw to it that not the slightest harm came to either her or child. Before daybreak they were brought into Gnadenhütten with the Death Yell. We saw their entry from the English camp. How we felt cannot be truely described. But what reassured us and kept us alert during those dark circumstances, was that the sisters remained calm and endured everything with patience. We saw the warriors walking around in our clothes, while we, at the same time, had only rags to wear."

Thus wrote the resigned, Christianly stoic Zeisberger. Heckewelder describes the plundering of his homestead and the seizure of his loved ones in a more vivid manner. He says:

"A band of Wyandots had already gone to Salem early in the morning and returned with a measure of honey which they set before us. They had gone there to search the house again, destroy my bee hives, and plunder and destroy my cabbage and beet beds in the garden.

Since Gnadenhütten and Salem were both on the river, during calm weather one could hear the bells and the dogs barking from one village to the other. A quiet night followed that day of plunder, and loud was the scalp yell from Salem, with which the pickets announced to us the success of their mission. We recognized on the three yells, that three persons had fallen into their hands, but whether they were dead or alive, we could unfortunately only determine upon their arrival. Finally, at mid-night, the band arrived with Michael Jungmann, whom they brought into our tent. "Good evening, brothers!" he called to us as we shook hands. "Our earthly journey appears to have ended. We stand at the edge of eternity. Let them put us to death. It is a just cause for which we die." Then he turned to me and said: "Cheer up, brother! Your wife and child are fine. The Indian sisters requested from the warriors that they be allowed to stay the night in their protection, they promised to bring them the next day to Gnadenhütten, and that was granted."

During the time of terror, the Wyandots from Chief Pipe's party acted humanely and honorably. On September 10, the semi- king returned from Salem and Schönbrunn with the band of plunderers, and then the devastation began in Gnadenhütten. With wild screams they ripped down the fences around the cornfields and gardens, drove their horses into them, in a drunken rage killed our pigs, cattle and poultry, wherever they encountered them."

"Under such circumstances," writes Heckewelder, we could no longer remain in our former homesteads and therefore we asked Chief Pipe himself to take us away. The next day, the 11th of that month, after everything had been prepared, we departed the area. Never had the Christian Indians left a country with greater sorrow. The three wonderfully thriving settlements, Gnadenhütten, Salem and Schönbrunn, they were to leave forever, leaving countless herds of young cattle and pigs, which were wandering about in the forests, the 300 acres of corn in the fields, ready to be harvested; in addition to large amounts of harvest, potatoes, carrots and cabbage, a treasure worth $120,000. Everything was lost, and what was most painful were our libraries and writings with the numerous schoolbooks for the children. Here indeed was patience necessary and the hope that God would grant us the strength and determination to overcome all of the difficulties and dangers. Schönbrunn was the largest and most beautiful city built by the Moravians in the West; it contained 60 dwellings, constructed mostly of hewn tree trunks. From its center, where the chapel stood, a wide street ran to the north, a second, the main street, from east to west. Gardens with proper post fences and wonderful fruit extended between the dwellings and the workshops."

From this former area of pastoral solitude and peace, the missionaries and their congregation were brought to Upper Sandusky. One segment made the journey to Sandusky Creek on the water; the others driving along the trail the herd of almost 100 cattle, mostly cows, and almost 100 horses, which Elliot had let them keep. At Goschocking, the perpetrator of this misery left them to report the success of this expedition to his friend and master McKee, who was waiting for him on the Scioto. As if the misery, pain and difficulty were not enough for the poor refugees, during the journey the most terrifying storms fell upon them, which ripped down the trees around their camp, tossing them across their boats on the Walhonding, so that two of the ones most heavily laden with food was sunk. It was a miracle that no human life was lost. The storms put out the campfires, and the poor women stood with their infants in their arms in water up to their knees. During the journey, the savages drove their captives before them, with the missionary families usually in the middle. For the entire journey, Indian women carried little Marie and Christian David, carefully wrapped in blankets on their backs, along the trackless path, where there was often one swamp after another.

After their arrival in Upper Sandusky, the refugees built small huts from tree stumps and bark for protection against the bitter cold. They had neither beds nor blankets and soon found themselves in the greatest of want and misery. Along the way, the savages had robbed them of the last of their possessions. Often the poor souls had nothing to satisfy their hunger; the Indians had to live from the meat of the cattle, which had pitifully died due to a lack of pasture.

Shortly after their arrival, an order from Colonel von Peyster summoned the missionaries to Detroit. Zeisberger, Heckewelder, Sensemann and Edwards went there, leaving behind Jung and Jungmann to protect the families. After unspeakable difficulties, the former reached Detroit clad in rags. Fortunately, in Governor von Peyster they found a humane, reasonable countryman, their benefactor and savior. In the council which was convened to examine them, he quickly recognized the falseness of the testimony so that the lying Pipe was at a loss for words. After several questions he promptly set the missionaries free, had them dressed in proper clothes, and ordered the return of many of the articles stolen from them by the savages. The German and English officers from the Detroit garrison, as well as the most honored citizens of the city soon gave them their fullest sympathy, and even Chief Pipe then slithered by to ask forgiveness for his reckless behavior; he claimed that he had been misled, a victim of Elliot's and McKee's trickery. The missionaries accepted his apology. For all that, in their hearts they felt relieved. They departed Detroit with the joyful hope that their enemies had been silenced and that the time of persecution was over. On the evening of December 22, they arrived again at the refugee camp, to celebrate Christmas in an uplifting manner in the circle of their families.

Chapter 15

The Massacre at Gnadenhütten. - The Revenge of the Delawares and Wyandots against the Murderers. - Death of Colonel Crawford at the Stake.

At the beginning of 1782, the sorely tested refugees could not even imagine that the year would bring them even worse calamities. Toward the end of January, a bitter cold set in, which became particularly bad during the nights. There was a severe shortage of firewood, and the low construction of their huts did not permit the burning of large fires. Their animals died from lack of feed, and starvation appeared even among the community. The missionaries were forced to reduce the daily ration of food to one pint of corn per person. Heart-wrenching were the cries of the Indian children for bread, whose poor parents could not even come up with one dollar for 2 quarts of corn meal, which was the normal price among the Indian planters of Upper Sandusky, all of whom had only a small supply. In a general council, the Indians finally came to the desperate decision to send some of their people back to their deserted cities in order to harvest the corn abandoned in the fields, to bury it in the woods, and when needed, carry it in sacks to their place of hunger and misery. After obtaining the permission of the half-king and the missionaries, they set out for their former homes in several groups of men, women and children.

Though the cold and hunger were bitter adversaries of Zeisberger and his companions, even more dangerous was the continuing hatred of their enemies, a hatred which was fed by the monster Girty. The nearness of the German Indians soon became a burden to the half-king and his people; they feared that the nearby missions would flourish as they had on the Muskingum and that the rejuvenated communities would seek revenge against the Wyandots for the latter's participation in their persecution.

In December the half-king had lost two sons at the hands of unknown border rowdies, which he blamed on the secret intrigues of the missionaries. Plagued by the avenging spirits of his own self-imposed guilt, he finally feared for his own life. Thus troubled he sent a messenger to Colonel von Peyster requesting that he remove the missionaries from his lands since he could not live peacefully in their proximity; if this were not granted, then he would take his own measures.

This threat had its desired effect. Concerned about the fate of his brave countrymen, the Colonel informed Zeisberger about the intent of the half-king and commissioned Girty to see to their transfer to Detroit. Fortunately for the missionaries, but unfortunately for their disciples who had returned to their former homesteads, the monster had set out with a war party of Wyandots against the Ohio valley settlements, where his path was marked by murder and plunder. In his place came the Frenchman, Francois Levallier, from Lower Sandusky, a humane and educated man, who cared for the German teachers with the greatest of respect.

While the refugees were preparing for the next day's departure to Michigan and the separation from their former community rested heavily on their souls, a runner came with the horrible news that the departed Indians, while harvesting the corn at their former settlements had been attacked by a group of white frontiersmen and murdered without regard for age or sex. Just how devastating to the missionaries was this latest horrible news, is indicated by the following devout lament in Zeisberger's diary from this date: "There is nowhere a spot on earth where we can live in peace. The world is too small. We can hope for no protection from the whites and so-called Christians and have no more friends among the pagan nations, but are just fair game. Praise God! The Lord, our God still lives. He will not abandon us."

The news of this latest unbelievable atrocity by the frontiersmen turned out to be true in every detail. Never dreaming of danger from this direction, the German Indians had been busy for weeks collecting and shelling the corn and hiding it in the forests. They had finished their work and had packed their sacks for a departure the next day, when a band of mounted whites from Pittsburg led by Colonel Williamson appeared before Gnadenhütten. The murderers had assumed that Girty's bloody campaign across the Ohio had had some sort of connection with the reappearance of the Indians in the German cities; they had come to seek revenge upon the very ones, whose innocence must have been recognized by almost all, for the murderous deeds of Girty and the Wyandots, not with a blind determination, but rather with a cool and careful calculation, with the epicurean presence of mind of bloodthirsty cannibals. During the three-day trip, no second thoughts had dampened their thirst for murder. A mile from the village, they came upon Joseph Schebosch, the son of the missionary, while he was busy rounding up his horse. Karl Bilderbach, one of the scouts, the brutal son of a German, sprang upon him and struck him down with his tomahawk. Even though the boy raised himself up on his knees and pleaded for his life with the words that he was the son of a white man, the monster cut his scalp from his skull with his hunting knife and finally killed him with a blow through the heart. Jacob, the unfortunate youth's brother-in-law, was at the time on the river outside the village, busily tying together his sacks of corn, when the murderous band appeared. He personally knew several of those from Pittsburg and was about to greet them, but was shocked when he saw them shoot down one of the brothers, crossing the river in a canoe en route to the cornfields. This sight robbed him of the presence of mind; rather than warn his friends, namely those in Salem where his father was, about the murderers, he fled fearfully in the opposite direction and hid for several days in a cave in the woods. Upon their arrival in the village, the murderous band found the Indians scattered in the cornfields; they beckoned them with hypocritical friendship, that they had come as "friends and brothers", to assist them in their adversity caused by their enemies, because, in times of adversity, they had proven themselves to be the best friends of the Americans. Not in the least doubting the sincerity of these assertions, the German Indians approached them. Williamson further informed them that several bands of frontiersmen from Virginia and Kentucky were out to murder them and that they should quickly cease their work and under his protection follow them to Pittsburg where all their needs would be generously met. Shocked at this news, but at the same time delighted at the prospect of their salvation, the poor souls agreed to his suggestion and hurriedly prepared for their departure.

While this was occurring in Gnadenhütten, the national helper, Johann Martin, was with his son on the other side of the river, busily burying the collected corn. Upon his return to the corn field, he was not just a little surprised to find the tracks of so many shod horses and no one working. He climbed a hill from where he could see the village and was surprised to see his brethren in groups, some peacefully talking with the newly arrived whites, others walking with them along the streets. Believing that the whites had been sent by God as saviors, so that his people would not perish in the wasteland of Sandusky, the old one sent his son back to the city in order to relay to his brethren the joyful news. They, however, were a bit more cautious and sent two emissaries, to ascertain the purpose of the newly arrived whites. Unfortunately, as they entered the city, their brethren greeted them cheerfully with the news that their tribulation was over, that the whites had come to bring them to new homes where the fathers in Bethlehem would surely honor their request and send new teachers. Colonel Williamson encouraged them in this belief and sent along a group of his murderous thugs to Salem as an escort, in order to bring those Indians with their effects to Gnadenhütten. There, the crafty rascals also won the confidence of the unsuspecting ones; they tossed about biblical phrases, discussed with their victims the true meaning of the word of God, praised their (the Indians) piety, which enabled them to build such a beautiful, spacious church in Salem. "Yes, these are true and good Christians, better than many of our whites," they said, while exchanging hypocritical glances among one another so that the Indians could hear this. As they departed Salem, the true nature of several of the betrayers came out and they threw fire into the church that they had so admired and also into several of the homes. Against the shocked resistance of the Indians, several of the more clever ones of the gang remarked that they were only being smart in that they would deny to their enemies, the pursuing frontiersmen, any sort of shelter. It was only when they were at the bank of the river, across from Gnadenhütten, when the unfortunate ones had their eyes opened. Here they came upon a spot in the sand where there were bloody pieces of clothing and disturbed earth, where one of their people had writhed, and nearby was a blood splattered canoe. The realization came too late for the unfortunate victims. As with their brethren in Gnadenhütten, they had surrendered all weapons, muskets, axes and knives to the "deliverers", who had promised to return everything upon their arrival in Pittsburg. Upon arrival in the city, their escort cast aside their deceitful pretensions; brutal curses against the "German Indians" now flowed out of their mouths and their approaching murderous accomplices, who in the meantime had become totally inebriated on the sacrificial wine, cheerfully chimed in on this animalistic cry for blood. Like a herd of sheep, mistreated and cursed at, the victims were led into one blockhouse; while the men, women, and children from Gnadenhütten were being guarded in another. After separating the women and children from the men, it was shouted at the unfortunate victims that they were not Christians but rather damned heathen dogs and wicked thieves; their horses wore brands, and were all stolen from the whites, as were their axes, shovels, buckets, ladles, in short, everything they owned. In vain did the victims argue that, in the manner of the whites, they marked all their utensils and horses with he first letter of their name, and that they could give an exact accounting for every one of the items in question, including the name of the trader from which this and that had been purchased. These protests were ignored. Colonel David Williamson called the murderous gang aside and took a vote as to the fate of the unfortunate ones. Of 80 to 90 votes cast, only 18 were against slaughtering all of them. After deciding upon death, the savages discussed the manner of the mass murder. Several wanted to set fire to the blockhouses and burn the unfortunate victims alive. Others, however, wanted to take some sort of victory symbols back to Pittsburg, and therefore suggested killing and scalping them, an execution which was generally accepted. In the meantime, the Indians had read their fate in the faces of their guards, and when the monsters approached to carry out the bloody deed, they begged for a time to prepare for death. After much delay they were granted this request. Christine

Mahei, a spry and honorable woman, who spoke English and German, made one last attempt to arouse the mercy of the gang; forcing her way through the throng, she threw herself at Williamson's feet and mentioning his own family begged for mercy for her own; with cold-blooded words the monster pushed her away saying he could not help her. Under a flood of tears the brethren took each other in their arms and said their goodbyes. Then they chose one of father Zeisberger's hymns of mercy and waited quietly for death.

When the prayer was over, one of the executioners took off his coat and rolled up his sleeves. Then he grabbed a nearby club, and, shouting with joy, entered the slaughterhouse and clubbed to death 14 persons who were on their knees, their hands folded before them. Judith, a pious 80 year old woman, was the first victim. Finally, the executioner's arms became tired of the gruesome chore, and he passed the murder weapon to another thug with the words; "that's a lot of work, you keep going, I'm tired." Like the women and children, the men gave no resistance, and 90 in number, including five educated national helpers who spoke English and German, three of them over 60, including Isaac Glickhican, a hero and speaker of the Delawares and a true friend of the American colonists. Many of those murdered were born of Christian parents, and belonged to those refugees which the Pennsylvania government had protected against the Paxton murderers in 1762 and 1764.

"They were here shamefully slaughtered," writes Heckewelder, "men and women along with their children, those same lovely children, whose harmonic voices had so often in our school, so wonderfully raised in hymns of thanksgiving to the Maker. Their tender age, their innocent faces, their pleading, their tears could not move the monsters." Only two young boys survived the slaughter. Even before it had begun, one had raised one of the floor boards and crawled into the cellar, where the blood from above flowed down upon him. As it became dark, he crawled to the door and used the opportunity to escape unnoticed into the woods. That evening, the other boy, although struck down and scalped, recovered his strength and followed his companion.

When the savage slaughter had ended, the tired executioners left the scene to get drunk on whiskey and the remains of the sacrificial wine. However, they soon returned to count the corpses and when one poor boy by the name of Able, although scalped and struck down, raised up under the pile of bloody bodies, they finished killing him. Then they set fire to the large slaughterhouses and departed yelling and singing as if they had carried out a victorious deed. Those hyenas, who had so heinously bathed in the blood of the best friends of their country, were never prosecuted. The law remained mute in this shameful deed, the likes of which has no equal in the annals of crime, and which forms an indelible spot in the history of the Ohio valley. With all its savagery against the Indians, even Spain never murdered her Christian friends. Even a segment of the press acted horribly in regards to this cowardly and sordid mass murder of Zeisberger's disciples. The "Pennsylvania Gazette" of April 17, 1782 praises it as a "victorious incursion into enemy territory, where much booty was taken and the hideouts of the enemy were destroyed."

Even Doddridge, the historian of this "Moravian War", attempts to play down the shameful deed and excuse its perpetrators. He writes,

"The people were not monsters and vagabonds, but many belonged to the most respected families of the territory. They were embittered at the loss of their relatives and the theft of so many items by the Indians."

But Heckewelder replies to that: "The Pittsburgers certainly knew how to differentiate our Indians from the murderers and brigands. Even disregarding years of maintaining a well-known friendliness, our people did not dress or paint themselves in the Indian manner, but rather wore simple and decent clothes, cut in the manner of the whites. In regards to the numerous murders and thefts of the Indians, it is well known among those who have lived among the Indians, that very often border settlers would dress and paint themselves as Indians, in order to attack and plunder settlements and travelers, in the firm belief that their crimes would be attributed to the Indians.

By chance the Indians of Schönbrunn were spared the fate of their brethren. Two of them, on their way to Gnadenhütten, discovered along the trail the marks of shod hooves and immediately thereafter the scalped body of the young Schebosch. They decided that Gnadenhütten had been attacked by white frontiersmen and hurried to warn those left behind. Before the murderers arrived, those from Schönbrunn were already in flight to Sandusky.

The massacre at Gnadenhütten did not quench the thirst for blood of Williamson's tigers. Still unsatisfied, and before they arrived in Pittsburg, they fell upon the camp of the Delaware tribe's peace party which was under the protection of the American government and murdered everyone who was not able to escape into the woods. Furthermore, in May, barely two months after the bloodbath on the Muskingum, the same murderous gang, reinforced by an additional 400 out for blood, with the same butcher Williamson and Colonel Crawford[1], Washington's land agent in command, set out to wipe out from the face of the earth those from Schönbrunn who had been spared so far and who were in Upper Sandusky. But the tragedy of Gnadenhütten had taught the Indians caution. Every white homestead on the Ohio, from Pittsburg to Cave Creek below Wheeling was watched by their scouts. And when Williamson issued the order to depart on a new journey of murder, fleet-footed runners brought the news at a gallop to the cities of the Wyandots. In the meantime, Williamson's band marched straight to the Moravian settlement; however, since those remaining had been warned and brought to safety in Detroit accompanied by a company of rangers sent by Colonel von Peyster, the Americans turned away from the deserted Moravian huts towards the Wyandot cities. That was exactly what the savages wanted them to do. One evening, when the murderers had reached a spot of open prairie, where a retreat to the protection of the woods was not possible, a war party of Wyandots and Wolves approached from all sides. Their very first murderous shots felled a large number of the rogues. The onset of darkness saved a few of those remaining, during which time the rest of the cowardly band, who could slaughter helpless old men, women and children, but would not dare face Indian warriors, took to flight. The savages chased after them, killed many of them fleeing in the woods, and took Crawford, Dr. McKnight, and five others prisoner. "Where is Williamson, the chief murderer?" screamed the warriors at them. Upon the negative reply, that the monster was one of the first to flee, the shout came from their mouths: "Revenge, revenge on those in our power for the murder of our people in Gnadenhütten and Pittsburg!" The following horrible chain of events was provided by Dr. McKnight, who miraculously escaped:

"A group of squaws and children fell upon our five companions, struck them with tomahawks, ripped off their scalps, and shoved the bloody skins into our faces. The colonel was then stripped naked, led to the side of the fire and beaten by the squaws with fists and clubs. The

---

[1] Colonel Crawford had at first refused to participate in this cowardly campaign of murder; but since a "Moravian War" was popular among the frontier settlers, after extended consideration and bowing to political pressure, he accepted "the command" in consideration of the desire of his patriotic fellow citizens". This fatal weakness, this miserable servility in the face of popular pressure, would reap a horrible punishment.

same happened with me. Then they fastened a rope to a stake sticking into the ground about 15 feet high, tied the Colonel's hands behind his back, and wrapped the rope around his waist. The rope was long enough so that the Colonel could sit down or move once or twice around the stake. In vain did he plead for mercy and stated that he had not taken part in the Muskingum atrocity.

"You marched at the head of the murderers of our brothers," was the dreadful reply. "No one on earth, not even the British king with all of his treasure can save you. The blood of those murdered on the Muskingum must be revenged."

"All right, then," called the colonel in distress, "go ahead and burn me, I will just have to suffer it patiently."

"Pipe, the chief of the Delawares, then gave a speech to the execution group, which consisted of 30 to 40 warriors and 60 to 70 squaws and children."

"When he had finished, they all yelled their approval of his suggestions. The men then took their muskets and fired powder at the Colonel's naked body from his head to his toe. At least 70 shots were fired against him. Then young and old surrounded him and, as far as I could see, one of them cut off his ears; when the throng thinned out somewhat, I could see that, as a result, blood was streaming down both sides of his head."

"The fire was about 6 or 7 paces away from the stake where the colonel was tied; it had been started with hickory sticks, which burned in the middle, and were about 6 feet long. Three or four Indians would in turn take the burning sticks and grind them from all sides into the colonels body, which had been blackened with powder. Several squaws shoveled up burning coals and ashes and tossed them against the victim, so that shortly he could only stand on fiery coals and ashes."

In horrible agony, the colonel begged them to shoot him; but no one paid attention. Soon thereafter his voice failed, but he still endured the fiery pain two hours longer with manly endurance. Finally his strength gave out, and he lay down; the Indians then scalped him and several times tossed the skin into his face and yelled: "Look, that is your great captain!" One old squaw (Satan could not have appeared more gruesome) took a board, scrapped up some more coals and ashes and poured them on the colonel's back and scalped head. Once more the colonel raised himself up and walked slowly around the execution stake; again the executioners shoved flaming rods into his flesh, but as before the victim seemed to be even more insensitive to the pain. I was then led to the house of Chief Pipe, which lay about 1 mile away from the execution site. The next morning I was brought to the Shawnee city, and we passed the site where the colonel had been burned; his bones were burned almost to ashes in the glimmering fire. The Indians said that that was my great captain and gave the scalp yell."

That was the grisly revenge of the Delaware warriors for the mass murder which the whites had carried out against their praying brethren on the Muskingum.

Chapter 16

The Battle of Blue Licks. - Major George W. Bedinger. - Clark's Campaign Against the Shawnees. - A Dying Person's Vision on a Cincinnati Hill. - The Praise of the Kentuckians. - End of the Revolutionary War. - Gen. Steuben's Mission to the West to Take Over the British Military Posts.

After the removal of Zeisberger and his communities from under British control, there were no more obstacles in the path of Elliot and McKee to unite all the Indian tribes of the northwest against the colonists of the Ohio valley.

Because of the newly inflamed hatred of the redskins against the whites, a result of the mass murders at Gnadenhütten and Pittsburg, the Kentucky settlements would have surely been destroyed had the alliance had a leader such as a Philipp or a Pontiac rather than Simon Girty. But this cowardly renegade, an expert only in trickery and deceit, was not the equal to the military leaders of the frontiersmen, Clark, Boone, and Kenton. On the 16th of August of that same year, he led a war party of 5-600 warriors across the Ohio against Bryant's Station, a post on the south bank of the Elkhorn, about 5 miles from Lexington. The station bore the name of one of Boone's in-laws, a cool and experienced Indian-fighter, who had recently been attacked and killed by Shawnees at the mouth of Cave Creek.

Because of the continuous Indian attacks, many of the station's original settlers had fled back to North Carolina, and the newcomers from Virginia, inexperienced in life in the woods, were unfamiliar with the Indian form of warfare; among them was Robert Johnson, the father of the eventual victor over Tecumseh and famous Vice-President of the United States, Richard M. Johnson. However, in spite of all their disadvantages, they held out and, with the help of reinforcements from Lexington, led by Boone and Colonel Todd, they beat back the repeated attacks of the enemy. Thus thwarted, Girty pulled back to the Blue Licks on the Licking river, secretly stalked by Boone and his companions, who sought to cut off their retreat across the Ohio. At this point the rogues had better luck. Upon seeing the redskins, Major Hugo McGarty, commanding the enemy center, plunged his horse wildly into the Licking and challenged everyone to follow him. The savages sensed their advantage and opened a terrible fire against McGarty's riders while another party, breaking through the right wing, fell upon Boone from behind and broke up his entire command in the woods with a loss of 76 men. Among those who fell on the battlefield were Colonels Todd and Trigg, Major Harlan, and Boone's son. In the unfortunate battle, Major George M. Bedinger, of German descent from North Carolina, who had been Bowman's Adjutant in the campaign of 1779 against the Shawnees in Old Chillicothe, won a name for himself as a brave and able officer[1]; he collected the stragglers and led them back to Colonel Logan's corps, which, for some unexplained reason, had remained behind at the station.

(95)

---

[1] *Historical Sketches of Kentucky* by L. Collins, pag. 485.

In order to avenge this heavy defeat, which filled Kentucky with grief, Clark collected a thousand mounted riflemen at the mouth of the Licking and set out at the end of September against the villages of the redskins in the Miami valley. His adjutants were Colonels Floyd and Logan; Kenton was the guide for the army through the wilderness. Even though the preparations for the campaign had been swift and in secret, the natives had heard about it and deserted their villages on both Miamis and the Mad River. Again burning torches were cast into the blockhouses and the fields devastated. Upon their return to the Licking, the troops stopped on the hill of Cincinnati, which now as Mount Adams has the observatory. Here, in the shadow of the oaks and beech trees they set down a stretcher, on which a brave forest warrior, Captain McCracken, lay, who the day before had been fatally wounded. It was the 4th of November, 1782. The sun was sinking in the glowing rays of the evening. The colorful glory of the Indian summer was reflected on the silvery surface of the Ohio, where the forests that surround the valley were still colorful. Unconsciously the foresters were riveted by the wonderful panorama of the wild forest at their feet. Even the one who was dying rose up from his stretcher and his eyes were aglow. The radiant wilderness caused a prophetic vision to appear before him; of a great, towered capital city, with its two sister cities on the Licking with numerous villas and gardens: "Comrades, he spoke, in 50 years a great and splendid city will arise in this valley. Who will then still be alive, to see this monument to the creative energy of our people?!"

Colonel Floyd seized upon this idea and continued: "Let us pledge with our word of honor and a handshake, those of us still living in 50 years, to meet again on this site, to celebrate the success of our campaign and the development of our fatherland out of the womb of the wilderness to a site of culture and peace."

A great, joyful cry of the Indian hunters proclaimed that these words had inflamed all the hearts. The rough sons of the woods shook hands to pledge a reunion on November 4, 1832.

It was a unique decision in that time of danger, where death waited at any moment in each bush for every one of them. The next day, its originator, Captain McCracken, breathed out his spirit and was buried in the vicinity of a lonely blockhouse near the mouth of the Licking. Even Floyd, the one who made the pact, would soon follow him. He was felled by a redskin's bullet at the Falls of the Ohio. The fifty years did pass, but for the wartime comrades the formal pledge was not forgotten[2]. Already at the beginning of 1832, survivors announced in the papers of the Ohio Valley the reunion on November 4. Responses from several areas proved that a number of former comrades were still alive and would appear at the remarkable reunion. The elderly hero Kenton wrote an announcement, which warmed all hearts. The city authorities and citizens of Cincinnati took preliminary measures to warmly receive the old pioneers, but unfortunately, cholera, which at the time was devastating Cincinnati and causing such grief, caused the reunion to be canceled.

The dying captain's vision on Mount Adams was realized. On November 4, 1782, there were just a few, scattered settlements in Kentucky, and Ohio was a complete wilderness. On November 4, 1832, both states already counted two million souls. In place of the beech and oak forest of 1782, stood on the day of the intended reunion an industrious city with more than 30,000 souls. In the history of the world, there have been no parallels of such growth and expansion.

---

[2] *Biographical Sketches of Simon Kenton* by John McDonald. Cincinnati 1838, page 247. Collins' Hist. Sketches of Kentucky, *Cincinnati Gazette*, Nov. 3, 1832.

But, since we have jumped half a century ahead of our chronological progression, let us return to the last date of our Chronicle.

On November 30, 1782, several weeks after Clark's return from his campaign against the Indians of both Miamis, preliminary peace arrangements were signed by representatives of England and the United States in Paris. The hostilities ended on January 20, 1783, and on the following 19th of April, the continental army was informed of the beginning of the peace, and on September 3 the revolutionary battle ended with a definitive peace treaty. However, even though the hostilities against the redcoats were ended, the battle against their former allies, the redskins, was continued even more intensely in the Ohio Valley. The peace treaty led a number of officers and soldiers discharged from the the continental army across the Alleghenies and the Ohio Valley became th the goal for these adventurers. They could not remain in the east, since commerce, factories, and professions lay prostrate. Agriculture and hunting were about the only areas to which they could turn. For these no capital was needed. A musket and ax were the only necessities. Block houses took the place of tents. Furthermore this wild region with its perils, was just the right place for people, who after the uncertainty of war could just as little fit into an orderly life under the law as they could manage in the rigid life in the cities of the devastated east. Here in the far reaches of the west, every vestige of authority was remote, and there was room for unlimited action. Earlier (in October 1779) Virginia had, by law, prohibited all settlements of its citizens northwest of the Ohio, but the greed of the land speculators and the pressure from the adventurers became stronger than the law. For the leading politicians, it became an obsession to open up the gigantic region on the other side of the mountains to settlement, but without driving the savage owners to despair and causing a new Indian war. In addition, it became necessary for Congress to take measures for the transfer of these areas from the states, who felt that they had a historical claim to them, to the federal government. On March 1781, New York gave up its claims under conditions accepted by the Congress; and Virginia, after several of its arrogant demands were refused by Congress, finally, on December 20, agreed to give up its demands for the entire territory northwest of the Ohio.

In the meantime, the government had taken steps to secure possession of the military posts in the ceded regions. Washington selected General Friedrich Wilhelm von Steuben as the man, whose enlightened military and political decisions made him the proper choice for this mission[3]. Among his eventual instructions were the following:

"In carrying out this mission, you will, where possible, receive from General Haldimand the assurance and the order for the immediate occupation by the United States of the posts in question or at least a relinquishment in the near future. Should this not be possible, then you will attempt to secure from him a definite and irrevocable guarantee, that he will establish, as soon as possible, a definite schedule for abandoning said posts, and that the troops of his British Majesty will not depart before receiving assurances that United States are in position to occupy the forts, as soon as the troops of the British majesty have departed."

"You will suggest to General Haldimand an exchange of cannon and artillery supplies on those sites, as you deem suitable in the interests of the United States, and you will reach agreement with the British commander that a similar number of cannon and a similar quantity and nature of supplies, as those above, be given to his British Majesty

---

[3] Kapp's *Life of Steuben*, page 503-507.

by the United States at a location and a time as determined by you."

"After completing your arrangements with General Haldimand, you will, in a manner best determined by yourself, visit the individual posts and forts on the border areas of the United States up to Detroit, noting their situation, strengths, and other conditions, provide an opinion as to their position and probable advantages for the United States, and immediately report to me, as to which posts, in your opinion, in the interests of the United States should be occupied. While transiting across Lake Champlain you will observe the width of the water on the northern end and the nature of the neighboring land and determine whether, south of the 45th Degree, or near our furthest boundary, there is a small piece of land available, upon which, should the Congress deem it necessary, fortifications could be constructed, which would control entrance to the lake from Canada.

In Detroit you will find an extensive settlement, consisting mostly of French Canadians. You will assure the latter that the Congress and the citizens of the United States are most concerned about their welfare and protection. At the same time you will make them understand, that we desire the self-same friendship from them towards us and the posts which we desire to erect there and towards all the future settlements, which might be established in their area by the citizens of the United States. Should the advanced season of the year or other unexpected obstacles make it difficult for a detachment of American troops to arrive before the British garrison departs, then in this case you will see to it that one or several sympathetic individuals of said district shall cause, at cost to the United States, to raise a militia company, should there be one available, or other armed individuals to guard the forts and buildings in return for appropriate payment and under what conditions. You will also pay particular attention as to whether the farmers and merchants in Detroit are willing and able to supply an American garrison at that post with provisions and other necessary articles."

In accordance with his instructions, Steuben departed immediately for Canada and arrived in Chamblee on August 2nd, where he sent Major North to General Haldimand, in order to announce his arrival. According to the wishes of the latter, they met on August 8 at Sorel, where Steuben took immediate preparations to complete his mission.

On August 23, 1783, he forwarded the following report to Washington:

"In regards to the first suggestion, which I was instructed to propose, General Haldimand replied, that he had not the slightest order to evacuate any post, but rather only had orders to cease hostilities and these he had strictly carried out, in which he had recalled not only the British troops but also the savages from carrying out hostile actions; however he would not give up one inch of territory until receiving explicit orders to that effect. I informed him that I was not instructed to demand an immediate evacuation of the posts in question, but rather instructed to visit the posts currently occupied by the British, in order to formulate the necessary arrangements in the interests of the United States, in accordance with which I sought his permission to visit said posts and a safe escort thereto. To this he responded, these measures were premature; the peace treaty had not yet been signed; he had only been authorized to cease hostilities and therefore could not permit me to visit a single British post."

"Similarly, he also did not intend, where it was in his power, to permit negotiations between the Indians and the United States;

he would keep the door to negotiations closed until receiving a definite order from the court to open it."

"My final suggestion was, that he should agree to inform the Congress three months prior to evacuation. But because of the reasons stated above, he refused to do this, explaining, that he would make no agreements or enter into any negotiations, as long as a definitive agreement had not been signed."

"I am truly sorry that I was unsuccessful in this endeavor, but the thought consoles me that Your Excellency will know that I have done all within my power to carry out your wishes and those of the Congress."

Since Steuben had not the slightest hope of achieving anything through further negotiations, he departed St. Johns on August 13.

The reason why Great Britain would not agree to handing over the military posts could be found in the unwillingness shown by several states, to ratify several conditions of the peace treaty, particularly the 4th, in regards to reimbursement for seized British property. Virginia stood at their head, because Britain had refused to return those negro slaves which had been taken as war booty to Canada and there set free. While this uncertainty concerning the western borders continued, European immigrants resettled around the domestic forts. In the spring of 1784, Pittsburg, under the guidance of Tench Francis, the agent for the properties of the Penn estates, who, having remained loyal to England during the Revolutionary War, had lost the majority of their holdings in America, was properly laid out and received several new buildings. The areas must have appeared rather lifeless and with little hope for the future, because Arthur Lee, the government commissioner, wrote in his diary about that year:

"Pittsburg has been almost totally settled by Scots and Irish, living in decayed blockhouses and are so dirty that, in general, they resemble their countrymen in Ireland or Scotland. However, a lively commerce exists here. In the shops, cornmeal and skins are taken as money. Within the city there are four lawyers, two doctors, but no clergy of any sect. I do not believe that the area will ever achieve any significance."

At the time, Lee was en route to Fort McIntosh for a council with the Indians. Shortly before, he had secured from the Iroquois in Fort Stanwix a renunciation of their rights to the Ohio Valley and then, in concert with R. Butler and George Rogers Clark, was commissioned to conclude a peace treaty at the above-named fort with the Wyandots, Delawares, Chippewas, and Ottawas, which he did. With this treaty, the border was exactly determined between the United States and the Wyandot and Delaware nations, the former (the United States) would be permitted to erect trading posts, but also required to subject any white, attempting to establish a settlement on Indian land, to any punishment desired by the natives.

Chapter 17

Captain Elholm. - Captain David Ziegler. - The Organization of the Northwest Territory. - The Founding of Marietta. - Governor St. Clair. - Ludwig Wetzel.

During the year 1784, and authorized by the laws of Virginia, the holders of military land grants began selecting good sections of the valley south of the Ohio. With the exception of the Henderson Company's holdings, the entire area between the Green and Cumberland rivers was distributed to Virginia soldiers.

Even Congress had, at various times in 1776 and 1780, authorized land grants to the men and officers of the revolutionary army, as well as to the families of those who had fallen. After peace had been proclaimed, General Rufus Putnam forwarded a request to the Congress from numerous officers of the New England states, requesting the implementation of those promises. However, that body was not in a position to act at that time; for it required that the states, which had restated their prior claims to the western territories, set aside their own self-interest and declare the lands to be in the public domain. In vain did New Jersey, Delaware, and Maryland, in the spirit of good politics and self-righteousness, suggest that the entire area which was still unsettled at the begining of the war, originally claimed by Britain but subsequently renounced in the Treaty of Paris, was indeed in the public domain, having been won by the blood and treasure of all the states. It was only in 1786 that the federal government was finally able to dismiss Connecticut's claims to these areas[1].

In the same year there were rebellious movements in eastern Tennessee. There the local settlers did not accept the governance of North Carolina; they seceded and organized an independent state under the name of "Frankland", and elected John Sevier (Xavier), son of a Huguenot family, to be governor. In this revolt of the backwoodsmen, a central role was played by Captain Caesar August Elholm, a German who had earlier served in Pulasky's Legion and been decorated in the siege of Savannah. Supported by a sergeant and three soldiers, he used a ruse to successfully capture 110 English under Captain French, as well as five vehicles with their drivers and seize 130 rifles[2]. In the end, the revolt of the east Tennesseans was put down, Sevier arrested and dragged deep into North Carolina, only to be soon freed by his friends. Later he became Governor and Tennessee representative to the US Congress.

In the Fall of the year 1785, a contingent of troops from Fort McIntosh under Major Doughty began the construction of Fort Harmar at the mouth of the Muskingum. The War Ministry had decided to construct this fort not only to protect the settlers south of the Ohio, but also to protect the Indian lands north of the river which were threatened with attack and seizure by a group of Kentuckians led by James Wilkinson. On May 4th of the following

---

[1] See page 14.

[2] Ramsay's *Annals of Tennessee*, page 382.

year, the area was occupied by a company of the 1st Regiment of the Line under Captain David Ziegler. Ziegler was born on August 16, 1748, in Heidelberg and was a soldier from head to toe. His avocation to the military had shown itself in his early youth, and since his small fatherland, the wine cellar of the Holy Roman Empire, kept him too constricted, he followed the beat of the recruiter's drum, which collected all the candidates for martial glory under the banner of Empress Catherine of Russia. During the campaign of General Weismann he had been decorated and mustered out after the seizure of the Crimea and immigrated to North America. He had arrived in Philadelphia in 1775. When the revolution broke out, he was one of the first to serve under Washington's flag and served honorably as a subaltern. Based on numerous wounds received on the battlefields of the revolutionary war, which testified to his bravery and heroics, he attained the rank of Captain. Furthermore, Ziegler was an experienced drill master in the manner of Steuben and a true leader of men, not an easy task in the remote border posts. For, according the reports of Dr. Hildreth, the soldiers manning these posts included the lowest and most unscrupulous ruffians in the country, who could only be controlled when just about every one of them received 100 to 200 whip lashes with the rod almost every day. Indeed, discipline was maintained not only with the rod, but also in the most barbaric manner with the bullet; in this manner Johann C. Dittmann and two other unfortunate warriors for Uncle Sam were shot on the order of the Major when they did not promptly return with their Corporal from a detail in the forest. In October of this same year, Ziegler traveled with 2 companies of his regiment to Vincennes, to reinforce General Clark, who, on orders of the government, was collecting 1000 Kentucky militia for service against the tribes of the Northwest, since, in spite of the treaties, the latter had not ceased their hostilities against the settlements. In the end, however, the mission of the expedition was totally thwarted because, due to the swampiness of the Wabash, the ammunition and provisions were stuck in boats at the mouth of the river. Put on short rations, the soldiers became impatient, while their trust in Clark disappeared, due to his constant drunkenness on whiskey. They refused to follow orders. Two hundred men threw their packs on their backs and marched home, to be followed shortly by the rest. Ziegler then returned to the Muskingum and from there returned as a recruiting officer to Philadelphia.

After Virginia abandoned its claims to the lands above the Ohio to the Federal Government, Congress issued an ordinance organizing the new territories, which gave the following bombastic names to the 10 states included therein: Sylvania, Michigania, Chersonesus, Assenisipia, Illenoia, Metropotamia, Saratoga, Polypotamia, Pelisipia and the fitting Washington. However, this decree was soon rescinded, since this wise body had overlooked provisions of a law from the year 1780, which had limited the area of the states to between 100 and 150 square miles. Thus these pretentious names were lost to posterity; Congress decided to distribute the territory into no less than three and no more than five states, and thus ensued the famous Ordinance of 1787 "For the Governance of the Territory of the United States Northwest of the Ohio," which forms the legal basis for the present states of Ohio, Indiana, Illinois, Michigan, and Wisconsin. The proclamation of this ordinance caused numerous groups and entrepreneurs in the eastern states to request of Congress the turnover of significant stretches of land for the establishment of settlements. The most famous of these was the New England Company headed by the above-noted General Rufus Putnam and Dr. Cutler, who obtained 750,000 acres on the Ohio, west of the Scioto, while Royal Flint and Joseph Parker obtained land westwards to the Mississippi, and John Cleves Symmes of New Jersey obtained the land between the two Miamis.

The Minister of War immediately ordered Colonel Harmar to Vincennes in order to obtain a peace treaty with the Wabash and Shawnee Indians. It was also hoped to work out something with the Wyandots and Iroquois. In order to counter any possible hostilities, troops were sent to Forts Pitt and McIntosh, to the Muskingum and Miami, to Vincennes and Louisville, while the Governor of Virginia was asked to keep the militia in the District of Kentucky prepared for an emergency.

During the Autumn of 1787, the Directors of the New England Company took steps for the settlement of the company's lands. During the winter and following spring, General Rufus Putnam with 47 men made his way along an old Indian trail over the Alleghenies. On the Youhiogheny they built boats and continued downstream until they reached their desired destination at the mouth of the Muskingum river, which they named Marietta to honor Queen Marie Antoinette's support for the American ambassador in Paris. On July 9, the governor of the territory, General Arthur St. Clair, arrived with his family at Fort Harmar which lay opposite Marietta. His arrival was accompanied by a terrible thunderstorm, similar to the storms which would mark his administration. The Governor was born in 1734 in Scotland and had enjoyed a classical education at the University of Edinburgh. His preference for the military life won out over his scientific talents and led him to General Wolfe's flag under which he participated in the storming of Quebec. After the Peace of 1763, he was given command of Fort Ligonier in Pennsylvania and a land grant of 1000 acres. At the outbreak of the Revolutionary War he became colonel of a regiment of Continentals, soon achieved the rank of Brigadier General, and was cited for bravery in the battles of Trenton and Princeton. At the same time, there were accusations of cowardice and incompetence from other quarters, even treason, when, after he was transferred as a Major General to Ticanderoga, he abandoned the fort upon Burgoyne's approach. The charges, however, simply reflected the anger of his detractors. The fortifications were not complete and could not have been defended against the assembled British force, a fact recognized by the court martial, which had been convened to examine the charges, and which completely exonerated the general. During 1785, while living on his wonderful farm in the Ligonier Valley, in Westmoreland County, he was appointed representative to the Continental Congress; soon to be elected President of that body. The Governor had a lovely family, a son and three daughters, highly educated and of glowing beauty. The one, Louise, was an excellent rider and hunter; a true Diana, she would gallop into the forest, with no fear of Indians, and shoot deer and squirrels with a rifle like a backwoodsman.

The settlers of Marietta, the first permanent city in Ohio, offered a stark contrast to those on the south side of the river. They belonged to the most respected and educated families of New England. However, they soon did not lack the company of the rough sons of the forest such as Colonel Peter Nieswanger, Jakob Weiser, Johann Warth, and most of all, the famed Indian hunter, Jakob Wetzel, all of whom, after the arrival of the governor, continued to remain in the vicinity of Fort Harmar as spies and scouts. The vast Ohio valley again resounded with the unique deeds and adventurers of this Renaldo of the west. Of his birth, his early experiences, and adventures, the following was told:

Wetzel's father, a German, was one of the earliest pioneers in the west. Scornful of the communal protection of forts or stations, he always built his blockhouses right in the heart of the Indian territory, where he cleared several acres for corn and pumpkin. In addition to his wife, the family consisted of four sons, Martin, Ludwig, Johann, and Jakob. One day, a band of Indians forced their way into their home, killed and scalped the father and took both boys, Ludwig and Johann into the forest. During the noise and confusion of the attack, the mother was able to escape. On that day, the oldest son Martin was away hunting. Ludwig, at the time a boy of 13, received a slight wound in the chest. On the second night after their capture, the Indians camped at Big Lick, near McMahon's Creek, and, because of the tender age of the boys, did not take the normal precaution of tying them up at night. As the Indians lay in a deep sleep, Ludwig whispered into his brother's ear: "Jakob, let's escape and go back home." They took off, but after putting just a few hundred paces behind them, their feet became so cut by the plants and thorns that they could not go on. They sat down on a tree stump and Ludwig said: "Jakob, without shoes we'll never get back home. You stay here and I'll sneak back to the Indians and get us 2 pair of moccasins." The boy did as he said, stole the shoes from two sleeping Indians, and returned to their hiding place. After a while the thought came to him, that it would be better for them on their flight to have weapons. This thought was put into action. Again Ludwig crept back to the Indian camp, grabbed two muskets and a hunting knife and, along with his brother, swiftly followed the path leading their home. The Indians quickly noticed their flight and theft and set out after the daring escapees. Ludwig, however, was aware of the cleverest tricks to confuse their pursuers and safely reached the bank of the Ohio with his brother. There they quickly made a raft and made it over to the other side to Virginia. Because of the pain and loss of blood from his wound, Ludwig was totally exhausted. Both boys were totally shocked when they found their burned-down cabin and the scalped body of their father. Over the smoky pile of ashes, both swore to shoot down every Indian that would cross their path in the future. And how terribly was this oath kept.

Ludwig Wetzel's life reflects the cunning, trickery and amazing sturdiness and individualism which developed in the border warfare with the Indians. He had been raised as a hunter and warrior. As a small boy he had learned to load and fire a musket while running full speed, to throw a tomahawk, and use the scalping knife.

In the year 1782, a short time after Crawford's death at the stake, the 18 year-old Ludwig Wetzel set out with Thomas Mills, who had participated in the campaign against the "Moravian Indians", to retrieve a horse which had been left behind in the area where St. Clairsville now stands. At "Indian Creek", a well-known forest stream, they suddenly came upon a group of 40 Indians who were lying in wait for the stragglers from a campaign. The Indians and the whites spotted each other at the same moment. Ludwig fired first killing an Indian, but at the same time a ball wounded his companion Mills who was soon captured and scalped. Four Indians threw away their muskets and took off running at full gallop after Wetzel, who reloaded his musket during his long strides. After running half a mile, one of the pursuers was only ten steps away from Wetzel. The young man turned around, shot him down, and, in the same manner as before, reloaded his musket in his breathless flight. Soon, another Indian came so close to Wetzel that, when he turned to aim at him, he grabbed the barrel with his hand and the two began a terrible struggle began for the decisive weapon. Wetzel succeeded in turning the barrel against the Indians' breast, pulled the trigger, and the Indian fell to the ground. In the meantime, the young man, along with his two pursuers had become fairly worn out by the constant running; Wetzel reloaded his musket and stood waiting for the two Indians. One of them went behind a young tree trunk which only partially covered his body, and with Wetzel's ball in his hip sank to the ground. With a loud war cry, the remaining Indian gave up the chase and returned to his companions.

The savages were often close enough to send Wetzel into eternity with their tomahawks; however, their intent to take him alive and burn him at the stake clouded their judgement and gave him an opportunity to escape. Wetzel had alledgedly killed 27 Indians in the area around Wheeling alone.

Soon thereafter we find Ludwig with a party of scouts sent out to pursue the Indians. In the Spring of 1787, a party of savages had crossed the Ohio at Mingo Bottom three miles below Steubenville, fell upon a settlement and killed all the inhabitants. In reaction to this, well-to-do inhabitants had circulated a subscription list which promised one hundred dollars to the first one to bring in an Indian scalp. Major McMahan, who had often led the border settlers in bloody skirmishes, soon raised a company of 20 men, among whom was Ludwig Wetzel. They crossed the Ohio and, with cunning and tenacity, followed the Indians' trail all the way to the Muskingum. There, the advance scouts discovered a horde of Indians encamped on the river bank whose number far outweighed their own small group. Since the Indians had not discovered their enemies, Major McMahan cautiously pulled his people back into the bushes in order to discuss further plans. The result of the discussion was, "since discretion is the better part of valor, a rapid retreat was the best solution." Believing that his companions were busy planning the best attack, Ludwig Wetzel remained sitting on a tree stump, with a musket on his lap and his tomahawk in hand. Upon the decision for a rapid retreat, it was carried out without delay; the stragglers departed leaving Wetzel resting. Noticing that he was not following, Major McMahan called to him whether he wished to return home with them. Ludwig replied to him that he would not run like a fool. "He had come on a hunt for Indians, he saw them out in front, and had not the least intent to turn and run like a coward. He did not intend to return home without an Indian scalp, regardless of whether he lost his own doing it." Neither friendly advice nor persuasion could move such a character, who had never before submitted to the control or suggestions of others. Therefore, his companions left him alone in the forest with a numerous and alert enemy. However, this solitary woodsman, although looking danger straight in the eye with the daring of one who is insane, had the cunning of a fox, the bravery of a lion, and trust in his musket and arm, which had never yet failed him.

As soon as he lost sight of his companions, he put his blanket and musket over his shoulder and took off in the opposite direction with the hope of encountering a lone straggling Indian. He stayed away from the large streams, since large parties often set up camp there. With silent steps, sending his eagle eye through the bushes, he stole through the enemy territory, until the evening of the next day, when he saw a puff of smoke raising from the bushes. Silently he crept to the fire and found two wool blankets and a small copper kettle. It was apparently the camp of two Indians and Wetzel decided to stalk and kill them. He hid himself in the thick underbrush so that he could clearly make out the number and movements of the enemy.

At sundown, one Indian returned to camp, lit a fire and began to prepare dinner. Shortly thereafter his companion returned. They both ate, began to sing and so entertain themselves with humming that their lively laughter resounded throughout the forest.

The poor souls had not the slightest idea that death in the form of their fiercest enemy, intended to make them an easy prey. Ludwig kept his eyes on the camp. Around 9 or 10 o'clock in the evening, one of the Indians wrapped himself in his blanket, put his musket on his back, grabbed a burning stick and left camp, probably with the intention of stalking a deer. The fire was supposed to keep away the horseflies and mosquitoes; for it is a well-known fact that deer are not frightened by the sight of fire, since they often see it in the Fall and Winter, when the leaves and grass are dry and the forest catches fire. The departure of the Indian bothered our hero quit a bit, and he kept hoping that the other Indian would return to camp at daybreak. But he was mistaken. The birds began to chirp, the wild cock gave out his shrill sound throughout the countryside, and Wetzel saw that the daybreak had come and that he could no longer wait with his deadly task. He silently crept to the camp and found his victim sleeping soundly. He swiftly pulled out his fighting knife and with all his strength sent the avenging steel into the Indian's heart.

A convulsive movement, a brief gasp, and the poor soul was with his ancestors. Wetzel scalped him and set out for home. He arrived home only one day after his companions, where he claimed the promised reward.

The praiseworthy hero of the Ohio valley was that sort of person.

The Ordinance of 1787 had established two levels of governance for the Northwest Territory. On the one hand, the legislative and judicial power resided in the hands of the governor and three judges, and this form was immediately put into effect upon St. Clair's arrival in Marietta. Misters Parsons, Armstrong, and Barnum had been named judges. The latter, an enthusiastic disciple of antiquity, ordered that the streets of the new city be named Campus Martius, Capitolium, Cecilia, and the main street Via Sacra.

According to Brissot, the bizarre judge was so driven in his hatred for the British, that he made a serious suggestion to give up the English language in the Northwest Territory and replace it with ancient Greek. It was at his suggestion that the name of the city was taken from the first and last syllables of the name of the French queen. In the beginning, they were satisfied to call the city Castripolis, a monument to an ancient camp fortified with uniquely shaped mounds found at the location of Marietta, which led to the conclusion that this land had once been occupied by a race more advanced than the Indians.

The immigrants now came in waves over the Alleghenies to the Ohio valley. Major Doughty, the commandant of Fort Harmar, reported that between February and June of 1788 alone, 4,500 persons had passed his post. They were all heading to the new Kentucky District, glorified by the land agents in the east, which was rapidly beginning to be populated. Already on August 18, 1787, the first newspaper, the "Kentucky Gazette", had appeared.

In January 1789, additional treaties were concluded at Fort Harmar with the Wyandots, Delawares, Ottawas, Chippewas, Pottowatomis and Sacs, which extended the provisions of the Treaty of Fort Stanwix. The United States and the named nations agreed therein, that members of both parties could hunt freely in those areas ceded by Great Britain to the United States. Trade with the nations was opened, but no white would be permitted to reside in the Indian villages or or as a trader in their hunting camps, without a signed and sealed permit from the Governor of the Northwest Territory or his representative. Should enemy tribes attempt to invade the Ohio Valley, then said nations were obligated to try and thwart this and report this intent to the Governor or to commander of the next military post.

The American Sovereignty

Chapter 18

John Cleves Symmes. - The Founding of Cincinnati. - The Pesthal Family. - Fort Washington. - The Wetzel Mob. - Karl Bilderbach.

John Cleves Symmes, already mentioned above as the original owner of the land between both Miamis, was born on Long Island and had already had a diverse career before he became the patriarch of the western wilderness. For example, he was at first a school teacher, then a surveyor, a soldier, one of the heroes of Saratoga, then lawyer and politician, a congressional representative, and Chief Justice of New Jersey. His two silent partners for the purchase of the Miami lands were General Dayton and Elias Boudinot.

On November 26, 1787, Symmes published a pamphlet which praised the advantages of the western lands and at the same time set out the contractual conditions and the price schedule. No one would be permitted to purchase less than one quarter section; the price was 62 cents per acre. The intrigues of the Kentucky land speculators, who had characterized the Miami lands as the "slaughter house" of the west, scared the peace-loving inhabitants of New Jersey from the wilderness and, in the summer of 1788 just a small group departed New York to settle the "new purchase" which was how Symmes' land was called. Among these was Mathias Denmann, who in addition to other sections, also acquired the county where Cincinnati now stands. Upon his arrival in Limestone (later called Maysville, founded by Ned Waller), he sold a third of this county to Colonel Robert Patterson and the rest to John Filson, a school teacher in the wilderness of Kentucky, who had become famous because of his book about the area. The three immediately decided that together they would establish a city across from the mouth of the Licking River, start a ferry, and clear a road through the forest to Lexington. At the time, the spot was a complete wilderness; however, there was a stockade constructed by Clark in 1782, for which Abraham Thomas in a story in the *Troy Times* took credit for cutting down the first tree. Directly opposite, at the mouth of the Licking stood a few dilapidated blockhouses. A narrow Indian trail to the British garrison in Detroit crossed the Ohio at this location, which so often had been the meeting point for the war parties of the Indians and for the Kentucky border settlers.

Filson, the school teacher, was given the task of naming the city. As with Barnum, Filson's head was swimming with thoughts of the ancient Greeks and Romans. He even sought to outdo the judge from Marietta and called the new community Losantiville, which means: ville-city; anti-across from; os-mouth; L of the Licking.

Near the end of September 1788, Losantiville's three owners, together with Symmes, the surveyor Isreal Ludlow and several settlers landed on the shore of the new city. Here they separated into two groups and, with rifles on their shoulders and supplies for several days, they scouted the neighboring areas. During this trip, the schoolteacher Filson became lost. In spite of all their efforts, they could not figure out what happened to him, and it was assumed that he had been attacked and killed by Indians.

Soon after, Denmann retured to Maysville with his companions. Ludlow, the surveyor, who had not paid one heller for his portion, took Filson's place. Denmann soon returned to New Jersey and left the job of settling the new city to Ludlow and Patterson.

The original price, which he had paid the judge for the land on which Cincinnati stands (between 700 and 800 acres), was the usual price for government land, namely five shillings per acre in continental certificates, which, at the time, were worth only five shillings per pound. According to the face value of the certificates, the land cost $500, but, in actual market value, it was only worth $125 cash.

It is remarkable, but the year and the day of the founding of Cincinnati are in doubt, since the founders themselves were of diverse opinions. Israel Ludlow and Colonel Patterson later swore in court that they had landed opposite the mouth of the Licking in the month of January 1789; whereas Denmann and William McMillian, the latter a member of the expedition and a very perceptive man, claimed in the same court hearing that they had founded the settlement on December 28, 1788. They all agreed that the company had departed Maysville on December 24. At the time the river was full of ice, and the journey of 65 miles could easily have taken 10 or 2 days. Thick forests of beech, sycamore, oak, and elm still covered the ground, and the settlers' first task was to clear the valley between Broadway and Walnut streets. The streets were then laid out through the forest, and the intersections were marked by three notches on the trees. The first blockhouses lay for the most part at the current landing, and their inhabitants consisted of 11 families and 24 unmarried men.

Since their scanty supplies soon gave out, the settlers ate fish and game; however there would soon be difficulties with the Indians, who watched the movements on their territories with hostile eyes.

Mrs. Rebecca Reeder, the last one remaining from the time of the first settlement, shared with the historical and pioneer society her memories of those weeks in a report, from which we have taken the following interesting details.

"On February 8, 1789, my father landed with my mother and seven children in Cincinnati, at that time still called Losantiville. Mr. Israel Ludlow, one of the owners of the area, and Mr. McMillan came down to the river to greet us. Both of these gentlemen were the surveyors of the Miami purchase. Just three small blockhouses, occupied by the surveyors and their assistants, were standing at the time. Their floor was the naked earth. In addition to my mother, three other women were already here, Miss De Mint, Mrs. Conney Zenes (later married to Mr. McMillan), Mrs. Pesthal, a German, and my mother, Mrs. Rebecca Kennedy. Only two families had small children, the German family and ours."

"Mr. Ludlow invited my father to move into one of the blockhouses until we could build our own house; but my mother thought that, because of the small children, it would be more comfortable in the boat. We stayed there until the river became full of ice and we were forced to move elsewhere. The few men who were here at the time, hacked our boats into pieces and from that built a small hut where we lived for six weeks. Then my father built us a large blockhouse, the first one in the area large enough to house a family. The siding from our huts were used for the floor. My father had wanted to build our house on the corner of Walnut and Water streets, but since he did not exactly know where the street was, he built it right in the middle of Water

Street. The streets were laid out but not opened, and the forest was so thick, it was impossible to say just where the street was.

"When we landed here, the army was stationed in North Bend. They suffered severely from a lack of bread. When the soldiers heard that we had landed with a sizeable quantity of flour and cornmeal, they came to my father and asked him for several barrels of flour for the army. My father told them that he had not brought flour to sell, but to protect his children from hunger here in the forest. They had their muskets with them and finally threatened to take the flour by force. At that point my father grabbed his rifle from the wall and said that he would defend his flour. They then returned to North Bend, and Judge Symmes sent my father a letter, in which he asked him to give the soldiers as much flour as they demanded, and he would replace it. This came to pass, and the judge kept his word."

In spite of his extensive land possessions, whose size overshadowed many a kingdom, Symmes was a most troubled person. It demanded a tough American nature in order for him to face up to all the obstructions and dangers. He had barely started his new settlement at the mouth of the Big Miami, when Blackbird, the chief of the Shawnees, appeared and asked by which right he was felling trees for a settlement. In the meantime, the judge had been named one of the judges of the Northwest territory to replace Armstrong, and he showed the chief his seal of office with its American seal. The chief examined it for a long time and, through a translator, finally said that that seal meant evil for his people. The eagle was extending its wings as if in flight, and that meant war; were they to be brought to rest, then that could mean peace. Furthermore, it was carrying a whip of branches in one claw and a bundle of arrows in the other claw, which left no doubt as to the warlike nature of the bird.

It cost the judge no little effort to calm the chief's concerns. But the hostility of the Indians was the least of his worries. The ice on the river had crushed the settlers' boats, drowned their animals, and inundated their provisions, so that they had to flee back to Kentucky merely to save their lives. The small garrison used up its supplies, which had finally been authorized by General Harmar in Marietta. Their Captain Kearsey had been ordered to construct a fort there to protect the settlers; but instead he fell in love with the pretty wife of a settler, which led to the ruin of the new city of North Bend and the beginning of Cincinnati's expansion. In his notes, Judge Burnett writes of the following important event:

"At Symmes' urging, the contingent of troops, which General Harmar had sent from Marietta, had landed at North Bend to construct a fort between the two Miamis. This fact attracted several settlers to the area, since the garrison provided valued security to the newcomers. While on patrol in the area around North Bend, the officer commanding this detachment fell in love with a delightful beauty with fiery eyes, unfortunately a married woman. Her alert husband recognized his danger and, in order to wisely avoid any disruption to his domestic harmony, he forthwith moved to Cincinnati. Immediately upon learning about the departure of his flame, the seductive warrior became of the opinion that the "Bend" was totally unsuitable for the erection of a military post. The pleas of the unhappy judge were in vain. A flood at the "Bend" reinforced the determination of the infatuated officer. The troops moved to Cincinnati and the establishment of Fort Washington began. The inhabitants of the thriving "Miami", who were more numerous than those in Cincinnati, could no longer remain. In two to three years, the "Bend" was totally deserted, the settlers had followed the troops, and the idea of establishing a city here had been given up completely.

"From this we realize," explains Judge Burnett, "what great results very often follow small events. The beauty of one female settler shifted Ohio's center of trade from its original cradle to the place where it is now. Had the beauty with her fiery eyes remained in North Bend, then the barracks and fort would have arisen there, North Bend would have become the center of the population, capital and business, and Cincinnati would have been an area of relatively little significance." As the abduction of Helen by Paris caused the destruction of the Greek metropolis, so here too the abduction of a Helen from Paris by her husband Maneläus caused the founding of the western capital.

The construction of Fort Washington under the direction of Major Doughty was completed towards the end of November 1779. It was a four-sided, two-story fortified building, constructed of hewn trunks; each side was approximately 180 feet long and connected at each corner with palisades made of bastions of hewn trunks, which extended out about 10 feet on each side of the fort, so that the cannon could sweep all its walls. The exterior of the fort was painted white and from afar, with the dark background of the forest, and with its esplanade surrounded with the palisades, comfortable officers' quarters and gardens, presented a picturesque view. The last remains of the fort can be seen today on Arch Street, between Broadway and Ludlow.

On December 29, General Harmar arrived from Marietta with 300 men and took possession of the fort.

The first official act of the general was the issuance of a proclamation on wanted posters, which promised a substantial reward for the arrest and deliverance of the famous Indian-hunter Ludwig Wetzel to the garrison at Losantiville. Ludwig, hated and feared by the Indians as an evil sorcerer, was honored and admired by the whites who saw in him the vehicle of their revenge against the redskins who had subjected the farms some distance away from the fort with murder and plunder. Several months earlier, Wetzel had escaped from Fort Harmar, where he had been held in chains, awaiting death on the gallows, because he not only had refused to recognize the peace treaty which Harmar had concluded with the tribes, but rather bumped off one Indian after the other. The news had soon reached the ears of the general, who issued the order for Wetzel's capture dead or alive. Unworried, Wetzel stayed with his friend Carr, whose farm lay on an island near the fort. However, the general's scouts found out about that and, one night, floated to the island, fell upon Wetzel while he slept, bound him hand and foot, dragged him to the boat, and brought him to Fort Harmar, where he was locked in chains and thrown into a dark hole. The shame of being chained hand and foot and bound to the wall was more painful than death to the free-spirited son of the forest. Soon after his capture, he demanded to see the general. Harmar came. Wetzel admitted that he had killed a sachem. But since he did not want to be hanged like a dog, he begged the general to hand him over to the Indians, a large number of whom had assembled at the fort. "Let them form a circle," he said, "with their scalping knives and tomahawks, give me a tomahawk, put me in the middle, and me and the Indians will fight it out as good as we can." Since the general could not grant this naive demand, Wetzel then asked for room to walk. He had never been imprisoned, he said, and if he could not see the sky and woods, he could not breathe and would die.

The general smiled and gave the officer of the watch the order to free him of the leg chains, but to retain the hand chains. He was then to be permitted to exercise at the mouth of the Muskingum, but to be carefully observed and not to be let out of sight. With a military guard,

Wetzel was barely outside of the fort, when he began to jump around like a wild foal that had broken out of its stall.

First he ran a few steps, as if attempting to impetuously escape, then he turned abruptly and returned to his guard. The next time he went a little further before turning around. In this manner he entertained and deluded the soldiers for quite a while, in which he went a little further each time. Finally he gathered all his strength and determined to gain his freedom or an early death. With mighty strides he jumped forward as before, but rather than turn around, he dashed into the protective underbrush of his beloved woods. All of this occurred so lighting fast and unexpectedly, that Wetzel was already 300 paces away, before the guards could recover from their surprise. The soldiers fired and missed. They quickly followed him, but he was soon gone from their sight. His friend Weismann, with whom he hid, freed him from the heavy chains and took him to Maysville, where he was safe from Harmar and the search of his Myrmidons. Here he hung around with hunters or went on raids against the Indians. He spent his free time in shooting matches, running races, wrestling, or boxing with other woodsmen.

While thus enjoying himself at Maysville, where he had become the toast of the town, a Lieutenant Lawler, enroute towards Fort Washington with a group of soldiers, landed before the city and encountered Wetzel in an inn. He quickly returned to the boat, selected several soldiers, and had Wetzel seized and carried off. In order to lose no time, he got underway, and that same night delivered his prisoner to General Harmar in Cincinnati. Again Ludwig was cast into chains for the murder in Marietta, while sentenced to being strung up. But the news of his capture and danger of death spread like lightning through the settlements. When their written requests to General Harmar for his release did not bear fruit, pioneers from both sides of the Ohio assembled to free Wetzel by force. The news of the storming of the Bastille by the revolutionaries in Paris had just arrived in Cincinnati and inspired the mob to storm Fort Washington, where Wetzel was imprisoned. A clash with the military seemed unavoidable. But, in order to avoid bloodshed, Judge Symmes issued a writ of habeus corpus. John Clayton and other hunters from Columbia vouched for Wetzel, who, as a result, was freed and brought by the people in triumph to Columbia, where a feast and ball were given in his honor.

At that time, Wetzel was 26 years old. The size of his chest and shoulders along with his muscular arms testified as to a Herculean strength. His long hair, always carefully combed, fell to his knees, his eyes were black as coal, and their sight left no doubt that one could not awaken his fury without revenge.

In his *History of the Germans in America*, Franz Löher attributes the final end of our forest hero to a secret avenger, who continually plagued him with an unknown tragedy. "We have never found out," he writes, "where his restless life ended and on which forest lake his bones lay bleached." The course of our chronicle indicates that Wetzel's eventual fate is well-known and interwoven with a tragedy, which is almost more romantic and notable than the adventures of his youth.

In contrast, during the summer of this year (1789), the wrath of the Indians met one of his wild friends and companions in several campaigns against the redskins, Karl Bilderbach, who had settled at the mouth of Short Creek, on the east bank of the Ohio, several miles above Wheeling. One day, believing that the enemy had deserted the west bank of the river, Bilderbach went across the Ohio with his wife Ruhama and his brother Jakob, to look after some of his cattle grazing there. After the trio had disembarked and walked several hundred steps into the forest, a group of Delawares fired at them from ambush and wounded Jakob in the shoulder. Thinking about their escape, the family split up. Karl was captured while trying to escape. Jakob had reached the canoe and fled back across the river, while, in the meantime, his sister-in-law hid herself under a pile of driftwood on the bank. Upon seizing Bilderbach, the Indians forced him, under threat of death, to call his wife from her hiding place. He complied in hopes of soothing their anger. Ruhama was a brave woman. She heard her husband, but did not answer, for a conflict arose within her breast. Should she come out of her hiding place to share the fate of her husband, or remain to return to her blockhouse and care for her two children, a son of three and a small daughter of two. With desperate words, Karl called for her a second time: "Ruhama, hurry, you can save me from death!" She then hesitated no longer, left her hiding place and surrendered to the savages. All of this occurred within sight of their blockhouse on the opposing shore, on whose threshhold the two children were playing. The savages, knowing that they would be followed as soon as news of the attack reached the stockade at Wheeling, immediately began their return trip with the captives. All that day and the following night they walked without giving any rest to the pair. The next day, the group split into two groups; one group leading Bilderbach in one direction, and the other group taking his wife in another direction. Certainly the revenge for the gruesome murder of the young Schebosh had arrived. After some hesitation he answered the group's questions with his name: "Karl Bilderbach!" Ecstatic the savages repeated the name and a devilish happiness streamed from their faces. They had their dangerous enemy in their hands. "You have killed many Indians," they said, "you are a great chief! You killed Schebosh and burned our people!" From this moment his death was decided[1].

After a few days, the band leading Bilderbach's wife reached the Tuscararas River and encamped on the bank. Soon after, the other band which had taken her husband arrived. In order to prove to the woman that he was dead, they carried his scalp on a rod and threw it into her lap. Immediately she recognized it by its red hair, but no word of lament came from her lips. That evening, her ears still smarting as a result of the terribly shrill cries of the savages, and overcome with weariness, she fell asleep until morning leaning against a tree. When she awoke, her husband's scalp had disappeared.

Shortly after Bilderbach's capture became known in Wheeling, scouts left to search for his trail; they found signs of the one party and followed it until they came upon Bilderbach's body. He had been killed with tomahawks and had apparently suffered a slow and painful death.

---

[1] Sketches of John McDonald of Ross County, in Howe's Hist. Coll., pag. 160.

Chapter 19

The First Popular Assembly in Cincinnati. - The First Court Session. - Conflict Between the Civil and Military Authorities. - The Change of the Name of the City. - The Cincinnati. - Stations Around the City. - Indian Attacks. - Jakob Wetzel and his Dog. - Harmar's Campaign.

In 1790, the Northwest Territory had no fixed government site. Laws were issued whenever necessary and announced from whatever place the territorial assembly happened to be in session. Naturally, the settlements in and around Cincinnati sprang up even prior to the establishment of the courts, even before the basic steps for the administration of justice in the territory were taken. To protect against the "actions and wantonness of evil persons and to promote the common good," all of the settlers on the Miami lands were called for this purpose to Cincinnati. The people met for the first time out in the open, under a majestic Elm on today's Broadway, under the direction of William McMillan. It produced a civil code for certain crimes, established a court with McMillan as judge and John Ludlow as Sheriff, and instituted a system of juries.

Prior to the convening of the court, everyone was obligated with a solemn oath to give full support to the application of the law. Shortly thereafter, a certain Patrick Grimes was observed stealing cucumbers from his neighbor's vegetable garden. The sheriff immediately issued an arrest warrant and convened a jury to hear his case. The accused was found guilty and publicly received 25 lashes on the back. Upon a second accusation, the accused fled to Fort Washington and the protection of the commandant. The latter sent McMillan a harsh note ordering him to cease the future operation of his court under threat of punishment. In a solid, honorable reply, McMillan responded that this massive intrusion by the commandant as unjustified. The tone of the note angered the commandant. Thereupon he sent a sergeant and three soldiers to immediately arrest the judge and bring him to the fortress. But McMillan was as strong as he was energetic; he barricaded his blockhouse against the soldiers, and when they finally forced their way in after much effort, they fought for 20 minutes. He knocked one soldier unconscious and the other two, battered and exhausted, had to give up and return to the fort. In the fierce fight, McMillan received a severe blow in the chest, from which he never fully recovered. He had a severe cough until dying in the prime of his life.

On January 2, 1790, Governor Arthur St. Clair arrived in Losantiville in an elegantly equipped keelboat, in order to organize the county, which, upon the suggestion of Judge Symmes, was so named to honor the current Secretary of the Treasury, Hamilton, and included the entire area west of the Muskingum. In order to honor the Order of the Cincinnati, of which St. Clair was a member, the city received its present name. The Order of the Cincinnati was organized by army officers under the following conditions.

On May 10, 1783, while the United States army was assembled on the banks of the Hudson, suggestions were made to the various line regiments for the establishment of a society whose members would consist of the officers of the army. As a result, each regiment named one officer, who, along with the generals, was to consider those suggestions agreed upon at a meeting held the very same day, at which Major General Baron von Steuben was the chairman. At this meeting, it was decided to form a standing committee, including Major-General Knox, Brigadier-General Hand and Captain Shaw, whose unanimous report of the meeting of May 13, 1783, was accepted at General Steuben's headquarters and begins as follows:

"In regards to the order of human affairs, the highest god of the universe has seen fit to cause the separation of the colonies of North American from the sovereignty of Great Britain, and, after a bloody war of eight years, to establish them as free, independent and sovereign states, who through advantageous alliances are allied with one of the mightiest princes and powers on earth.

In order to eternally promote the memory of this occasion as well as the current treaty of mutual friendship, made under the pressure of common danger, and in some cases made even closer by the blood of comrades, the officers of the United States Army unite, constitute and join together in festive manner into a society of friends, which should last as long as there are male heirs or, in case of the lack thereof, of relatives, who are found worthy of being the bearers and members of that society.

The officers of the United States Army, most of whom are American citizens, greatly honor the character of the famous Roman, Lucius Quintus Cincinnatus, and whereas they have determined to continue this honored example into civilian life, therefore consider it their right to call themselves the "Order of the Cincinnati."

The following constitution remains unalterable and forms the basis for the Society of the Cincinnati: a constant effort to maintain inviolable those noble human rights and freedoms, for which they have fought and spilled their blood, and, without which, the honored position of an intelligent being remains a curse rather than a blessing.

An inalterable agreement between the various states, which demands and encourage the unity and national character so necessary for the welfare and future honor of the American nation.

In the sincere desire of the officers to ensure eternal respect, the spirit of brotherly love will guide all of its relationships, and in regards to the treasury of the society, extends particularly to the welfare of those officers and their families, who unfortunately fall into adversity."

Thereupon there was given a series of rules for the direction of the Society, whose leadership would consist of a President, Vice-President, Secretary, Treasurer, and Vice Treasurer, each of which would be elected at a meeting held every three years. The Society is divided into various state organizations, organized in a similar manner, who possess the authority to direct themselves. The meeting to be held every three years will consist of officials and a delegation of not more than five persons from each state.

"All officers of the United States Army, those honorably discharged after three years of commissioned service, or those who are discharged as a result of congressional orders to reorganize the army, as well as those who served to the end of the war, have the right to become members of this society," assuming that, within six months, they sign the statutes, and make a monthly payment designed for the establishment of a fund, the interest from which shall be dedicated to support the families of those who fall.

As an indication of the respect for the memory of those officers who remain in the service, a similar privilege will be granted to their oldest male descendent, as well as to those French officers, who served in the revolutionary war with the rank of Colonel and above. Honorary members, but only for their lifetime, are eligible in the ratio of one to four.

"A decoration has been authorized, consisting of a gold bald eagle, to be suspended on a dark-blue ribbon with white stripes, the latter to commemorate the alliance between France and America. In its claws, the eagle grasps golden olive branches, whose enameled leaves extend completely around the figure, forming a wreath above its head, to which the clip will be attached. On the breast of the eagle is the figure of Cincinnatus receiving a sword from three Roman senators, as well as other fitting figures in the background. Around the entire device runs the inscription: "Omnia reliquit servare republicam. (Give up everything to serve the republic). On the reverse side one sees the honor, which crowned Cincinnatus with a wreath, as well as the motto: "Esto perpetua! (Let it be forever!")

Thus was founded the Order of the Cincinnati, with General Washington as President, General Knox as Secretary and General McDougal as Treasurer.

Unjustified derision and hostility of their contemporaries, who saw therein the establishment of a military nobility and a patrician class, hindered the thriving expansion of the Order. But such was not the case with the city that bore its name. From the few blockhouses of Losantiville, she rose up, not just as the Queen of the Ohio Valley, but also to be a capital of scientific culture, trade and commerce in the far west.

At the beginning of Spring, John Dunlap and several companions, laid out the fortified Colerain Station on the Big Miami, 17 miles northwest of the city. Similar stations were established in the neighborhood, such as Ludlow's, Garrard's, Corvette's, White's on the third ford of Mill Creek and the station in Round Bottom. Harmar stationed several soldiers in each of these locations. The Indians laid siege to several of them. At the head of a Shawnee war party, Girty himself attacked Colerain Station, but was driven off by Colonel Kingsbury's cannon. The only safety for the settlers was in these stockades. Whoever dared to go to work in his fields, did so at the risk of his life. Among the numerous adventures of that year is the saga of Jakob Wetzel, the brother of the famous Ludwig, which demonstrates just how dangerous it was at the time to hunt in the area around the city.

The path along the Ohio leading to Storrs and Delhi was broken by an arm of Mill Creek just below the junction of Front and 5th Street. On October 7, 1790, the lowland was covered with a thick forest of birch and maple; the underbrush of roots and wild vines made the area a safe hideout for wild animals and Indians. On that evening, while laden with a rich catch from hunting, Jakob was returning to the city along that path, when he threw himself down next to a rotting tree stump to rest and find a horse to finish the trip back into the city, since the burden of the slain animal was beginning to hurt his shoulders. As he was drying the perspiration from his brow, his dog suddenly began to growl at his feet. Realizing the danger, Jakob sprang quick as lightning behind a tree stump. Looking around he suddenly saw the dark figure of an Indian, halfway hidden behind an oak trunk, standing with a raised musket ready to fire. The Indian had heard the dog's growl, which suddenly began to bark loudly. At the same instant both opponents raised their muskets and fired. The Indian dropped his rifle, for the hunter's ball had shattered his left elbow, while Jakob remained unscathed. Before the copper-skinned, wounded warrior could reload his musket, Wetzel pulled his hunting knife and jumped him; but the latter had already pulled his own and parried the strike with such skill and force that the hunter's knife flew thirty feet away from him clattering into the bush. Undeterred, Wetzel grabbed the Indian around the body and right arm which held the knife. But his gigantic opponent was every bit his equal in wrestling and the battle's outcome was completely in doubt. With all his strength, the savage attempted to free his arm; while Wetzel continued to hang on; the legs of the two fighters became entangled and they fell to the ground, the Indian on top, which freed his arm from the hunter's grip. With almost supernatural strength, he tried to turn the tip of his steel against the deadly enemy, but he could not do it since Wetzel forced him onto his right side where he could not use his arm. Finally he was able to make the fatal turn; with a loud victory yell he forced Wetzel down with renewed energy, sprang over his body, and raised the knife for a fatal thrust. Wetzel saw death before his eyes. At this critical moment, his faithful dog, who during the battle had kept his eyes on his master, sprang at the Indian's throat with such force, that his weapon fell and Wetzel swiftly grabbed it. Then Wetzel shook off his enemy with the last of his strength, and before the other could even rise up, the knife was half way into his heart. After a few convulsions the savage was no more. Wetzel quickly grabbed both muskets and fled homewards. He had barely put a short stretch behind him when his ears heard the war cry of a group of Indians. Like the wind, Wetzel ran to the river where his luck continued. At the mouth of the creek he found a canoe and, without any additional danger, made it to the foot of Sycamore Street. The Indians recognized the dead one as one of their bravest chiefs and their horrible yells followed the brave victor.

In 1790 the population of Cincinnati increased by about 40 families. Six craftsmen established themselves in the area: a blacksmith, a shoemaker, a tailor, a stonemason, and two carpenters. During the year, 15 to 20 settlers were killed by Indians; almost as many casualties were suffered in the newly established Columbia (established by Benjamin Stites near the mouth of the Little Miami). These continuous hostile attacks, and particularly the news of the establishment of a new wartime alliance against the white intruders among the Miamis, Shawnees and Delawares, whom traders had led into the Wabash area without St. Clair's knowledge, forced the government to take energetic measures to protect the settlements. Only with great reluctance did Washington give in to the pressure of events; he was aware that, based on all previous treaties, the Indians had never conceded to the Americans the rights to any segment of the Northwest Territory. France and Great Britain had always guaranteed them. At the conclusion of peace, Great Britain had transferred to the Union the former disputed claims to the Ohio Valley by the Six Nations, as well as the claims against the Union by southern tribes on segments south of the Ohio. It had never conceded one acre of the lands of the Miamis, Shawnees, the western Delawares, the Wyandots, and the tribes residing further north. Congress assumed the position, that the peace treaty had included the entire Northwest Territory and that, as a result of their hostilities during the Revolutionary War, the Indians had lost all title to the land. It was not necessary for the Union to buy land from the former owners, but rather only to dictate the peace and determine the boundaries of its counties.

Heckewelder, on the other hand, gives the Indian side in his *Narrative*: "We are addressed as if we are slaves, who must submit to the dictates of a proud conqueror. It is said that, since we supported our father, the British, that we have lost territory and homeland. Our entire country belongs to them, and it is only at their mercy that we are permitted to live and hunt here. Could we have acted differently without exposing ourselves to the wrath of the British. And what do the Americans have in mind for us? In Pittsburg, our representatives were told: 'All of those who stayed at home and did not participate in the war, would become a great and happy people.' Did they not deceive us? Did they not kill the Christian Muskingum Indians, who never raised weapons against the colonists, but were dedicated to farming and serving God and showed them only goodness? Did they not seek to slay those remaining in Sandusky, who, according to their own demands, remained peacefully at home? Did they not promise us trade and friendly interaction, and that depots for our supplies were to be opened in Pittsburg and Fort McIntosh? And did they not simply murder our people, who had traveled there with skins and pelts, many of whom were in the process of trading with them? And are they not presently spreading over our land in order to steal our horses and, during our absence, even the pelts from the drying racks? And are we supposed to tolerate such thieves and murderers as neighbors? If we simply ignore this, then our race will be destroyed, and our entire land will fall into their hands. Did not God put us into these forests and give us the strength and ability to resist such murderous intruders? Does He not expect us to pass on the land of our forefathers to our descendants? Which Indian nation would permit itself to be driven off its land by another nation? Is it not the law among us, that, should members of another tribe be encountered while hunting on our land, to take them prisoner, seize their horses, flints, pelts, even the clothes from their bodies, and send them home naked, under threat of death should they reappear? And should we accept from white intruders, that which we avenge in such a manner with our red brothers? There can be no peace with them. If we desire to make a treaty with them, then we constantly hear complaints about our acts of violence, but from their own misdeeds they wish to know nothing. They justify robbing us of our land, on account of bloody deeds, which they caused or carried out themselves."

In this manner the Indians testified as to the taking away of their lands in the northwest. As the Ohio now became a chain of forts, with the settlements constantly advancing, and, now cut off from their rich hunting grounds south of the river, there grew in the minds of the Indians the determination for a new, united resistance, which no treaty of the American government could appease, and it soon became clear to both sides that these two races could not live side by side, where the one, with an inbred hatred for the other, desired to open the land to culture, and the other, with similar hostile feelings, wanted to maintain the wilderness for the sole purpose of hunting. The hostility of the savages was encouraged by Great Britain, which felt that it might some day be able to reclaim the land. From the western posts, which it refused to give up to the Union in spite of the peace treaty of 1783, Great Britain provided the natives with all the necessities for carrying on the war.

In light of the threatening danger, Governor St. Clair, in accordance with on an act of Congress passed the previous year, sent a request to Virginia to provide 1,000 militia for an impending campaign, and to Pennsylvania to provide an additional 500 men. Of these, 300 men were to assemble in Fort Steuben (today's Jeffersonville, across from Louisville), in order to support the garrison at Vincennes against the Weas and Kickapoos of the Wabash; 700 were to be sent to Cincinnati and 500 intended for Wheeling in order to march with the federal troops at Fort Washington against the seven villages of the Miamis and Shawnees at the junction of the St. Mary and St. Joseph rivers, where the savages had assembled their army under the leadership of Little Turtle.

This chief and first counsel of the Miamis, already known to the reader for his clever response to one of Bolney's ideas, had, to his own disadvantage, been exposed to culture. His kitchen and cellar were arranged in the European manner, his preference for alcoholic drinks had brought the gout to this gastronome.

He was acquainted with the leading men of the nation. While visiting Washington in Philadelphia, he found out that Kosziusko was also currently in the city. He immediately went to visit Poland's hero. Even though ill and confined to bed, Kosziusko called the son of the wilderness to his bedside and conversed with him for a long time. The proud, unbounded self-confidence, which, like the fresh forest air, uplifted the chief's words, pleased Kosziusko tremendously. Upon departure, he presented to his visitor two splendid pistols inlaid with gold and silver, with the words: "I have carried these weapons in numerous battles in the defense of the oppressed members of my race, and I give them to you with the wish that their first shot hits the man who attempts to rob or subjugate you, the free men of the wilderness."

In three decisive battles, the hero of the Miamis had proven that Kosziusko's pistols were in good hands and used according to the Polish hero's wish.

Before the end of September the militias from Kentucky and Pennsylvania had arrived in Cincinnati rather poorly equipped for military operations. The mustering officer, Major Ferguson, reports: "The Kentuckians had brought neither camp pots nor axes. Their weapons were unserviceable. One had a musket without a firelock, another one without a stock. Many of their officers expressed to me their surprise that about half of all the weapons to be found in the entire district of Kentucky were such as were to be found in the hands of these people[1]. The Pennsylvania militia was even more poorly armed; many had no rifles; many were cripples, old men, or boys wet behind the ears. Their Major Paul explained to me that many of his men were so inept and untrained that they could not even unscrew the firelock from the barrel to oil it, and they could not properly set the flintstones in order to be dependable while firing."

Out of a deep-seated reluctance to serve next to the regular military, which they despised, the best soldiers of the wilderness, the veteran Indian hunters, had not joined the militia. Adding to this confusion which these unserviceable elements brought to General Harmar, who had assumed the command of this expeditionary corps, was the jealousy and difference of opinion of the militia officers and their followers concerning the various commands. The situation was finally cleared up when Colonel Trotter was given the command of the Kentuckians while Colonel Hardin was given the command over the Pennsylvanians and Virginians, who constituted a battalion under Lt. Colonel Troply and Major Paul. Including the federal troops under Majors Doughty and Wyllis, who amounted to 320 men, Harmar's army counted 1453 men.

On September 30, Harmar departed Fort Washington at the head of the federal troops; the militia had already left. On October 13, the army arrived in the area of the Indian villages, and Harmar sent out Colonel Hardin with a detachment of 600 militia and a company of federal troops, to surprise the enemy and keep him in his forts until the main body with the artillery could arrive.

However, when Hardin reached the enemy villages he found them deserted. Along with the articles of the French traders, he burned the villages with their abundant supplies of corn and then returned to the main army, which, in the meantime, had arrived at Chillicothe, the capital of the Shawnees. At this point Harmar started acting like an idiot. The Indians appeared to have retreated across the St. Joseph

---

[1] These Kentuckians possessed a genuine Yankee spirit. They had heard that their weapons would be repaired in Fort Washington and that the unserviceable ones would be replaced, and thus thought that this presented a fitting opportunity for a good trade.

and so the general dispatched independent detachments in several directions against the allegedly fleeing enemy, all of which eventually returned half wiped out.

At the initial enemy fire, a terrible panic gripped the Pennsylvania militia. They had thrown away their rifles without firing a shot and, disregarding the orders of their officers, like a mob threw themselves back upon the federal soldiers, thus bringing disruption into their lines. In an order of the day written on October 20 in a camp near one of the Shawnee villages, Harmar thus expressed his disgust:

"The reason for yesterday's defeat of this detachment is due totally to the weak, cowardly action of the militia, who ran and threw away their rifles without firing a single shot. During the return to Fort Washington, should officers or troops leave the ranks, or not march in the manner as ordered, the General herewith makes it clear, that he will fire the cannon at them without mercy. He hopes, however, that the defeat suffered yesterday will result in his orders being followed in the future.

Josiah Harmar"

On the 21st, when the defeated army was returning to Fort Washington, a scout brought the news that the victorious Indians had reoccupied one of their villages. In order to soften the bitterness of this defeat of American arms, Harmar again sent Colonel Hardin with 300 militia and 60 federal soldiers under the command of Major Wyllys to the attack. Treacherous scouts led one segment into an ambush while Little Turtle threw his entire force of warriors against the main body, casting destruction in its ranks with muskets and tomahawks. Majors Wyllys and Fountain fell, struck by numerous bullets; 51 federal soldiers remained on the field; the total of dead and wounded amounted to 180.

Harmar now had to begin a retreat head over heels, leaving the wounded behind to the scalping knives of the savages. Only four years later, during Wayne's victorious campaign, could their bones find a proper burial.

Harmar's threat to fire cannon against the militia should there be a repetition of the disobedience during the march appears to have made little impression, because even before the army reached Fort Washington there were new difficulties. While at the former Indian village of Old Chillicothe, on the Little Miami, one segment of the militia, to show their disregard for the published order, fired their muskets. In order to make an example, Colonel Hardin ordered one of them to be bound to a six pounder and given six lashes by the drum major. His comrades became angry, and led by their officers, they attempted to free the prisoner by force. Cursing, Harmar ordered the federal troops to advance to the site to disperse the mutineers with the bayonet, and carry out the punishment. This action thoroughly embittered the frontiersmen against the army and was the reason why, during later campaigns to protect the settlements, they greatly resisted being placed under the orders of the federal officers.

Harmar returned to Cincinnati on November 3 and soon thereafter placed the command of Fort Washington into St. Clair's hands. Several years later he died in seclusion on the banks of the Schuylkill.

Chapter 20

Major David Ziegler defends Marietta. - St. Clair's Defeat. - Ziegler Commandant of Fort Washington. - Colonel Schaumburg. - Gen. Wayne's Campaign. - Major Rudolph.

The war parties of Chief Turtle followed Harmar's army to the hills which surrounded Cincinnati; from that point they combed the area for all the stragglers they could find and either killed them or chased them back into the stations. Many of these fortified sites were subjected to such a determined siege that a shortage of ammunition arose, and the women were forced to donate their tin spoons and plates to be melted into bullets for the common defense.

Not only the area around the young city, but also all of the settlements north of the river suffered under the wild attacks of the victorious savages. On the evening of January 2, the red bands forced their way into a new settlement in Big Bottom on the Muskingum, 40 miles above Marietta, and slaughtered the entire population, men, women and children. Marietta saw itself doomed to destruction. At the time, the garrison at Fort Harmar counted only 20 men while the entire male population in the Muskingum Valley counted barely 280 able to fight, the majority of whom were only poorly armed. In this emergency, Governor St. Clair sent his most capable officer, David Ziegler of the 1st US Infantry, who had recently been promoted to Major by Washington for bravery in Harmar's campaign, along with two companies to aid those in distress. Ziegler's fitting and energetic measures as commandant of Fort Harmar soon saved the Muskingum area from the threatened devastation and earned him the gratitude of the population and the love of a charming young settler from one of New England's most educated families. The young lady was Miss Lucy Anna Sheffield, sister-in-law of Mr. Charles Green, one of the founders of Marietta. A few months later, the happy warrior led his beauty to the altar.

From that point on, various and diverse attempts were made by the Federal Government to secure a peaceful transfer of the contested area from the Indians. However, since they were all unsuccessful, a new army corps was formed under Governor St. Clair to subdue those resisting and bring the desired peace to the settlements. The plan for the campaign was devised by Washington himself. As a veteran of the Indian wars, he did not fail to notice that the location of the Miami villages at the confluence of the St. Joseph and St. Mary rivers was a suitable site for the construction of a fortress. St. Clair's campaign was to connect Fort Washington, via a chain of military posts, with that site to be conquered from the Indians and upon which a great fortress would be constructed for the purpose of containing the hostile attacks of the natives.

In order to subdue the Wabash Indians, a squadron of mounted riflemen from Kentucky under Brigadier General Scott, as well as a small corps under General Wilkinson, departed Fort Washington. However, this expedition did not complete its mission; both wings became bogged down in the swamps of the Wabash and Eel rivers and returned after destroying several Kickapoo villages and cornfields.

In the meantime, the recruits for the new campaign gathered at Fort Washington under similarly miserable conditions, which would serve to eventually hasten Harmar's defeat. Again the Quartermaster Department was a shambles: the tents, packsaddles, tornisters and powder bags were for the most part unusable, even the powder was defective, the rifles unserviceable, and there were no tools on hand for repair. The troops who had been recruited from all parts of the upper Ohio valley were undisciplined and everyday caroused drunk through the streets on the arms of the Kentucky militia. In order to assist the defenders of the fatherland to avoid further temptation, St. Clair moved the army to Ludlow's Station; even though he reduced the problem, he more than doubled the costs of provisions. On September 17, 1791, the colorful army, which numbered two thousand three hundred men, finally began its advance towards the Miami valley and, after arriving there, erected Fort Hamilton as the first link in the chain of planned posts. After installing a small garrison, the march was continued; approximately 40 miles north of Fort Hamilton, a halt was made, and a new military post was constructed six miles south of today's Greenville, in Darke County, which received the name of Fort Jefferson. On October 24, the exhausting march through the wilderness was renewed, unfortunately with provisions of flour and forage for only three days. Many horses soon perished due to a lack of grain; on the 31st, groups of Kentucky militia openly deserted, and a group of Pennsylvania militia followed them. St. Clair had to send Major Ziegler with the 1st Infantry regiment after them, since it was feared that they might grab the supply wagons along the way and use them to continue their flight back to the Ohio.

On November 3rd, the army reached a forest brook, fifty miles from the Miami villages, and established a camp with two lines on a rise with a brook in front. The right wing, consisting of the battalions of Butler, Clark, and Patterson, commanded by General Richard Butler, the second in command after St. Clair, constituted the first line; the left, made up of Major George M. Bedinger's and Guthrie's battalions and the 2nd Regiment of the US army under Colonel Darke, made up the second line. St. Clair held the right flank, covered by the steep bank of the stream where he had posted a troop of riflemen as a reserve. The cavalry and their pickets protected the left flank. Disregarding the bad experience his predecessor Harmar had experienced in regards to the unreliability of the militia, St. Clair had given them the most dangerous position, namely, that which was on the far side of the stream, a mile away from the main army, and arranged in the same manner as the main force. This shortsightedness could not even be excused by the reason that the general did not expect an attack at all, but rather merely dug a light entrenchment to protect the field packs while he intended to await Ziegler's return with the 1st Regiment of the Line, so that he could then advance to the Miami villages and offer battle on the enemy's own land and territory. But something else was to happen. Militia pickets reported the approach of the enemy to General Butler; however he was ill-disposed against the senior commander and neglected to forward that report. Shortly before sunrise the next morning, when an icy fog enshrouded both camps, the horrible war cry of the savages suddenly sounded and their musket fire immediately thundered into the camp of the unprepared militia. Totally surprised, ignoring the commands of their officers, and abandoning their weapons, they fled through Major Butler's camp, there spreading a similar panic and rout. Dashing wildly, the Indians chased those fleeing and threw themselves with all their force against the right wing. For a few minutes the fire of the first line stalled that raging storm, but the enemy threw themselves with renewed vigor against this and the center of the second line, where the artillery had been positioned. The artillerymen fell almost to the last man before the shots and tomahawk blows of the redskins; Lieutenant Schaumburg and Corporal Mott were the only ones who were barely able to save themselves. Then St. Clair, who had been confined to his tent with the gout and chest pains, sought to turn the day's fortune with a bayonet charge by the federal soldiers under Colonel Darke. Like battle-hardened veterans, the men rushed forward and drove the Indians back two to three hundred paces; but, in spite of their gallantry, they had to retreat, since they had no riflemen to support them[1]. At that same moment, the enemy forced their way through the left flank, driving back those soldiers who had been stationed there. At that point General Butler fell[2], supposedly by the hand of his own son, a Shawnee half-breed, along with every officer of the second regiment except three. Since the artillery had been lost and half of the army had fallen, everyone sought safety in a panic-stricken flight, leaving the camp and field devices to the enemy. The Indians chased the remains of the army for four miles and then, luckily for the latter, turned back to divide the fruits of victory and carry out a terrible revenge against those who had fallen into their hands. Those still living had their members torn individually from their bodies, the unfortunate women who had accompanied the army as cooks and launderers were raped with flaming torches.

St. Clair left the wounded who might hamper the retreat in Fort Jefferson and hurried with the remnants of the army behind the protective walls of Fort Washington. His defeat was as horrible as that of Braddock. Of the fourteen hundred enlisted men who had stood in the heat of battle, 894 had fallen, while sixty-one of eighty officers had fallen or had been wounded.

A young second lieutenant of artillery from Virginia, who arrived in Cincinnati on that very day, sadly, and with his arms crossed, watched the return of the pitiful remains of St. Clair's army. Inwardly he had pledged someday to dedicate his future to restoring the country's lost military honor. This young man, who, in keeping this pledge, made a name for himself as a general and statesman of the Northwest Territory, and whose fame would lead him in the election as President of the United States, was William Henry Harrison.

This second humiliation of American arms spread horror and fear throughout the Ohio valley. Even the inhabitants of Pittsburg imagined the barbaric enemy to be before the gates of their city and sent to Governor Miffen pleas for military assistance; the populations of Wheeling and Ohio county did the same thing with frantic pleas to the Governor of Virginia.

During the horror and confusion which the arrival of the nearly destroyed army aroused in Cincinnati, whose citizens expected an attack by the victors at any day, Governor St. Clair handed over the command of Fort Washington to Maj. Ziegler and hurried to Philadelphia, in order to explain to the government the reasons for his defeat. Evidently, the citizens of Cincinnati felt relieved that, in that dark period, the most competent commander was leading the troops protecting them, but the officers did not share that feeling. That xenophobic spirit, which had shown itself during the revolutionary war against General Steuben and all foreign officers, stirred itself in Ft. Washington against Ziegler. He was accused of insubordination against the Secretary of War and of drunkenness. The correspondence between General Wilkinson, who followed Ziegler in command, and Captain John Armstrong[3] leaves no doubt as to these secret activities. Disgusted by this shortsighted, maliciously envious persecution, Ziegler not only voluntarily gave up the command of Fort Washington, but he also resigned from the army.

---

[1] Major Jakob Fowler of Covington, who participated in the battle, described the tragic results of this attack in a most vivid pioneer manner: "During Colonel Darke's last bayonet charge, the dead and dying lay thickly around us and the freshly-scalped skulls steamed in the heavy morning fog and looked like so many pumpkins in a December corn field."

[2] To honor the hero, Butler County (OH.) was named after him in the year 1803.

[3] Cist's *Miscellany* I, pag. 233.

During that year, Cincinnati's population did not increase at all. Half of its population had been in the army and many of these had fallen in the battle. Its tragic fate caused several citizens to fear for their safety, and they resettled in Kentucky.

From all sides, bands of Indians swarmed across the area and even disrupted the connection with Columbia. The *Chronicle* chose to describe the following strange case: As a youth of eleven years, Oliver M. Spencer, the father of the recently deceased Judge Spencer of Superior Court, was visiting in Cincinnati from Columbia where he lived, in order to participate in the Fourth of July celebration. In order to avoid the dangerous land journey for the return home, he joined with three other persons to travel to Columbia in a canoe. About one mile above the mouth of Deer Creek, one of the men, drunk on whiskey, began to shake the canoe so severely that Spencer, who feared capsizing and could not swim, pleaded that he and the drunk should be put on shore. At the same instant, a band of Indians appeared on the bank and captured Spencer, scalped the drunk, and fired at the canoe which turned over in the excitement of the moment. Jakob Licht, a German who was steering, was shot in the arm but, as he was a good swimmer, he was able to reach the shore. Mrs. Coleman, the boat's other passenger, a lady of 60 years who could not help herself was, in spite of how impossible it seems, held above the water by her extremely wide skirt, and carried by the current to Cincinnati, where a citizen rescued her. The Indians led the young Spencer to one of their villages near the mouth of the Auglaize; only after a period of three years did they permit him to return to his home.

The widow Bilderbach had somewhat better luck. When the Indians reached their villages on the Big Miami with their captives, they adopted Ruhama as one of their own, and she lived among the savages until her release. She did a squaw's work, carrying home the meat from the hunt, set it up to dry, making moccasins, leggings and other articles of clothing for the family to which she had been given. Even though not treated poorly, nevertheless she suffered severely from the rough and squalid lifestyle of the Indians. Several months after her capture, friendly Indians made it known to the commander of Fort Washington, that a white woman was being held in the Miami villages. The commandant traded for her freedom, brought her to Fort Washington, and sent her back with her two orphaned children to the lonely blockhouse of a relative[4].

After numerous attempts by the Federal Government to begin negotiations for peace had ended with the murder of several of their emissaries by the Indians who, blinded with their great victories over Harmar and St. Clair, felt themselves to be invulnerable, Washington called the brave Revolutionary War general, Anthony Wayne, to replace the deposed St. Clair as commander-in-chief and raise a new army of the west. In June 1792 Wayne arrived in Pittsburg to begin work on this latest attempt by the Americans to subdue the Indian confederation with overwhelming power. The new army received the name: "Legion of the United States," and was divided into four sub-legions. Their weapons drill lasted until December of that year. Washington had particularly emphasized to Wayne that the first priority for a campaign against the Indians was to train competent marksmen, and that he should spare neither powder nor lead in this effort to achieve this goal.

Wayne's appointment had caused ill will in the southern states, particularly in Virginia, which had suggested General Henry Lee for command. Even among the officer corps in Cincinnati after Wayne's arrival, a hostile

---

[4] Soon thereafter, the widow Bilderbach wed John Green and moved with him in 1798 to the Hockhocking Valley where she bore the first white male child in Fairfield County, three miles west of Lancaster. She died in the year 1842.

divisiveness had arisen, caused by the ambition of General Wilkinson, who himself had sought the senior command. In his "Notes", Judge Burnet describes the commandant of Fort Washington as a cavalier with the most refined manners, a celebrated man of the world, whose talents unfortunately combined the ambition of a Caesar with the confidence of a Napoleon. His love for pomp knew no bounds. Therefore, he had his own barge built and magnificently outfitted for pleasure trips. Twenty five men rowed it against the current. Often the general would give regal banquets on board his favorite vessel for his officers and for the leading citizens of Cincinnati. A band played compositions from Gluck and Hayden; the selected foods and drink and the popping of the opened champagne transported the guests away from the wilderness of the Northwest Territory and into the Lucullian life of the European aristocracy.

Mr. John Breckenridge from Kentucky writes in his memories from Gallipolis about one of these banquets which he attended as a boy: "My senses were overpowered. To me the vessel seemed like an Elysium. The splendor of the furniture, the elegant, expensive clothes of the party, the richness of the table blinded my senses. The General's face was blessed with a constant smile, his objective appeared to be to make everyone in the party happy, and his spouse, a delightful soul, stood faithfully by his side and enlivened the conversation with the spirit and grace of her soul."

Since his hospitable home represented the the center for Cincinnati's social circles, it was no wonder, that the General acquired a following among the officers as well as the citizens, who approved his intrigues against Wayne and joined them. Amazingly enough, his house guest, Colonel B. Schaumburg, was an exception. Judge Burnet describes Schaumburg's character, which his service in the west through his military abilities swiftly brought him promotion from Lieutenant to Colonel, in the following manner:

"Colonel B. Schaumburg, born a German, was extremely respectful of his immediate superior, and actively engaged in furthering the superior's interests, which is due to a superior officer. The colonel's bravery was as well known as his charity and, since he had served in Europe, he let himself be governed by the proper role of an officer in the above-mentioned dispute[5]."

With the exception of Schaumburg, all the officers stood on one side or the other. But Wayne's friends were more numerous as a result of the popularity which the hero of Stony Point had won among the people represented among the militia officers.

Another German under Wayne's command, the true antithesis of the venerable Schaumburg, was the Dragoon Major Rudolph, whose corps, an advance party of the army, had spent the winter of 1792 in Fort Washington. It consisted of three companies of light dragoons, one company of riflemen, and infantry. Rudolph had been reared in the wilderness of lower Virginia, and, as is demonstrated in the following events, was a rough, tyrannical officer.

In the Spring of 1793, seven of his troops, tired of their harsh treatment, deserted to the Ohio river, where they got a boat and fled down river towards Spanish territory. However, at the Falls of the Ohio they were apprehended by Lieutenant Clark and sent back to Fort Washington. A court martial condemned three of the unfortunate ones to the gallows, two to running the gauntlet, and the remainder to a long period of close arrest in irons. John Brown, Seth Blin and J. Gallaher were the ones sentenced to death by hanging. The execution was to take place the next day. The gallows were erected below the fort, south of the former United Reformed Church in today's Hamilton.

---

[5] Burnet's Notes, pag. 25.

Five hundred soldiers were assembled around the gallows to witness the death of their unfortunate comrades. The appearance of the condemned and their deportment on the platform won the sympathy of all the spectators. They were three intelligent, young men, in the flower of youth; their braids were loosened, and the wind played with their long hair, which waved about their shoulders. John Brown was the son of a respected family in Albany in the state of New York. The love for a poor but worthy and virtuous girl had brought down on him the displeasure of his parents, who had already selected a bride for him from one of the richest families. Despairing and with a broken heart, he had left his father's house and enlisted in a Dragoon company. The service brought him to the west and, unfortunately, under Rudolph's iron discipline. The constant insults to his honor led him to desert. When the Sergeant, who was serving as hangman, according to custom asked him a last question as to why the force of the law should not be extended to him, he replied with a hateful look at his tormentor Rudolph, that he would die nine hundred deaths rather than be subject to the orders of such a devil. Without a complaint he departed this world. Seth Blin was the son of a respected widow, who lived in the state of New York. His struggle against death lasted a long time, since the noose had been applied by an unexperienced hand. Three times he raised his legs to the platform, but finally the exertion broke his neck.

Immediately after the guilty sentence had been delivered, a friend of the accused hurried to Fort Washington to seek a pardon from General Wilkinson. He was successful, but unfortunately, the obstinate Major had ordered that the execution take place immediately and the messenger arrived 15 minutes too late.

When General Wayne had arrived at the post, he was so outraged at Rudolph's maliciousness, that he gave him the choice of either being cashiered or submitting his resignation. The tyrant chose the latter and returned to Virginia. In his place came Major Jonathan Cass, the father of the statesman Lewis Cass. But the nemesis soon caught up with the scourge of Fort Hamilton. In partnership with a merchant from Norfolk, Rudolph bought a ship for a business trip to Europe. In the Mediterranean, pirates from Algiers captured the ship and nailed Rudolph to the mast of his own ship. Loud was the joy when this news reached Wayne's army.

The troops who had been recruited during the Summer and Fall of 1792 arrived in Cincinnati with General Wayne in the Spring of the following year. After camping there for two or three months, the march through the wilderness began. The first stop occasioned the construction of Fort Greenville. There the army went into winter quarters until the following July. In the fall of that year, measles broke out among the troops at Fort Washington and spread so severely through the area, that almost a third of the soldiers and citizens fell victim to it. On July 26, General Scott arrived at Fort Greenville from Kentucky with 1600 riders and two days later the legion began to move toward the confluence of the Auglaize and the Miami, where Wayne built Fort Defiance. This occurred on a well-settled site, a former large French Canadian and Indian trading post, where there was an abundance of vegetables and fruit. Huge cornfields, apple and peach groves spread out here, and, after the previous harsh difficulties and deprivations, the army reveled in this Capua in the wilderness. Here General Wayne received valuable information about the strength and position of the Indians, and about the assistance which they could expect from the French militia in Detroit and from Major Campbell, commander of a British post on the Miami. After considering the impatience of both his militia and regular troops, he decided to rapidly advance and attack the enemy. Beforehand, however, in the spirit of his instructions from President Washington, he sent Christoph Miller as a special emissary to the united tribes urging peace and promising them the protection and friendship of the United States. Christoph, the son of a German, had, as a boy, run away to the Shawnees in the wilderness and had been adopted by them. In a remarkable coincidence several weeks before Wayne's arrival on the Miami, he had been captured by his own brother, who was serving as a scout under Wayne. The brothers soon recognized each other, and it did not take much convincing to win the deserter back over to the interests of the whites, against whom he had turned his back. Unfortunately, the mission of the German Indian was unsuccessful. The chiefs demanded a period of ten days in order to decide on peace or war, a demand which Wayne denied, in that he gave the order for a rapid advance. On the 18th, the army, numbering about 2000, after deducting the garrisons and wounded in the various posts and forts, arrived in enemy territory and erected Fort Deposit to protect the baggage during the impending battle. The allied tribes had selected an area between the Miami, an area of almost impenetrable underbrush as the battle ground; huge barricades of fallen trees protected their front. Led by King Schingask, Little Turtle and the Shawnee chief, Blue Jacket, two thousand warriors awaited the attack of the Americans. Even though he advanced slowly and carefully, Wayne became aware of the enemy's presence through a murderous fire which swept his forward party from the underbrush. He immediately ordered a halt, arranged his troops in battle formation and let the Kentucky riders attack the Indian flank. While they were slowly making their way through the underbrush and breaking through the fallen trees, Wayne ordered the first line of the legion forward, in order to drive the enemy out of their cover with the tips of their bayonets and subject them to a well aimed fire in their rear. With fixed bayonets and wild cries the brave legion charged the underbrush and drove the Indians from their ambush. The red bands had barely reached the openings in the forests when salvo upon salvo smashed into them and threw them into panic and confusion and, before the other segment of the army could even hurry to their assistance, the first line had routed everything before it and stormed the Indian camp over piles of bodies. Only 100 Americans fell in this murderous storm, which drove the Indians off into all directions, so that they could not reform and abandoned their fields and villages to the enemy. This severe lesson caused the savages to ask for peace. On August 3, 1795, General Wayne signed a treaty with all the warring tribes at Fort Greenville, which ended the long years of hostilities and gave the new settlements a period of peace and security.

However, Wayne's glorious victory did not silence his numerous critics; on the contrary, they became even more bitter. At a dinner meeting in Wilkinson's home, Major Campbell Smith attributed the victory on the banks of the Miami not to Wayne's talent, but rather to the disunity among the chiefs of the various tribes. Barely half the Indians were present on the field at the start of the battle. Had the superb plan of Little Turtle, which Blue Jacket had ignominiously rejected, been carried out, Wayne's army would have been irretrievably lost. On this same occasion, Major Gmion also spoke out against Wayne with scathing humor. All of these stories caused much bad blood, and Cincinnati's chronicle points to many a duel as a result.

Chapter 21

Secession Attempts in Kentucky. - The Intrigues of Spain and France in the Ohio Valley. - The Whiskey Rebellion. - Ludwig Wetzel's Captivity and Death.

During the six-year campaign against the Indians, Kentucky had become the scene of stormy political movements, which, in order to understand them, we must go back several years in our thread of chronology. The reader has already been made aware (page 77) of the demands which Spain had raised in regards to the Mississippi valley. Even though they were diminished somewhat in their extent during the revolutionary battles, American diplomacy was not successful in convincing the cabinet in Madrid to give up control of the main river. In January 1781, Spanish troops had stormed Fort St. Joseph and claimed the northwest in the name of his Catholic Majesty; on the 15th of the following month, Congress, at the urging of the eastern and middle states, instructed Ambassador Jay to relinquish the right of free navigation on the Mississippi below the border of the United States, lest this endanger the completion of the pending treaty with Spain concerning boundaries and trade. This surrender of their best interests caused utmost bitterness among the population of the Ohio Valley. It appeared to them that the only course remaining was between battling or joining Spain, and, at any rate, that independent action was necessary since the trade with New Orleans was their life blood. The question was not to remain long in doubt. Troops were raised for a campaign against the Spanish territory, Vincennes occupied, the property of Spanish traders on the Wabash and Illinois seized, and all traders from that nation were expelled from American territory. The agitators even sought to throw themselves into the arms of Great Britain, should the eastern states condemn their independent action. The Virginia legislature did not hesitate to act against the movement. It ordered a return of the seized property, arrested the plot's ring leaders and brought the affair before Congress. The latter permitted the government in Vincennes to occupy the town with federal troops and disperse the agitators.

But this action so little influenced the reigning agitation in the District of Kentucky that the state's attorney, Harry Innis, felt himself compelled to write to the Governor of Virginia, that, because of the bitterness among the population, he would not be able to try those arrested and added: "I am definitely of the opinion, that the western territory will act in its own special interest and will establish an independent government." Even the great statesmen of the time were completely blind to the question of life or death of the west. Thus Washington expressed his willingness, to give his approval to a temporary cessation of navigation on the Mississippi, since he believed that this measure would bind the new western colonies even closer to the Atlantic states, and they would support one of his favorite projects, the construction of a canal to link the Ohio with the Potomac and the James rivers. It is no wonder that, because of such views of their national leaders, the most respected individuals of the west would waver in their devotion to the powerless and worthless union of states, and the dissatisfaction among the people increased daily. Spain nourished this dissatisfaction with all the sorts of cunning diplomacy. Through its secret emissary Gardoqui, it assured the Kentuckians that, in case of a split of the territory from the Union, the Mississippi would, under the most advantageous conditions for both parties, be opened for the export of their goods.

The outbreak of the French revolution and the arrival in the United States of its ambassador Genet, hindered the success of the perfidious Spanish politics. In the meantime Kentucky had been preparing for statehood, and was admitted as the newest member to the Union on February 4, 1791. Genet thought that he could use the bitterness of the western population in regards to navigation on the Mississippi to raise troops in the Ohio Valley and use them against Spain, the enemy of the French republic, for the purpose of conquering Louisiana. In November 1793 his agent Lachaise appeared in the Ohio cities, and the recruiting was as open as was the issuance of officers' commissions in the name of the French republic. Even Kentucky's political founder, George Rogers Clark, joined the army as a Major General of the French army and commander of the revolutionary forces on the Mississippi. Washington immediately took steps to squelch the activities of the plotters. To Governor Shelby of Kentucky, Governor St. Clair, and General Wayne went orders for the alerting of troops; Fort Massac was renovated and received a garrison, but more than these military preparations, Washington's successful efforts to have Genet recalled caused the strange affair to fail. Disregarding this setback, in 1796 the government of France sent two new agents, the generals Collot and Warin, to the Ohio valley, in order to again stir up the population against the federal government and inflame them in a war against Spain. But Washington's alertness again defeated the undertaking. The famous Volney almost became entangled in the revolutionary intrigues of his countrymen. In 1796, after a tiring journey on foot through Kentucky, the author of the "Ruins", carrying under his arm his modest wardrobe wrapped in oil cloth, arrived in Cincinnati, where he found accommodations in Yeatsman's Hotel on Front Street. The traveler's monosyllabic, taciturn behavior caused Governor St. Clair, Judge Burnett and others to suspect, that he might belong to the French agents, who were seeking to break the West away from the Union, and it was only with extreme effort that he was able to allay their suspicions and avoid confinement in Fort Washington[1].

When all hope for French assistance had to be abandoned, many Kentuckians secretly courted the idea for a union of the West with Louisiana. The glorious leaders of this movement were Judge Sebastian, State Attorney Innis and General Wilkinson. Baron de Carondelet supported them with money, weapons and men. Among others he sent an Irishman by the name of Owen, who had previously lived in Cincinnati and knew the country and the people, in a barge, loaded with weapons and money on board, to the Ohio. But at its mouth, the Spanish crew stabbed Owen to death and fled to the Northwest Territory with their captured booty. In addition, an Englishman, Thomas Powers, arrived in Cincinnati from New Orleans in a vessel manned by many armed individuals, and anchored on the Kentucky shore. He sent his companions ashore, ostensibly to buy horses. However, it was generally believed they really intended to recruit troops, the command of whom was to be assumed by an officer from Fort Washington.

Not just the Federal Government, but also the State of Kentucky did not hesitate to act swiftly against the secessionist traitors. It

---

[1] Transactions of the historical and philosophical Society of Ohio, pag. 13.

was proven of Judge Sebastian, that he had received from Spain an annual salary of 2,000 dollars for services performed. The Kentucky House of Representatives put his case on its agenda and found him guilty of maintaining seditious contact with the agents of the Spanish government and treason against his fatherland through the acceptance of bribes. Before the guilty verdict had been given, Judge Sebastian resigned his office. In addition General Wilkinson was brought before a court martial on the same charge, but acquitted due to lack of evidence.

Incidently, the closure of the Mississippi was merely one of a series of serious complaints, which had made the population of the Ohio Valley hostile towards Washington's administration. The defeats of Harmar and St. Clair were attributed to the government's inadequate measures; the army was unpopular; people saw in its establishment the beginning of a system of a standing army, the western posts were in the possession of Great Britain, the frontier areas devastated by the savages, and then came the oppressive domestic taxes, among which the tax on distilled spirits wase most detested. Since the farmers and speculators could no longer bring their products to New Orleans, they had turned them into whiskey. Therefore, at the suggestion of Treasury Secretary Hamilton, Congress had applied a heavy tax, during which time all farm products remained untaxed. The bitterness of the western Pennsylvania population, especially the German farmers, encouraged revolutionary activities against the tax officials. A group of masked individuals ambushed the collector from Allegheny and Washington counties, took away his horse, shaved his head, tarred and feathered him, and left the severely mistreated person in a lonely spot in the forest. But the barbarity of those same persons, who performed the atrocities in Gnadenhütten, would increase to savage barbarism against the unfortunate federal officials. In October 1791, Tax Assistant Wilson began to register the distilleries. On the very first day of his office a masked band fell upon him, dragged him to a blacksmith five miles away, there they tore the clothes off the unfortunate person and tossed them into the fire; then they seared his body with glowing irons, tarred and feathered him, and left the tortured victim naked and bleeding with the blacksmith. Soon thereafter a certain Roseberry experienced the same fate, since, during a conversation, he had uttered the unwelcome observation that the population of a county could not expect the protection of a government, whose laws they so stubbornly resisted. The audacity of this revolutionary gang was so brazen that they seized and kidnapped two persons who were to testify in court against Wilson's tormentors.

But even as Congress eased somewhat the pressure of the hated financial code in order to mollify the anger of the population, resistance continued in western Pennsylvania. Agents were warned that they should not open any offices, and when Captain Faulkner, against public sentiment, fixed up an office for the tax administrators, a mob armed with knives and pistols fell upon him and threatened to scalp him and burn down all his houses in Pittsburg, should he complete the rental contract. The captain complied and was happy to get away from the hands of the crazed mob with his whole skin.

At the head of this mutinous movements stood David Bradford, who was also the leader in all of their acts of violence.

Against these rebels the government appeared to be totallly helpless. It did not dare to bring the perpetrators before the court but suggested the following measures for a gradual throttling of the resistance: 1) legal action against all unlicensed distilleries, but only when this could occur without acts of force. 2) seizure of all illegally produced spirits on their way to market, when it could occur without inciting a riot.

3) By ordering that only those spirits upon which the tax had been paid would be purchased for army use. Even though the effect of these measures were partially circumvented by the introduction of whiskey from the Northwest Territory, where the tax law was not applicable, the leading distillers, upon further consideration of their pecuniary interests, abandoned Bradford's group and resumed their business anew. However, the appearance of Genet's agents reinflamed among the dregs of society the former resistance against the federal government. Those distillers submitting to the law had their houses, mills, and barns containing the harvests burned. The offices of the tax officials were stormed and their books burned. But, in response to these acts of violence, the federal government did nothing to exert its authority other than to order that the criminals be brought before the federal court by the US Marshal. This caused the real catastrophe to break out. The federal court held its sessions in Philadelphia, where the accused were brought for examination. Then was heard the cry that the federal government was dragging people from their homes, that it had become as tyrannical as the British government, which carried American citizens to overseas courts. The slogan for all was rebellion and secession. In Pittsburg, mobs gathered and, under Bradford's leadership, descended upon the house of Tax Inspector, John Neville, in order to burn his books and all his possessions. Aware of his unpopularity, Neville had armed his negroes, barricaded his door and windows, and when the raging mob attempted to burst open his door, he opened fire upon them. Six of the attackers were wounded, one fatally. This rash, thoughtless act increased the general uproar. The next day, the leaders openly gathered mobs from the areas around the city and the settlements on Mingo Creek in order to renew the attack on the inspector's house. The latter had wisely fled, but had left a small group of troops from Fort Pitt led by a relative, Major Abraham Kilpatrick, to protect his property. The attack was not long in coming. The leaders laid siege to the building and opened an hour long barrage against the guard, who returned the fire. In order to force a quick end to the affair, the mutineers set on fire eight houses in the neighborhood; the massive heat and the danger of a fiery death, should the fire spread to Neville's house, forced those inside to capitulate. During the battle, one of the leaders was shot to death and three wounded. Neville's house shared the fate of the adjoining buildings and was burned to the ground. Bradford then traveled throughout the countryside calling upon settlers to arm against the Federal Government, which finally recognized that it was time to take definite steps to subdue the rebellion. On September 25, Washington ordered the militia from Pennsylvania, New Jersey and Maryland to be placed on a war alert and ordered their commander, the Governor of Virginia, Henry Lee, to subdue the rebellion. At the approach of the troops, however, the mutineers scattered in all directions. Bradford and several of those most involved fled to Spanish territory. In order to hinder a renewed outbreak of the rebellion, and establish a subsequent respect for the law, an armed force under General Morgan remained in the upper Ohio Valley for the entire winter. Thus ended the so-called Whiskey Rebellion after an expenditure of 669,992 dollars.

For Ludwig Wetzel this settlement was to mean freedom from a horrible situation. Bitter about the treatment he had received from Harmar, the brave Indian fighter departed for Spanish territory. In Natchez, where he continued as a frontiersman, he made himself the favorite of the settlers, as he had done on the upper Ohio. But then he was to become the victim of a malicious deed. Even though Ludwig could neither read nor write and put the least value on money, he was arrested for counterfeiting. His accuser was a certain Piatt from Pittsburg, an individual who, because of a crime committed on the upper Ohio, had sought refuge in Louisiana, and was probably trying to get the heat off himself. Based on the testimony of this person, Wetzel was sentenced to life imprisonment in the New Orleans jail. The news of his misfortune soon reached the upper country. Therefore, upon arrival in New Orleans, the boatsmen considered it their first duty to visit the prisoner and, through all sorts of friendly deeds, ease the severity of his situation. Petition after petition for Wetzel's release reached the Spanish governor, but in vain; this official refused to issue a pardon based on the grounds that his sovereign wished strict compliance with the sentences of the courts against the numerous counterfeiters in Louisiana. The poor soul had already spent 4 and 1/2 years in a dark, damp hole, totally without all the comforts of life, among society's lowest criminals. He had given up all hope of regaining his freedom. For even his friends, who had earlier made tireless efforts in his behalf, had long ago given up all attempts at freeing him and believed that only death would free him from the chains. A dark resignation had beaten the free spirit of the brave son of the woods and convinced him that he would be cut off from the light of he world for the rest of his days. But then a ray of hope fell into his cell. Bradford, who had fled because of his leadership of the Whiskey Rebellion, arrived in Louisiana. Because he was a person of high education and fine manners, he became a favorite at the court of the Spanish governor. Wetzel's sad state, of whose character and popularity among his countrymen he was well aware, soon reached Bradford's ear and touched his heart. Bradford then made it his immediate priority to free his old friend from the horrible prison, where he was dying inch by inch. His urgent requests to the governor had success. In order to avoid a conflict between Wetzel's release and the royal instructions, a subterfuge had to be arranged. It was necessary that Wetzel suddenly become sick and die. His body was laid in a coffin and given over for burial to his friends, among whom was Bradford. That evening, Wetzel stepped out of the coffin in the crypt where he had been temporarily brought, and the empty coffin was laid in a fresh grave in New Orleans. Under an assumed name, Wetzel journeyed to his cousin Sicks who was living in Natchez, with whose family he remained for several years. Unfortunately his long imprisonment in the damp hole in New Orleans had ruined his health so that he could not live on the frontier. Robbed of their former movement and action, his members had lost their former agility and strength. The mighty form was broken, Wetzel had become an invalid, dependent upon the support of his friends.

After the purchase of Louisiana by the United States, Sicks accompanied Wetzel to the Brazos in Texas. On the banks of this river, in his beloved home, the far wilderness of the whispering forest, rest the ashes of the daring German Indian fighter. Even in his final days he could not forget the injustice inflicted upon him by Harmar. He died with a curse on his lips against Piatt, who had already met his nemesis. For after the sentence had been given against his victim, Piatt had been brought to the jail in New Orleans, where he remained for nine years for the murder of an Indian on the Red River. Then, after a court verdict, he was taken from his cell and hanged on the gallows[2].

---

[2] From the Hon. E.R. Eckley's report on Wetzel's death, and according to the memoirs of his father, who had been engaged in river trade, who knew Wetzel personally in Louisiana, and had often visited him in his prison in New Orleans, as well as later in Natchez. Taylor's *History of Ohio*, pag. 532.

Chapter 22

The Founding of Gallipolis, Chillicothe, and Dayton. - Volney and Brissot (write about) the German Settlers. - The First Church and School in Cincinnati. - The first Jail - The First Sheriff and the First Execution. - The Courts and Lawyers. - Distribution of the Northwest Territory. - The End of St. Clair.

On October 16, 1790, four hundred Frenchmen arrived in Marietta in 6 Kentucky boats. They were the advance party of a large immigration party, formed in Paris at the beginning of the French Revolution, for settling the Scioto Valley, encouraged by a confidence man by the name of Joel Barlow. This person had distributed pamphlets in Paris as well as throughout all of France, in which he passed himself off as the agent of a Scioto land company, offering the most wonderful land on the most beautiful river in the world, with a heavenly climate which knew no winter, for 5 shillings per acre. Volney writes: "The pamphlet described to the reader the American forests in a fairy tale-like fantasy; where sugar grew out of trees, exotic plants produced breadfruit and lights, with no fierce animals and snakes, no taxation, military service, military quartering, etc., filled with the ideas of Rousseau, embodying Washington's republic in the distant wilderness, which the philosophers and literati of Paris reinforced, particularly Brissot de Warville, who, with his own travel descriptions, added to the swindle. Soon, the only topic of discussion in the Parisian social circles was the paradise on the Ohio, and the free and happy life in the forests of the Scioto valley. The buyers of land, belonging mainly to the wealthy class, soon crowded into Barlow's office; entire families spent their fortunes and counted themselves lucky to be able to participate in such an excellent undertaking."

At the head of these unfortunate dreamers stood Count Malartin, a captain in the guard of Louis XVI, and a natural scientist, Dr. Sangrain. The majority of the colonists consisted of sculptors, painters, goldsmiths, coach makers, barbers and wigmakers to his Majesty and other artists especially ill-suited to life in the wilderness; representing the practical element, there were a few genuine farmers in three cornered hats and wooden shoes, including one Alsacian family, Schumann. After the hazards of the sea and land journey, the colorful party reached its chosen site to find out that the land sellers did not own a single foot on the Scioto, and that they had exchanged all of their possessions to reach a wilderness, whose makeup they did not understand, in a foreign country with a foreign tongue, where the Indians brought death and destruction to every homestead. The settlers in Marietta took pity on the poor souls and supported them with the best of their efforts. General Putnam built them a village, to which they gave the name Gallipolis. Now they were to start clearing the surrounding land, which, in their French fantasy, they expected to be made a present of by Congress. But, thickly forested with huge sycamores and oak, this was not an easy job even for an American woodsman. With joy and determination, to the accompaniment of opera songs, the painters and wigmakers began this new work. Tying ropes to the branches, a dozen would work on a tree trunk with axes, hatchets, and other cutting tools, while others would pull with all their might to bring down the giant, which was not without danger for them, when the trunk would come crashing down and they would scatter in all directions. But when the giant finally lay felled on the ground, there was the other problem of hauling it away or burning it. Then an enlightened idea struck the French fantasy. While several would cut off the branches from the trunk, others would dig a large ditch alongside the tree, into which several of them would strain to roll the fallen enemy. Given such exertion, it is no wonder that the area around Gallipolis did not present a picture of culture. Here and there a small garden arose-but the settlers had to get the majority of their supplies from boats on the river, as long as they had the means. Then came the Indian wars. Somewhat discouraged, Count Malartin left the settlement and joined the army. St. Clair made him his adjutant for the lost battle[1] during which he was wounded. The Count then returned to Philadelphia and from there continued on to his sorely beloved France. In the meantime, those remaining behind endured terrible fortunes. Several of them were attacked by Indians while working in the fields and scalped; soon one did not dare to till the gardens. Among those remaining behind was the baker Franz Thiery, from whose mouth Ludwig Philipp, who visited the settlement, heard the stories of the various adversities. In order to mislead the Indians, Thiery's wife tilled the garden dressed in men's clothing. After a terrible winter, not at all like that promised by Barlow, there were constant feverish sicknesses, the result of bacteria coming from a swamp behind the city. But regardless of how sad the situation was, the French levity was not disheartened. Twice a week, the entire colony came together to dance away hunger and cares to the fiddle; several times this terrified the Indians lurking in the underbrush, who hurried back to their camps with the news that he whites had already started their war dances. But even the French joy of life gave way before the hunger and misery. The settlers scattered mostly to Detroit and Kaskaskia. In reaction to the descriptions from the lawyer Duponceau from Philadelphia, Congress granted to those remaining 24,000 acres across from the Big Sandy River, and in 1798 increased it another 1200. Since then this stretch of land has been called the French Grant.

Volney had seen Gallipolis in its most miserable state and naturally found the idea reinforced, which he had already stated while visiting Vincennes, that the French workers were totally unsuited for the American wilderness. "In contrast to the German settlers," he writes, "out of passion, unrestrained enthusiasm or restlessness, the French embark upon settlement projects without counting the costs or difficulties. Germans, who have advanced into the forests or even into Indian territory, are often successful in establishing farms and even villages, which I cannot say about our own countrymen, who, like in Vincennes, spend their time in idleness or in liaisons with the Indian girls; their women have no understanding of farm life and they throw their money away on ornaments and baubles."

The famous friend of liberty, Brissot de Warville, is even more generous with his praise for the German pioneers. He writes, "The Germans are considered the sincerest, most industrious, simplest and most economical planters. They do not make debts and, of all the Americans, are the least blustery. In addition, they have large families, often 12 to 14 children. They have been accused of being of low intelligence, but from such as these have come Rittenhaus, Mühlenberg and Kühne."

The Anglo-American Morse and the Englishman Weld gave the German settlers of the west similarly eloquent praise.

---

[1] The battle occurred on the border between today's Mercer and Darke counties (OH.).

Even more important to the thriving development of the Northwest Territory than the founding of the French colony was the settlement of the so-called Virginia Reserve, a stretch of land between the Scioto and the Little Miami Rivers, which Virginia granted to the officers and soldiers of its army, an act which the Congress recognized in 1790. Nathaniel Massie, an enterprising young surveyor 27 years old, was the first one to advance into the depths of the Scioto wilderness and in mid March 1791, founded the city of Manchester on the Ohio River, 12 miles above Maysville. Among the pioneers, who surrounded this fourth settlement in today's Ohio with a palisades for protection against the Indians were the Otts, of thoroughly German stock, whose men were true giants, who were as familiar with the dangers and joys of the forest as were the Indians. Accompanied by these half wild warriors, Massie undertook exploratory trips through the wilderness during the dangerous period from 1791 to 1796, the year that Wayne's treaty finally brought peace to the settlements. In August of that latter year, Massie laid out the now thriving and expanding Chillicothe, in a thick forest on the west bank of the Scioto. Since he gave a free home site to every settler, at the end of the war many of Wayne's soldiers, drovers, and camp followers, a rabble, streamed in, and for a long time gave the place the name of "The City of Gamblers and Drunkards." From here began the settlements of the Scioto Valley. In the inn called "General Anthony Wayne," on the corner of Water and Walnut streets and in "The Green Tree," on the corner of Paint and Water streets, the streams of immigrants took their rest, who later felled the giant trees of the Scioto Bottom and soon turned Ross County into the most thickly farmed county in the state of Ohio.

Kraus, Maunz and the Otts belong to these earliest of settlers. The first house in Chillicothe was built by McArthur out of tree trunks. The blockhouse city became the seat of the territorial government, and 7 years after its establishment, in November 1802, Ohio's first constitution was drafted there. Palatial buildings now stand where 60 years ago Indian wigwams stood.

Wayne's peace treaty also caused the establishment of Dayton and the settlement of the hill lands and the wonderful forested flatlands on the Miami and Mad, which are considered the best lands in the state of Ohio. On November 4, 1795, the city was laid out by Governor Arthur St. Clair, James Wilkinson, Isreal Ludlow, and General Jonathan Dayton, a partner in Judge Symmes Miami lands, after whom the city received its name. The first building sites were given away free to settlers based on a lottery. In Cincinnati, 46 persons had committed themselves to resettling there; but the harshness of winter scattered many of them again; others had been scared off by the dangers of this far off outpost, and at the beginning of spring only 19 kept their promise, including the Germans A. Gaßmeier and S. Goß.

This hesitation to participate in a dangerous expedition was easy to understand. At the time of Wayne's peace treaty, with the exception of Cincinnati and its nearby environs, the entire country between the Miamis was a dark wilderness. Mill Creek Station, which lay 11 miles away, was considered the boundary of the Miami Valley, further out only a few individual adventurers had sought homesteads. Here, in 1795, in Warren County, one mile below today's Lebanon, in a lonely double blockhouse in the forest, lived Captain Robert Benham, already known to the reader through his adventures on the Licking; his next neighbor was Daniel Bonte, an elderly German, near to whom several other of our countrymen settled, including Johann Brill and Peter Jäger. The nearest protection against the Indians in the north, built before the settlement, was Fort Piqua, whose last commandant, H. N. Vischer, enjoyed a reputation as a brave and careful officer. One year before, two loaded garrison boats, manned by one officer and

23 men, were attacked by Indians near the fort, and every person was massacred. Bischer heard the firing, but because of the weakness of his command, could not provide any assistance. The Indians had planned to lure him out in order to destroy the entire garrison and lay the fort in ruins and ashes.

Let the reader now return to the settlements on the Miami lands of Judge Symmes. After paying for their lands and bringing in their families, many of the newcomers in Cincinnati had used up all their means of support. Others wandered in without a cent in their pocket, hoping to get small building plots at no cost, which the original buyers had let go because they could not build the structures stipulated in the purchase contracts. This class of newcomers was the most numerous. Their situation was pitiful, since settling in the forest was certain death, and in the city they were subject to starvation because there was no work. Hunting, fishing, and perhaps the profit from a small building site near the city offered them the only means to maintain themselves. Before the signing of the Treaty of Greenville, with the exception of the three-storied, comfortably equipped Quartermaster General's house in the fort, which was called the yellow house, there were only blockhouses in the city. Next year, the population increased by about 50 persons, mostly immigrants from New Jersey. Soon thereafter the first church was built. It was Presbyterian and stood almost on the same site where the handsome new Presbyterian church now stands, near Main Street. Cincinnati's original house of God was made from boat planks, fastened with wooden pegs. Later it was transported to Vine Street, below 5th, where in 1838, it was used as the gathering site for the first German Methodist congregation[2]. A little west of the church stood the first school. The first jail was built on Water Street around 1793. Two years later, the inhabitants had increased to such an extent, that a roomier blockhouse had to be constructed on the corner of Church Alley and 5th Street. On the site of today's Middle Market was a swamp overgrown with alder bushes, which constituted the city limit. On the northeast corner of Main and 5th Streets stood the city's most notable public inn, run by George Avery. The court sessions took place on its first floor and the croaking of the frogs competed with the arguments of the lawyers. Close by stood the signs of the current justice, gallows, pillory, and whipping post. Jacob Mays was the first criminal to be hung by Sheriff John Ludlow. His deputy was Levi McLean, who was also the jailer, assayer, butcher, constable, and voice teacher; he also played the violin and led the dances at parties. The prisoners, mostly unhappy debtors, had to suffer somewhat under this guard, who, after drinking a glass to quench his thirst, put on a "Flogging Frolic," i.e. a thrashing bee, where he beat every prisoner in a genuine communistic manner, without differentiating between criminals and debtors.

On the southwest corner of 3rd and Main street, Francois Menissier, a refugee from the glories of Gallipolis, maintained the first coffee house with the sign: "Pegasus and the Fallen Poet." With this particular device, the unhappy Frenchman probably wanted to publicize the terrible event, brought about by his own fantasy and the Rousseauan lectures, which caused him to leave beautiful France for the unattractive Ohio wilderness. Menissier turned the entire city block, which he paid for with an old saddle, into a vineyard, and thus must be recognized as the patriarch of grape cultivation in Ohio. For the block across the street, now worth more than a million dollars,

---

[2] At the time, this first church was so far away from the settled parts of the city, that the churchgoers were forced to take their muskets along with them to church for protection against the Indians. Whoever failed to do this was subject to a fine.

his neighbor at the time paid two silver dollars. The first newspaper appeared on November 9, 1793. It was called: *The Sentinel of the North Western Territory* and was edited and published by William Maxwell.

On the corner of Broadway and Front Street, where the Spencer House now stands, a German by the name of Barthel ran a grocery store. During these primitive times, the man had great difficulty with small change, which, as elsewhere in the west, was one of the biggest obstacles to trade. In the beginning, pelts were used instead of money. A muskrat pelt was a quarter, a raccoon pelt a third of a dollar. A doe skin was a half dollar, and a buck skin was the almighty dollar. However, this pelt currency lasted only a short time.

The garrison and the campaigns against the Indians brought tidy sums of Spanish dollars into the community, which nevertheless did not help with the lack of small change. But the settlers helped themselves; they divided a silver dollar into 25-cent pieces and from these even made smaller pieces of 12 1/2 cents each. When this wedge-shaped money made its way back east, it would be brought to the US Mint in Philadelphia to be recast and restamped. Amounts of less than 12 1/2 cents would be equalized by the merchants with needles, writing paper and similar articles. In 1794, the above named grocer Barthel brought in from the east a barrel of copper coins, which so angered his neighbors that they almost mobbed him; for, at the time, the distrust of copper coins was so great that whoever offered them could only expect insults, since whoever accepted them was considered petty and stingy.

After January 11, 1794, trade with the east was carried on with two keel boats, which traveled every 4 weeks alternately between Cincinnati and Pittsburg. These vessels were armored with steel plates, had firing ports for cannon, a six pounder, and an arsenal of flints and ammunition for the passengers, as protection against the Indians on the Ohio.

For this city, which was so totally cut off from the civilized world, the officers and army civil servants set the tone for the social life, and this was not very stimulating. Idleness, gluttony, and gambling were the daily routine. Judge Burnet explains that, with the exception of two or three, all the officers from Fort Washington were marked drunkards. The lawyers were not far behind them; with the exception of Burnet's brother, who died of tuberculosis, all nine lawyers drank themselves to death. Such a sad state of affairs in the morals of the upper classes can provide us with an indication of just how comfortable the life was in Cincinnati. To the lower classes of the population, St. Clair represented more the domineering soldier than the republican official. In order to bring some sort of order into this wild life, he vigorously applied the despotic Territorial Code which recognized whipping for continual drunkards, loafers and vagabonds.

On October 27, 1795, the Federal Government finally completed a treaty with Spain which established the western borders of the United States, granted to its citizens free travel on the Mississippi and granted them access to the port of New Orleans for a period of three years as a shipping point for their goods. With that, the continuing uproar in the Ohio valley was put aside and further attempts at secession were defeated. Another no less fortunate occurrence the next year was the transfer of the military posts in the Northwest Territory from the English. This led to the formation of the new Wayne County, which included northwest Ohio, northeast Indiana, and all of Michigan.

Up to that point, the Northwest Territory included only four counties, Washington, Hamilton, St. Clair, and Knox. The territorial courts convened in Marietta, Cincinnati, Kaskaskia and Vincennes, and also Detroit. At the time when this small city was chosen as the seat of government for Wayne (County), it was a garrison post, with narrow streets, built in the style of the French cities and totally surrounded with palisades. The citadel, an imposing building with an esplanade, was located within these entrenchments. In addition to its military significance, Detroit was at the same time a great trading site, the main depot for pelt commerce in the northwest, in which numerous English and Scottish merchants participated. When it was time for the courts to convene, the judges and lawyers had to travel there by horse through the wilderness, and in his Notes Judge Burnet describes several interesting adventures he experienced in the Indian cities along the way. But all the deprivations of the journey were weighed against the glamor of Detroit, which, in relation to the pleasures of life, was considered a small Paris.

The pelt trade required great capital and was subject to frequent fluctuations. The participants would earn large sums in one year and lose a relatively similar amount the next. Upon their return from their dangerous excursions to the cold regions of the west to their comfortable houses decorated with european luxury, these adventurers would recover with lucullian feasts, whereby the finest of wines would flow. Barely a day passed, without which such a feast would occur, to which every honest stranger, who happened to be in Detroit would be invited, and the true hosts of the wilderness were pleased when the party became wild and the heads became foggy. The servants at these dinners were usually Pawnee Indians, whose nimble courtesy Judge Burnet could not praise enough. They were slaves, according to an ancient law, that had been instituted upon the initial settling of upper Canada, which was based on the right of the Indians to sell prisoners-of-war. This custom was recognized upon transfer of the land to the United States; but it soon died out, since the public opinion, which increased with the population, was against it.

The native French of Detroit were all God-fearing people, who regularly gave their tithes to the priests and damned Judge Symmes, when, in an address to a jury, he spoke out against the many holidays and excessive church attendance.

According to articles of the Ordinance of 1787, the legislative power of the Governor and the Judge was replaced in 1799 by a General Assembly, which was elected by the population and by a legislative council appointed by Congress. The General Assembly elected W.H. Harrison to be a representative to Congress. In March of the following year, Congress partitioned the Northwest Territory, in that it established the new Indiana Territory, for which Harrison became governor. Chillicothe became the seat of government of the Northwest Territory and Vincennes for the Indiana Territory. The construction of the first state capital began in Chillicothe in 1800. In the meantime the legislature convened in a two story, hewn blockhouse, which stood on the corner of 2nd and Walnut Street; its upper rooms were equipped with billiards and tables and cards and dice cups, which were extensively used by the wilderness solons.

The City of Gamblers and Drunkards showed itself to be ungrateful for the honor of being elevated to be the capital city of the territory. On two evenings, the city's entire population, gathered together drunk and, angered by the issuance of an unpopular law, drove the governor and the legislators out of the state capital with curses and stones. As a punishment for this uncivil behavior, the seat of government was removed back to Cincinnati. This occurred on November 24, 1801. In the following year, Ohio was admitted as a state to the Union. Among the members of the convention which drew up its first constitution were the Germans Jakob Grubb and Nathan Up de Graff. In that year, St. Clair resigned his office. His extensive unpopularity, which he owed at no small extent to the fact that he was a foreigner, accelerated the state organization process. The constitutional convention had remembered the occasion that, during the last session of the legislature, he had vetoed 11 of 30 bills; therefore they denied this right to the governor of the new state, an action which was also included in the second constitution.

After resigning his office, St. Clair returned to the Ligonier Valley, impoverished and without any means of support. Unfortunately, he was too old and weak to embark on a new career. During two winters he petitioned Congress for reimbursement of the sum of 2000 dollars, which he had spent out of his own funds for the purchase of a number of pack horses and war supplies used in the Indian campaigns. He received the reply, that his claim was too late and that he should also be satisfied because a fire in the building which destroyed the records of the Ministry of War in Philadelphia probably also destroyed his receipts. This crass insult to his sense of honor hurt the old warrior even more than the shabby refusal of his just claim. Several representatives from Pennsylvania, who felt sorry about the old man's adversity, finally introduced a bill before Congress which granted to him a small annual pension. Unfortunately it became lost during its third reading. After the poor, otherwise proud man had lived for a time supported by his friends, he returned to the Ligonier Valley broken in spirit and body, where a widowed daughter, who was as poor as he, shared her remaining resources with him. The state of Pennsylvania finally granted the sorely tested Revolutionary War veteran an annual pension of $650, which maintained him during his remaining days. But he did not long enjoy it, for shortly thereafter, on August 31, 1818, he died as a result of a fall from a horse.

The brick house, which St. Clair had built in Cincinnati while governor of the Northwest Territory was, at the beginning of the century, still admired by the settlers as a grand palace. The unassuming box still stands today behind the bookstore of the Methodist church on the corner of 8th and Main Street.

Chapter 23

Cincinnati in 1800. - David Ziegler, Mayor of the City. - The Founding of Vevay. - German Wolf Hunters. - Burr's Conspiracy. - Justus Erich Vollmann. - The First German Property Owners in Cincinnati.

In 1800, the area of cleared land in Cincinnati would barely equal one of today's city blocks. Across the canal and west of Western Row was forest, where here and there shabby blockhouses stood, connected to the settlement with winding cow paths. South of the turn of the canal, where today the city hall and the cathedral stand, was a half-cleared field surrounded with raspberry bushes, where the young people would pick the fruit while in danger of being bitten by snakes. On the site of the Mozart Hall and the Mechanics Institute was an extensive wheat field. Beginning at Lower Market a ravine extended to Congress Street, which, before the settlement of the city, formed a series of beaver swamps, which the rains and the annual flooding of the river often swelled into lakes. Only Front Street showed any sort of pretense of being a city. From Walnut Street to Eastern Row, today's Broadway, there were block and frame houses built close together, and it even had sidewalks (trottoirs). Here lived the rich and the merchants; here was the hotel of Griffin Yeatman. Near to that, on the corner of Front and Sycamore, was built a small wooden business building, on whose columns sailors would tie up their barges and other vessels whenever the river was high. Starting on the northeast corner of 4th Street and Broadway, the entire block was fenced in; in its midst stood an imposing frame building, built by Winthrop Sargent, the Secretary of the Northwest Territory. From 4th Street to the river extended the military reserve of 16 acres around Fort Washington; here were the bastions and stockades; here the fort's flagpole rose into the air, and mornings and evenings was sounded reveille and taps. In 1803 Fort Washington was abandoned, and soon thereafter the area was divided up into lots and sold. The post office was on the east side of this military square, near the corner of Lawrence and Congress Streets. Here, once a week, the large amount of mail from the east was brought in, and the ever-busy and always cheerful Postmaster Ruffin would distribute the letters and newspapers with his own hand. On the block between Lawrence and Pike Street and 3rd and 4th Street, formerly called the "Lytle Square", stood a solitary house, built by Dr. Allison, and a field of several acres extended to the east and north. It was known in the town as the "peach grove".

In January 1802, the territorial legislature incorporated Cincinnati as a "town."

In order to make up for the jealousy and insults which the officers of the fort and the federal government had shown towards Major Ziegler, the citizens, at the first opportunity to exercise their municipal prerogatives, attempted to make up for this as best they could. They elected the major to be the first Mayor or President of the city.

The history of the Germans in Cincinnati therefore begins with a German as the first city official. And this forthright act of justice, which initiated the municipality, brought blessings. The city began developing in stages to its current size and population.

Following his resignation from the army, Major Ziegler ran a grocery on Front Street, a business that was as ill-fitting to his military customs and behavior as it was to his inability to "make money." In 1803 he gave it up, as indicated in the following, bitter advertisement in the "Western Spy", which followed Maxwell's newspaper.

"David Ziegler herewith announces that he wishes to sell his goods and rent his shop to a 'hard working man', who can then make as much money as possible. The principal reason why I am giving up my business lies in the shortage of money and the shamefulness with which some people refuse to pay their debts. To those who do not visit me to get goods on 'credit' I say to you my thanks; to those delinquents in my account books, the 'Squire' will soon pay his 'compliments'."

As indicated above, Cincinnati's first settlers were immigrants from New Jersey, in whose footsteps soon followed Pennsylvanians, Virginians, Marylanders, New Yorkers, and finally New Englanders. Among these, the first two were the most numerous; Pennsylvania provided the strongest element of the American settlers. Among the first European immigrants were English and Scots and then the Germans.

These first individual German inhabitants were former settlers from the east; the earlier mass immigration direct from Germany had been slowed by the general European war which the French revolution had spawned. For the most part, those few German arrivees in the eastern seaports did not even have the right of free choice over their own or their family's work; they were slaves, who had indentured several years of their work to pay for their journey. But the German scientific spirit accompanied those first American pioneers into the Miami wilderness and had given the world a glimpse of its treasures. Long before Humboldt, Christoph Daniel Ebeling, one of Germany's ablest scientists, had with his collection of travel journals from the American west, published from 1780 to 90, as well as through his economic collection of 1784-97, described the land and climatic relationships and won for himself the gratitude of Congress. The famous Freiherr von Bülow, one of the first German anarchists appeared in Cincinnati and in the far west. But since his murky ideas of freedom had had just as little effect as had his excessive speculation with glass items among the Indians, so upon his return to Europe he achieved his revenge with a sarcastic book about the United States, which nevertheless did contain something of true scientific value. Cincinnati's situation he described in exaggerated colors. "The Ohio," he wrote, "the Po of the new world, flows here through a great valley, which will become amazingly similar to the culture of Lombardy." When the poor soul died in prison in Riga, the victim of cowardly Prussian internal politics with Napoleon, German vintners were already busy in the Cincinnati, ready to try out the accuracy of his reports. For in 1796, the French Swiss, Johann Jacob Dufour, had been sent to America by a stock company of the Swiss canton of Waadt to introduce the cultivation of wine in the west. Along with his brother Daniel and several relatives and vintners, he founded in 1802 the well- known vintner colony Vevay in Jefferson County, Indiana, which soon let loose a stream of German families into the Cincinnati area; there the colonists had purchased 3700 acres of land. They were given a period of 12 years to pay off the debt, beginning in 1802. This vintner colony would soon enter into a close trade with the thriving capital city of the west.

The theater and horse racing both appeared in the news chronicles of Cincinnati on the same day, namely September 30, 1801. At that time, wolves were quite numerous, lurking around the seat of the muses and the circus. Among the wolf hunters, who received $3-6 for every wolf pelt from the county commissioners, appeared the German Nimrods, Jacob Meisner, Michel Rüdesel et al. These hunters obtained the genitalia of a female wolf in heat and rubbed their soles with it. The wolves then followed the trail in packs and were killed with ease. These hunters chose their hunting outfits according to the colors of the season; they were brown in the fall, white in winter, and green in summer.

During the year 1806, Aaron Burr's secret, wild endeavor in the west was the theme of the latest gossip in Cincinnati. It was known that preparations were made in the immediate area, in Marietta and on a neighboring island. Among the plotters, this limitless desire for excess, the desire for the unusual, which typifies the irascible American character, shows only shadowy agitators and arch traitors, who sought nothing less than to destroy the Union, and from its western remains build a new great new empire in alliance with Mexico. A remarkable group of unique and contrary characters made up the leaders of this alleged secret conspiracy. In addition to Aaron Burr, the rising American politician, and the former republican Vice President of the United States, who, next to Jefferson, was the leading man of his party, we find a smooth Irish intellectual, Blannerhasset, who, in the midst of the western wilderness, lived for the arts and sciences, whose wife, a charming and extremely talented woman, turned her attractive island in the Ohio into the seat of fairy tale hospitality, and another, a Yankee manipulator, by the name of Swartwout (under Jackson's administration said to be robbing the till), and the famous German of the world, experienced physician and merchant, the Doctor Justus Erich Vollmann. Even before this period, the name Vollmann had become famous in its day, where he was the object of much speculation both in Europe and America.

Vollmann was born in 1769 in Hoya in the state of Hanover, where his parents lived in respectable but not very well-to-do conditions. Since the family was quite large, a near relative, city councilman Brauer, took him to Karlsruhe. Here the north German youth found a very pleasant life, where in addition to a strict law and order, a free spirit could thrive. Well prepared by prior scientific studies, he entered the university of Göttingen, where he earned a doctorate and gained a thorough knowledge of English language and literature. In the Fall of 1791 while in Mainz, he studied under the famous physician Hofmann, and the great anatomist Sömmering, and became well acquainted with the world sailor Forster, who was working there as a librarian and professor. Due to petty intrigues, which in such a small circle could arise quickly and be of great importance, his presence was no longer desired and he returned to Karlsruhe from Mainz. Furthermore, it was time for him to make his choice and seek out a life in the wide world. He went to Paris, which was very hospitable to German doctors. But he did not like the constant pressure there. To his cousin, the city councilwoman Brauer, he wrote after a few weeks: "The national assembly can in a short period of time be the object of praise, of ridicule, or of hatred. In general it is a raging gang, a large assemblage of passionate, scheming, selfish, ambitious people, among whom an honest person would be buried in idleness. There are plenty of aristocrats, even more democrats, and ocassionaly one could find two people who agree on something. There are as many types of democrats as there are modish colors. The smartest ones know how to suffer in silence. Many are democrats only out of stubbornness and despair. Some are truly taken with the idealistic beauty of the French constitution. They do not realize that it is only an ideal, like Plato's Republic.

Among the many acquaintances which he made in Paris, was Madame von Stael, Necker's daughter, the wife of the Swedish ambassador. She became the reason why he again left Paris in the Fall, to save her lover, the Minister of War, Narbonne, who was on the Jacobinite list of those to be executed on August 10. With a false passport under the name of a German by the name of Hirsch, Vollmann brought Narbonne to London. He was barely eight days in that world city, when the rich Narbonne sent him a legal document, in which he obligated himself and his heirs to pay to his benefactor 50 Louis d'ors for as long as he lived, to show gratitude for services rendered. But Vollmann returned it to him with the words, that he was not accustomed to profiting from such endeavors.

In London Vollmann sought entry into one of the offices of Pitt or Greenville, in order to start a political career. There he became acquainted with the famous countess de Laly Tolendal and princess d'Henin, both close friends of Lafayette. In their charge or at least through their urging on behalf of that third person, the venerable hero of two worlds, Vollmann traveled to Prussia. Tolendal had written a paper which clearly showed the innocence of that falsely arrested person, unjustly imprisoned in Germany. Vollmann was supposed to use some ruse to bring this document to the king in Berlin, lend his personal support for it with the ministers, sooth any misgivings, and set the affair in motion. But the attempt failed. For the prisoner was no longer in Prussian custody, but had been delivered into Austrian custody, since the Austrians had successfully argued that, during his trip from France, Lafayette had first encountered and had been detained by Austrian outposts, and then, just by accident, had been further escorted by Prussian troops. Lafayette was now an Austrian prisoner and was held in close custody in Ollmütz. The widespread sympathy for the prisoner, even in enemy countries and circles, so strengthened Vollmann's hopes, that he decided that, in some clever manner, he could successfully free Lafayette by force. He hurried back to London and Lafayette's eager friends. In some wondrous, secret manner, they had received urgent letters from the prisoner, who pleaded with them to attempt to free him. The most urgent requests to risk all and everything for Lafayette's sake arrived from the United States. With the American ambassador in London energetically directing the effort, anything that could be of assistance was considered. It was acknowledged that, in order to accomplish an escape by force, no one other than Vollmann had all the requirements needed for this desperate undertaking. Well supplied with recommendations and letters of credit, Vollmann again departed London for the continent in the summer of the year 1794 to carry out his daring plan. In Vienna he found a fitting helper and accomplice, Francis Hüger from South Carolina, who died just two years ago. In correspondence with the prisoner, arranged by a woman who brought him milk everyday, whose inventiveness and speed were perfectly genius, the prisoner was kept informed about the arrival of his benefactors. Since the next day had been selected for a walk which Lafayette had been permitted out of health reasons, it was chosen as a fitting occasion. The two met Lafayette somewhat far from the city, riding in an enclosed wagon, with a guard next to him, a soldier driving the coach, and another standing on the rear. In a moment the two jumped out, ordered the coachman to stop, and while Hüger dismounted to hold the horses ready for the escape, Vollmann also dismounted in order to help Lafayette mount. Upon the cries of his benefactors, the latter had opened the coach door and, along with his guard who was desperately hanging on, forced himself onto the road. Both lay wrestling on the ground. At that moment Vollmann sprang forward, freed Lafayette, and forcibly restrained his opponent whom he had disarmed. In the meantime, the other soldier had sprung from the coach and fled into the field, the other one in the driver's seat, having remained unnoticed, turned the coach around and raced back into the city. Vollmann had let his opponent go free who, now alone and without weapons, could do nothing else but race after the wagon. Thus stood the freed Lafayette with his two friends whom he had never seen before, on the open road, and it was imperative that all three to flee rapidly. Having been left alone during the fight the horses panicked, and one broke away. In this emergency, Lafayette's escape was the only goal. Vollmann gave him a few verbal instructions of what was most necessary, a slip of paper with written information, a purse with money, and ordered him to mount the remaining horse and continue on alone on the main road towards Silesia. But soon Lafayette went in the wrong direction and was arrested near Brauneisen, after his requests for directions put him under suspicion. A shop keeper recognized him while he was being led to the village magistrate. He was taken into close custody and returned to his earlier prison. For him this was the end of a daring and miraculously half successful undertaking. As is known, he remained another three years in prison when the Austrian government agreed to trade him for other prisoners held by the French republic.

Vollmann and Hüger were separated and each was thrown into a dark dungeon. Initially they were sentenced to 14 years imprisonment, but, at the urging of a Russian nobleman, and, after the government was convinced that the garrison at Ollmütz had not participated in the conspiracy, they were released after 7 months. Vollmann soon thereafter went to the United States and established a business in Philadelphia. Lafayette's countless friends soon joined him and promoted his business to be a great success. He soon achieved great respect and welfare, and lived treasured and loved among his new fellow citizens, in whose midst he was also held at home by the hand of a lovely wife. A happy marriage gave him two daughters. His circle of influence continuously widened; he made long trips through the entire breadth of the United States, through the Ohio Valley, to the furthest mountains beyond the lakes.

It must be obvious just how important the support of such a man could be for Aaron Burr. That Vollmann, who, as a Federalist and an enemy of revolutionary intrigues, would knowingly dedicate himself to the cause of a political opponent, would argue against the assumption that he had joined a highly treasonous project. A number of the boats which Vollmann's companions were taking from Blannerhasset's island to Fort Massac were stopped and searched at Cincinnati. On June 18, 1805, Major Ziegler had resigned the office of Federal Marshal for Ohio, which he had held since the beginning of Jefferson's administration.

Vollman's subsequent arrest was reported in the Cincinnati Gazette of January 22, 1807, enclosed in large boxed letters in a story by Senator Jeremiah Morrow, who, later as the Governor of Ohio, welcomed Lafayette to Cincinnati. It read, "Today Doctor Erich Vollmann and Swartwout were taken to Washington under heavy military guard and lodged in the navy base. Everyone is interested in the outcome of the trial."

But events did not progress that far. Vollmann was freed when the case against Burr was thrown out. The shining role which our hero later assumed in Austria in 1814, during a daring endeavor to restore the shaken Austrian financial system, lies outside the limits of our story. He died in Kingston, Jamaica in 1821 while the director of the Baring Company. Just a few years ago, both of his daughters, Caroline and Elizabeth lived happily in that country.

The Burr episode had barely passed when Cincinnati's population was again shaken by a sensation and consternation by an alleged new traitorous act in their midst. For eastern newspapers had namely spread the story that the famous General Moreau, who at the urging of his rival Napoleon, had been banned from France, was traveling through the west to measure the attitude of various individuals and seek their help in stirring up the area against the Federal Government. It took a while for the people to digest the news that the victor of Hohenlinden, who was living quietly on his farm in Morrisville, not far from Philadelphia, was thinking of nothing less that treason against the country which had granted him asylum.

In addition to those named above, the first German settlers and property owners of Cincinnati were Martin Baum, Ludwig Lang, Eduard Stall, Georg Strohhuber, Franz Kebsheimer, Fried. Höflich, Andreas Boden, Jakob Kautz, August Erich, Mich. Hahn, Friedrich Alter, Heinrich Hafer, Caspar Fahs, Fried. Fegekorn, David Muselmann, Heinrich Bechtle, Robert Bohl, Christoph Ehrenfeiht, Heinrich Seiz, Georg Leibin, Wilh. Tilly, Fried. W. Beinbrecht, Georg Juppenlatz, Peter Knöpfly and others. Their family life does not appear to be totally pure, as the following announcement in the "Spy" indicates:

"The year 1800 has arrived and I herewith
warn everyone against loaning anything to
my wife Susanne, since I am not responsible for it.

Andreas Westfahl."

Evidently someone else wanted to begin the new century with a new page in his life.
Several weeks later, the following appeared in the advertisement section of the "Spy" under the heading of "Something Special":

"Everyone should note that my wife Elizabeth
Hildebrand has left my table and is living
with a certain Jakob Grimm, against which I
warn everyone.

Lorenz Hildebrand."

During this early republican period, Germans appear to have participated in politics. In the Fall of 1805, during a convention of delegates which took place in Pittman's Hall, Adrian Hagemann was named to the ticket with Governor Edward Tiffin to represent Hamilton County. During the presidential election of the preceding year, all of Ohio had barely produced more electoral votes than are currently counted in the German 12th Ward.

Judge Burnet contends that President Adams' administration found general approval among the citizens of Cincinnati; that in 1800, only 9 voted for Jefferson, including Major Ziegler. In contrast, the Aaron Burr conspiracy caused quite a bit of ill will and John Smith, representative from Hamilton County and a long-time acquaintance of Burr's, saw his political career closed, because he had sheltered the leader of the conspiracy in his home.

Chapter 24

German Boatsmen on the Ohio. - Michel Fink. - Martin Baum. - Settlement of the State of Ohio. - German Pioneers in the Various Counties. - The First German Newspaper.

In the primitive period between the beginning of trade and travel on the Ohio and Mississippi and the introduction of steam navigation, a race of men appeared on these peaceful waters with unique ways and customs. It was the former Indian fighters, who, after the return of peace, could not give up their natural wandering life, refugees from the civilized classes of society, who found a special attraction in the adventurous life of the boatsmen. This class of original profiteers increased on the Ohio, after Louisiana, ceded by France to Spain in the secret Treaty of St. Ildefonso in 1800, had been sold in 1803 to the United States and the products of the Ohio Valley now had an unhindered outlet to New Orleans and to the French plantations.

Among the most famous of these boatsmen, who brought to the Mississippi the newly won treasures of culture, Michel Fink stands out above all. Even today there is practically no location between Pittsburg and New Orleans, where he did not play a significant role in local traditions. Michel was born in 1780 in Allegheny County, Pennsylvania, and just his initial adventures in the small city of Pittsburg would fill a book with wildly romantic tales which illustrate the bloody nature of the Indian wars. As a young lad, Michel Fink, like Wetzel and others, had joined a group of scouts who fought the Indians in their own manner and who were just as happy over the victorious taking of a scalp as were their wild enemies. During these bloody and desperate skirmishes in the forest, Fink developed admirable courage and brought his bodily strength and abilities to fruition, which made him so famous as a boatsman. No one was a better marksman than he. Once when he was passing by Wheeling on his flatboat, he spotted a Negro approaching the shore, a tin pot on his head, happily singing a song. Even though the distance from the boat was not inconsiderable, Michel shot the tin pot from the head of the deathly terrified singer. And to entertain the boatsmen, he would often shoot a tin cup off his brother Albert's head from 30 paces. One time his bullet cut off the shoe sole of a negro swinging on a gate in Louisiana. Morgan Neville and Hiram Kaine poetically glorified Fink's deeds and adventures on the western waters.

One of the most experienced boatsmen on the Ohio and Mississippi was the elder Wittmer from Lancaster. Judge Symmes had originally offered to sell to him the land on which Cincinnati stands for $1.25, before Denman bought it. The judge's constant bragging about the land just made the old boatsman even cautious, and he preferred to buy a farm near Buffalo, where he died several years ago.

Another German by birth, who was very active in the Ohio Valley river trade with New Orleans was Vincent Nolte, who later settled as a merchant in this city. A depiction of his experiences was published in English and in German. During the course of a long life, Nolte gained riches, lost them through changing fortunes, undertook extremely long journeys, and tried just about everything possible. He had built a fleet of flat and keel boats on the Ohio and was present when Robert Fulton launched his first steam boat; he was one of the richest and most respected merchants in North America and for a time was in the debtors' tower in London; he had concluded contracts with Napoleon involving enormous loans and done the same with Indian chiefs concerning possible trade. He arranged a loan for the Pope in Rome, and on another occasion translated some documents for the monks of San Lorenzo just to stay alive. At one time he was an army supplier and at another time published a small newspaper in Hamburg, he had millions in his hands, was in contact with all the significant business houses of the world, and wrote articles for American newspapers to earn his bread.

The first improvement in navigation of the Ohio was the replacement of the flat and keel boats with sailing barges. Martin Baum and Heinrich Bechtle were the first to introduce them in Cincinnati. During the years of 1807-17, their ships made two trips annually to New Orleans. The industrious Baum stood out ahead of all the citizens, whose patriotism and desire for the public welfare brought Cincinnati's growth to fruition. When Joel Williams, who had purchased Denman's property, had, under false pretenses, gained control of the landing place between Broadway and Main, Front Street and the River, and had already begun to erect a brick building on it, he (Baum) raised funds to defend the city's right to this property and headed it with success. In the memoirs of Doctor Daniel Drake, Ed. D. Mansfield notes about Baum: "One of the first merchants and community-minded citizens of this region was Martin Baum. He was born in Germany and started a business in Cincinnati prior to the year 1800. For 30 years he was in business and in the trades and during the entire time established a reputation for honesty and administrative talent. He was president of the City Council and of the Miami Export Company, which was founded in 1803 for the purpose, when, during a period of recession, farm products were not worth the cost of getting them to distant markets. He collected the best agricultural products from the farmers and brought them to New Orleans on his own vessels. In addition, Baum was a co-founder of the Western Museum, the Society for the Arts, and one of the original landowners of Toledo."

The city soon thrived through 3 different streams of immigrants. As in all the larger cities, so too settled New Englanders in the so-called Western Reserve; in the central counties and the Miami lands were immigrants from New Jersey, Pennsylvania, Germany and Ireland. Kentuckians and Virginians, intermixed with Germans, preferred to own the stretches on the Scioto, the Muskingum and upper Miami.

In 1797, in exchange for a grant from Congress of three stretches of land on the Hockhocking, Ebenezer Zane opened a road through the wilderness between Wheeling and Maysville which passed through Lancaster. For the longest time, this military road constituted the only connection between the eastern states and Kentucky. Zane also laid out Lancaster; he named it in honor of the Pennsylvania-German farmers, who had settled there and came mostly from Lancaster in Pennsylvania. Initially the town was called New Lancaster but did not thrive, since many of the settlers seemed to be incorrigible drunkards. Since there was no civil code, the sober ones among the settlers banded together and ordered that, from then on, anyone seen drunk on the streets, would have to dig out a tree stump, of which there were still many, or receive 12 lashes on the back. The delinquent was given the choice of punishment. "After several penalties were given out," says the chronicle of Lancaster, "everyone became sober and happy." Here in Lancaster (1807) appeared the first German newspaper in the State of Ohio, "The Lancaster Eagle," naturally written in the gibberish of the Pennsylvania German country newspapers.

Perry County, named after Commodore Perry, and bordering Fairfield County, was first settled in 1802-03 mostly by the Germans, Daniel Scherer, Peter Obermeyer, W. and J. Dusenberg and others. Johann Fink erected there the first blockhouse. In Pickaway County, Daniel Driesbach was among the first settlers on the land of Jäger and Watt near Circleville; in Fayette County Peter Eimann. This latter area was initially built up mostly by Kentuckians and Virginians. Among the former was a family of German descent by the name of Funk, widely known for their nefarious deeds. All the men, from the old man Adam to the youngest son Absalon were of gigantic stature, excellent marksmen, wild fighters and ruthless in the use of the hunting knife. One of the sons, Jakob, was arrested in Kentucky for passing counterfeit bank notes. His friend Trumbo paid his bail. But when he did not appear for the opening of his trial, Trumbo, with several dozen of his friends, all well armed, set out to take Jakob by force and bring him back to the authorities in Kentucky, to avoid losing the bail money. The Funks had heard the news of the impending attack by their former friends and prepared to resist. The doors of the blockhouse were barricaded; the old man took his seat at an old table in the middle of the room, musket in hand, in order to give orders to his sons, all of whom were armed with knives and pistols. When Trumbo and his friends appeared before the house, he ordered them in a hoarse voice to leave; they, however, were not afraid, forced the door and crowded into the room. One Kentuckian by the name of Wilson grabbed Jakob, and the shooting now began on both sides. Wilson and Absalon fell mortally wounded. Jakob had grabbed Trumbo and was about to stick his knife through his throat, when old Adam cried, "Let him live, his father once saved my life from an Indian." Thus Trumbo was released and his friends were glad to get away with their skin intact. The old blockhouse where this battle took place stands today, with bullet holes as reminders, on the east fork of Paint Creek, about 8 miles from the county seat of Washington. All of the Funks were well known lovers of whiskey. One day, old Adam was with several of his friends in a neighboring pub where numerous glasses were downed to quench their thirst. Upon leaving, the patriarch wanted to take a gallon of whiskey along home, but there was no container on hand to be found, not even a wash basin. Then Adam spotted a grazing pig. He bought it for a dollar and skinned it. After plugging up the holes, he poured the whiskey into it and returned home with his friends, where they all became totally drunk on the contents of the pigskin. Thus was one of the joys of the life in the forest.

The central county of Franklin was formed from Ross (County) on April 30, 1803, and named after Benjamin Franklin. On the site where Columbus now stands, was a Wyandot city with extensive corn fields. Here a famous chief, Leatherlings by name, was accused of sorcery by Prophet, Tecumseh's brother, and murdered with tomahawks. The initial settlement in the county took place in 1797. The Dierdorf and Selz Brothers, Johann Grob, Johann Dill, Jakob Obertür, were among the first builders. Franklinton, across from Columbus, was the first city to be built in the Scioto Valley north of Chillicothe. And many Germans also settled in Licking (County), formed out of Fairfield (County) on March 1, 1808, and named after its main river. Its capital city of Newark was laid out according to the plan of General Wm. C. Schenck. In Columbiana, Jefferson and Washington, formed on May 25, 1803, at least one third of the settlers were of German origin.

In the northwest sector stood numerous Swiss huts, surrounded by hops and vines, which can still be seen to this day. The name Columbiana is a strange combination of a pioneer fantasy of Columbia and Anna. When the legislative permission was in process, one member proposed that his wife's name of Maria be added, so that the county would in the future thus be called Columbianamaria. But when another member wanted to add the name Elizabeth, the whole addition was defeated with wild laughter.

Probably the first settler in Clermont County was Jakob Ulry, who settled in Bethel in 1798, and who, like their arch enemy Wetzel, was hated and feared by the Indians. In the same year, the only building between Lancaster and Wheeling was at Zanesville. Georg Beymer, a German newcomer from Somerset, PA., maintained here an inn and a ferry. Eight miles away, his brother Simon Beymer laid out the village of Washington.

In 1880, German immigrants were already streaming into today's Harrison County (formed on January 1, 1814, from Jefferson and Tuscararas). Jakob Haberfeld, Jakob Scheppler, Michael Wachsler, and the brothers Johann, Joseph and Eilhelm Hoff were named among the first pioneers. The latter was a famous hunter and Indian fighter. After the peace of Greenville, one Indian was boasting in a tavern in his presence that, in his life, he had scalped over 50 whites. That evening the Indian started on his way back to his wigwam, which he would never reach. The next day someone found his body, with a bullet through the brain. When the neighbors started to surmise about the murder, Hoff, with a nonchalant expression for everyone to see, said that he had seen the Indian sitting next to a tree trunk, a pipe in his mouth; he looked him straight in the eye and thought about his boasting about scalping so many whites. Suddenly the pipe fell out of the redskin's mouth, and when he went over to him, he was already bent over in the throes of death. Also in Jefferson County, founded upon St. Clair's proclamation on July 29, 1797, many Germans settled, mainly in the area around Steubenville. The former Mingo village, Logan's home, lay three miles below the city, with which many historical occurrences were connected. Here, Logan's father, mother and sister were murdered by Virginia frontiersmen; only the child of the latter was spared because his father was a white man, Colonel George Gibson of Carlisle, PA. Here lived the avengers of those murdered, who, near the Scioto, seized Cressap's brother, the Cayugas' murderer (see page 62), and beat him to death. Here, Williamson and Crawford assembled their murderous gangs for the destruction of the German cities. In Hocking County, the first settler was Christian Westenhöfer. Among one of the most practical of farmers, he arrived in 1798 and left behind an army of descendants. In Highland, one of the first planters known was Bernhard Meyer, the discoverer of the famous rock cave in Virginia; in Holmes (County), Jonas Korn; in Knox (County), Kreuzer, Glick, Welker, and Hauk; in Logan (County), Körner. In the latter county can be found the grave of the famous Simon Kenton. Next to him lies the German pioneer, Salomon Praetor. Among the first settlers of Miami County was Johann Knoop. In the Spring of 1797, he came down the Ohio to Cincinnati and cultivated the first harvest on David Ziegler's so-called "Stonehouse Farm," 4 miles above Cincinnati. During the summer of 1797, as an assistant on a surveying trip, he made a journey through Indian territory, using the opportunity to select the land which he settled in 1798. The first apple tree in the county, grown from a seedling by his wife, still stands in the yard of the family holdings. In that same year, the first white child was born in Miami County, Jakob, Knoop's son. Here was established the "German Station," built by the German settlers for protection against the Indians. In addition, among the first settlers in Montgomery County were many of German origin, for example Gunkel, Emerich and Schaeffer[1]; similarly, Butler County, formed in 1803 from Hamilton (County) was named after General Richard Butler who fell during St. Clair's defeat. Isreal Ludlow laid out the capital city, Hamilton, on December 17, 1794; the town was originally called Fairfield. The first settlers were from Chillicothe, discharged soldiers and camp followers, a debauched rabble, who spent their time drinking, dancing, gambling and fighting; even the judges and lawyers often participated in the drinking bouts and brawling, and carried away colorful reminders of the fighting. The strict Themis often wore a dunce's cap. The natural humor made itself known even during court proceedings. It is said that, in the absence of a Bible, Arthur St. Clair, the governor's son, as district attorney, once swore in all witnesses using "A Thousand and One Arabian Nights." Normally, the Ohio county courts, convened in taverns. The stalls were used as a jail. On one occasion, a judge reprimanded two young lawyers, who were involved in a personal dispute. That really tickled one young, Herculean woodsman dressed in a flannel smock, who was leaning against the bar, and he called out in a loud voice to the judge who was squinting with one eye: "Give it to 'em, old Squint Eye!" "Whose is that?" thundered the judge. The woodsman then rose up to his full height and yelled, "here, it's the old plug horse!" Without letting himself become excited, the judge ordered the Sheriff: "Sheriff, take that old plug horse out to the stall and see to it that he's not stolen before tomorrow."

The first court in Butler County convened in Torrence's inn, later in H.S. Ehrhardt's house.

In April 1801, a society whose agent was John Reilly founded Rossville. Middletown was laid out in 1802 by Stephan Bail and James Sutton. Dierdorf's mill was the first in the neighborhood. In that year (1802), the *Western Agriculturist* reports that a hunter by the name of Keenes shot the last buffalo in the state of Ohio at the head of Symmes Creek. Thus it took 62 years for this wild animal to be exterminated in Ohio. The paths which the buffalo took on their journeys to and from the salt licks in Jackson County can still be seen and appear to be well-used wagon trails, which lead across hills, valleys and rivers.

---

[1] Germantown, named after the city in Pennsylvania, was laid out by Philipp Gunkel in 1814.

Chapter 25

Zeisberger's Return to Ohio. - A Moravian Settlement in Indiana. - Fiery Death of a German Mohican. - The End of Zeisberger and Ziegler. - The Earthquake of 1811. - Growth of Cincinnati. - The War of 1812. - Introduction of Steam Navigation. - German Arrivals in Cincinnati. - The First German Congregation.

With his sorely tested flock, which we left while on their wanderings towards Michigan, Zeisberger again appears in the Chronicle of the Ohio Valley. On July 20, 1782, the patriarch had founded a new settlement in Michigan and gave it the name of New Gnadenhütten in memory of the massacre site on the Muskingum. But soon hunger and the hostility of the Chippewas again drove the congregation away from there and the poor souls wandered aimlessly between the Walhonding and the Huron. But the Continental Congress acted generously on behalf of the martyrs of culture. The American people had almost unanimously condemned the terrible deeds of Williamson and his gang and, pressed by the general outrage of the national conscience, granted to the refugees the stretch of land they had once occupied on the Muskingum. Charles Thomson, Secretary of Congress, wrote Bishop Ettwein that he would be very pleased were he to become the tool to save the precious remains of the German Indian congregations and see to their continued undisturbed welfare. He turned the affair over to James White, Indian Agent for Southern Ohio, as well as to Richard Butler, Indian Agent in the northern district, where the land grant lay. But in spite of this support from the government, Zeisberger did not dare return to his beloved Muskingum. The frontier settlers threatened to murder any Indian who arrived there; the former hatred had continued and found new roots. Therefore, Zeisberger founded the settlements of Pilgrims Rest (*Pilgerruh*) and New Salem on the Huron River, below Milan, a scenic area surrounded by the remains of earlier races, artificial mounds, palisades, as well as circular and four-cornered bastions. But the heathen Indians again drove the congregation back to upper Canada, where the tireless patriarch founded Fairfield on the Thames River.

In 1797, General Rufus Putnam, the Federal Surveyor, laid out the land granted to the Moravian congregation in three areas of approximately 4,000 acres each; they included the earlier cities of Gnadenhütten, Salem and Schönbrunn. Heckewelder and Benjamin Mortimer were sent by the Directorate of the Society in Bethlehem to bring this news to the congregation in Fairfield. In October, Zeisberger returned with a number of disciples to the Muskingum and, on the Schönbrunn grant, founded the village of Goshen 7 miles from Gnadenhütten. Unfortunately he would soon be visited by the former difficulties. In spite of the Treaty of Greenville, monstrous whites continued to murder peaceful Indians; for example, among others an entire camp on the Scioto, where not even women and children were spared. Even Thomas White Eye, son of that treasured friend of the German cities, who was reared and attended Princeton College in New Jersey at the cost of the Federal Government, was murdered by the beasts. Whiskey dealers attempted to demoralize the inhabitants of Goshen until Zeisberger finally traveled to Cincinnati and got the legislature to forbid the sale of alcoholic drinks on Indian land.

The Delawares on the White River (an arm of the Wabash) had often invited the German Indians and their teachers to establish a settlement on their land. Therefore, in 1801 the preachers Natuge and Luckenbach were sent by Bethleham with three well-educated Indian families from Goshen, including Joshua, the musical director of the community. The mission did not succeed. For among the Shawnees, the prophet Tecumseh, who was planning a new crusade against the whites, arose against them. He told the Indians that the whites were sending sorcerers of their own blood among the tribes, in order to turn them away from the warlike customs and religion of their forefathers, and then deliver them as slaves to the whites; he, however, had the task of driving out these usurpers, and it was the duty of the tribes to burn them to ashes at the stake. The Indians went in droves to hear the speeches of the wandering prophet in order to discover who were the traitors to their nation. While listening to his words, he often accused several of being sorcerers, who in turn were seized and burned on the spot. Among these was Tatapaschkse, Chief of the Delaware Turtle clan, who had signed the Treaty of Greenville as a representative of the nation. He was taken from his village, where the meeting had occurred, brought to the German mission, and burned near there. When the gruesome scene was done, the executioners forced their way into the houses of the missionaries, let themselves be well fed and inquired as to the music director Joshua. However, he had departed the day before, and the Luckenbach family, where he was staying, were greatly concerned about his fate. And rightly so, for the poor soul had ended his life on that same day on the pile of wood. The savages had erected their Auto da Fe right in front of the village of the German Indians, in order to distract them from Joshua until it was too late to come to his rescue. The unfortunate Mohican had sung German hymns on the pile of wood until his strength ceased and death brought an end to his pain. His family belonged to the first and truest disciples of the Moravian religion. Joshua's father was the first native baptized in 1742 by Zinsendorf himself in Bethlehem. From his early youth Joshua had lived with his German teachers; he spoke and wrote fluent German and English and was an expert smith, carpenter and instrument maker. As the community's musical director he also played the organ. The hardest blow which fell upon him in life was the murder of his beloved children, two daughters, by Williamson's murderous gang. In his later years he often spilled the bitterest of tears. He was 85 years old when he was burned at the stake. Since the missionaries had no hope for success in their efforts, they departed the settlement in 1806 and returned to Bethlehem.

On November 17, 1808, the venerable David Zeisberger, founder of the cities of the Ohio Valley, died at Goshen. His colleague, Benjamin Mortimer, wrote the following obituary for the "Pittsburg Gazette" as taken from the "American Register" Vol. V, Part 1, for 1809:

The senior missionary of the United Brethren among the Indians, the honorable Zeisberger, died today at the age of 87 years and 7 months. He was born in Moravia on April 11, 1721 and in his early youth went with his parents to Herrenhut in the Oberlausitz. In 1738 he arrived in the United States, that is in Georgia, at a time when the United Brethren were preaching the Bible to the Creek Indians. From there he moved to Pennsylvania and actively assisted in the founding of the settlements of Bethlehem and Nazareth. Since 1746, a period of 62 years, he lived, except for a few short intervals, among the Indians and spoke several of their languages with masterful fluency.

Zeisberger possessed a daring, active, enterprising spirit, dependability during adversity and danger, and sound judgement in determining the best means to overcome them. Countless were the indescribable exertions and privations which he endured during his long life among the Indians. He was often subjected to the bitterest persecution and exposed to mortal danger. Yet none of this could deter him for even a moment, but rather merely increased his resolve. He often experienced the satisfaction of baptizing converts, who just a short time before had raised a murder weapon against him. With a cheerful calmness and trust in God, he always finished the task given to him. At the same time, he was blessed with the most unpretentious humility; he always thought about himself last; a general love for his neighbor filled his heart. He was the most devoted husband, a true, always dependable friend; every aspect of his character showed him to be a sincere, concerned, venerable soul. On the evening of the day when his mental strength began to waver, he was prepared for his journey home with quiet determination. "Lord, take my soul to you!" were his last words. A respectful group accompanied his body to the grave. For the benefit of the various listeners, the funeral service was held in the German, English and Delaware languages. The venerable soul did not concern himself with earthly goods. The Onandago (one of the languages of the Six Nations) and Delaware language, and several other related languages he spoke very fluently. In 1768, he wrote two grammar books about the former language, in German and in English, and an extensive dictionary (German and Indian) containing over 1700 pages. In the year 1776 he published his first edition of a spelling book in the Delaware language, of which a second, improved edition appeared in 1806. Two of his other works were sermons for children and a song book, which in its 360 pages contained more than 500 songs translated from German and English, and which is used in the Brethren congregations. In manuscript form he left a grammar of the Delaware language written in German, which P.S. Duponceau, Esq., translated in Philadelphia into English for the American Historical Society, as well as a translation of the Psalms and Bible into the Delaware language."

Noteworthy is the advanced age which all of these Ohio valley pilgrims attained. Bernhard Adam Grube died in Bethlehem in 1808, age 93 years and 3 months. Johann Georg Jungmann in July of the same year age 88 years and 3 months. Gottlob Sensemann died in 1800 in Fairfield, 87 years old. Johann Heckewelder on January 31, 1823 in Bethleham, age 79 years and 11 months.

In 1806, Cincinnati was still a small dirty village. But that year began a growth in population, commercial success and the professions, which has not been bettered in the history of the country. In 1810, Dr. Drake, a local physician and scholar, published an amazing pamphlet entitled: "Information about Cincinnati, its Topography, Climate and Diseases." Five years later appeared his "Picture of Cincinnati and the Miami Country." In it the doctor prophesied that in 1820 the state of Ohio would contain a population of 492,000 souls, and since this was hard to believe, he gives as basis for his assumptions the richness of the soil, the prohibition of slavery and the enormous expansion and the cheap prices for the state lands. Drake's prophecy was more than confirmed. For in 1820 Ohio already counted 580,000 souls, thus 100,000 more than the doctor had prophesied.

In the year 1810 the city counted 388 buildings, mostly frame houses, with 2400 inhabitants. At that time, Pittsburg had 4768 and New Orleans 17,242 inhabitants. Elmore Williams had the first brick house and the first cellar, on the south west corner of Main and 5th street, constructed in 1795.

On September 24 of the year 1811 our German hero David Ziegler died at home. The "Western Spy" printed this news in a necrology surrounded with a black field, which ended in the following manner:

"An unpleasant experience at the time caused the Major's departure from the army. Having returned to private life, he settled in our midst, where, in the profession of a merchant he operated a successful business, until a sickness forced him to give it up several months before his death. Thus America lost another of its revolutionary officers, who was a good husband, a true neighbor, and an honorable man to the fullest extent of the word."

The federalist "Liberty Hall," Ziegler's political opponent, also agreed to publish this necrology.

"At the time of his death, Ziegler held the municipal post of Cincinnati Harbor Collector and the state office as Adjutant in the Ohio militia. The funeral procession was very interesting and was described as follows in the 'Spy': "Last Thursday the body was buried with military honors. During the procession, which was unusually large, the Harmony Society played various wind instruments. On both sides of the procession walked the major's comrades in arms, Captain Torrence, Major Ruffin, General Gano, Captain Carr, Major Stanley and Colonel Riddle. Following the coffin, and led by a soldier, the major's horse with saddle holster and pistols, the clergy and physicians. Then came the military; the infantry under command of Captain Mansfield, the artillery under command of Captain Jenkinson, the cavalry under command of Captain Sloan with reversed weapons. Then came the carriages of the mourners, militia officers and citizens."

On the following 6th of October, the Reverend Joshua L. Wilson gave an eloquent speech on the hero's death before a packed auditorium in the Presbyterian church, in whose church yard (Ziegler) was buried.

According to his will, which was probated in the Hamilton County Probate Court, Ziegler died a very wealthy man. To his sister, Mrs. Susanna Elizabeth Detrosch, he instructed the Ohio Secretary of State to pay $3,000. He also remembered his nephews and nieces. One of the former, Mr. Joseph Pierce, the executor of his estate, received, in addition to the sum of $500, the major's gold watch and iron chest, the seal and diploma of the Order of the Cincinnati and all accompanying privileges. Another nephew, Charles R. Green, received $500, Ziegler's sword and walking stick with a golden stud; each of his four nieces $500. To his wife, Lucy Anna, fell the elegant house, 7 lots in the city, west of Broadway, 30 acres of wood lands, a mill with a half section of land on Greenville Creek, in the then Miami county, 2 shares from the Ohio Land Company, a farm in Columbia, his capital and stocks in the Miami Exporting Company and in the Bank of Pennsylvania in Philadelphia. Mrs. Ziegler is also pictured as a very generous lady; in 1823 she remained Treasurer of the Dorcas Society to support the poor and then moved to Dayton where she died.

Since the death of the former soldier, more than one generation has followed him to the grave; from this unknown spot in the world, a capital city, the Queen of the West, arose, in which every third person was a countryman of Ziegler's. After the former churchyard of the Presbyterian church yielded to the pressures of trade and the professions, a result of the vastly improved conditions, the overturned gravestone of the hero was discovered under the refuse and bushes. The short biographical inscription resurrected the merits of the departed back into the thoughts of a new world. In 1844, the numerous German military companies accompanied the ashes of first German pioneer when they were moved to a new and final resting place.

On December 16, 1811, a terrible earthquake, centered in New Madrid, on the Mississippi, occurred in the Ohio Valley. Even though Cincinnati was 400 miles distant, the houses moved and shook like ships at sea, and many chimneys collapsed. The shaking continued for several days, accompanied by terrible, continuous underground thunder. Many families packed their valuables and hurried to leave their houses, since they believed that the earth would open and swallow the entire city. The first steamboat on the waters of the Ohio, built in that year by Captain Rosefeld in Pittsburg, during a trip to New Orleans, came upon this earthquake and was just able to avoid being stranded and wrecked by the high, stormy waves of the Mississippi. During this year, complaints against Great Britain had increased, which in 1812 led to the new war with that power, and to a significant disruption of American trade by the blockade system, the forcing of American seamen into British naval service and the agitation of the western Indians in connection with the plan to destroy the Union, led by Ambassador Henry. Just the year before, Tecumseh, at the head of the Shawnees, rose against the Americans under the pretense that the 1809 land purchase treaty of Fort Wayne with the Delawares, Miamis and other tribes, was unjust and illegal. The battle in the swamp at Tippecanoe (fought on November 7, 1811) brought a massive setback to the Shawnee chief and caused him to throw himself completely into the arms of the British perpetrators. Upon the outbreak of the war, Governor Hull of the Michigan Territory was given command of the American troops for a campaign against upper and lower Canada. To support this campaign Ohio supplied two regiments, which, before their departure, were concentrated in a camp in Urbana county. Among the staff officers of Col. McCarthur's regiment was Adjutant Wilhelm Heinrich Puthoff, a highly competent soldier, brave, energetic, and punctual in carrying out his duties. Daniel Womeldorf led a mounted squadron to the camp from Gallia county. In addition, the already noted Simon Beymer from Guernsey county appeared as the captain of a company. Gen. Findley, one of the pioneers of Cincinnati, commanded the Miami area regiment. Several companies were formed by Cincinnati volunteers. The entire population was moved to accompany the "Conquering Army of Canada" upon its departure from the city. The bright sky, the warm June sun were no warmer and brighter than the expectations and hopes of the people in regards to the success of this campaign, which was to suffer such a shameful end.

For in mid-August of this year, because of Hull's military incompetency, the entire Northwest, with the exception of two forts, fell into the power of the English and the Miami Indians. The 1,400 man strong American army, which had been sent out to conquer Canada, surrendered without a shot to 700 English soldiers and Canadians. It was Brigadier General of the Militia E. Munger from Dayton, who, through a letter to Gen. John Gano, sent this sad news to the city and therewith mobilized out the militia. A great excitement was brought by the news that the German merchant, Jacob Gerhard Koch, in Baltimore, had offered to the penniless and creditless government a loan of half a million dollars and at the same time declared himself ready to buy and equip a warship. His example awakened a slumbering patriotism which performed many heroic deeds and fought numerous noteable battles at sea and on land. Strangely enough, it was also given to the only German general in the United States army the task of informing the country about the expulsion from the US army of General Hull, who was sentenced to death for his surrender. The "Cincinnati Gazette" carried the following notice about that:

"Order from the General Office of the Adjutant and Inspector-General. The rolls of the army are no longer dishonored; it no longer contains the name of Brigadier General William Hull. The general court martial is herewith absolved. Upon the order of

J. B. Walbach, General Adjutant.

Washington, April 15, 1814.

In 1782, Walbach joined the French army under Louis XVI. After his capture, he left the service and until the year 1785 remained under the Kaiser's flags on the Rhine and in the Netherlands, where he covered the retreat of the Duke of York at the battle of Dunkirk. In 1795, Walbach sailed to Domingo where, eight years later, he left the foreign service and went to the United States, in order to visit his father. In the year 1793 he joined McPherson's Volunteers. Soon thereafter he was artillery adjutant and remained in federal service where he attained the rank of general. Several years ago, Walbach died at an advanced age in Baltimore while commandant of Fort Henry.

While the east suffered a serious depression as a result of the break with England, at the same time the break caused the settlement of the west and brought about large expenditures to the army and contractors, who as a result even more rapidly helped to develop the natural riches and resources of this segment of the country. But the most important event which suddenly raised Cincinnati to be the capital of the west, was the introduction of steam navigation on the Ohio, in which Captain Shreve played such an outstanding role. The huge mass of the states on the Ohio now appeared on the world market as a competitor to the older, less productive regions of the east. Its natural central point, Cincinnati, therefore received a massive push into a gigantic arena of commerce and manufacturing, to which it has now grown.

It is no wonder that the east now looks with envious eyes at its new competitor, which has begun to greatly reduce the east's economic and commercial realm. Dr. Drake complained in his statistical work, "Cincinnati in 1815," which appeared then that, in particular, the business barons of New England unabashedly tried to stem the loss of competent craftsmen and farmers much in the same manner that the Tory barons tried to stem the immigration to America. Among others, someone tried to prevent a house painter from immigrating to Cincinnati with the story that he would have to wait half a year before he would have a house to paint, and that he would then be paid in potatoes.

Among the German newcomers in Cincinnati during this period, the bakers were the most represented. Among those was Abraham Böbinger, who built the first brick building on the north side of Middle Market, which is now Hart's shoe store, wherein he operated a tavern along with his bakery; A. Hafer, Georg Juppenlatz, J. N. Grüner, Jakob Fabler, Martin Benninger and August Eiteljörg. And even the German pioneer who passed away in 1861, A. H. Ernst, the founder of the Horticultural Society, which was well known for developing the growing of flowers and fruit, worked at the baking ovens. Originally from Böringen in Hanover, he arrived here in 1807 with his father, Johann Zacharias, who likewise died in 1821. The first confectioners were also Germans, August Zeumer, also known as a passionate hunter, who had his confectioner's shop in the Columbia Hotel on Lower Market, where the theater was located, and John Meyers, known for his constant help to any of his countrymen, and through the cultivation of any worthy German undertaking, was called the father of the then German community. Right behind the bakers came the gardeners. In the "Gazette" of November 28, 1815, Jonathan Stäbler advertised himself as a German gardener and, from his shop near the new market hall, offered seedlings for sale. Later, he arranged Longworth's gardens and thereby earned $500. For that job, Longworth had offered him two acres of land, where the flea market now stands. But Jonathan's wife felt that, with that amount of money, one could buy an entire farm, and urged him to refuse the offer. At her urging, Stäbler bought a farm in a neighboring county, which today is worth several thousands, while the flea market property is worth hundreds of thousands. On the corner of 3rd and Broadway was Hechinger's vegetable garden, while Gode's was on Deer Creek. On 12th and Vine Street leading to the hills, were the vegetable fields of Licht, Danzer, Link's tavern, Dannheimer and others. The centers of amusement and promenades were at that time restricted to the lower parts of the city. The Columbia Garden, the mound and the river bank were the gathering points for the fun seekers on foot, since in entire Cincinnati there were only two coaches. Following the bakers came the meat cutters with Jakob Waltenrath, Jonas Hecker, and John

Reiß at the head. Among the mercantile firms, the German Bühring and Breuning, was already known in 1816.

The Germans can certainly claim to have brought local music to an advanced state, but they were not the first pioneers; for in 1816 the Americans had already formed a music club under the name of the "St. Cecilia Society," and from a report from the same year in the Boston Courier, we know that there were dozens of pianos here, but no tuner, even though the piano teacher, Adolph Wupper, advertised himself as such in the Gazette of December 18, 1815. The second music club was the "Apollonian Society" which held its meetings in the salon of the baker, Georg Juppenlatz.

The initial German clubs in Cincinnati were religious. Already in 1810, the Methodist preacher Behm held a German language prayer service in the schoolhouse. The first appeal to form a German Catholic congregation occurred on December 11, 1811. The meeting was called together in the home of Jakob Fabler, but nothing came of it. At the beginning of 1814, Dr. Dreher preached the teachings of the United Brethren in Christ in front of somewhat empty seats. The German element in the neighborhood was too sparsely represented to form a church congregation, and several German settlers showed themselves to be migratory birds, as indicated by the register of the old land office in Cincinnati.

It was 1814 before the English Lutheran congregation succeeded in forming the Germans into a liturgical community. For this purpose they employed the Reverend Joseph Zäslein and rented the Cincinnati public school building. Zäslein had been trained for the ministry in a Swiss seminary. He was trained in the old school, one of the best speakers in either English or German, who ever preached in the west. The Moravians of Bethlehem, who recognized his abilities, soon sent him as a missionary to Ohio. Unfortunately, he died in 1817, before the congregation had achieved a firm footing.

From the church records of St. John's parish, it is indicated that the first German infant baptized by Zäslein in October 10, 1813, was, similar to the first child born in Ohio, a Heckewelder, Pierson, son of Thomas Heckewelder and Marie, nee Seyers. The second was Friedrich Wilhelm Beinbrecht, son of a Prussian of the same name. In 1814, there was one German baptized, in 1815, four, in 1816, five and in 1817, ten. The leading members of this first congregation, these German pilgrim fathers, were Andreas Hoppel, Zacharias Ernst, Johannes Herz, Ludwig Schäfer, Wilhelm Steg, August Zeumer, H. G. Höfer, Jonathan Strickler, Bernhard Gilbert, et al. The first German couple to be married in 1817 in this church was Andreas Ernst and Elisabeth Höfle.

After Zäslein's death, the United Brethren in Christ, who ran a nearby mission, became the guardians of the orphaned congregation, mostly Würtembergers and Swiss. But the preachers from the Brethren were untrained youths, with such a rough gibberish that even the less educated in the audience were finally alienated by their preaching. Not less offensive were their public manners and Mrs. Bogler, who was somewhat of a German Ninon, and who assumed the task of protectoress of the old-world culture, and whom these begging preachers often visited to partake of her cooking, bakery items and Vevay wine, finally banned Brother Ebinger and his colleagues from her house, as did the church congregation. At everyone's urging, Mr. Jakob Gülich assumed the office of pastor. The congregation had moved into a decaying plank building, a former schoolhouse, on Arch Street, between Broadway and Ludlow, where, under Gülich's leadership, the church services were held from 1817 until 1820. It counted 60 to 80 members including many Catholics. The most enthusiastic members of the congregation were Franz Link, Jakob Hummel, J. W. Frühlingsdorf, Martin Benninger, Abraham Bixler, Johann Bubritt, David Aupperle, Jonathan Stäbler, Geo. Gettier, Friedrich Herzog, Friedrich Schmidtlapp, J.G. Höfer, Jakob and Karl Hanselmann et al.

From the very beginning, the congregation was unfortunately torn by an unbreachable split between the Swabians and non-Swabians, which the projected construction of new church brought to culmination. One beautiful Sunday, this dispute became so heated that the floor collapsed during a fight, and the battling pilgrim fathers and mothers all tumbled together into the basement.

In 1820, Gülich passed his office on to the Reverend Ludwig Heinrich Meyer, a Hanoverian, under whose leadership, the first German church, built with brick, was constructed on 3rd Street, between Broadway and Ludlow. Even though out of an overall population of 9602, the German community counted 3 to 400 souls, their financial means were so limited that the funds for the construction of a small church had to be collected in the east. In addition to the above-mentioned Germans, the following resided here and were particularly active on behalf of this church congregation: the still living Dr. Ritter, Misters Tron, Autenheimer, Kapp, the Main Street merchant, Vogelgesang, Techhans, Bömeler Sprigmann, the Hessian captain Joh. Jakob Schröder, who died in Miamisburg, Jos. Schiele, Jakob Suter, and above all, Albert Stein, the German engineer. In the year 1817, the latter, under contract to Colonel Davies, an Englishman and subsequent mayor of Cincinnati, built the water works. Using draft horses, the water was first pumped into the reservoir and from there fed into wooden pipes across Martin Baum's property up to the foot of 5th Street and then along 5th Street to Sycamore Street. On July 4, 1819, the first water fed into the city sprang about 20 feet out of a fountain block; at the corner of Lower Market and Sycamore Street a stream jumped up 50 feet. Later, Stein built the famous extensive water system for New Orleans and also for Nashville.

On Martin Baum's property in Deer Creek valley lived at that time as a recluse, Christian Burkhalter, former secretary to Count Blücher and later well-known as a Shaker and editor of the "Western Mercury". Totally immersed in his religious devotion, he wrote sermons and songs for the congregation. In addition, an excellent German natural scientist, the Swiss Freiherr Julius Ferdinand von Salis, cousin of the famous lyricist Johann Gaudenz von Salis lived here at one time. He came from the Orient and here in the seclusion of this western commercial spot, he wrote of his experiences and impressions of this ancient cradle of mankind, until death took the pen from his hand. The simple stone monument, purchased from his estate and erected by his friend, Dr. Ritter, was, in 1820, torn down by Judge Burnet in a fit of xenophobic arrogance, because the body of the "Dutchman" was occupying a few feet of his noble soil and earth. Another educated German traveler, Joh. L. Friedr. v. Jenner, the son of a Berne official, died here in 1821.

Two German physicians had a successful practice here, Dr. Horwitz and Dr. Franz Jos. Constantin Oberndorf (who died here on November 15, 1860).

Early in 1819, our German pioneers conceived of the plan for a mutual aid society. The commendable club came into being under the presidency of Reverend Meyer, after each member had donated $10 to fund the aid society. Unfortunately, the flesh was willing but the spirit was weak at that time of weak economy. For several months later after a stone mason, who had broken a leg while working on new construction, drew upon the mercy of the fund for three weeks, our philanthropic Germans revolted. The majority feared that the patient would use up the entire financial support. On a beautiful morning, they stormed into the victim's home and forced the repayment of the funds. Naturally, when this fund dried up, so also was extinguished this first blossom of German corporate humanism.

Chapter 26

Cincinnati as a City. - The First Catholic Churches in Ohio. - Fr. Friedrich Rese. - German Life in 1825. - The Swiss Colony at Vevay. - Lafayette in Cincinnati. - The First German Newspaper. - The First Synagogue.

In 1819, the citizens obtained a charter from the state legislature, through which Cincinnati would be incorporated as a city. Even though often amended and modified, it remains the basis of the current municipal authority. This legislative edict granted the rights of a city but not the appearance. At the time, it consisted of 432 stone and brick buildings of a somewhat uniform construction and 1458 wooden houses, altogether 1890 buildings, of which 887 were shops, warehouses, and public buildings. In the past five years 820 new buildings have been built. The most significant building, which on a photograph lend the appearance of a city, was the courthouse erected in 1816, on the site of today's building, a clumsy towered box, which many readers may still remember. Its predecessor stood on the east side of the public landing and was constructed in 1802. It had a front of 42 feet with a depth of 52 feet and was decorated with a wonderful, 20-foot tower, which resembled a cathedral. It burned down because of the negligence of soldiers who had been quartered there during the campaign of 1814. Next to the courthouse rose out of a field of shingled roofs the Presbyterian church on the corner of 4th & Main, which has since also been replaced by a new structure, along with the Methodist church on 5th Street, the House of Friends, the Cincinnati Lancaster Seminary, the current "Merchants Exchange", and the Cincinnati factory. The tallest building in the city was the 110-foot-high steam mill of George Evans, which was constructed in 1812-14. It stretched along the landing from Broadway to Sycamore. The foundation and first floor alone required 6,600 measures of stone and 90,000 bricks; its walls were an unbelievable 10 feet thick, otherwise unheard of in the history of Cincinnati.

The *Cincinnati Directory*, published by Census Reporter Rice in 1819, gave the number of municipal dwellers as 9120. Since 1813 this had more than doubled. According to the contemporary census of the city council, it was 4000. Of the character of the population of the time, Rice writes: "its greatest number comes from the middle states. However, we also have numerous foreigners among us, and it is not unusual to hear three to four different languages on the street. With such a cosmopolitan society, there can not be the slightest hint of provincialization, which is to be found in the older settlements. Certainly these newcomers from various countries and climates increase the amount of knowledge and practical experience, which could never be found among those who grow up together; the settlers of Cincinnati are adventurers seeking fortunes; their principal characteristic is a restless spirit of endeavor and the search for quick property and fortune."

In that year, the "General Pike" was the first passenger boat to travel between Cincinnati, Louisville, and Maysville.

Except for the above-mentioned, intermittent disputes between the Swabians and non-Swabians, there was at the time no other split among the German popul-lation. Every Sunday, Protestants, Catholics and Reformed would gather harmoniously in the 3rd Street church, as well as in the amusement park which was opened by Kothe and Ott on Deer Creek. On festive occasions this amusement center did not lack for a German dance orchestra. Sebastian Renz played the clarinet, the so-called Fat Henry the violin and Jacob Schnetz, the gardener's brother, played the piccolo. The Bacchanalian atmosphere, achieved by Lauterbacher, which this trio of virtuosos provided, simply banished any lack of spirit. The diminutive Ott was not just an able and attentive host, who provided his guests with the best of simple comforts, but he was also a philosopher, a politically calculating person. Later, he moved to Madison, Ind., and married the daughter of Mr. Ritter from Philadelphia, the first German book dealer in America, and even later served in the United States diplomatic service as a consul in Switzerland. But even though he was an excellent host, he could not conceal the fact that the beer was poor. Not even the construction of the first German brewery by Billiod and Jonte could avert this national calamity. The beer brewed at that time would not stay fresh in the summer, and better ingredients had to be brought in from Germantown, where the elder Schulze ran a mashing tub. The Englishman Embree built the brewery which produced the first beer, but it was of poor quality.

The financial depression between 1817-23 had brought great adversity to the new settlers of the Ohio Valley. Under the then-current system for selling government land on credit for $2 an acre to genuine homesteaders, the settlers had assumed huge debts, which probably exceeded the entire amount of money in the western states. In 1820, the various land offices owed the government 22 million. Neither the farmers nor the speculators could repay. Nineteen out of twenty people would have lost their land had not the Congress issued a relief act. The shortage of money was great and widespread. The banks suspended cash payments; there was no credit, and one could not borrow money at any rate. General bankruptcy threatened. Then Congress enacted a law which gave credit to the settlers for the money they had paid, and established for the remainder a long term repayment with no interest. Thus the Ohio Valley was freed of a great burden. From 1823 onwards began a period of increasing population, land improvements and commerce. Just about everyone in Cincinnati gave and took credit, and almost everyone was engaged in business. Doctors became merchants, while clerics and lawyers (became) bankers and speculators. Gen. Harrison, Doctor Drake, Oliver M. Spencer and Richard Burnet established workshops, factories and banks as well as museums and literary clubs. Manual laborers and farmers laid out cities and villages. In an area 100 miles around Cincinnati rose hundreds of new villages, including Gellertsburg, Germany and others, which according to the guarantees of their owners, had the best chance of becoming a second "Paris and London", but unfortunately remained unknown in the new geography.

The first Cincinnati steamboat (1816) was the "Vesta." In 1817 two were launched and in 1818-19, eight. Before 1820 there were only 11 steamboats built. Burnet, Harrison and others had built large iron foundries and steam boiler factories, all of which failed in the financial storm of 1819-20. Burnet lost $80,000, which was everything he had earned in twenty years of law practice, but the increase in value of his rich properties in and around the city soon replaced this loss. In 1825, to repay $25,000 in debts, he relinquished to the bank of the United States that magnificent block, where now stands the Burnet House, the post office and the 2nd Presbyterian church. He had unsuccessfully offered it to the city for a municipal park. From the Cincinnati Directory, published in the year 1824 by Harvey Hall, we quote the following table of the various countries of birth of the city's population:

Pennsylvania 394. New Jersey 337. New York 233. England 190. Massachussetts 184. Maryland 170. Connecticut 143. Virginia 113. Ohio 52. Kentucky 42. Vermont 36. Delaware 32. New Hampshire 30. Maine 28. Rhode Island 20. District of Columbia 11. South Carolina 10. North Carolina 7. Tennessee 3. Indiana 2. Michigan Territory 2. Ireland 173. Germany 64. Switzerland 17. Scotland 39. Wales 21. France 19. Holland 2. Portugal 2. Austria 1. Poland 1. San Domingo 1. Sweden 1. Unknown 43.

Names, Occupation and Addresses of the Germans.[1]

(Translator's Note: Klauprecht filled this original space with many names, all printed so small that they were hard to read. In order to make these family names more accessible, I have included them as an endnote beginning on page 199.)

In the role of officials appear Friedrich Fecorn as the municipal health official and Juppenlatz and Meyers as officers of the R.C. Harmony lodge of the Freemasons #2, founded in 1791. In the foreword to his "Directory" Hall says: "The majority of the women came from Pennsylvania and New Jersey, and thus the greatest number of Cincinnati's young newcomers originated from these states. In addition, we find among our citizens emmigrants from all the states and almost every country of Europe. And to their honor it must be said that the greatest cooperation and harmony remains between these diverse nationalities and languages; everyone acts like brothers, united in the natural results of emigration. The safety of the citizens is such that the city council decided that a night watch was unnecessary."

A Roman-Catholic community was formed in 1818 with 100 members, mostly Germans[1]. They erected a frame church in the Northern Liberties

---

[1] In 1810 only ten Catholic families lived in Cincinnati.

on the corner of Liberty and Vine Street. But it was the arrival of Fr. Edward Fenwick, the first to reestablish the Roman church in Ohio since the early attempts of the French Jesuits among the Indians, who gave strength to the Catholic development. Fenwick, a Marylander, had, along with his nephew, N. D. Jung, from the Dominican order, founded the first Catholic chapel (St. Joseph) on December 6, 1818 in Perry County, two miles from Somerset, in a congregation with 10 members. Both had been ordained by Dr. Flaget, who at the time was the only Catholic bishop between the Alleghenies and the Mississippi. This chapel in the wilderness was built with tree trunks and later received a stone annex. There was soon a monastery at its side, inhabited by the Marylander Jung, the Irishman Thomas Martin, and the Belgian Vincent de Rymacher. New congregations then formed in Somerset, Lancaster, Zanesville, New Barnabas, in Morgan County, Rehoboth and St. Patrick, 7 miles from St. Joseph, in Sapp's settlement; even in the furthest settlements, the white robes of the Dominicans appeared in the darkness of the forest[2].

Dr. Fenwick had been consecrated a bishop in 1822[3]. His diocese included not only the state of Ohio, but also Michigan and the Northwest Territory with the Indian missions. The bishop had arrived in Cincinnati as poor as an apostle of the original church. The house he rented was a dismal frame barracks. He slept in the attic; the rooms below constituted chapel and office. Often the bishop could not pay his rent, and he even lacked the few cents to go shopping. The above-mentioned Catholic church--if one could call the barn-like, plank hut a church--was in the woods, one mile distant from the city, and on rainy Sundays the bottomless muddy path was almost impassable. In the lower parts of the city, a site to build a church could not be secured. Finally, success. The attempt to move the plank church with a team of oxen to the site on Sycamore was unsuccessful. During the move, it totally fell apart and finally had to be rebuilt on the spot. Shortly before the bishop's arrival, a German Catholic priest, the Hanoverian Friedrich Rese, had arrived. At the request of the bishop, he twice traveled to Germany seeking funds to propagate the faith in Cincinnati. He had the most success in Vienna. Löher even credits him with the establishment there of the Leopold Foundation, whose purpose was to support the American missions. Next to the plank church put up in 1823 was erected an imposing brick building and soon thereafter a beautiful gothic cathedral, whose plan was designed by Michael Scott and held 800 persons. The altar had a beautiful painting by Verschoot which portrayed the investiture of a nun.

The city's German population received a delightful addition not only from the east, but also, strangely enough, from the west, namely the above mentioned Swiss settlement of Vevay. Weary of the cultivation of vineyards were such returnees as Captain Weber, the founder of the Wilhelm Tell Exchange on Middle Market, J. Massard, J. Marc, Dr. Ritter and others. We have already indicated that this rather unassuming Swiss colony, laid out in 1802, maintained a rather significant trade with Cincinnati. In 1810 it had achieved its first notable harvest of 2400 and in 1817 of 5000 gallons. The expectations of the vintners were, at the time, so lofty that, in a letter to the Gazette, they foresaw an abrupt end to the importation of French wines and prophesied that Vevay alone would supply the entire United States with wine.

---

[2] *United States Catholic Magazine* for January 1847.

[3] The first Catholic priest ordained in America was Father Badin. He was known throughout the far west and died at the age of 98 on April 16, 1853, in the home of the archbishop of Cincinnati.

While the men of Vevay were running the winery, the women made straw hats which they sold in Cincinnati and also to the trading boats traveling down the river. Dufour's sister had taught them this trade. The people of that colony were interesting, educated and happy. In addition to its founder, Johann Jacob Dufour, who also had an excellent college education, where he had also been elected chancellor, the others included Misters Montraux, Siebenthal, Bertens, the merchant Jex, who was always making the best wine, the mineralogist Los and his son Carl, the town surveyor, the hardware dealer Denkler, and the merchant Ange, Dr. Flügel, his son-in-law, later the consul in Leipzig. He became famous in Germany for his translations of classical German poetry which appeared under the title "Flowers of German Poetry". However, among German-Americans, he was even more famous for his eccentric, almost servile warning to President Pierce, in which he warned that the German immigrants of 1848 intended to seize a portion of the Union and turn it into a New Germany. Another interesting personality of Vevay society was General Lefevre Desnouettes, a follower of Napoleon, who claimed to have been sentenced to death by a duly constituted court martial. Desnouettes erected a maple sugar factory across from Vevay. With Desnouettes's assistance, Dufour had formed an excellent artillery corp manned by the young colonists, which won Lafayette's praise during his visit in Cincinnati. However, this also brings up another interesting occurrence worthy of note.

As a result of a Congressional invitation to Lafayette to visit the scene of his earlier victories, General Lafayette arrived in New York aboard the American merchant ship Cadmus on August 15, 1824. During his extended travel throughout the United States, he was everywhere enthusiastically received as a guest of the nation. So too preparations were made in Cincinnati for a glorious reception, for which the city council had voted a sum of money. Since, at the time, there was no military unit in existence, a Hussar corps was organized to escort him for this particular occasion. The organization of the festivities was given to a committee, headed by the later US President, W. S. Harrison and Peyton S. Symmes, a nephew of the original founder of Cincinnati. Accompanied by his son, his secretary Lewasseur, and a faithful German servant, Bastian of Gonsenheim, Lafayette arrived in Covington, Kentucky, from Lexington, Kentucky on March 19, 1825. The committee welcomed him there and transported him across the river in a festively decorated barge with sea cadet Rowan at the helm. As the boat touched the Ohio shore, it was greeted by cannon salutes from the Vevay artillery company, which had come expressly for this occasion, and by the shouts of thousands of people assembled at the landing. Governor Jeremiah Morrow received the guest of honor in the name of the state of Ohio, and General Harrison greeted him in the name of the City of Cincinnati. With Harrison and Symmes on each side, he was led to the Cincinnati Hotel, where began the welcoming ceremonies, which plague every celebrity in America. Later the General went to the residence selected for him, the home of the Alsatian merchant, B.F. Febriger, in Vine Street. The real festival began the next day. In order to greet him, the entire population arrived on foot and by horseback. Led by Marshal Carr, the great procession began at 11 o'clock and escorted Lafayette through the main streets of the city to the festival area, a clearing in the woods between Elm Street and Western Row where Schaller's Brewery now stands. There a pavilion had been erected for the General and those accompanying him as well as for the speakers, raised high enough to permit a view of the tremendous crowd. The General sat down with those accompanying him, and Mr. Joseph S. Benham, a lawyer (Kentuckian), gave the speech of the day. It was a poetic vision of the glorious future of the West, which actually became reality in a miraculous manner. He finished with "when the names of Washington and Lafayette first echo in the valleys of the Rocky Mountains, then and only then may we call to the heroes and wise ones who planted the "Freedom Tree": "Fruitur fama." Lafayette rose to answer. He was greeted by an enthusiastic greeting from the huge crowd. As he began to speak, total stillness reigned. His first words had barely crossed his lips when a lively exchange of words interrupted him. Our gallant countryman, Dr. Ritter the Hussar guard on the steps to the pavilion, was attempting in vain to turn back a German farmer's wife who would not let herself be dissuaded from greeting the general at that very awkward moment. The impatient crowd began to murmur. "Order, order!" called out the thunderous voice of the president. However, in an instant, the woman who had caused the disturbance pulled herself free, ran up the steps to the general and extended a wrinkled hand. The amazed general shook her hand. "Don't you recognize me anymore?" screamed the woman in a shrill voice.

"My dear woman, I don't remember ever seeing you before."

"But General, don't you remember the milkmaid who brought you the letters from Mr. Vollman in the Ollmütz prison?"

A most amazed surprise streamed from Lafayette's face and with unabashed sincerity he shook the hand of his former benefactor, whom, as once with Vollman, a remarkable twist of fate had brought to the far west. The woman was the gardener's wife, Mundhenk, who along with her husband Heinrich, ran a kitchen spice nursery in the so-called hops garden, where the city hospital now stands. In the 1830's she was still well-known at the market there. This remarkable episode disturbed Lafayette's oratorical efforts and interrupted the celebration to such an extent that the crowd had to leave without even hearing a speech from the guest of honor.

That afternoon, the general witnessed a shooting contest between the Vevay artillery company and the city's American company held on the city landing. The Germans fired nine times, each time cooling down their barrels, whereas the Americans fired five times, but without taking that safety precaution. That careless spirit of competition cost them dearly. While loading, the red hot barrel ignited a powder charge and blew off the legs of one of the cannoneers.

That evening, at the conclusion of the celebration, there was a glittering ball at the Cincinnati Hotel. The elder Tosso led the orchestra while Johann Meyer provided the dessert, which itself was a marvelous product of the confectioner's art - a pyramid of sugar, 6 feet tall, richly decorated with appropriate marzipan statues, arabesques, and inscriptions. All of those attending were highly impressed with the cake, and Johann's fame as a fancy confectioner spread throughout all the cities of the west.

In 1826, nuns from the Order of Poor Clara arrived from Europe and opened a free school with 60 children. In that same year appeared Cincinnati's first German newspaper "The Ohio Chronicle". However, it soon failed for lack of support. At that time, of the city's total population of 15,540, there were about 500 to 600 Germans. In 1827, Professor F. Eckstein from Berlin (an "intelligent and extremely gifted artist", according to assurances of Drake and Mansfield's Cincinnati in 1827) founded an academy of fine arts.

The first Jewish congregation, founded in 1822, held its services in a frame building on Main Street between 3rd and 4th streets.

Chapter 27

Columbus and its German pioneers. - Goshen and Zeisberger's Grave. - The Rappists and Zoarites. - The First German Settlers of Pittsburg. - Lenau's Farm.

From its initial organization to the year 1816, the government of Ohio had no fixed site. Until 1810, the legislature held its sessions in Chillicothe, from 1810-12 in Zanesville; and again until December 1816 in Chillicothe, at which time time the legislative body met regularly in Columbus. On February 14, 1812, the legislature approved a law to establish a fixed capital city for the government. And, based on the recommendations of the pioneers Sterling, Johnson, McLaughlin, and John Kerr, all of whom eventually came to own the town, the legislature approved the establishment of Columbus, in the midst of the forest, on the upper bank of the Scioto River, across from Franklinton. Chillicothe remained the temporary capital until the completion of the capital building. According to pre-arranged agreements, the owners of the town were responsible for the erection of the state capital and the public buildings. Under the direction of Moses Wright, the city was surveyed and laid out in the Spring of 1812. On June 18, the day when war was declared against England, the first public sale of the construction sites was held. The state prison was erected in 1813, but did not receive its first prisoner until 1815. The state house was erected in 1814. The first newspaper appeared in 1814. It was called the "Western Intelligencer and Columbus Gazette" and became the basis of today's "Ohio State Journal". During the first years the population of Columbus grew swiftly. Newcomers came from all sides. However, it soon became clear that they had chosen a poor settlement, since Ohio's capital city was a rough and lonely clearing in the woods, far from any main roads. The East-West Highway ran through Zanesville, Lancaster, and Chillicothe, and the mail was delivered on horseback, via forest paths. In 1816, Philipp Zinn ran a stagecoach once a week between Chillicothe and Columbus. The bleakest years for Columbus were 1819-26. However, from that time on it progressed rapidly as a result of the construction of the national highway and the reservoir to the Ohio Canal.

Among the first settlers of 1813 were W. Altman, Daniel Kuser, Jacob Heer, and Christian Heyl. The latter is still alive and recently celebrated an anniversary, about which the "Westbote" carried the following interesting notice:

"Golden Anniversary! Mr. Christian Heyl, one of the original settlers of Columbus, celebrated on Saturday evening with his dear wife his golden wedding anniversary. Mr. Heyl is 77 and his wife is 73. Their five sons were present with their families. In the year 1800, as a boy of 13 years, Mr. Heyl came with his parents from Germany to America. Because of contrary winds, the trip from Bremen to Baltimore lasted 23 weeks! Thus the family was almost an entire half year on the ocean. After staying 6 years in Baltimore, they then moved to the area of Lancaster, Ohio, and settled in Columbus in 1813. Since that time, Mr. Heyl has been a constant witness to the development and blossoming of our capital city. Several sites which are now occupied by proud houses, were then covered with forests. Mr. C. Heyl was not merely a pensive observer, for his fellow citizens entrusted him with important posts.

For 16 years he was a member of the city council, county treasurer for 7 years, and for 14 years an associate judge. Let the "newly married" couple remain a witness to the growth of our beautiful city for many years to come!"

In the first days of Columbus, hunting was one of the settlers' major occupations. The number of squirrels was particularly large. Since they were doing massive damage to the cornfields, there was soon a law to protect the fields, which set a bounty for pelts. The "Columbus Gazette" of August 29, 1822, carried the following story about the squirrels:

"Big squirrel hunt! The squirrels in the area are increasing so rapidly, that they promise to ruin the hopes of the farmers for the coming fall. A lot of good could occur, when all those citizens, whose conditions permit, would participate for 2 or three days on a general hunt in order to reduce the hordes of these pesky neighbors. It is respectfully suggested that the various townships elect 2 or 3 citizens to attend a meeting about the hunt in the home of Christian Heyl on Sunday, the 31st of this month, at 2 o'clock in the afternoon. Should the time be too short for this, then the following men are requested to attend this meeting in Columbus."

Among those named were the following German hunters. For Hamilton County: Andreas Dill. For Madison County: Nicolaus Goetschius. For Washington County: Peter Salz. For Jackson County: Ulrich Conrad and Nicolaus Huber. Among the signers of the request: Christian Heyl. A later paper reported that the hunt went as planned. The number of pelts taken was 19,660.

Now for the last time the reader should direct his attention with us away from Columbus and to the first settlements of the Ohio Valley. According to the land patent of 1798, the directors of the Moravian community in Bethlehem were given the administrative rights and guardianship over all the Indians settled on the Muskingum lands. The Moravians had established excellent institutions for civilizing the natives and had spent, among others, sizeable sums for the construction of roads, schoolhouses, mills, etc. The village of Goshen, near to the burned-to-ashes Schönbrunn, laid out 3 miles south of present-day New Philadelphia, was the collection point for all the scattered Indians and any other newcomers. Unfortunately, the character and customs of the Indians became worse as the neighboring areas became increasingly populated with whites. In addition to the general hatred of the whites for the Indians, the War of 1812 resurrected the old prejudices. As a result, the militia attacked an Indian village near Urbana which was under federal protection. They would have massacred the entire population had not the venerable Kenton prevented them from carrying out that terrible deed. Even Goshen was often similarly threatened. A few Goshen settlers maintained an opportunistic trade with the Sandusky Indians, a few of whom were considered enemies by the Americans. The murder of several whites on the Mohican near Richland increased the animosity. After the death of Zeisberger, Abbot Luckenbach led the settlement until 1823. In vain did the poor man attempt to restore the customs of the charges of his honored predecessor. But the interaction with the whites steadily worsened all their prospects. Even though the Ohio legislature passed a law which imposed a heavy fine for selling alcoholic beverages to Indians, it was violated or simply ignored. Constantly, drunken Indians were wandering about the county seat and in their own village of Goshen to the laughter of the children and the wizened old-timers. Even though a large segment of the Moravian lands were leased, the Directorate profited little from that. The entire costs of the mission and the support for the sick were paid for by the spiritual guardians. Based upon this perception, the Congress took measures to remove the Indians and relieve the Moravian Directorate from administering the lands.

On August 4, 1823, Lewis Cass, Governor of the Michigan Territory, at the request of the government, signed a preliminary agreement with Ludwig von Schweinitz, Agent for the Moravian Directorate, for the return of land to the federal government. According to this agreement, the Moravians surrendered their custody and received from the United States $6,654, for their buildings and improvements, barely half of that which they had expended during their custodianship. In order to complete the agreement, the owners of the city, the Indians of Goshen, along with the descendants of Killbuck and White Eye traveled to Detroit and there, in an agreement with Governor Cass, gave up their right to 12,000 acres in Tuscararas County for 24,000 acres in a territory to be determined by the United States along with a yearly payment of $400. The majority of these Muskingum Indians, however, moved to the Moravian mission on the Thames river in Canada. According to an act of Congress of May 26, 1824, their earlier inheritance, the stretch of land including Schönbrunn, Gnadenhütten and Salem was divided into farm tracts and sold by the federal commissioner, James Patrick, in New Philadelphia. The next year, the Ohio canal was plotted; it runs close to the three former German villages. After the Indians' departure, the population of the county rapidly increased; and its composition as well as the appearance of the land changed.

Goshen, Zeisberger's last settlement, is now the homestead of a German farmer. A wooded hill, which overlooks the former village, is being worked as a coal mine, whose yield is delivered to the nearby canal boats. But there still remains a spot dedicated to the memory of the first settlers. If one goes down the south side of the hill towards the Zanesville road, one will come upon a deserted forest stream, which is bordered on the opposite side by a steep bank. Climbing that, one happens upon a small leveled cemetery, guarded by low forest, underbrush, and wild flowers. Here is the grave of Zeisberger, as announced by a small marble tablet with his name, the date of his birth and death. Next to him rest the ashes of his companion Edwards and several German Indians. The nearby Gnadenhütten is a village of several hundred souls, with a pretty church and rectory, inhabited mostly by Moravians. About 100 yards east of the village is the old cemetery. One can still find the very stone foundations of the blockhouses and traces of the fire, which consumed the bodies of those murdered in 1782, burned corn cobs, etc. Apple trees planted by the missionaries still stand amidst wild dwarf bushes. At one time, an avenue of Lombardy poplars surrounded the village. Of these only one remains, undamaged by time, a natural memorial to the former German pilgrim fathers.

But this passing memorial to the martyrs of the initial culture in the Ohio valley was not sufficient for the piety of the settlers. On October 7, 1843, several craftsmen and farmers from the town and the neighborhood, joined together to fence in the site where the victims were resting and erect a fitting monument to their memory. The society elected Rev. Sylvester Walle as President and Mr. Ludwig Peter as Treasurer. The first and second articles of the constitution which they adopted declared that the purpose of the Gnadenhütten Monument Society was to establish appropriate gardens on the site of the former Indian village and erect a fitting monument to the memory of the death of 96 Christian Indians who were murdered here on the 8th day of March, 1782. Thanks to the generous efforts of the officers of this society, Mr. James Patrick, Judge Eb. Lane et al., that monument at long last, has come about in memory of the men who, as Taylor says, "preached the gospel in the depths of the wilderness among the atrocities of the frontier wars and became the martyrs of the new, great era of material development and spiritual freedom, which have raised Ohio to be the Union's third stage of development.

During the time of the French Revolution, the wars against Napoleon, as well as the dismal years after his fall, the Ohio Valley was the object of attention of numerous Gemans who were simply fed up with Europe. After his spirit had become clouded following the sad result of Austria's war against Napoleon in 1809, Germany's great patriot and statesman, the venerable Freiherr vonm Stein, spoke and wrote about immigrating to Kentucky. Obviously the immigration did not have the huge dimensions as the earlier ones. From 1794 to 1815, on the average only 3,000 Germans immigrated annually, including the Rappists under their leader Rapp in the year 1803.

Johann Georg Rapp was born under Duke Carl in the year 1757 and was a weaver and brewer in Iptingen, in the church district of Maulbronn. Through diligent study of the Bible, he came to the conclusion that, basically, mankind could free itself from the selfishness of its earthly nature only when it could renounce the ownership of private property and embark upon communal work and earn the necessities of life therewith. In his 24th year he began to teach that one had to return to the life of the early Christians. Initially he joined the many Pietists in the country, but did not find there the desired reception and so he began to assemble his own community, to which he preached in his own home. When the French Revolution came, there arose among the Swabian country people a significant interest in spiritual things. Rapp then witnessed an increased response to his sermons. When he declared various church customs to be useless, for example the baptizing of children, persecution arose against him, and he and his followers were brought before the police and court, which sought to force them to go to church; in 1791, a plea to Duke Carl requested that they be expelled from the country. But he let them stay. During the persecution, his congregation had increased, and Rapp was the head and selected their elders. Then the thought occurred to immigrate in order to win the space necessary for a new communal life. A book came into Rapp's hand which invited settlers to Louisiana; in 1803 he turned to the French government, which replied that Louisiana had been transferred to the United States. From merchants in Holland, Rapp acquired reports and thereupon traveled with his son Johannes and two companions to Baltimore. Here and in Philadelphia, where he preached several times, he found a friendly reception and support through small donations. He then traveled to western Pennsylvania and, eight hours north of Philadelphia, purchased approximately 6,000 acres of forest land. In the Spring of 1804, he returned to Baltimore and on the 4th of July there received the first group of his community in Baltimore and a second segment in mid-September in Philadelphia. After they had all been assembled on the purchased land, a communal agreement was signed on February 15, 1805. Everyone donated their possessions and obligated themselves to a communal life under elders whom they themselves elected. Rapp became the spiritual, his adopted son Friedrich the temporal Leader; three elders held coordinated leadership positions, in that they constituted the community's council, administration and court. The new city, which was laid out, was called Harmony; it included 130 large and small houses, nearby were three suburbs: Ramsthal, Edenau and Oelbrunn. All the workers were divided into groups according to their profession, at the head of each was a leader, who maintained order at work, delivered the products and goods, and supplied the household necessities to everyone. After exhausting efforts and even more exhausting disputes, as a result of which several families departed, the colony achieved a surprising growth. Fields and cattle thrived, wool weaving, dying, flour mills, sawmills, hemp and grinding mills, tanneries, distilleries, iron and copper smiths, all prospered and produced quality goods. Later they also introduced wine and fruit cultivation and also raised sheep, which they imported from Spain. Americans came from near and far to see this new sort of model economy. The credit of these Germans was soon so firmly established, that the Rapp currency was soon accepted without question in all areas of the States.

Harmony was maintained until the year 1815. In that year, Rapp sold the property to a Pennsylvania German for 100,000 and, with his liquid assets otherwise worth another 45,000 dollars, moved further west to the state of Indiana, where he purchased 30,000 acres of woodlands on the Wabash and established the colony of New Harmony. Within ten years, this new colony also thrived to the same degree as the former one and in 1824 was sold to the well-known Owen in 1824 for more than 200,000 dollars.

A third colony was then established on the Ohio River, on the Pennsylvania border, which was named Economy. Five years elapsed, and in 1832 this settlement received a hard blow, because of an adventurer, whose real name was Bernhard Müller, who had promoted himself, under the name of Broli, as the long-time head of a sect in Offenbach near Frankfurt, and who now appeared as Count Leon before Rapp with about 40 persons, including two well-known families from Frankfurt. He sought a unification, but there soon arose disputes, and in order to rid themselves of the burdens, the colony, after a legal proceeding, had to pay a settlement of 105,000 dollars. With 400 souls from the Rapp colony, Broli settled today's Philippsburg, 12 miles below Economy on the Ohio, where, with Wm. Nast and others he sought to establish a new Jerusalem. However, the new congregation fell apart, its property, sold in increments; Broli himself, greatly reduced by sickness, died of cholera in 1833 in Natchitoches.

In August 1847, nearly 90 years old, Rapp died and since then the colony's affairs have been administered by Misters Bäcker and Henrici, two versatile and energetic businessmen. Currently the colony counts only 150 souls, mostly people over 50 years old.

Similar to the Rapp colony was the settlement of the Zoarites in Tuscararas County, Ohio. It also demonstrates how simple and sincere German farmers and weavers could embrace communism and how wisely they could make it work. The overzealous religious convictions of the old Swabian villages also brought these people into conflict with the police and so, in the Spring of 1817, with about 150 souls, they left their fatherland and arrived in Philadelphia in August. During the journey, Joseph Bäumler, a young person, won the confidence of his companions through his clever and tactful behavior; he was first a weaver, then a teacher, and finally he developed his unusual talent for organization. For an inexpensive price and long-term credit, Philadelphia Quakers sold the society 5600 acres of land, that had been originally a military reserve near the former Fort Laurens in Tuscararas County. The people arrived in the middle of winter. They were poor and devoid of all means of making their life even somewhat bearable, and their animals and utensils were similarly in need. Suffering from cold and dampness, while attempting to maintain themselves in dismal huts, the fever ran rampant among them. But their religious fellowship held them together. After one year of working individually, they thought it better to join together for the purpose of producing common property and livelihood, in order to overcome the obstacles through community efforts. The cholera of 1832 brought widespread death into their midst. Fifty members fell victim to it. However, from then on they continued to thrive every year. Their assets soon climbed to well over a million dollars including one tract of 9000 acres, the best herds of cattle, oil-, saw- and grist mills, two smiths, a cloth factory, and at the same time carried on significant trade with their products and deposited vast sums in the banks.

Their pastor was anyone who felt the calling. Throughout the entire settlement, however, there was a strict code. Many young persons who disagreed left and then received for their own settlement extensive equipment from the community's assets.

Until his death on July 30, 1853, Bäumler was the leader of everything, and, in the manner of the patriarchs of old, he incorporated the position of pastor, judge and physician. Though earlier very active, he gradually reduced his efforts, since everyone had more than enough. After him, the one most respected was Kreuzner, also an old man and widely known as a veterinarian; he had learned his profession through experience and the study of nature.

In the year 1812, C. Volz, a partner of a Baltimore company, arrived in Pittsburg, ran an extensive business and kept an open door for any educated German traveling the Ohio Valley. In 1832, the German poet Lenau, on his way to Ohio, found there a most hospitable reception. Volz later became the water tax assessor, but died a few days after the great fire of April 1845 when the wall of a burnt-out house fell upon him. His son Ferdinand was later twice elected Mayor of Pittsburg.

At the same time as Bolz, a Prussian major, C. von Bonnhorst, and the merchant Passavant from Frankfurt am Main arrived in Pittsburg. The former married a rich American, lived 7 miles from Pittsburg on a country estate and later moved into the city, where he competed with Volz in attempts to host traveling Germans. Leading musicians were particularly welcome at his home, for Bonnhorst was himself an excellent violinist and composer. Until 1837 he held the office of Justice of the Peace. He wrote a brochure about Broli's scam, which was published in Germany. He died in 1838. His son became postmaster in Pittsburg.

Passavant moved from Pittsburg to Butler County, Pennsylvania, to the immediate vicinity of the colony left by Rapp, and established the village of Zelionopel, named after his wife Zerline who still lives there. He died in 1849. One of his sons, a preacher in Pittsburg, founded a hospital and girls' orphanage, as well as a boys' orphanage in Zelionopel.

One of the earliest settlers in Pittsburg was Georg Anschütz. He settled there at the beginning of the century and was a respected, energetic merchant. He died in August 1853.

Johann Oppermann arrived in 1813 and ran the most popular German inn, to which streamed most especially the immigrants of the 30's, because there they could not only receive sound advice, but also material support when needed. Oppermann was elected Chief Constable by his fellow citizens. In 1839 he moved to his country estate near the German settlement of Sachsenburg, in Butler County, where he died in 1843.

Along with Oppermann came Johann Reis from Württemberg. Unable to pay for his sea passage, he was sold as a servant to a meat cutter in Philadelphia, who moved to Pittsburg. There he learned meat cutting, and with his saved-up earnings bought the area which now constitutes Pittsburg's 6th and 7th wards; in 1854 he died of the cholera, a well to do man. Several years later, the Swiss Jost Rush and Johann Gast arrived in Pittsburg. Both bought land, ran an extensive dairy and a nursery, and acquired great wealth. Even a confectioner from Göttingen settled in Pittsburg in the year 1815.

In 1822 the Swiss Vögtly and Riekenbach arrived, for a time ran a country inn on a small farm in the right bank of the Allegheny and died rich men several years later. For their properties constituted what is now a part of the 3rd and 4th ward of Allegheny City and Duquesne Borough. In 1828, Dietz from Basel put out the first German newspaper under the title of the "Allegheny Demokrat." It folded in 1831. In 1833 Etzler founded the "Pittsburger Beobachter," which turned into the "Pittsburger Adler," which ceased publication in 1839. The first German-trained physician in Pittsburg was a Dr. König from Hanover. He arrived in 1830 and moved to Texas in 1835. J. Schimmer and J.N. Straub founded the first German breweries in 1832. The former established the first vineyard in Duquesne Borough. The first music teachers were E. Heidelberg from Braunschweig and H. Kleber from Darmstadt. They arrived in 1830 and 1831 and are still to this day feted by the artistic Pittsburg public.

The site where the first Protestant church stands was a grant from William Penn. The foundation stone was laid in July 1833, and the church completed in 1834. In 1836, the first German Catholic priest read Mass in St. Patrick's Church, which has now disasppeared, on what was then the Pennsylvania Canal.

The public properties in Crawford County, Ohio, came onto the market in 1820, at a time when the forests still swarmed with bears, wolves, deer and foxes. The German immigrants, Jacob Schäfer, David Stein, F. Markgraf were among the first settlers. Here in the swampland of the Sandusky plateau, Ab. Hahn discovered the skeleton of a mastodon and Kneisely a rich sulphur spring 7 miles from Bucyrus. In this County, near the little village of Washington, lies the farm of the unfortunate German poet Nicolaus Lenau. It consisted of a section of US Congress land, forest, a few cleared acres, and several blockhouses, which the impractical poet had selected in that swampy area, which was often totally isolated from any traffic. When a homesickness for his former culture and literature carried him back to Germany, he left it to be administered by a German farmer by the name of Gärtner. Part of the low leasing price was to cover the tax payments, and a segment sent to him in Germany.

But Lenau had barely arrived in Stuttgart, when Gärtner abandoned the harsh tenancy. The clearing grew over and, since the taxes were not paid for several years, it was sold by the sheriff.

A farmer from Alsace by the name of Jung bought it. Under the hard-working hands of this enterprising man, a decent farm arose out of the deserted swamp with a comfortable brick farmhouse, fruit orchards, and fertile corn and wheat fields. Years later, after the venerable poet had suffered his tragic fate in the insane asylum at Winnenden, he remembered the piece of land, which he had left behind, when tired of America, and instructed a business house in New York to sell it to the best advantage of the unfortunate owner. His efforts came to naught, however, since Jung had a notarized bill of sale from Crawford County for the property which had been auctioned by the sheriff. For Lenau the property was lost. The matter came to the ear of Mr. Stanislaus, the late Prussian consul in Cincinnati who, as agent for the Bank of Norwalk, was personally acquainted and friends with Lenau, and with praiseworthy energy, the hardy soul protected the interests of the unfortunate poet.

A return of the farm by Jung was unthinkable. For, in addition to the sense of satisfaction, which he had in his legitimate title, he had also dedicated a small fortune and the sweat of years into improving the farm. However, Mr. Stanislaus explained to him the full story behind the county's shameful deed, in which Lenau had been cheated of his fortune for a few tax dollars, and, after a long, hard argument, convinced Jung to pay a reparation of 1000 dollars.

The money arrived in Germany too late. According to the opinion of his physician, Dr. Menkel, Lenau had become insane because he feared that he did not have sufficient financial means for a happy, carefree relationship with a young woman he loved.

Chapter 28

German Citizens of Cincinnati from 1790 to 1830. - The Immigration of 1830. - Cholera and Floods. - German Newspapers. - Schools and Churches. - Julius Weise. - Friedrich Gerstäcker. - The Explosion of the Moselle. - Expansion of the German Sectors of the City across the Canal. - German Military Corps and Wine Planters.

On May 20, 1828, the first boats arrived in Cincinnati via the Ohio Canal which had already been partially navigable since 1827. The opening of a new waterway into the heart of the state was commemorated with a festive celebration and was not just minimally responsible for an increase in commerce as well as immigration.

With the year 1830, the stream of German immigration began to pour into Cincinnati. Newcomers from all parts of the former Fatherland entered into the city's diverse businesses, factories, and professions. Especially the immigration from northern Germany was simply huge. Until 1826, the north Germans were represented by the hatmaker Hermann, the shoemaker Windeler and two brothers by the name of Kennings. But then came Timmermann, Stegemann, Dettgen, Havekotte, Speckmann, Kattenkamp, Oehlmann, Döbbelen, Willmann, et al. in large groups. On the average, these newcomers were truly the opposite of the immigrants to St. Louis, but consisted of scholars, officials, students, and similar individuals, namely, solid, business-like people accustomed to work, who were the followers of the country adage to "help yourself". As if by magic, new streets and boroughs arose. Similar to the population increase from 25,000 to 50,000, so too the houses increased, from 3,000 in 1830 to 6,781 in 1840. Everywhere there was life, activity, an increase in material wealth, which had never existed before and which was only temporarily interrupted by Cholera in 1832-33. And while they appeared with a quiet determination in all areas of business, the newcomers entered the political areas with fanaticism, where the great struggle between General Jackson and Henry Clay had developed and where the new Democratic party opposed the new Whig party.

During the era of good behavior under Monroe's 8-year administration, as well as under John Quincy Adam's quiet, sedate, and non-controversial governmental leadership, the German inhabitants of the city had paid little attention to politics, since most of them were busily concerned with their own existence and hardly thinking about attaining citizenship.

The official records from 1790 to 1830 indicate that only the following Germans became citizens during this time:

From 1790 to 1812 none.
In 1812 two: Joseph Seemann from Saxony and Ludwig Schäffer from Hannover in December 1812.
In 1813 and 1815 one each: Johann A. Gessner in October 1813 and Friedrich Wilhelm Beinbricht from Prussia in 1815.
In 1816 three: Friedrich H. Klein, Andr. H. Ernst and Zacharias Ernst in July 1816.
In 1818 four: Anton Link from Switzerland, Wilhelm Frühlingsdorf from Prussia, Karl G. Ritter from Saxony and Abraham Bebinger in September 1818.

From then until 1824 none. But then in that year eight: Joseph Kessler, Thomas Miller, Jacob Strodtbeck, C.F. Hanselmann, Friedr. Herzog and Jacob Burget in March 1824; Johann M. Massard and Johann Meyers in November 1824.

In 1826 eight: Gottfried Schober, Hermann T. Windeler, Johann Kaiser and Anton Kahni in September 1826; Friedr. Baumgärtner, Simon Euler, Wm. Riek from Prussia and Jacob Reiß in November 1826.

In 1827 six: Joseph Cartrecht, Joseph Davis from Prussia, Johann Hoffmann, Carl Schmidt from Prussia, Ludwig Krauskopf and Johann A. Kothe in August 1827.

In 1828 six: Gregor Leitner and Friedrich Autenheimer in February 1828; Georg Juppenlatz and David Weber from Switzerland in August 1828; Innocenz Thränle and Ludwig Frey from Switzerland in November 1828.

In 1829 seven: Friedrich Diserenz from Switzerland, in February 1829; Jacob Roh in August 1829; David Pfister, Jacob Haltenwerth from Prussia; Johann H. Greven from Prussia, August Eiteljörg and Heinrich Biemer in November 1829.

In 1830 six: Friedrich Tauber and David Aupperle in February 1830; Franz Eberhard, Anton Donners and Johann Rieter from Switzerland in August 1830; Heinrich Brachmann from Prussia in November 1830.

Thus, within this period of 40 years, only 52 Germans became citizens in Hamilton County.

At the beginning of the 30's, most if not all of the old German pioneers belonged to the Whig Party (already in 1831-32, Misters Carl von Bonge, Lange and Heinrich Brachmann published a political paper to support the Whig Party), whereas the spokesmen for the newcomers, filled with memories of the July days, the Polish Revolution, and the Hambach festival, turned to the party which called itself democratic.

The leaders of the 20's, i.e. of the Whigs, were Misters Brachmann, Bodmann, Hanselmann, Darr, Dr. Ritter, Schulz, Juppenlatz, Fleischmann, Panning, Autenheimer, Frey, Kronenbold, Libeau, Ruß, Gieße, et al. Those (leaders) of the 30's were Misters Rümelin, Rehfuß, John and Gottlieb Meyer, Carl and John Belser, the Wolf Brothers, the senior Zimmer, Ellwanger, Kurfis et al. The latter divided themselves into supporters of Van Buren and McLean in the second Jackson period. Their speaker was Heinrich Roeder, who already in 1835 published the Prospect as a German McLean paper, but which met little success.

At the beginning of the 30's, the public gatherings of the Germans normally occurred in Captain Kothe's coffee house, who apparently played a significant role in all endeavors. The captain, a highly educated man, later moved to Miamisburg where he died on May 25, 1852 at the advanced age of 74.

In 1832, cholera arrived in Quebec aboard an immigrant ship; it spread up the St. Lawrence and around the Great Lakes and came to the Ohio Valley after sweeping across the upper Mississippi. Scott's troops, marching to the Black Hawk wars, brought it there from Buffalo. On September 20, it broke out in Cincinnati. The reports of the Health Committee began on October 10 and ended on November 3. The total number of deaths was 351.

As with the great floods which occurred in February of that same year, the pestilence severely hindered the city's expansion. On February 9 the river began to rise. On the morning of the 18th it rose swiftly where it stayed for a time at a height of 63 feet above the low water mark and then began to recede slowly. The inundation of the city was five feet higher than in 1772 and 1815 and had the most horrible results. The entire lower part of the city was devastated; hundreds of families were without shelter. The water spread across

35 city blocks of the most densely populated parts of John Street in the west to Deer Creek, in the east and northwards across Lower Market and Pearl streets. West of John Street, the land was flooded for miles. Businesses, professional people and home owners suffered unspeakable damage. Many buildings were washed away, a great number of their foundations were wiped out. All commerce ceased and money disappeared, prices for groceries and heating materials had reached huge heights. All empty buildings, the ground floors of the churchs, school buildings, were used to shelter the homeless, for whose support the Beethoven Society sponsored a concert in the 2nd Presbyterian Church on 4th Street.

Cincinnati's second regular newspaper appeared on October 7, 1834 edited by Hartmann. It was called the *World Citizen*, had a Whig leaning and, after several editions had appeared, turned into the German *Franklin*, initially a Van Buren paper, edited by Benjamin Bossinger. His transfer into the ranks of the Harrison papers generated the establishment of the *People's Paper (Volksblatt?)* by a stock company in 1836. For the latter, the company chose Heinrich Roedter as editor. While, during the next 15 years, the political catfights of the Germans provided a poor imitation of American party brawls, German life in another area developed healthy and happily. In March 1834, the German Society was formed with Carl Libeau as President, Ludwig Rehfuß as Secretary and Karl Rümelin as Treasurer. This respectable club, which during all the changes of the years, and through all the bickering of the political and religious intolerance, whose colors remained faithful to the united German colors, is still in existence today and several years ago celebrated 25 years of existence.

Along with the increasing population, the church life naturally made major advances. The increase of the Germans can be seen in the baptismal lists. While under Gülich and Meyer from 1817-22 an average of 10 children were baptized, from 1823-26 there were on the average 14 baptized, from 1827-29 there were on the average 23 baptized; in 1830 already 35; in 1831 43; 1832 up to 54; in 1833 69; even though, in that same year, a new Protestant congregation had formed and the Catholic Church counted numerous additional members. Because of the continuous growth of new members, the church of the Protestant St. John's congregation soon became too small for its members. Therefore they sold their first site on 3rd Street and in 1832 bought a former Episcopalian church on 6th Street, which they to this day still own under Pastor Kröll. In that same year and from that same congregation the Evangelical Protestant St. Peter's congregation was formed, which, since their means were limited, bought a frame church on Elm Street, between 3rd and 4th Streets, for the sum of 350 dollars. This church was carefully dismantled by one of their trustees, the sturdy pioneer of German life, Mr. Philipp Reiß, and with considerable effort and hard work rebuilt on property leased on the corner of 13th and Walnut St. On August 11, 1833, the first church service was held there by Pastor Hauser. His successors in that church were the Reverends Niemann, Beyer, Schaad, Hofsümmer and Spindel.

A third Protestant church arose in 1834 on the site of Wood's Theater under Reverend Raschig.

The former intra-German feuds, which even during the pioneer times had spawned regrettable disagreements, caused a new split among the original church. The south Germans accused Reverend Meyer of unfairly favoring the north Germans. The dispute finally became so unbearable that Meyer resigned in 1825 and moved to New Bremen, a north German village founded by an uncle of Judge Stallo. The Reverend Baptizans H.W. Lauer then assumed the pastorship but had to resign in 1837. Then it became necessary to choose between Pastors Wilhelm Möllmann from Osnabrück and Steinmaier which caused a complete break in the community. The preliminaries to the election were played out with such emotion, that Steinmaier returned to Germany in disgust. He currently holds a professorship at the university in Bonn.

The members from Osnabrück and surrounding area departed the congregation and founded the North German Church, on the west side of Walnut, between 8th and 9th streets. In order to avoid any future difficulties, the new congregation included in their constitution the requirement that every trustee had to be able to speak Low German. The congregation's first pastor was Mr. Möllmann. However, he died soon thereafter as well as his successor, the happy man of the world and excellent violinist, Pastor Seib. However, the selection of Pastor Suhr over Pastor Clemen caused another split in this congregation. One segment left, purchased a Presbyterian Church on Columbia, and selected Mr. Sträter as their pastor. He was followed by Mr. Göbel. Later the congregation again sold their church property, moved across the canal and built the Paul's Church on Elm Street. Their pastor was Mr. Gerwig, followed by the present pastor, Dr. Eisenloh.

In 1833-34, Mr Wilhelm Nast, the tireless apostle and founder of the German Methodism, began preaching in places of work, in private homes, on street corners and in various houses of God in the city. As already reported, his first congregation formed in the old building of the First Presbyterian church, on the west side of Vine, between 4th and 5th streets.

In contrast to the Protestant churches, the German Catholic community greatly thrived with complete unity. Already on October 22, 1831, appeared the first edition of the *Catholic Telegraph*, on January 19, 1833, the first orphan's fair was held by several young ladies in the Broadway Hotel and earned 160 dollars. Near the end of 1832, Bishop Fenwick died, and on October 13, 1833, Dr. Johann Baptist Purcell, formerly president of St. Mary's College in Emitsburg, Maryland, was consecrated as his successor. He founded the Athenäum, the first Catholic university, where the German language was also taught, and the St. Xav(i)er Seminary for the training of young clergy. Rese, strongly criticized by the Irish clergy because he energetically represented the interests of the German Catholics against the Irish, went as bishop to Detroit. His successors in the recently built Trinity Church on 5th Street, were Misters Henry D. Junker, the first German priest to be consecrated in Cincinnati, Mathias Wurz, John M. Henni, Franz L. Huber, Franz Hammer, and others. On January 27, 1837, the St. Aloysious Society was founded chiefly due to the efforts of Fr. Henni with J.B. Germann, President; J. Schulte, Vice-president; J. H. Berte, Secretary; C. Dietrich, Treasurer; the honorable Mr. J. M. Henni, senior administrator for the Bishop of Cincinnati; Officers: A.B. Rohmann, Andreas Groß, B. Kuhlmann, Mathias Behringer, Ursus Frey, Ferdinand Stuntebeck; Collectors: Jos. Gohs, Jos. Schwegmann.

On February 26 it was decided to publish the constitution of the St. Aloysious Orphan Society, and on April 9 Misters Clemens Dietrich, Andreas Groß, Heinrich Schnittger, Heinrich Plaspohl and Adam Dick were appointed to a committee to make preparations to publish a paper, as a result of which the first edition of the *Friends of Truth* appeared on Thursday, July 20, 1837.

The initial small number of members soon was significantly increased to such an extent that in the year 1850 there were about 1600. In order to counter the circulation successes of the *Friends of Truth*, the Lutheran Synod authorized the publication of the *Protestant*. Its editor was George Walker, a theologian educated at Tübingen University, who for the prior three years had been the pastor of a poor congregation in Tuscarawas County. The paper soon went under due to lack of support, and, in the meantime, after the German *Franklin*, which had become the Ohio

State Newspaper, ended in a fire, Walker joined with Mr. August Renz to publish the *German-American*. But this paper was also not to last long. German social life now began to develop in earnest. Public amusement parks sprang up one after another, including a magnificent open air park, which Jacob Reiß had already laid out in 1828, in whose picturesque signs, Franz and Georg Frankenstein, who later became famous German landscape painters, displayed samples of their early art. Later the park passed on to that well-known friend of the (stage)lights, Georg Fein. The same happened with Hasselbeck's Tivoli on the site of today's St. Mary's Church and the amusement park of Georg Schnetz in Deer Creek Bottom. Festivals were celebrated, including even a repetition of the 1839 Hambach festival in Dayton.

But the German population was quite attentive to serious German questions, particularly in regards to the schools. Thus they sent Georg Walker as a delegate to the Pittsburg convention, which founded the teaching academy in Phillipsburg.

In 1836, an immigrant school arose on the northeast corner of 9th and Race Streets, under the direction of the founders of the gymnasts, Salomon and Julius Weise. Both men were unique individuals. In addition to his school, the former toiled over a number of outlandish inventions, for which he obviously lacked the scientific training. Thus he invented a 16-sided, welded steam boiler which could never explode (for the simple reason that no boilermaker would ever make the awful monster), a saddle which would fit a horse as well as a buffalo, a wild boar, in short, any four-legged animal, and, finally, a locomotive, which used carbonic acid as fuel. Salomon explained that he had been been put into prison in Erfurt for establishing athletic clubs and for participation in the murder of Kotzebue. He thanked a wooden boot jack for his freedom. He told the following interesting story: since he was arrested at night and his friends could not find out where he was imprisoned, therefore every morning he introduced himself in a loud voice as Oelmüller Salomon from Erfurt to a wooden boot jack, which he happened to find in his cell. This conversation, continued for several days and finally aroused the interest and laughter of the soldiers standing watch in the corridor next to his cell. Thus the news spread around town that a crazy fool was in cell #1 of the prison, calling himself Oelmüller Salomon, who talked with his boot jack every morning. Thus his friends found out about his sentence and could set his freedom in motion. Salomon's partner, Julius Weise, was a loyal, intelligent, former student activist and a poetic soul. He composed various poems for the German festivals and an excellent song book for the immigrant children.

In the 40's Weise returned to Germany; but the conditions there were highly unpleasant and so he sailed to California in 1850. He wrote thus to a friend: "This time I entered America through the back door, having completed the long ocean journey around Cape Horn (6 months), where I suffered mightily from the cold in the months of July and August. In Valparaiso (Chile) I stopped for four days; it is a friendly, beautiful area with a wonderful climate, excellent wealth, and pretty scenery. I met many Germans there, all of whom, without exception, felt at home. We northerners sat there in a garden, where German beer (brewed by a German) was served, beneath fig, lemon and orange trees as if in a fairy tale, and for the first time I had the pleasure of picking oranges from a tree and eating them."

In California, Weise settled with the German Miners of Los Angeles in Annaheim. His humor and constant good humor he retained to the end of his life, as for example, one of his last reports to the *California Democrat* shows. He wrote:

"Recently I received a copy of the *Democrat*. There I saw that someone had suggested naming the streets in our neighborhood after well-known types of wine. The idea is original, and with care and good taste, it could be carried out; therefore I wish to propose the following unofficial ammendment, the cross streets should be named after the delicacies which go with wine, e.g. Swiss Cheese Street, Sausage Street, Porkchop Street, Oyster Street, etc. Just imagine how pretty and attractive the following would look like in a letter: 'Mr. N.N., corner of Hand Cheese and Greenberg- 3 Men Wine Street,' or 'Mr. N. N., of Lacrimae Christis, between Collared Pork and Liverwurst Street.' Even a map of our city would be a truly appetizing menu. For those sections of the city of lesser importance, which are constantly used for the somewhat baser needs, one could choose drinks of somewhat lesser quality, e.g. Berliner White Beer, Corner, etc." The old rascal died in California in the Spring of 1864.

We should not forget the third person in this pedagogical alliance, Julius Schwarz, son of a professor in Heidelberg. He had come from the mines of Mexico, where, as an assayer for the Düsseldorf Company, he had gathered a small fortune, aided by the publishing of original Christian poetry, until he found it necessary to work on the canal, from whence Salomon freed him.

In his book about America, Raumer had widely mentioned his eccentric, Old Testament project of establishing a new Jerusalem. Among other things, the pious founder had some very unusual dress ideas. The inhabitants of his Jerusalem were to wear wide-brimmed, golden hats with diamond-encrusted air pipes and wide knickers, with the undergarments fastened in such a manner, that one could slip into both at the same time. An ingenius time saver! The route to market for the gardeners and farmers of the new Valley of Josaphat had already been determined; thus every morning the gardeners, on black horses, and the farmers, on dune colored horses, would enter through the Zion Gate and return home through the Bethel Gate. With a brilliant fantasy, the streets of the new Jerusalem were named according to various precious stones. There would be an Emerald Street, an Amethyst Street, a Topaz Street, a Sapphire Street, a Ruby Street, an Azure Street.

The German immigrant school, whose leaders were those indicated above, with Salomon as organist, was established by the Presbyterians and, therefore, did not enjoy general confidence. The fear of conversion-oriented preaching by the clergy and the fact that the German citizens were already forced to pay taxes to support the English Free Schools, finally brought about an attempt, via an amendment to the public school law, to permit the introduction of the German language in those districts of the city where it was desired by the citizens. With admirable energy, it was insisted that the Democratic candidates support the modification, which sought to maintain the German language among the newcomers. After numerous attempts in the political arena, which extended over several years, this important amendment was wrung from the legislature, and in 1840 the German-English Free School came into existence with Misters Joseph Anton Hemann and Georg Labner as teachers. But additional bitter battles with the local school officials became necessary; the trustees refused to pay teachers' salaries claiming that the general educational law did not apply to the city of Cincinnati, which already had its own special schooling. While the new legislative edict to remove this obstacle was in the balance, the German citizens had to pay the teachers from their own funds, and when it finally did appear, the trustees wanted to grant to the German citizens only primary schools, i.e., ABC and spelling classes, but allow no advanced instruction in their language.

This battle for the upper classes lasted to the mid-40's. Among those men, whose tireless efforts earned the most praise for finally attaining this great achievement for the the Germans, include Misters Stephan Molitor, August Renz, Dr. Häusler, Pastor Seib, and Dr. Rölker. The schools filled so rapidly that it soon became necessary to hire more teachers. Among those candidates for a teaching position and who had passed an examination before a committee was a young man from Hamburg, whose intelligent appearance along with his garish clothes aroused attention. He wore a blue coarse striped jacket, fastened with a belt, into which were stuck a hunting knife and a tomahawk, wide trousers from the same material, and a weather-beaten, rolled-up straw hat. With a musket on his shoulder, he had hunted and hiked the entire distance from New York. During the years 1837-41, one after the other, he was a pharmacist's helper, a silver smith, a firestoker on a steamer, a keeper of horses, a speculator in Arkansas cane, and he was known as one of the first to help in case of a fire. His favorite haunt was among the prairie dogs, raccoons, porcupines and owls of a small private zoo, with whose aroma, its owner, a German optician by the name of Gerhard, had filled his workshop as well as the house of the lawyer Fox on 5th Street, where the zoo was located. That candidate for a teacher's position in the local German free schools later became the famous travel writer and novelist, Friedrich Gerstäcker.

The German Catholics soon distanced themselves from this movement for German-English Free schools. Under the direction of their clergy, they founded their own schools in each parish, which were soon filled. Opened in November 1840, their high school, St. Xaver Collegium, was staffed by newly immigrated French and Belgian Jesuits under President Fr. D. A. Elet.

During the time frame of 1835-47, all of the scenes of dramatic terror which the authoress of *Uncle Tom's Cabin* so faithfully depicted, occurred in Cincinnati. At that time, Cincinnati was the main battlefield between freedom and slavery. Not a month passed, when some occurrance refocused attention on this great conflict; often there was the destruction of an abolitionist press, then the mob would demolish the house of a free black man, or there would be a related complaint in court, a public discussion, a slave would escape, an armed attack on a black neighborhood, or the destruction of a black school, or the arrest of a black who had killed his wife and children in prison rather than subject them to being sold again. Founded in Cincinnati in 1833, the abolitionist press was destroyed five times. On one occasion at midnight, the mayor dismissed some rowdies, who had destroyed the homes of several blacks, with the merciful words: "Well, boys, let's go home, we have done enough!" In 1841, slave hunters, supported by the base element of the mob, and egged on by several politicians and merchants, attacked the black neighborhoods. Several houses were even blasted flat with cannon.

For several days the city was given over to every act of violence and crime. The black sections were plundered and laid to ashes; Negroes trying to protect their property were killed and their maimed bodies tossed into the street, women were assaulted by the rowdies and soon died from the mistreatment; houses were laid to ashes while men, women and children were captured in the confusion and cast into slavery.

The governor hurried from Columbus, proclaimed martial law, and mobilized the militia, which finally succeeded in suppressing the uprising.

During the same period, there was a horrible accident in which 200 German immigrants lost their lives in the harbor at Cincinnati, namely the explosion of the steamer Moselle.

This steamer, newly constructed and elegantly fitted out, departed its dock on April 26,

1838 under the command of Captain Perrin for a trip to St. Louis. He first went upstream towards Fulton to take on board a traveling family. While the steamer was docked for this purpose, the captain, with criminal negligence, had held back the steam, which the fire had built up in the meantime, in order to demonstrate the vessel's speed while passing the entire length of the city, and also to catch another boat ahead of him, which had just shortly before departed for Louisville. For the "Moselle" was a so-called "Brag Boat" and had recently completed several extremely fast trips to St. Louis and return. The lines had been barely pulled in and the wheels began turning under the pressure of the built-up steam in the cylinders, when all of the boilers blew up with a thunderous roar. With that there was a horrible loss of human life. Bodies and parts of bodies flew into the air accompanied by the screams of the horribly injured. The explosion occured when the boat was 30 feet from shore and, torn open from the men's staterooms, it turned into a complete wreck. When it started sinking, the remaining uninjured passengers in the staterooms jumped panic stricken into the river. Fifteen minutes after the explosion the boat sank. It had been packed full with between-deck passengers, including 250 German immigrants, most of whom drowned in the river. Because of the force of the explosion, the Captain was tossed into the city, where his horribly maimed body was later found. The pilot flew 100 feet into the air and found his grave in the Ohio. Countless parts of bodies were scattered all along the river bank.

After the cholera epidemic, which lasted from 1832-34, Cincinnati's commerce and industry emerged from its doldrums and suddenly experienced a wonderfully rapid growth. The city may thank its expansion and welfare partially to the plans for the construction of public works which were carried out, for example the Cincinnati and St. Louis Railroad via Lawrenceburg (chartered in the year 1832), the little Miami Railroad, the Cincinnati, Columbus and Cleveland, the Mad River and Lake Erie Railroad (chartered in the year 1836), the White Water Canal, the Covington and Lexington Railroad. In 1836 the city counted a population of 38,000 souls, and its commerce at that time amounted to only 10 million dollars annually.

In 1840, of a total population of 45,000 the number of Germans already amounted to 14,000 souls. In addition to the Catholics, Protestants and Methodists, the German Jews were also increasing. Their synagogue was on the east side of Broadway, between 5th and 6th Streets. Their Rabbi was Mr. M.A. Moehring.

During the stormy presidential battles of that year, the German citizens had increased tenfold in comparison to 36, and were enthusiastic fighters in the ranks of both parties. The *Volksblatt* (People's Paper) battled the *Westliche Merkur* (Western Mercury) to represent the Whig principles; for the first time, its party was victorious in Hamilton County; in 1841 it became the *Deutschen im Westen* (Germans in the West), published by Burghalter and Hefley, which in 1842 became the *Volksfreund* (People's Friend) of Rudolph Maltiz, followed in that same year by the still existing *Republikaner* (Republican), which the jovial Captain J.H. Schröder led in Louisville. In the same year appeared the *Volksbühne* (People's Stage) (democratic), edited by Walker and Renz, the *Lichtfreund* (Friend of Light), edited by Eduard Mühl, who later resettled in Hermann, MO., and the *Christliche Apologete* (Christian Apologetic) under W. Nast, organ of the German Methodists. The German population, which prior to 1830 had settled mainly in the lower parts of the city east of Main street, soon departed this area and left it to the Americans and Irish. From there they expanded to the west and northwest from Main Street and, from the gardens, fields and underbrush, created the almost pure German sector of the city across the canal, which the Americans soon named the "Rhein". As an initial indication of this resettlement, was the rise of the Protestant St. Peter's Church, followed by the

Catholic Mary's Church, the St. John's Church on Green Street, the Elm Street Church, the St. Paul's Church on Walnut, the Methodist Church, etc.

The sale of the Pendleton property by Carr and the Bank of the United States on Elm Street further extended the German families east and west. In the year 1842, the section of the city known as Texas was merely undeveloped land covered with grass and bushes. At that time, the German population celebrated a wonderful May festival in the shadow of its natural park on Eichert's property. Several recently estabished German guilds had participated in the festival, including the support organizations for the tailors, masons, furniture makers, and smiths. With music ringing, the German military companies from Louisville enlivened the celebration along with Pastor Kröll, who gave an eloquent speech for German unity on every occasion. The necessity for this unity did not last long among the German military companies. The original conflicts, caused by individual arrogance as well as sectional differences, continued which, in turn, caused the formation of new corps for new disputes. While, at the time, the Americans had only one military company, the Grays, the Germans counted a Lafayette Guard, a scout company, a rifle company, a light infantry corps, which bore the name of Kosziusko Guard, and a German Jackson Guard. A committee of the latter had informed the ex-President about the establishment of this corps, and thereupon received from him on June 8, shortly before his death, a letter from the Hermitage, which ended with words that are fitting to the current situation:

"I hope that the German militia soldiers will, when needed, be found in the front ranks to repel foreign attacks or local traitors, who, by severing the states, seek the destruction of our glorious Union as well as the destruction of our republican system of government."

Certainly, in spite of dangers threatening from all sides, the lack of unity among the German citizens was demonstrated on August 9th of that same year, when the scout company, under the command of Melchior Heckel was attacked at the San Souci House by a group of nativist rowdies, just as they were coming from a generally bloody conflict between Germans and Americans, which by itself was accompanied by a lot of maiming and injuries, a lot of bad blood and a number of criminal cases. The decisions at a mass meeting presided over by Philipp Reiß suggesting to that corps the necessity for a reconciliation had no success. This was only achieved two years later with the establishment of a German battalion under Lieutenant Colonel August Moor.

On January 11 of that year (1842), public agitation broke out against several banks. The Miami Exporting Company had assigned all of its effects while the Bank of Cincinnati closed its doors. Because of this bankruptcy, a crowd of people assembled on the morning of that day in front of the doors of that institution, broke in and destroyed all the property and books they could get their hands on. The City Guard under Captain Mitchell, which hurried to the scene, fired on the mob but had to retreat under a hail of stones. Two persons were injured on this occasion.

Beginning with this period, Cincinnati's Germans began to shine not only in Ohio but throughout all the states with their active and happy life style. At the numerous festivals and social gatherings, the fiery Catawba soon began replacing the native Rhein wines. Already in 1825, Mr. Nicolaus Longworth had received this vine from Major Adlum in Georgetown, D.C. and caused a vineyard to be planted by a German vintner by the name of Amen.

During the 30's and the beginning of the 40's, the cultivation of this vine had been greatly expanded by the German farmers. When, on June 3, 1842, the former President of the United States, Martin Van Buren, arrived in Cincinnati during his trip through the west, a delegation of German grape growers, whose leader was Karl Rümelin, presented him with samples of excellent wines to taste, which had been grown during his administration. Mr. Van Buren compared them to the best wines he had tasted in Europe.

Among Cincinnati's Germans, the period of 1840-48 saw the development of a series of wonderful and useful events. There arose the Reading and Development Club, the founding of a German library, and a series of educational and entertaining presentations on the evenings of the winter months, a club for western settlement, the founding of the city of Guttenberg in Iowa, and a singing club, "Liedertafel", under the direction of the accomplished musician, Mr. Scheidler[1].

In June 1844, the historian, Friedrich v. Raumer arrived here during his travels through the United States. The elderly gentleman wrote widely about America, where he complained in a conversation with a lady as to how he had lost his heart, and when she asked for the name of his loved one, he admitted that it was the beautiful, rich and wonderfully thriving Republic of Ohio, the pearl of the world.

A German theater arose because of Christian Thielemann, who, after several attempts by traveling actors, the most noteworthy being those performances of R. Riese (who died in the poor house on Blackwell's Island on September 10, 1860 after poisoning himself), collaborated with Icks. In reaction to the Oregon dispute, the German Oregon Guard was formed under Captain Stephan Fehr. The war with Mexico caused the organization of the 4th Regiment under Colonel Charles H. Brough and LTC A. Moor. Coming mostly from the Ohio Valley, the German units of the American troops demonstrated particular bravery in this campaign. It was these dependable groups, among others in the center of the line under General Butler, who participated in the terrible assault on Monterey. Those particularly outstanding were: Ludwig Heimann, the German adjutant of a regiment from upper Tennessee, a professional stone-mason; Mathias Hett, who, as the First Lieutenant of a German company from Cincinnati, met a hero's death, and Dr. Egry, Lieutenant of the German company from Dayton. The reports of the elderly general Scott praised the bravery of the German troops under their leader Moor on the trip to Mexico, where, among others from Cincinnati, Captain Hermann Kessler, an educated German artillerist originally from Saxony, was killed by a guerilla's bullet.

In order to support the freedom movement in Germany, a patriotic club was formed in 1846, which sent considerable funds to those harried patriots Wirth, Seidensticker, Jordan, and to the children of martyred Weidig. Simultaneously, the following year, without regard for religion and politics, all the Germans joined together and generated eight thousand dollars for those suffering in Germany. Several national festivals were celebrated in the now gone Unitarian Church on the corner of 4th and Race Streets, for instance, on March 25, 1840, Richter's birthday and Goethe's death. Professor Calvin E. Stowe was the key-note speaker.

In 1847, Georg Fein from Braunschweig gave several historical presentations in Cincinnati, and, during an extended stay in Cincinnati, the historian Franz Löh(e)r wrote his well-known *History of the Germans in America*, published by Eggers and Wilde, and which last year experienced a reprinting in Germany.

---

[1] Misters Salmon and Schragg had founded the first German men's choir in January 1840. The choir gave its concerts in the North German Lutheran church.

Chapter 29

The period from 1848 to 1860. - Development and expansion of Germanculture in the Ohio Valley. - Its struggles and achievements.

Through the efforts of its pioneers, the German life in Cincinnati already acquired had a firm basis, when the movements of 1848 and 49 brought a new era.

There was countless emigration[1] which filled the areas of Switzerland, France and England. The unlucky ones came from all the provinces of Germany. Whoever had stood on the barricades in Vienna against the Black and Gold League and fought against the Szerencs of Jellachich, whoever from Prussia fled from Wrangel's and Brandenburg's soldiers; anyone in Dresden defending the Imperial constitution with arms, whoever took the field as a republican soldier in Baden against the combined army of princes - regardless of whether they were Liberal, Democrat, Republican or Socialist. Members of the most diverse political persuasions and interests were all united in the same exile and misery. But these immigrants were to receive a better welcome than the German pilgrims of the 20's and 30's. Rather than a simple marketplace passing itself off as a city, the newcomers found a thriving and rich capital city of commerce and industry, whose exports ran into 65 million dollars[2], where the German heart greeted the essence of the Fatherland in a thousand forms, and where the German ethic was presented with an opportunity for rapid advancement in the numerous business opportunities founded by it. The population of Cincinnati was then 111,435 souls, of whom 33,530 were Germans (that figure itself probably too conservative). If one includes the Germans living in the precincts, that number would probably increase to 50,000.

Their increase continued according to the immigration. German immigration in 1821 was 2200 souls. Until 1830 there was only one year where that figure increased to 15,000 souls. In 1832 it rose to 24,000, and in 1837 to 34,000. However in 1843 it fell again to 23,000. Yet, after that, it grew swiftly. In 1844, Germany sent approximately 44,000 immigrants. In 1845, 67,000 and in the famine years of 1846 & 47 more than 106,000. In 1848, 49 and 50, during the years of revolution and banishment, there were 80,000 to 90,000; and in 1851 more than 113,000. It has been estimated that the capital brought by these settlers totaled $80,000.

A large segment of these newcomers settled in the Ohio valley. On November 21, 1848, the first happily thriving Turner Club was founded.

On August 29, 1848, was founded the first lodge of the Special Brothers,

---

[1] In London, Marx, Blind, Füster, and other refugees published a plea to the Germans in North America to support these hard pressed immigrants. Collections were taken up in Pittsburg, Cincinnati, and Louisville and met with great success.

[2] Just how much the property values increased is indicated in a note from W. B. Barr, on whose land many German citizens settled. In the year 1811, his father had paid $33.50 per acre. If calculated according to $30 a foot, this totals $9,304,000 and does not include the buildings.

the Germania Lodge, now with 700 members; on December 12 the first Lodge of the Order of Druids. The first German theater on the canal, built by the Wolf Brothers, opened in October of this year under the direction of Thielman, and is enjoying the greatest of popularity among the public. In September the Synagogue Bnei Ishurun was opened on Lodge Street with an appropriate ceremony. The speaker was Mr. Gettheim. Among the political clubs, the National Reformers gained a lot of attention with lively meetings, parades and a wonderful banquet held in September in the Masonic Lodge to which were invited all the "friends of humanity".

In addition to the political refugees, there soon appeared members of different religious orders, including a group of 80 Trappist monks in 1848. They purchased 14,000 acres near Bardstown and in their frugal manner soon turned them into gardens and fields. In 1848/49, the Benedictines settled in the mountains of western Pennsylvania. In the Latrobe monastery (in Westmoorland County) there were 13 priests and 20 young people studying Philosophy and Theology, 8 younger students doing preliminary studies, and no fewer than 30 lay brothers. The monastery owned 3600 acres in four different communities. The lay brothers, students, and priests all worked at farming andmanual labor. The German populations in the counties of Westmoorland, Indiana, Cambria, Blair, Clearfield, Elk and Warren, are under the spiritual guidance of these Benedictines. The Germans are mostly from Bavaria. Former King Ludwig, Bishop Ziegler of Linz, the Mission Society in Munich, and several abbots of the order in Bavaria were instrumental in the founding of this monastery.

In addition, the famous Einsiedeln Abbey founded a branch near St. Ferdinand in southern Indiana.

In regards to the German settlements which arose about this time in St. Joseph, Marshal and Wetzel counties in Virginia, the following was reported to the *Deutsches Volksblatt*:

"This settlement lies in the pleasant, water-blessed valleys and slowly rising mountains of Marshal and Wetzelcounties, VA. Glorious and virgin forests cover the hills. Trees of 150' height are common. Medicinal herbs of all types are found in great quantities. The larger waterways are Fish Creek, Lumenkamp and Wetstone, the latter of which drives three grinding and two saw mills in the immediate vicinity of the settlement. There 8 German farms, some of which have been given German names by their owners, e.g.: Einsiedeln, Franzburg, Sonnenhof, Dennhof, etc. The families living there are mostly from Wheeling and expect six more to arrive shortly. Many more have already purchased (land) there, and the number is estimated to be 37. This will soon be one of the most pleasant German settlements, since everything there is so suited to make it that way."

In the Fall of 1848, the German singing clubs, the Liedertafel, the Workers Club, and the Swiss club decided to hold a festival, and invited all the then known German singing clubs inthe Union. Several clubs accepted this invitation. Thus the first German singing festival in the west took place in June 1849 in Cincinnati to the satisfaction of all the participants, who approved this first attempt. The main effect of that festival was a closer union of the representative clubs which formed the "German Singing Society (Sängerbund) of North America" and elected an executive (central) committee, which in the name of the society established contact with all the singing clubs in the Union. Since then, a national singing festival has taken place every Spring, in different communities. Of the various clubs, more and more joined the society so that there are now almost 20 (member clubs). The activity of the society slowly spread to Germany, where they established initial contact with the choir composers such as A. Zöllner, F. Abt, J. Otto, and others.

Shortly after the first singing festival, which took place on June 3 in the Armory Hall, a cholera epidemic broke out in the west and in a period of several weeks claimed many victims in Cincinnati. The "Central Watchmen" saw fit to blame the pest on the large, unruly German singing festival on Baldhill, an opinion accepted by a lot of bigots.

In that year, February 9, 1849, the Kentucky Gazette ceased publication. It had been born 60 years prior to that time in Lexington, when Kentucky was still a part of Virginia. The housing for its press was carved from limestone by friends of the undertaking. At that time, it was the only paper in the entire region, where today at least 700 newspapers circulate. On the proud rivers, where formerly only immigrant flatboats and Indian canoes navigated, there are now 600 stately steamers. And that fruitful region, formerly traveled only by Indians and buffalo, now encompasses 12 to 13 states with a population of 8 to 9 million.

The popular German, Friedrich Hecker, arrived in New York with his family on September 15, 1849. During his stopover in Cincinnati, he was given a festive reception in the courthouse by the Germans. Mr. J. B. Stallo delivered the welcoming speech with warm words and in an eloquent manner.

In that year, the Cincinnati City Council voted to donate one million dollars towards the construction of the Cincinnati to St. Louis railroad. There were also funds earmarked for the construction of a bridge over the Ohio. The number of acres within a radius of 20 miles from Cincinnati dedicated to wine growing was 743. These were built by 264 German owners and tenants. The average yield in the good year of 1848 was 300 gallons per acre. In 1849, the worst year, the yield was 100 gallons (per acre). One two-acre vineyard's of Johann Wenz produced 1300 gallons.

The pioneer of wine growing in the Ohio Valley, Johann Franz Dufour, died the next year, on June 3, 1850. In the Necrology of the Vevay Palladium, the following notes on his life appeared: "Mr. Dufour originated the cultivation of fine grapes in Kentucky. In 1803 he was sent on horseback to Washington with a bottle of wine from the first outstanding harvest in the Ohio Valley, to present to President Thomas Jefferson, a taste of the first wine harvested on this side of the Alleghenies. By coincidence, at the same time of the arrival of the wine in Washington, there also arrived bottles of water from the headwaters of the Mississippi, sent by captains Lewis and Clark. The author of the Declaration of Independence drank the first wine produced in the great valley of the west mixed with the waters of the father of waters.

In October 1802, Mr. Dufour moved from Kentucky to Vevay, which at the time was still thick wilderness, and built the first blockhouse, which to this day can still be seen on Main Cross Street. In 1810 he caused the founding of a post office and was named the first postmaster, a position he held until 1835, a quarter of a century. After the organization of Switzerland county, he was named territorial governor's clerk, and elected justice of the peace and surveyor. After the founding of the community government, the trust of his fellow citizens called him to numerous honorary as well as important posts. He was the county clerk, representative in the legislature, probate judge, and finally, in March 1849, Switzerland County judge. While busily carrying out his official duties, he died suddenly after a three week illness. His brother Daniel Dufour died a few years later on January 11, 1855.

In 1850, during the celebrations of the Hambach festival, on 27, 28 & 29 May, a large German marksmanship festival took place on Jackson hill. Carousels, target shooting, barrel rolling, gymnastics, music and dance, joyful parties and rounds of singing, all were enveloped in a cordiality, which released a natural spirit; the common dress and harmony which gripped all the festival participants fulfilled the high expectations of the founders of that festival and enjoyed the active participation and approval among the German community. Even the Americans felt sincerely moved by the spirit of the costumes and conviviality. The following report of the evening *Times* gave this impression:

"The main theme of the entire festival was cordiality, an unspeakable depth of feeling, spread with magnetic swiftness from host to guest, from Germans to Americans and Americans to Germans. It was a pleasure to see the happy faces of the Germans. From each side of the hill, they could look down on the city and see that there was no area in whose improvement they were not participating, in effort and reward, in prospects and hopes-Americans all, the only exception being language and birth, living under the same laws, protected by, and protecting the banner, whose stripes and stars were as dear to their eyes as to those native-born. Let every future annual festival bring us all together and make us closer, and let "Liberty, Equality and Fraternity become for us a reality, and not just rhetoric as in France".

A memorial to the festival was published by Eduard Bühler: "Dedicated to our brave countryman, August Moor", who had been appointed by the Ohio legislature as Major General of the first militia division.

The Burnet House, a glorious hotel of the Queen of the West, celebrated its opening on May 1 of this year. Not only the power and elegance of Cincinnati, but representatives from Louisville, Dayton, Columbus, and other communities appeared, surrounded by protective cavaliers in the gaily decorated rooms, glowing in the richest and most colorful glamor of the latest fashion. Even the serious old-timers danced in the aisles, it was the comrades of the old pioneers, who had cut down the oaks around Ft. Washington and hunted elk and buffalo. What a magical change! Between the first bivouac of the original border settlers and the festive evenings in the Burnet palace lay a half century, during which had arisen a capital city of a hundred thousand souls, whose luxury rivaled that of the old world. Mr. Karl Rümelin, already famous in Ohio law, who fought to give the Germans in Ohio recognition by causing official notices to be published in German, was elected to the convention which drew up Ohio's constitution. Records of the discussions indicate that he was one of the most active and sharpest members of that body.

Along with an increasing population, the church life also increased. The registers of 12 Catholic churches show for the year 1173 marriages, 3397 baptisms, and 2742 deaths. In March the third German Methodist church was opened on Buckeye and Main streets. On July 21 the cornerstone of the Protestant orphanage on Mt. Auburn was laid, and it was opened in September of the following year. A fair to raise funds for this social institution raised nearly $5,000.

A Justice of the Peace election at the end of this year ended with the victory of Mr. F. H. Röwekamp, formerly a representative of the 9th ward. For the first time, Cincinnati had a German Justice of the Peace.

During the past few years, the German population around the city has increased. The Northern Freedoms, Covington, (KY), Newport, (KY), St. Bernard, Sedamsville, Lockland, Fairmount, Cumminsville grew and prospered under their hard-working hands. As the following report indicates, the value has risen enormously: in the year 1838, Mr. Donnersberger, a German, bought 2 1/2 acres on the west end of 8th street for $5,500. He sold the topsoil for several thousand dollars and the property itself to Judge Short for $52,000. The area where the hospital now stands was developed in 1818 for $3000. At that time, its distance from the city was just right for a pleasant trip. The value of that same property is now estimated at $400,000. It will shortly be in the midst of things, because the business world is pushing its boundaries ever outwards.

At the singing festival which took place in Louisville this year, the singing clubs "Liedertafel" and the "Workers Singing Club" won prizes in the form of silver trophies.

On February 22 of this year, the first regularly scheduled trains ran to Columbus.

Unfortunately, cholera appeared again this summer. During a period of 7 weeks, the Board of Health reported 2031 deaths.

As a result of the uprisings in the eastern cities, in 1850 there was much suffering among the working families. Their call for help was heard in Cincinnati by members of several German workers clubs and also by a temporarily defunct chapter of the National Reformers. They collected money for their hard-pressed brethren. This joining together in the public interest formed the basis for a German workers' union which came into existence on November 19, 1850. Its purpose, the education and edification of its members, also had the purpose of achieving material profit through practical cooperation by forming a grocery co-op. Wilhelm Weitling's paper, **The Workers' Republic**, cast the first sparks of discord into the club, which for its own purposes purchased a small frame building in Walnut Street, where the spacious Workers' Hall now stands. The fortunate choice of its executive leader, Gottlieb Braun, had given the club a solid foothold in the business community, and enabled the club to continue developing, in spite of the storms of the communist, socialist, and religious persuasions, represented by Weitling, Magnus Gross, Seidensticker, and the recently founded Freemen's Club, led by Hassaureck, Dr. Steinmetz, Rittig, Rothacker and others. The club built a new hall, one of the most beautiful buildings in the German section of the city and sponsored a grocery business, which supplies its members' families with necessary articles at cost, takes care of widows and orphans, offers dramatic plays on its stage, in addition to scientific andscholarly presentations in the winter, and a reading library which provides its members diverse means of education and entertainment.

The Freemen's Club, whose primary goal was to oppose religious oppression in the United States, built a spacious hall at Vine and Mercer streets in 1850. Its mouthpiece soon became the *Hochwächter*, originally founded by Hassaureck and Wachsmuth, whose proselytising activity soon caused the establishment of similar clubs in all the major cities of the West.

In addition, the gymnastic clubs (American "Turners") had gained numerous members and enjoyed a high degree of success in attracting the public to its laudable efforts in building mental and physical health. In November of this year, the gymnastics club built a splendid hall on Walnut Street and began the production of a monthly publication under the editorship of Heinrich Essman in January 1851.

On October 15 of this year, the German Catholic orphanage was destroyed by fire. In the ensuing excitement, three children unfortunately perished. Gottfried Kinkel, the popular German poet, arrived in Cincinnati on November

1

and was ceremoniously welcomed by Mayor Taylor. The purpose of this trip to America was to raise the sum of 2 million thaler to finance a new revolution in Germany. This effort was supposed to begin in London by Misters Kinkel, Willich, and Oscar Reichenbach. A segment of Cincinnati's German population took it to heart and donated to this "German National Fund". Unfortunately there soon arose a great deal of competition among other revolutionary organizations led by Amand Goegg, Sigel and others. It resulted in an end of the whole project. Even the Governor of Hungary, Ludwig Kossuth, at one time visited Cincinnati to promote his plan for freeing Hungary by selling shares. He met Kinkel in the Turner's Hall, and spoke to the Germans in Paul's Church. And the Hungarian bonds soon enjoyed as great a popularity among our people as did those of the German National Fund, which, according to an audit by its treasurer, Mr. Reyfuss, stood at $2663.08 on May 5, 1852.

Among the five cadets sent by Ohio to West Point in 1851, was one Gottfried Weitzel, the first student in the German-American Free schools, decorated in the War of Secession as a Brigadier General. In September, the Cincinnati, Hamilton and Dayton railroad was opened. The railroad cuts through the entire area of Hamilton and Butler counties, the northwest corner of Warren county, and almost all of Montgomery county. The Miami and Erie canal joined them to Miami and Shelby counties. This entire region, the Miami Valley, known as one of the most fertile areas in the entire west, already has a population of 500,000 souls and boasts a population increase of 42 percent.

When the US Army under General Hull marched from Cincinnati to the Great Lakes in the year 1812, the keel boats which supplied the army with food and munitions, required two weeks to reach Dayton. The poor condition of the roads forced the choice of this mode of transportation over wagon transport. Now one travels there in three hours and in six hours to Lake Erie. This wonderful progress of the Miami Valley took place within a single lifetime. In that year, the Germans were represented in the city council by ten representatives: Misters Goepper, Eichenlaub, Stolz, Diehl, Schulz, Gott, Bonte, Rothert, Klein and Van Seggern.

During this year's world's fair at the Crystal Palace in London, the Ohio wines of German vintners won European recognition. The royal commissioners awarded Misters Duhme and Schumann from Cincinnatti a medal of merit for the Musk Catawba wine which they had entered.

The first German tribe of the Red Men, the Seneca Tribe #7, was founded on August 2, 1852. The first Sachem (medicine man) of the-German Red Men in Ohio was Lehmann Schloss.

The famous German jurist, Mr. J. B. Stallo, was appointed by Governor Wood in January 1853 to fill a vacancy as a Judge of the Common Pleas Court. During the popular elections which took place the following Autumn, he was returned to that position by a wide majority of the people. Mr. J. B. Schiff joined the Senate and Mr. Joseph E. Egly joined the state house of representatives. Misters Unzicker, Oehlmann, Wieser, Eichenlaub, and Schiff sat in the Board of Education.

On May 29, 30, and 31 of this year, the large gymnastics festival for the west took place in Louisville. The speakers were Fenner of Fenneberg and Theodor Dietsch.

A German marksmanship festival as celebrated in Columbus in September.

In the Spring of this year, the hostile demonstration of the ultra radical Catholic Party against the state free school system generated a hostile feeling among the non-Catholic population of the West. And the speeches of Fr. Gavazzi, who had come from Europe at the same time also generated a noticeably increased hostility. "War with the Papists, war with the Romans" was, according to Fr. Gavazzi, the only way to free the world. On October 17 of this year, he gave his inspiring talks at Smith and Nixon Hall in Cincinnati. The arrival of the Papal Nuncio in the following December, Cardinal Bedini, provided a suitable opportunity for numerous demonstrations against the activities of the hated Ultras. The Cardinal had been accused of having Garibaldi's chaplain, Ugo Bassi, and others, brutally shot by Austrian Carabinieris.

Friedrich August Hobelmann, who in 1848 as a teacher and editor of the Spring Messengers and, as a fearful "Red Man", had fled Bremen for participation in "death squads", was at the time the editor of the *Watchman* (*Hochwächter*). The Cardinal had barely arrived on December 21, when Hobelmann published a gruesomely colored biographical sketch of Bedini, which ended with the threat: "Here and no further!" This article set the blood of the Freemen to boiling. In order to appease the article a demonstration against the "bloodhound of Bologna" had to take place.

During an open-door meeting on Sunday, December 25, the Freemen community decided to stage that same evening a march on the archbishop's palace, where Bedini was staying, and formally burn him in effigy to the accompaniment of grunts and cat meows.

After deciding on this inquisition, a straw man in a Cardinal's vestments and a bishop's crown on its head was hung on a gallows. Then signs were hastily made bearing the inscriptions: "Down with Bedini," "No Papists", "Freedom, Equality, and Fraternity". Late in the evening the procession began on Vine Street with 800 to 1000 men and women. Going up Marshall, it came to the Turners' Hall, where the gymnasts were to be invited to participate in the procession. The leaders of the Turners recognized that the hour and time selected for this undertaking were not right, and wisely refused to participate.

Bolstered by curious onlookers from both sides of the street, the procession moved to Walnut and 9th Streets and then wound to the right into Plum Street.

Naturally the police were well aware of this movement. The mayor was absent from the city. Rather than release the officers after reading the watch list, the new police captain, Luken, had kept all of his police on duty in city hall. With his squad of 75 well-armed policemen, Luken hit the procession from the side, just as it was calmly passing the corner of 9th and Plum and approaching the archbishop's residence.

No talks went on between the leaders of the demonstration and Police Captain Luken; no warnings were given to the demonstrators to honor the Sabbath laws and disperse.

Evidently the police sought to handle the demonstration as a dangerous riot. Rather than read the riot act, which would have called on the people to disperse, Luken gave the command to arrest all the demonstrators. The police carried out the order in a brutal manner. At the outset of the first attack a shot was fired, no one knows by which party, to be followed in an instant by several dozen more. Then those in the procession, some armed with swords and pistols, and who outnumbered the police ten to one, broke and scattered wildly, accompanied by the screams of women and children. The police, seized by their sudden victory, fell upon those fleeing and arrested them in droves, striking and hitting them with a savage fury while dragging them to the police station. Bedini, the gallows, the signs, and other articles fell into the hands of the police.

Several innocent bystanders, who happened to be passing by, for example ex-city councilman Stolz, clothier Wolf, a farmer from Indiana, and others were shamefully attacked with lead slings by the police, knocked down, and severely mistreated. Two of the policemen were wounded. James Carroll of the 2nd ward received a bullet in the leg and Lt. Huesmann had a thumb broken. Karl Eggerlin, a young German, received a gunshot in the lung and leg. He died shortly thereafter. Several police officers had blindly fired shotguns into the midst of the crowd.

While the charges of rioting against all the participants in the Bedini demonstration turned into a fiasco, the counter charges of the Freeman against the police for the murder of Eggerlin and mistreatment of their companions likewise ended without any result. The only satisfaction for the leaders of the auto-da-fe against Bedini was that the straw effigy was eventually burned in front of the archbishop's residence. Even the citizens of Covington joined together to burn Bedini in effigy. Captain Lukens even received a polite invitation for his police "to pitch in".

The year 1854 witnessed a lively political life for the newcomers of '48. In Louisville, the Germans united on a platform created by Heinzen, Domschke, Bürgeler and Wittig, which declared war against slavery and religious oppression. To this end, the representatives of 17 Ohio clubs assembled at the end of March in the Freemen's Hall in Cincinnati, under the direction of a Mr. Müller from Cleveland. They developed a platform similar to the one in Louisville.

On September 18, Germans from the northern states convened a congress in Wheeling which presented to the political parties of the country a program of more progressive development, and (amazingly) called for the annexation of all of Europe to the United States while the surrounding robber states would be annexed by Europe.

In addition to some advanced ideas, many profane ones also came to light. According to repeated reports of the "Indianapolis Free Press", there was a club founded with the very modest name of "The Dirty Dogs". Its main regulations were the following: Each member had to drop a sample of his dirty-dog nature. In particular, the Captain or Praeses had to do this, in order to be a collossal dirty dog. The club's motto was the old saying which Goethe had taken from Lichtenberg: "We feel as cannibalistically comfortable as 500 sau's."

The railroad from Cincinnati to Louisville was opened in June of this year. In August a general German immigrants' club came to life. At its very first meeting, the resolution was reached directing that the contributions to Kinkel's fund for the revolution in Germany, should be turned over to the club to support the immigrants, rather than be used for some impractical scheme. Mr. Kinkel protested vigorously against that understandable request. The money for the revolution in Germany is still in his hands.

In March, Captain Theodor Schrickel organized a German artillery company.

In the autumn elections, the so-called Know-Nothing (American Reform) Party battled to its first major victory. But the leaf turned when it became known that its hostility against the Catholic hierarchy was matched by its hatred of all things foreign. In the following year's Spring election (April 2, 1855), the Know-Nothing Mayoral Candidate in Cincinnati, Taylor, was soundly defeated. When the outcome became known that afternoon, a Know-Nothing mob, ready for anything, broke loose to murder and destroy anything foreign, taking the law into its own hands.

The Mayor and police were intimidated and carried out their duties only at the pleasure of the mob.

The main act of the mob would be played out in the 11th Ward on the evening of the election. Embittered at the plurality which was unrolling against them in that ward, the Know-Nothings started a rumor that masses of falsified ballots had been cast there. Supposedly even small boys had been allowed to vote. The heightened mood of their "Bullys" was even further sharpened by the victory salvos, which were constantly being fired by Captain Salomon from Jackson Hill in honor of Jefferson's birthday. The Know-Nothings were not aware of the true purpose of the salvos and assumed they were s sarcastic expression of a victory celebration in honor of their anticipated defeat.

Meanwhile, the above-noted rumor spread throughout the lower sections of the city, and the lies became bigger and uglier with every block. The rage of the brutal band about their defeat suddenly exploded in every direction. In groups, the loafers and Know-Nothing rowdies, faces inflamed with whiskey, streamed on foot, on horseback and in buggies towards Hamilton Road, yelling like savages "Hurrah for Pap Taylor!". Even before they arrived, there had already been a bloody fight between a Dr. William Brown, a Know-Nothing from the 3rd ward, and Mr. George Röder, a foreman at F. Link's brewery. The former stabbed the latter with a knife in the abdomen and Röder fell mortally wounded. This act was the signal for general fighting. Brown was badly beaten up, arrested, and taken to the Bremen street stationhouse, only to be promptly freed by his numerous companions. No fewer than 30 persons were injured to varying degrees.

After these preliminaries, the army of Know-Nothings, around 500 strong, arrived in other sections of the city. The bullies split up. One group went up Jackson Hill and beat up Captain Salomon and his artillerymen. In spite of the fact that they had sidearms, the artillerymen stoically surrendered their cannon, flags and powder. The bullies dragged the equipment to the polls in the 11th Ward, where (it was already 6 o'clock) a terrible fight had broken out. The few Germans who resisted the insults and taunts of the Know-Nothings were beaten.

Mayor Snellbaker rode up on a lame nag and watched the riot for a while in painful lethargy. A crowd of thousands of Germans, Americans, and Irish surrounded him and the voting place. Constantly passing wagons and horses raised a thick cloud of dust. Then a gang of about 30 Know-Nothing rowdies broke into the polling place and, encountering no resistance, grabbed the ballot box, smashed it to pieces to the shouts of "Hoorah for Pap Taylor", and, with the Stars and Stripes waving, tossed the ballots into the air.

Mayor Snellbaker and city councilman Dale, who tried to stop this destruction, lost part of their clothes in this attempt. The latter was beaten with a chair leg and knocked down in front of the door. After spreading the shards of the voting urn, they went to the 9th ward where they expected to do the same damage. The doors of the voting place had already been locked up and the ballot box brought to safety. Enraged at this, they savagely attacked two German bystanders, Mr. Selker and the tailor Schuhmacher. Finally, they fired the cannon, loaded with stones, into the throngs of men, women and children who fled in all directions. They shot down a harmless worker and then, with a savage cry, and their Taylor flag waving, went through the streets to the office of the *Enquirer*. There they serenaded with grunts, threw stones and bricks through the windows, and continued on to the 13th ward to continue their mischief.

However, there they were met by a band of determined Irishmen. Firing shotgun blasts and throwing stones, the Irish attacked the cowardly band, which in turn fled in all directions, and recaptured the cannon originally taken from the Germans.

On the day after the election, when all the excitement of the parties would normally abate and the normal business would be resumed, a Know-Nothing mob of about 400 persons forced its way into the firehouse, where the judges themselves, all of them Know-Nothings except the German city councilman Erkel, were busily counting the votes. The mob grabbed the ballots, poll books, and voter lists and tossed them into the fireplace. Then the mob hoisted the American flag on the tower of the firehouse, saluted it with savage yells, and then departed. As explained in the *Times*, the pretense for this new shameful act was that there were 52 more votes found in the ballot urns than there were names of voters in the poll books.

In order to further agitate the Germans, a crowd which had gathered in front of the fire station on Vine street near the canal, demanded that Captain Salomon return to them the cannon which he had gotten back from the Irish and for which his company had paid a bond of $1000. In order to ease the agitation and keep the mob from violence, Sheriff Brashears suggested that Captain Salomon compromise and turn the cannon over to General Moor. The Germans felt that such a disarmament would be a humiliation and decided to keep their cannon, a decision which the sheriff relayed to the crowd. In spite of the moderation urged of Mr. Spooner and others, it was decided to attack the Germans.

That evening, mobs assembled in the lower parts of the city and threatened to mob the Freemen's and Turner Halls. At the central market, fanatics urged the mob to attack the Germans. Numerous handbills, printed on red paper, were distributed urging the mob to unite.

In the meantime, the Germans fortified themselves on Vine street as well as on Walnut street where it joins Mercer street. The Freemens' and Turner Halls were filled with armed men, determined to repel any attack.

At 10 o'clock, the American mob, with a drummer and fifer in the lead, showed up at the Freemens' Hall and began to load their weapons. The Germans fired from all sides and the crowd, which had not expected a determined resistance, fled like rabbits.

The shots had a bloody effect. One of the leaders, G. B. Monroe, a man from Indiana, who was staying in the Farlowe house, received a bullet in the head and fell dead[3]. William Grey, a barrelmaker, was hit by a ball in the abdomen. A third person by the name of Boggs was shot in the throat. John Coleman, Patrick Dorey from Covington, and others were also severely wounded. The mob then fled back to the Vine street bridge, which, during the day, it had chosen as its headquarters.

The news of the bloody reception of the Know-Nothing mob inflamed passions even further in the lower sections of the city. Mobs gathered at the central market. Many urged that the Americans should storm the canal en mass and take revenge for the blood which had been spilled. However, out of fear of a determined defense by the Germans, and following the urging of several speakers with good lungs, the move did not take place.

Even more horrible scenes were to occur during the elections in Louisville and principally against the Germans. The Know-Nothing Blacklegs and professional gamblers had wagered large

---

[3] A roll of counterfeit banknotes was found in his pocket.

sums of money on the election results. In order to ensure their wagers through trickery and force, hundreds of armed bullies were transported into the city. Their plans were forged in the Know-Nothing lodges and would be faithfully carried out during these terrible days. By 4 AM the 1st and 3rd wards, strongly Democratic, had already been occupied by the Know-Nothings. While a few former democratic friends would be allowed to vote, any German or Irishman who approached would be driven of by thrown rocks or by being threatened with bowie knives. Even Americans who did not know the secret signs and signals would be refused. By 10 o'clock, Louisville was under control of the mob, and neither life nor property was safe. The first serious fight broke out at 11 AM in the 1st ward at the corner of Shelby and Green Streets. Germans, Irish and Americans took part. The former were beaten back. Several of them, who had fled into a house, had to flee with broken bones and limbs. On Shelby Street, the rage of the Know-Nothing mob grew with every step, and as they reached Green Street, their thirst for blood was insatiable. There, while they were preparing for a fight, a shotgun blast greeted the Americans, and the mob exploded. After scattering the Germans, the mob started to destroy the coffee house of Christian Meier on the street corner. Windows and doors were broken, all the furniture in the building destroyed, and the people inside forced to flee. In a short time, this army of vandals had been continuously reinforced by armed citizens from throughout the city. The news of the beginning of the fight had spread everywhere. First the mob approached the house of Conrad Kitzler on the corner of Walnut and Shelby streets. Conrad was sitting calmly with a beer, puffing on a pipe. His neighborhood had never been the scene of any disturbance. But this meant nothing. All his possessions, for which he had worked the best years of his life, were destroyed and the life of his family threatened.

During this time another Know-Nothing gang began a fight on the street, in which a German living on the corner of Shelby and Madison streets was murdered. Mr. E. M. Saatkamp, a German baker who lived on Walnut Street, received several stab wounds in the head. In addition, several other Germans were injured. After completing the destruction of Kitzler's house, the mob turned on the German Catholic (St. Martin's) church in Shelby Street. Had it not been for the intervention of Mayor Barbee, it would have been plundered and burned.

Calm had only partially returned to the area, when suddenly a wagon, escorted by 50 men armed with muskets and bayonets, rumbled menacingly up the street. Under the leadership of Captain D.C. Stone, the mob went up Main street and then up Jefferson. The following terrible deeds were then carried out:

The large Armbruster brewery was set on fire and the workers injured. Armbruster was not in the city at the time. The pretense given for the destruction was that someone had fired out of a window at someone else chasing a German. Carl Heybach's factory was leveled to the ground, and a man by the name of Fritz shot in the chest. Daniel Schmuck's sugar bakery was attacked and the women inside driven to the floor, where they almost suffocated from the smoke from the burning brewery. The Becker house next door, was bombarded with stones and heavily damaged. Carl Becker's bakery was totally destroyed.

During the attack on the brewery, the drover Saddler was seriously wounded and his poor wife forced across the bridge. In vain she sought refuge with friends, who had barred their doors against the savages. Burghold's grocery was sacked. Joseph Hook's shoe store received similar treatment. While the mob was satisfying its thirst for destruction, there occured the most terrible scenes. Unfortunate women, children in their arms, carrying costly momentos from the fatherland, fled in all directions. In vain did their men plead for mercy from the mob, over which waved the Stars and Stripes. At 12 midnight, a frame grocery on the corner of Madison and Shelby street was burned down. Between midnight and 1 AM, Garrety's cooperage, on Main street, above Woodland Garden, was reduced to ashes. Garrety was bedridden for several days.

On Main street, Eduard Prim's barrel repair shop was burned down. During the battles which developed in the afternoon, Johann Vogt, a German who lived on Clay street, near Madison Street, was shot dead. His wife received a stab wound in the chest, and his child was injured. A German by the name of Kaiser, who lived on Marshal street, was killed.

Walther Murphy, an Irishman, was chased by the bloodthirsty ruffians and shot down. He died of his wounds the next day.

Johann Feller and Georg Edgeton received similar stab wounds. A German ropemaker was beaten to death. The above shameful occurrences, of which an even greater number could be described, took place in the east end of the city. In the 5th ward Henry M. Smith was attacked by the murderous band. A couple of friends along with his weeping wife, who threw herself and her children between him and the murderers, were barely able to save him.

In the 6th ward, an Irishman peacefully going on his way was felled with slingshots, stabbed with a pitchfork, and then dragged to the jail. The monster with the pitchfork, from which the fresh blood still dropped, led the procession. The victim was tossed into the jail, while the murderers at their leisure carried out additional evil deeds.

In the lower parts of the city the disturbance began at the corner of Chapel & Main. At 5 o'clock, a certain Rhoades chased an Irishman into a house. He (Rhoades) was shot down. At about the same John Hudson was shot to death in the 8th Ward. William Graham, a foundry worker, attempted to help Rhoades and was shot in the back by an Irishman named Barrett. Barrett was seized, shot and hanged. He was then dragged off to jail where he died later that night.

At 8 o'clock, a heavily armed mob surrounded a row of brick houses at 11th & Main. The junk shop of an Irishman named Long was fired on with the cannon and set afire. At the time his three sons were in the building. One ran out while the remaining two perished in the flames. The fire spread to the adjoining three-storied building, owned by the Irishman D. Riordan, which was used as a feed store. It was reduced to ashes along with Charles Kyan's boarding house and two empty houses. The next row house was occupied by the cigar maker McKinne. It suffered the same fate. Then came the brick building of Patrick Flinn, which was occupied by several families. Numerous other buildings were partially burned or destroyed. On 11th Street the fire destroyed two houses. In all, twelve of the buildings were the property of Patrick Quinn, who was the brother of an Irish Catholic priest who was living one of those same rooms. The unfortunate (Quinn) was shot, beaten, and burned.

On the other side of Main street the houses of Jonathan Fitzgerald and Mrs. Trainer were burned down.

However, the fires themselves were nothing in comparison to the terrible acts which were being carried out at the same time.

The unfortunate ones who tried to escape the flames met death in other forms. As soon as one would appear on the doorstep, he would be shot down. Many were dragged away seriously wounded; others, bloodied and maimed, crawled back into the flaming houses to avoid falling into the hands of the savages. One man, trying to escape in woman's clothes, was discovered and shot to death. Another seriously wounded man, wrapped in a blanket and supported by his wife, was pulled from her and shot dead in cold blood as soon as he crossed the threshold.

It was impossible to flee from the houses without being killed. It is impossible to tell how many of these unfortunate people were trapped in their homes and burned alive. Two sons of Mr. Long, who had a feed store at 11th & Main, were shot to death. George Hubert, a harmless old German, who was returning from his business in Portland Avenue, was surrounded by the mob. They fell upon him yelling "Let's beat the old dammed Dutchman to death!" Hubert pleaded for his life. One of the mob said cruelly, "you'll have to die because its fun." The unfortunate (Hubert) fell dead to the ground, shot through the breast. Another elderly German on Portland Avenue crawled under his bed at the outbreak of the disturbance. The murderers pulled him out and shot him through the heart. The reports of these bloody acts came from the Louisville newspapers.

Over 100 German families took their furniture and goods and moved to the northern states. Most of them went to Wisconsin.

It was the former spirit of barbarism, inherited from the border settlers, who, under Williamson, had reduced the German cities on the Muskingkum to ashes, which now precipitated the acts of murder and destruction against the foreigners. Louisville became deserted in the wake of these shameful acts. A curse seems to have hastened onto its future welfare; for the horror described above was carried out against the hardest working and most valuable segment of its population. Shortly before these bloody days, an interesting work appeared from the pen of the American A. M. Casseday, a history of the city of Louisville including statistics of its trade and commerce. A special segment was dedicated to the Germans, of which the following is a portion:

"Of the current population of Louisville, there are no fewer than 18,000 Germans. This number increases daily with newcomers from the fatherland. The least that can be said is that these foreigners belong to the best class of our population. They are a thoughtful, happy and hard working people, of a quiet, thoughtful and peaceful nature, the majority of whom are well-bred and professional. Every day this better class of the population gains in public esteem. And while in one respect they identify with the native-born citizens and are becoming Americanized, so too the influence of their philosophical spirit, their deep consciousness, their love of beauty in art and nature, are being incorporated into the social life of the city and each improves the other. In its higher development, the German character is deveoping many beautiful characteristics, which are lacking in more than one respect in our own native population. From the educated Germans we can learn to sincerely love and cherish the spiritual and beautiful in all its forms, which is ingrained in its character and gives pleasure to life. At the same time (the German character) can learn from us, that the basis of its philosophy must be practicality, and that without a certain mixture of that principle its theories are self-centered castles in the sky. Thus each class takes from the other that which it can use the most, and society reaps the fruit of this blending." Thus an American described that segment of the population, which, during those August days, fell victim to the fury of the mob.

Even in Columbus, Ohio, on the 4th of July, there was a collision between a nativist mob and a group of Turners. Together with the Grenadiers and the Men's Chorus, the Turners had held a celebration in Mauerer's Wood. Upon their return they were attacked with stones by rowdies in front of the United States Hotel. Someone tried to take their flags. The Turners halted and fired on their attackers, three of whom were wounded. One of those was the leader of the band, Henry Forster, a blacksmith. He breathed his last soon after. On an earlier occasion, on May 25th of that same year, after an outing in the suburbs of the city, the Turners had been assailed by a massive crowd of rowdies, falling upon the peaceful Turners who had unloaded weapons. The mob tore up their flags and scattered the Turner ranks by throwing stones. The Turners were a bit more careful on the 4th of July and, with manly resistance, made their attackers pay on this second occurrence.

As with the Bedini uproar in Cincinnati, so too in this instance the police behaved poorly and openly took the side of the mob. The hostile atmosphere prevalent as a result of the bloody scenes during the year between the nativist mob and the foreigners, was underscored with many violent acts. Among the victims was Captain Ismael, who suffered a fatal gunshot wound on the evening of April 19, in front of the Telegraph Office. As a result of these incidents, German immigration was significantly reduced. The New York Immigration Commission reported a drop in immigration of 111,803 against the previous year. On August 22, 1856, only 90,450 had arrived as against 202,267 the previous year.

The bloody Know-Nothingism had a positive effect on the German population, in that the Germans drew together even more than before. But the seriousness of the time did not dampen their festive spirit. The singing festival of the western singing clubs took place in Cleveland in that year with 250 singers participating. The following cities took part: Akron, Canton, Cincinnati, Columbus, Detroit, Milwaukee, Mount Easton, Pittsburg, Sandusky. There were also single or groups of delegates from other cities such as Chicago, Davenport, Iowa, Buffalo, and others.

And the third general Turner festival for all the clubs in North America from September 13 to the 20th, attracted Cincinnati's German population. An air of the conviviality was turned towards Turner Hall and Ross Hill. There was a significant participation by clubs from afar. About 30 cities were represented including: New York, Brooklyn, and Rochester, New York; Williamsburg, Syracuse, Philadelphia, Baltimore, Pittsburg, Wheeling, Cleveland, Milwaukee, Detroit, Chicago, Dayton, Madison, Indianapolis, Louisville, St. Louis, Circleville, Maysville, Kentucky; Portsmouth, Ohio; Columbus, Sidney Ohio; Terre Haute, Lafayette, Indiana; Memphis, Newport (Kentucky) and Covington (Kentucky).

There were even military and other clubs participating in the festival. This included: the German military company under command of Major Franz Link; the Dragoons under LT. Oesterle; the Hunters under Captain Becker; the Lafayette Guard under Captain Müller; the Steuben Guard under Captain Amis; the Jackson Guard under Captain Kühnle; the Cincinnati Liberty Guard under LT. Thole; the Sharpshooters under Captain Salomon; the Hunters and Sharpshooters; the Liedertafel; the Singers Union; the Germania and the singing group of the Turners, the Workers Club and the Freemen's Club.

The parade was one of the grandest ever seen here. The spirited marches of the six music bands, the waving flags, the shining uniforms, the ranks of strong young men in picturesque gymnastic garb, presented a picture of strength, which the German element could employ against the murderous nativist rowdies.

Mr. Wilhelm Rapp, Editor of the Turner newspaper, gave the moving keynote address in a manner attesting to the popularity of this hard-working man of letters. Gymnastics, now a part of the curriculum of the city schools, was introduced in August of that year by School board counselor Röwekamp into the schools of the First district.

The increase of the Germans in Cincinnati was also demonstrated by, among others, the arrest in July of that year of the Austrian officer Friedrich Posner. At the urging of the English Consul Rowecraft, Poschner is said to have recruited German troops for the Crimean War.

The members of the German company were arrested at the railroad station of the Little Miami Railroad by a strong cordon of police, in order to be booked for violation of the neutrality laws. At this year's awards for the best American wines, which were tested in New York, Misters Q. & P. Bogen, M. Werk and Ludwig Rehfuss received medals. The latter gentleman died on July 31 of this year. Having settled here in the beginning of the 30's, he had always participated enthusiastically in all the German affairs. After retiring from the hectic business world, he had spent the last year living in the country, where he dedicated his extensive earlier experience to the improvement of wine growing and agriculture. He was suddenly taken by the sickness which tore him from the side of his grieving family in the prime of his years.

On Pentecost Monday of the following year (1856) there were numerous confrontations between the Turners and the mobs in Covington.

During their picnic on the field beneath Whitehall, the Turners were constantly plagued by a group of youths from 10 to 14 years old, who had followed them from Covington. Constantly offering insults, they (the youths) threw sticks and stones and finally, one of them ripped a glass of beer out of the hand of one of the Turners. The affected Turner hit the boy in the mouth, whereupon the boy pulled a pistol and the spectacle began. The boy ran to Covington and spread the rumor that the Turners meant to murder 9 to 10 young Covington boys. Naturally the Turners remained ignorant of the resultant excitement. Between 5 and 6, with music playing and the Stars and Stripes waving, they began their way home.

Near Whitehall, bands of young people had gathered and began to attack the Turners with stones. As they came closer to Covington, one man stepped up, laid a hand on one of the Turners, and attempted to pull him out of the ranks. The Turner resisted and his companions came to his assistance. The man (who stepped out) was Marshal Butts of Covington. The Turners did not recognize the man or his office.

The procession continued; the crowd following with growing excitement. The marshal stayed close to his man and several times tried to apprehend him. Finally general fighting broke out, stones flew from both sides and pistols were fired. Marshal Butt's arm was shattered, and Deputy Sheriff Harvey was seriously wounded in the arm. The Turners marched through Covington, followed on both sides by an agitated crowd. They crossed the Licking bridges and passed through Newport, making for the ferry landing, where they intended to cross over.

During this time, the Covington fire bells were ringing, which further increased the crowd. The Turners formed up in rows and columns on the east side of the landing, with their front facing west. The crowd stayed below York street, from where they began throwing stones at the Turners. In response to the attack, the Turners fired several shots in return. The shots increased the overall anger of the crowd, most of whom were from Covington. Many of these individuals appeared to be almost insane, calling on "Old Kentuck" to destroy "the Dutchmen". Several rushed to the garrison and demanded assistance from the troops. Mayor Fearons later repeated that request; however, the officers refused to participate in the fight without authorization from Washington. The Turners straightened up their rows. In their gray linen jackets and caps topped with greenery, they posed a striking contrast to the mob. Several had muskets armed with bayonets. They stood peacefully and quietly, strictly obeying the orders of their officers. Sheriff Stricker and Police Officer Miller earnestly tried to calm the mob and forestall a bloody fight. The Turners remained quiet and made no difficulty. At that point, the mayors of Covington and Newport arrived on the scene. The former, Mr. Foley, immediately demanded that the Turners surrender their weapons and place themselves at the disposition of the civil authorities. The mob supported this demand and indicated that it would not be appeased if the weapons were not surrendered.

At that moment, the ferryboat "Bee" of Captain Air's Line approached the shore with a huge number of passengers from Cincinnati on board. Mayor Fearons would not let the boat land there. The passengers were disembarked onto a float, opposite the garrison. In response to the demand to surrender their weapons, Captain Müller, the Turner Commander, stated that his men would not hesitate to comply, if they could do so in safety; however, since that was not possible due to the presence of the hostile crowd, they would have to retain their weapons for self- protection. The police, however, would encounter no opposition in arresting those persons guilty of breaking the law.

The police moved through the ranks without encountering any opposition and arrested four Turners.

This did not appease the crowd, which demanded that the Turners lay down their arms. The officials again repeated this demand. The captain respectfully declined, but at the same time ordered the bayonets to be dismounted and sheathed.

That was a critical moment. The offials were powerless, the Turners quiet and determined, the crowd aroused to a frenzy. "Go and finish'em! Where are you, Kentucky Fellows?" screamed several voices.

Finally the Turners decided to seek refuge in the Turner Hall. Several stones flew against them; but not a word, not a curse came from the rows of Turners. They went up York street. Across from the courthouse and again at the corner of Orchard Street came the demand to the group in the name of the mayor to give up their weapons. The answer could be read in the faces of the Turners, who, to the astonishment of all who were following the events, reached their hall with every one of their men and without a wound.

Again Mayor Foley demanded that the Turners surrender their weapons. However, Judge Stallo replied that, since he (the mayor) could not defend the Turners against the mob, the Turners would have to do it themselves. On their part, the Turners guaranteed that no one would leave the hall and they would surrender the following morning to the authorities for disposition. Sheriff Stricker needlessly surrounded the hall with a cordon of Kentuckians, to prevent anyone from escaping. The crowd slowly dispersed.

After a long debate, it was decided that all of the prisoners would be given over to Kenton County authorities.

After deliberating for 7 days, the preliminary hearing, conducted by two Justices of the Peace, recommended to the Kenton County court in Covington that felony charges be brought against 31 Turners. Each one had to post $2000 bond, to ensure appearance before the court. The entire bond of $62,000 was immediately put up in Newport (Kentucky) by two honored Germans, Misters Daniel Wolf and Peter Constanz.

The trial dragged through several sessions of the County court and ended with an acquittal for every defendant, whose defense was conducted in a masterly fashion by Judge Stallo.

On January 20 of that year, the Settlers' Club of the Turners Union met for the first time in the Turner hall. In March of the following year the state commission was elected which in turn would select the state and community (for future settlement). After an extensive exploratory trip through the west, the commission decided upon New Ulm, Minnesota, which had already been founded by a German society. Very soon, numerous settlers, many of them Turner members, turned their steps to New Ulm. Since the town was to be renamed, in the interim it was called "Hutten" (Jahnshausen not having yet been discovered). Nevertheless, there were as many names suggested as there were patrons. Here is the list: Concordia, Thusnelda, Germania, Ulrichshain, Franklin, Sparta, Carthage, Constantinople(?!), New York, Nibelungen, Teutonia, Turnville, Humboldt City, Corinth, Wyandott, Cincinnati, Freiburg. Since a new name could not be agreed upon, it was decided to stick with the old one.

Simultaneously, the city of Buffalo in Buffalo county, WI, was founded by the "General Settlers Club" of Cincinnati with about 350 shareholders. That location currently has 350 to 400 souls and has a steam-driven corn and sawmill, which is associated with an incorporated furniture factory.

In 1857, another settler's club from Cincinnati founded Tell City, Indiana, on the Ohio river. On April 3, 1859, the inhabitants exercised their sovereign rights for the first time. The number of voters in Tell City was 204. The Swiss colony of Highland also sent many settlers (to Tell City).

The first Singing festival of the German Singing Society of North America took place in Cincinnati on June 12, 1857. The following cities were represented: Detroit, Sandusky, Ft. Wayne, Cleveland, Baltimore, Canton, Philadelphia, Dayton, Lafayette, Milwaukee, Tiffin, Wheeling, Columbus, Louisville, Pittsburg, Indianapolis and Erie. The high point was the festival on Ross Hill. The keynote address of Judge Stallo detailed in an eloquent manner the educational tasks of the Germans in America. Mr. Hans Balatka, a hard-working musician and composer from Milwaukee, received the prize for the best composition of the festival, an honorary cup, the work of art of a Baltimore goldsmith. One notable personality traveling the Ohio valley that year, was the famous Jewish emancipation fighter, Dr. Gabriel Riesser of Hamburg, former Vice President of the Frankfurt Parliament and Minister of Justice under the Imperial Administrator Johann.

The cornerstone for the new Free Mason Hall was laid on July 22, 1858. The first German Grand Master was Mr. E. F. Hanselmann, who was elected in 1841. The German Free Mason lodge Nr. 208, named after him, was founded on October 12 of that year and counted 80 members.

The Union of Special Brothers already had the following lodges: Germania Lodge 113 U.O.S.B. (Union der sonderbaren Brueder-Union of Special Brothers), founded on August 29, 1848, counted 577 members in 1860; Teutonia Lodge 177 U.O.S.B. founded on March 15, 1851, with 274 members in 1860. Hermann Lodge 208 U.O.S.B., founded on February 18, 1855, counted 242 members in 1860. Humboldt Lodge 274 U.O.S.B, founded May 18, 1855, counted 227 members in 1860. The William Tell Lodge 335 U.O.S.B., founded June 2, 1858, counted 85 members in 1860.

The autumn election of 1858 was accompanied with unusual excitement, to which a German worker, Karl Lucas, fell victim. He was murdered on the doorstep of his apartment by a brutal party lackey. Friends from both parties joined together to assist his family during that emergency.

In the following year, 1859, began the construction of the Catholic hall (Mozart Hall) on the north corner of Vine and Center streets, known as one of the most beautiful buildings in the city. Among the notable German festivals that year was the celebration in honor of Humboldt in the National Theater and the 100th birthday celebration of Schiller.

Let us examine the wonderful picture offered to us today by the combined effect of three periods of German immigration to Cincinnati, which covers barely 35 years. Mr. Rufus King, President of the Board of Education, states that it has been exactly 20 years since the founding of the German free schools in Cincinnati. Immediately following the passage of that law (1840) there were two schools equipped for that purpose. They had five teachers and 250 students. In this year (1860) the number has grown to 49 teachers and 4,788 students. Among the nine Catholic parish schools, there are a few (e.g., St. Mary's Church) which has 6 to 7 hundred students. We estimate the total (of the Catholic students) to be only about 4,000. If one counts the 172 students of the Talmud Yelodim Institute, then the total number of German children in school went from 500 in 1837 to 10,000 in 1860.

In 1840 there were a total of 6340 voters in Cincinnati.

During the presidential election of 1860, the five German wards alone produced a third more votes, namely 9499. If the scattered German votes in the other wards and townships are counted, then the total of German votes in Hamilton county in 1860 are more than all the votes in the county in 1850, when only 14,782 ballots were counted.

The value of the real estate and personal property of Cincinnati's Germans, which in 1830 was barely 100,000, had, in a conservative estimate increased and, due to a thousand-fold increase in their business activities, reached a height of 40 to 50 million dollars.

The German immigration engulfed not only the so-called Rheinland, but had also persevered in large businesses and banks in the midst of the economy and in German communities and in somewhat more than 30 churches, and had already spread to all major metropolitan areas.

As in the city of Cincinnati, so to did the German influence increase throughout the state. The following shows the country of birth of the foreign settlers who were naturalized in the year ending July 1, 1860:

$$\begin{aligned}
&\text{England, Scotland, Wales}\ldots..2632\\
&\text{Ireland}\ldots\ldots\ldots\ldots\ldots\ldots4186\\
&\text{Germany}\ldots\ldots\ldots\ldots\ldots13210\\
&\text{other countries}\ldots\ldots\ldots\ldots2113
\end{aligned}$$

Germans 60%, Irish 20%, English, Scots and Welsh 12%.

The last original inhabitants of Ohio had long since been transferred out west. The Delawares had left the state in 1830. In August 1831, the Shawnees, in conjunction with the Senecas, had ceded their last lands in Allen County to the United States, and in September of the following year were moved to the Indian areas on the Kansas River. The upper and lower Piquas[4] had retained in their headquarters until they were driven out by the Kentuckians when they came to St. Mary's and Wapakonetta (OH). The latter, a village settled primarily by German settlers, was named after a club-footed sachem who led the migration to the west. The remaining Wyandotts, 700 in number, departed the state in July 1843, led by a giant of a chief named Jean Baptiste, a unique figure with a horrible face, which was capped by an enormous nose, blue as a potato, which shook like jelly whenever he laughed.

Indiana entered the Union as a state in 1816, and on June 29 of that same year the consitution was created and proclaimed by 41 county representatives. In 1800 there were, not counting the Indians, only 4875 whites, in 1810 24,520. In contrast, in 1860 the state already had a population of 1,350,428 souls. During the last decade, it increased 362,000, or more than 36% of its population of 1850.

---

[4] *Piqua*, in Shawnee, means a man formed from ashes.

The Illinois territory was founded in 1809 and by 1818 had sufficient population to be admitted to congress as a state. The name came from the large river which flows through it and also from the Indian language which meant something like a man thriving in his strength. Prior to 1803 the entire territory was occupied by the following tribes: the Kaskaskias; Sacks and Foxes; the Piankeshaws; the Ottawas; the Chippewas; and the Pottawatamies, who gave up their last few territories to the Union in 1816. Illinois increased in population more than any other state in the Union. In 1800 the population was barely 600. In 1810 it was only 12,282, which included 11,501 whites, 168 slaves; and 613 freed blacks. In 1830 Illinois counted 157,445; in 1840, 476,138; in 1850, 851,470; in 1860, 1,711,951. Thus, in the past decade, its population has increased 101.06%.

In conclusion, we will now look at the German population of the states touched upon by this chronicle.

The Ohio Valley, meaning the entire area of the Ohio River and its tributaries and adjoining land, includes West Virginia, West Pennsylvania, Ohio, Indiana, Illinois, Kentucky, and Tennessee, and encompasses an area of 233,000 square miles. According to the census of 1860, approximately 400,000 Germans lived there.

They are:

In the state of Ohio: 1317 Austrians; 17,117 Prussians; 26,206 Bavarians; 19,025 Badeners; 12,234 Hessians; 1,136 Nassauers; 14,511 Württembergers; 76,574 from unknown German countries; 11,078 Swiss. There are altogether 179,278 out of a total population of 2,339,511.

In the state of Indiana: 351 Austrians; 8610 Bavarians; 5740 Badeners; 4298 Hessians; 738 Nassauers; 12,067 Prussians; 3956 Württembergers; 30,945 Germans from unknown countries; 3813 Swiss. A total of 70,518.

In the state of Illinois: 2,106 Austrians; 12,437 Bavarians; 9508 Badeners; 10,184 Hessians; 1,585 Nassauers; 24,547 Prussians; 5096 Württembergers; 65,341 from unknown countries; 5748 Swiss. A total of 136,552.

In the state of Kentucky: 116 Austrians; 3,973 Bavarians; 2,975 Badeners; 1,669 Hessians; 310 Nassauers; 2,964 Prussians; 1,480 Württembergers; 13,740 from unknown countries; 735 Swiss. A total of 27,980.

In the state of Tennessee: 75 Austrians; 222 Bavarians; 269 Badeners; 131 Hessians; 13 Nassauers; 354 Prussians; 165 Württembergers; 2,640 from unknown countries; 566 Swiss. A totalof 4,435.

Those from Alsace and Lorraine are not included in the above German census, but rather are counted in the French population.

The 1860 census gives the German population of the three largest cities of the Ohio valley as the following: Pittsburg 6,094; Cincinnati 43,931; Louisville 13,374.

Names, Addresses & Occupations of the Cincinnati Germans (from page 159)

Aupperle, David; Smith; Sycamore Street between 2 and Lower Market.
Autenheimer, Johann; worker; 4th Street between Main and Sycamore.
Benninger, Martin; worker; Water street between Walnut and Vine.
Dänzer, Georg; gardener, 5th street, East Broadway.
Dannheimer, Christian, wagon drover, corner of Ludlow and Congress Street.
Dross, Friedrich, watchmaker, 152 Main St, (Switzerland).
Dubois, John; tailor; Sycamore St (Switzerland).
Eckstein, Friedrich; schoolteacher; 4th Street between Vine and Race.
Elstner, Caspar; tailor; corner Walnut and Main street (Dutchman).
Ernst, Andreas H.; confectioner and producer of mineral water; 151 Main Street.
Ernst, Heinrich M.; grocer; Broadway between 5th and 6th.
Faber, Jakob; wood cutter on Deer Creek near the oil mill.
Fecorn, Fredr(ich); porter house, Front street between Elm and Plum.
Fegly, Caleb; butcher; #5 6th street between Smith und Mound.
Franks, Fr.; portrait painter; corner Smith and Longworth Street.
Frühlingsdorf, Wilhelm; stone mason; between Broadway and Ludlow.
Fritz, Johann; plumber; Broadway between 4th and 5th.
Gärtner, Heinrich; baker; corner Ludlow and 2nd Street.
Gruner, Auguste, 130 Main Street.
Hafer, Heinrich; grocer; 25 Lower Market.
Hechinger, Joseph; gardener; corner Symmes and Lawrence.
Herzog, Friedrich; shoemaker; 3rd street between Broadway and Ludlow.
Heckeren, Jonas, wood cutter; corner Ludlow and Congress St.
Hoffner, Jakob; baker; 196 Main Street.
Hoffmann, John; grocer; Water street between Main and Walnut; (Austria).
Hummel, Jakob; worker; Sycamore between Front and 2nd. (Switzerland).
Hanselmann, Carl; wagoneer; 5th Street corner Broadway.
Jupenlatz, Georg; baker; 26 Main Street.
Jarhanns, Philipp; cabinet maker; Deer Creek above the oil mill.
Keny, Anton; gardener; Sycamore above New Market.
Kessler, Fried.; worker; alley between Wayne and St. Clair.
Kniest, Friedr.; Glaser alley.
Knoblauch, Fried.; tailor; 12 Broadway.
Kopp, Jakob; gardener; High Street corner Deer Creek.
Krugmann, Peter W; shoemaker; 204 Main Street.
Letner, Gregor; moulder; Sycamore between 6th and 7th.
Libeaw, Valentin; gun smith; 127 Main Street.
Link, J; worker; Race Street above St. Clair (Switzerland).
Link, Anton; grocer; Front between Broadway and Ludlow.
Linke, Anton; gardener; Vine Street, above St. Clair (Switzerland).
Menken, Salomon; businessman; 88 Main Street.
Mehnke, Karl T; apothecary; 7th Street between Western Row and John.
Mehlen, John L; smith; New Market between Main and Sycamore; (Switzerland).
Miller, Thomas; wagon driver; 5th Street corner Broadway.
Mundhent, Caroline; baker; alley between Wayne and St. Clair.
Meyer, L H; German Lutheran preacher; 4th Street between Vine and Race.
Myers, J; confectioner; 66 Main Street.
Oberdorf, Franz J C; doctor; London and John.
Reininger, Caspar, joiner, 5th Street between John and Smith.

Reidinger, Barbara, corner John and Richmond.
Ritter, Karl G., confectioner and cordial distiller, 128 Main Street.
Rudolph, L., Walnut Street, between 5th & 6th.
Schroeter, Jakob, grocer, Broadway and 2nd Street.
Sellet, Anton, Corner Ludlow and 3rd Street.
Schäfer, Ludwig, wagon driver, Water St. between Walnut and Vine.
Schofer, Gottfr., shoemaker, Front, between Broadway and Ludlow.
Sieg, Peter, Cooper, 5th St. between Main and Walnut.
Schmidtlapp, Caleb, baker, 158 Main St.
Schmidtlapp, Fried., 158 Main St.
Stabler, Jonathan, gardener, Deer Creek near Symmes.
Sutter, Jakob, grocer, Sycamore, between Front and 2nd (Switzerland).
Tuffly, Peter, confectioner, Nr.. 13 Lower Market (Switzerland), Tuffly and Richard Co.
Tron, Fried., weaver, Sycamore, between Front and 2nd St.
Weber, David, innkeeper, 29 5th St. (Switzerland).
Weimann, Georg, meat cutter, 5th St. corner of Broadway.
Weimer, Georg, worker, 5th St. between Vine and Race.
Zeumer, August, confectioner, Loring's Row (Prussia).

INDEX

The following is the complete family name index of the book
Deutsche Chronik in der Geschichte des Ohio-Thales
by Emil Klauprecht.
(Cincinnati:1864)

(Note: Entries marked with an [*] are also cited in the Bibliography.)

Aaronburg, Mr. 11
Abel 92
Abt, F. 182
Adams, President John 143, 170
Adlum, Major 178
Allison, Dr. 138
Alter, Friedrich 143
Altman, W. 163
Amboy, NJ 57
Amen, Mr. 178
Amis, Captain 193
Anausseracheri. David Zeisberger's Iroquois name. Means "One Resting on a Pumpkin." 37
Anne, Queen of England. 10, 14, 15, 18
Ange, Dr. 161
Anschütz, Georg 168
Anton. Moravian Indian 54
Arbuckle, Captain (Matthew). Commandant of Fort Randolph (Point Pleasant) WV According to Klauprecht he
    was responsible for the seizure and subsequent deaths of Cornstalk, Red Hawk and Ellinipisco in 1777. 67,
    68
Armstrong
    Captain John 121
    Judge 105, 108
Aupperle, David 155, 159, 171
Autenheimer
    Friedrich 171
    Johann A. 156, 159
Avery, George 134
Bühler, Eduard 183
Babin, Fr. Peter 160
Bacon, Nathanial 14
Bail, Stephen 148
Baker 62
Balatka, Hans 196
Baptiste, Jean. Last Wyandot Chief in Ohio (1843) 197
Barbee, Mayor of Louisville, KY, during the Know-Nothing riots there in August 1855. 190
Barlow 132
    Joel 131
Barnum, Judge 105, 106
Barr, W. B. 180
Barrett 191
Bassi, Ugo. Garibaldi's chaplain 186
Bastian of Gonsenheim 161

Batte, Captain 14
Baum, Martin (1761-1831) Founded the Miami Exporting Co. in 1803. 143, 145, 156
Baumgärtner, Friedrich 171
Bavaria 71, 181, 198
Beach, William 52
Beaujeu, Captain (Daniel Hyacinth Maniede de) 29, 30
Beaver, Delaware Chief. See Schingask.
Bebber
    Jacob 72
    Mathias 72
    Rhoda 72
Bebinger, Abraham 170
Bechtle, Heinrich 143, 145
Becker
    Captain 193
    Carl 190
Bedinger, Major George M. 4, 95, 120
Bedini, Cardinal. Papal Nuncio 186, 187, 193
Behaim 9
Behm, Rev. 155
Behnam, Joseph S. 161
Behringer, Mathias 173
Beinbrecht, Friedrich Wilhelm 143, 155, 170
Belser
    Carl 171
    John 171
Benham, Captain Robert 77, 133
Benninger, Martin 154, 155, 159
Berte, J.H. 173
Bertens 161
Beverly, William 14, 19
Beyer, Rev. 172
Beymer
    Georg 147
    Simon 147, 153
Biemer, Heinrich 171
Bienville
    Captain Celeron de 22, 25
    French governor of New Orleans in 1736 16
Bilderbach
    Karl 4, 90, 110, 111
    Jakob 110, 111
    Ruhama 110, 111, 122
Billiod 158
Bixler, Abraham 155
Black Hoof, Shawnee Chief. 42
Blackbird, Shawnee Chief 108
Blannerhasset 140
Blin, Seth 123, 124
Blue Jacket, Shawnee Chief. Marmaduke Van Swearingen. 125
Blücher, Count 156
Boden, Andreas 143

Bogen
	P 194
	Q 194
Boggs 189
Bohl, Robert 143
Bonapart, Napoleon 123, 139, 143, 145, 161, 165
Bonge, Karl von 171
Bonnhorst, Major C. von 168
Bonte 185
Boone, Daniel 4, 53, 54, 61, 62, 65, 70, 76, 95, 133
Bossinger, Benjamin 172
Boudinot, Elias 106
Bouquet, Heinrich (1719-1765) 42, 43, 44, 48, 49, 70
Bourbons, Ruling Family of France 18
*Bowen. *Wheeling, WV City Directory of 1839*. 61
Bowman, Colonel John 76, 95
Brachmann, Heinrich 171
Braddock, General Edward 28, 29, 30, 31, 42, 43, 70, 121
Bradford, David 128, 129, 130
Bradstreet, Colonel (later General) John 41, 49
Brashears. Sheriff 189
Brauer 140
Braun, Gottlieb 184
Brebouef, Fr. S.J. 7
Breckenridge, John 123
Brill, Johann 133
Broadhead, Colonel Daniel 76, 79, 81
	Known to the Indians as Great Sun. 81
Broli. See Müller, Bernhard 167, 168
Brother
	David (Moravian) 86
	Lucas (Moravian) 86
Brough, Colonel Charles H. 179
Brown
	*Henry. *The History of Illinois*... 7, 12
	John 123, 124
	William, Dr. 188
Bubritt, Johann 155
Bürgeler 187
Bulge, C. 53
Bullitt, Thomas 53
Burget, Jacob 171
Burnet, Jacob 136, 109, 123, 127, 135, 136, 143, 156, 158
Burgoyne, General John 73, 102
*Burkhalter, Christian. (With a Mr. Hefley co-edited the 1841 Cincinnati newspaper *Germans in the West*.
	Also cited as *Deutschen im Westen*.) 156, 177
Burr, Aaron 140, 142, 143

Butler 120
	Richard 99, 120, 121, 148, 149, 179
	*Mann *History of Kentucky...* 66
	Simon (Simon Kenton's alias) 52
Butts, Marshal 194
*Byrd, J. *Progress to the Mines of Virginia* 15, 79
Bäcker, Mr. 167
Bäumler, Joseph 167
Böbinger, Abraham 154
Bögtly, Mr. 168
Böhler, Peter 35
Bömeler, Mr 156
Bühring and Breuning Co. 155
Bülow, Freiherr von 139
Büttner, Gottlieb 36
Cabot 14
Cadillac, de la Motte 7
Caesar 123
Calhoun, Dexter 46, 47
Cammerhof. Moravian missionary 37
Campbell
    John 53
    Major 124
Cannastego, Onondago Chief 19
Capp 160
Carl, Count 166
Caroll, James 187
Carondelet, Baron de 127
Carr 109
	Captain 152
	Marshall 161
	Mr. 178
Cartier, Jacob 13
Cartrecht, Joseph 171
Cass
	Governor Lewis 165
	Major Jonathan 124
*Casseday, A. M. *The History of Louisville...* 192
Catherine, Empress of Russia 101
Cecilia 105
Champlain, Fr. S.J. 7, 22
Charles I King of England. 21
Charles II King of England. 14
Charlevoir, Fr. 7, 9, 11
Chartier, Peter 17
Cholmac, Fr. 84
Christ 33
Christian, William 63
Cincinnatus, Lucius Quintus 113, 114

Clark 120
    Captain 182
        George Rogers 4, 62, 65, 74, 75, 76, 78, 79, 95, 96, 97, 99, 101, 106, 123, 127
Clay, Henry 170
Clayton, John 110
Clemen, Rev. 173
Clinton 22
Colbert 78
Coleman
    John 189
    Mrs. 122
*Collins, Lewis *Historical Sketches of Kentucky* 53, 55, 66
Connolly 61, 62, 63, 79
Connelly, (John) 53
Conrad, Ulrich 164
Consoly, Hermann 65
Constanz, Peter 195
Cooper, James Fenimore 8
Cornstalk, Shawnee Chief 62, 63, 67, 68
Foley. Mayor of Covington, KY 195
Miller. Covington, KY police officer. 194
Stricker. Covington, KY Sheriff. 194, 195
Craig
    *F. *An Account of...* 66
    *Neville B. *The Olden Time*...40, 47
Crawford, William 51, 89, 93, 103
Cressap, Michael 62
Crevecoeur, (Michel Guilleaume St. Jean de) 26, 28, 29, 41
Croghan, George 50
Cutler, Dr. 101
Dale, Cincinnati City Councilman 188
Dannheimer 154
    Christian 159
Danzer 154
Darke, Colonel (William) 120, 121
Darr 171
d'Artiguette. French Governor of Illinois in 1736. 16
David, Christian 33
Davies, Colonel 156
Davis, Joseph 171
Dayton, Jonathan 106, 133
Demint, Miss 107
Denkler 161
Denman 145
Denmann, Mathias 106, 107
Dennhof 181
Desnouttes, General Lefevre 161
Detrosch, Susanna Elisabeth 152
Dettgen 170
d'henin, Princess 141
Dianna 102

Dick, Adam 173
Diehl 185
Dierdorf Brothers 146
Dieskau, Baron (Augustus von) 31
Dietrich, C. 173
Dietsch, Theodor 185
Dill
    Andreas 164
    Johann 146
Dimmew, Jacob 18
Dinwiddie, Robert. Governor of Virginia 21, 24
Diserenz, Friedrich 171
Dittmann, Johann C. 101
Domschke 187
Donners, Anton 171
Donnersberger, Mr. 184
Dorey, Patrick 189
Dorfeuille (Museum in Cincinnati) 13
Doughty, Major (John) 100, 105, 109, 117
*Drake, Daniel Dr. 145, 151, 154, 158
Dreher, Rev. Dr. 155
Dreybach 84
Driesbach, Daniel 146
Dross, Friedrich 159
Dubois, John 159
Dufour
    Daniel 139, 182
    Johann Jacob 139, 161
    Johann Franz 182, 182
Duhme 185
Cumberland, Duke of 22
Dumas, Captain Jean Daniel 29
Dunbar, Colonel Thomas 28, 29, 30, 31
Dunlap, John 114
Dunmore, Lord. John Murray, 4th Earl of Dunmore. 61, 63, 64, 65
Duponceau, P.S. 10, 132, 151
Duquesne, Captain 76
Durlach 71
Dusenberg
    I. 146
    W. 146
Dänzer, Georg 159
Döbbelen 170
Ebeling, Christoph Daniel 139
Eberhard, Franz 171
Ebinger, Brother 155
Eckley, E.R. 130
Eckstein, Friedrich 159, 162
Edgeton, Georg 191
Edwards, William 83, 84, 88, 165
Eggerlin, Karl 187
Eggers and Wilde Publishing House 179

Egly, Joseph E 185
Egry, Dr. 179
Ehrenfeiht, Christoph 143
Ehrhardt, H.S. 148
Eichenlaub 185, 185
Eichert, Mr. 178
Eimann, Peter 146
Eisenloh, Rev. 173
Eiteljörg, August 154, 171
El Dorado 11
Elet, Fr. D.A. 176
Elholm, Cäsar August 100
*Ellet, Elizabeth F. *Women of the West* 66
Ellinipsico, Son of Cornstalk 68
Elliot, Captain Matthew 73, 81, 83, 84, 85,86, 88, 95
Ellwanger 171
Elstner, Caspar 159
Embree, English brewer 158
Emerich 148
Erich, August 143
Erkel, Cincinnati city councilman 189
Ernst
    Andreas H. 154, 155, 159, 170
    Heinrich M. 159
    Johann Zacharias 154
    Zacharias 155, 170
Essman, Heinrich 184
Ettwein, Bishop Johann 4, 59, 149
Eugen, Prince 34
Euler, Simon 171
Evans, George 157
Faber, Jakob 159
Fabler, Jakob 154, 155
Fabricius. Moravian murdered at Gnadenhütten, PA 38
Fahs, Caspar 143
Fairfax, Lord 24
Farlowe House 189
Fat Henry (Speckheinrich) 158
Faulkner, Captain 128
Fearons, Mayor of Newport, KY 195
Febriger, B.F. 161
Fecorn, Fredrich 159
Fegekorn, Friedrich 143
Fegly, Caleb 159
Fehr, Captain Stephan 179
Fein
    Georg 174, 179
    Johann 63
Fellebaum, George 73
Feller, Johann 191
Fenneberg, Fenner von 185

Fenwick, Bishop Edward 160, 173
Ferguson, Major 117
Filson, John 106, 107
Findley, General 153
Fink
      Albert 144
      Johann 146
      Michael 144
Finley, John 52, 54
Fitzgerald 191
Flaget, Bishop 160
Fleischmann 171
Flinn, Patrick 191
Flint, Royal 101
Floyd, Colonel 96
*Flügel, Dr. *Flowers of German Poetry* 161
Foley, Mayor of Covington 195
Forbes, Colonel (later General) John 31, 41, 42, 43
Forster
      Henry 192
      Professor 140
Fountain, Major 118
Fowler, Major Jacob 121
Fox, Mr. 176
Francis, Tench 99
Frankenstein
      Franz 174
      Georg 174
Franklin, Benjamin 22, 27, 28, 29, 51, 70, 146
Franks 71
      Fr. 159
Franz I, Emperor 13
Franzburg 181
Frazier 26
French, Captain 100
Frey
      Ludwig 171
      Ursus 173
Friedrich the Great (1712-86). King of Prussia 31
Friedrich II 41
Fritz, Johann 159
Frontenac, Louis de Baude, Comte de...et Palluau. Gov. of New France 7, 12
Frühlingsdorf
      Wilhelm 159, 170
      J.W. 155
Fullenweider, Peter 73
Fulton
      Robert 145

Funk 4
    Absalon 146
    Adam 146
    Jakob 146
Gage
    Captain 29, 30
    General Thomas 51, 57
Gallaher, J. 123
Gallisoniere, Marquis de 22
Gano, General John S. 152, 153
Gardoqui 127
Garibaldi 186
Garrety's cooperage 191
Gast, Johann 168
Gates, Horatio 73
Gavazzi, Fr. 186
Gaßmeier, A. 133
Genet 127, 129
Genovesa. Also known as Tegah Kuita 84
George III. King of England 28, 36
Gerhard, Mr. 176
Germann, J.B. 173
Gersdorf, Frau von. Grandmother of Christian David-Founder of the Moravian Church. 33
Gerstäcker, Friedrich 176
Gerwig, Rev. 173
Gettheim 181
Gettier, Georg 155
Geßner, Johann A. 170
Gibault, Fr. Pierre 75
Gibson, Colonel 76
Gieße 171
Gilbert, Bernhard 155
Girty, Simon 72, 73, 76, 81, 89, 90, 95, 114
Gist, Christopher 24, 26
Glickhican, Isaac 54, 55, 63, 68, 76, 92
Gluck, Christoph Willibald (1714-1787) 123
Gmion, Major 125
Gode 154
Goegg, Amand 185
Goepper 185
Goethe, Johann Wolfgang von 179, 187
Goetschius, Nicolaus 164
Gohs, Jos. 173
*Gordon History of Pennsylvania 16
Goß, S. 133
Gott 185
Grün 5
Graham, William 191
Grant, Major James 41

Great
    Spirit 7, 44
    Sun, Natchez Chief 16
    Sun, Indian name for Colonel Daniel Broadhead 81
Greathouse, Jacob 62
Green
    Charles 119
    Charles R. 152
    John 122
Gregor, Christian 56
Greven, Johann H. 171
Grey, William 189
Griffin 9
Grimes, Patrick 112
Grimm, Jakob 143
Grob, Johann 146
Gross, Magnus 184
Groß, Andreas 173
Grubb, Jakob 136
Grube
    Bernhard Adam 151
    Leonhard Adam 80
Grün 5
Gruner, Auguste 159
Grüner, J.R. 154
Gunkel 148
Guthrie 120
Gärtner, Heinrich 159, 169
Göbel, Rev. 173
Gülich
    Jakob 155, 156
    Rev. 172
Haberfeld, Jakob 147
Hafer
    A. 154
    Heinrich 143, 159
Hagemann, Adrian 143
Hagen, Moravian missionary 37
Hahn
    Ab. 169
    Michael 143
Haldimand, General Frederick 97, 98
Halkett, Sir Peter 28, 30
Hall
    Harvey
    *James. The Romance of Western...7, 12
Haltenwerth, Jacob 171
Hamilton
    Alexander 128
    Governor Henry 68, 69, 72, 75, 76, 83
    Governor of Pennsylvania 23
Hammer, Fr. Franz 173

Hand, Brigadier General Edward 113
Handbury 20
Hannibal 50, 75
Hanselmann
    C.F. 171
    Carl 159
        E.F. 196
    Jakob 155
    Karl 155
Hardin, Colonel (John) 117, 118
Harlan, Major 95
Harmar, Colonel (later General) Josiah 102, 109, 110, 114, 117, 118, 119, 120, 122, 128, 129, 130
Harrison
    County, PA 147
    General 22, 158
    William A. 136
    William Henry 121
    William S. 161, 161, 172
Harrod, James 55, 65
Hartmann, Mr. 172
Harvey, Deputy Sheriff 194
Hassaureck, Friedrich 184
Hasselbeck 174
Haus
    Andreas 65
    *Johann 65
Hauser, Rev. 172
Havekotte 170
Hayden 123
Hechinger 154
    Joseph 159
Heckel, Melchior 178
Hecker
    Friedrich 182
    Jonas 154
Heckeren, Jonas 159
Heckewelder 5
    *Johann 4, 5, 8, 10, 40, 44, 45, 46, 47, 58, 59, 60, 62, 64, 67, 73, 76, 82, 83, 84, 86, 87, 88, 92, 115, 149, 151
    Johanna Marie 83
    Marie nee Seyrs 88, 155
    Sarah 86
    Pierson 155
    Thomas 155
Heer, Jacob 163
Hefley, Mr. See *Germans in the West* 177
Heidelberg, E. 168
Heimann, Ludwig 179
Heinzen 187
Helen of Troy 109

Helfenstein, Peter 72
Helm, Captain Leonhard 74, 75
Hemann, Joseph Anton 175
Henderson
    Colonel Richard 100
    James 65, 78
*Hennepin, Fr. Louis *Amplissimae Regiones*...7, 9, 10, 12
Henni, Fr. John M. Editor of the *Wahrheitsfreund*. 173
Henrici, Mr. 167
Henry
    Ambassador 153
    Patrick 63, 72, 74
Hereford, R.P. 23
Hermann
    Hatmaker 170
    Johan 55
Herrman, Valentin 53
Hertel, Capt. 7
Herz, Johannes 155
Herzog, Friedrich 155, 159, 171
Hett, Lt. Mathias 179
Heybach, Carl 190
Heyl, Christian 163, 164
Hildebrand
    Elisabeth 143
    Lorenz 143
*Hildreth, Dr. S.P. *Pioneer History*...3, 9, 23, 63, 72, 101
Hirsch (alias of Justus Erich Bollmann) 141
Hobelmann, Friedrich August. Editor of the *Frühlingsboten (Spring Messenger)* and the *Watchman (Hochwächter)*. 186
Hof 4
Hofacker, George 53
Hoffmann
    Johann 171
    John 159
Hoffner, Jakob 159
Hofmann, Dr. 140
Hofsümmer, Rev. 172
Holderness, Earl of 25
Holsteiner, George Michael. Also known as Michael Stoner or Michael Schuck 62
*Homann, Johann Baptist. *Regni Mexicani*...9
Hooks, Joseph 190
Hoppel, Andreas 155
Horwitz, Dr. 156
House of Friends 157
Howard, John 17
*Howe, Henry. *Historical Collections of Ohio* 3, 42
Huber
    Fr. Franz L. 173
    Nicolaus 164
Hubert, George 192

Hudson, John 191
Huesmann. Cincinnati policeman 187
Hull, Governor William 153, 185
Humboldt, Alexander von 139, 196
Hummel, Jakob 155, 159
Hutchins, Thomas 49
Häusler, Dr. 176
Höfer
    H.G. 155
    J.G. 155
Höfle, Elisabeth 155
Höflich, Friedrich 143
Hüger, Francis 141, 142
Icks, Mr. 179
Innis, Harry 126, 127
Isabella, Queen of Spain 5
Ismael, Captain 193
Jackmann, Johann 53
Jackson, Andrew 140, 170
Jacob 90
Jäger 146
    Georg 4
    George 52, 53
    Peter 133
Jahnshausen 196
Jarhanns, Philipp 159
Jay, Ambassador 77, 126
Jefferson, Thomas 78, 79, 140, 142, 143, 182, 188
Jellichich von Buzim, Joseph Graf (1801-59) 180
Jenkinson, Captain of Artillery 152
Jenner, Johann L. Friedrich von 156
Jex 161
Johnson 163
    Colonel 8, 10, 31, 41, 42, 49
    Colonel John 58
    Richard M. 95
    Robert 95
    Commissioner for Indian Affairs 50, 51
Jones
    Gabriel 65
    *Hugh *The present state of Virginia...* 15
Jordan, Mr. 179
Joshua, Mohican Indian 150
Jouges, Fr. Isaac S.J. 7
Judith 92
Jumonville, Ensign Coulon de 26, 27
Jung
    Michael 80, 83, 84, 86, 87, 88
    Mr. 169
    N.D. 160
Jungmann, Johann Georg 80, 84, 86, 88, 151

Junker, Rev. D. 173
Juppenlatz, Georg 143, 154, 155, 159, 171
Kahni, Anton 171
Kaine, Hiram 144
Kaiser, Johann 171
Kapp, Mr. 156
Kebsheimer, Franz 143
Keenes 148
Keith. Governor of Pennsylvania 15
Kennedy, Rebecca 107
Kenning Brothers 170
Kenton, Simon 4, 52, 53, 76, 95, 96, 164
Keny, Anton 159
Keppler, Admiral Augustus 28
*Kercheval *History of the Valley of Virginia* 71
Kerr
    Hamilton 63
    John 163
    Susanna nee Nieswanger 63
Kessler, Fried. 159
Keßler
    Captain Hermann 179
    Joseph 171
Killbuck, Delaware Chief 81, 165
Kilpatrick, Major Abraham 129
King, Rufus 197
Kingsbury, Colonel John 114
Kinkel 185, 185
    Gottfried 184
    Wilhelm 187
Kitzl, Conrad 190
Kleber, H. 168
Klein 185
    Friedrich H. 170
Kneisely 169
Kniest, Friedr. 159
Knoblauch, Fried. 159
Knoop 4
Knöpfly, Peter 143
Knox
    General Henry 113, 114
    James 53
Koch, Jacob Gerhard 153
König, Dr. 168
Kopp, Jakob 159
Kossuth, Ludwig 185
Kosziusko 117
Kothe, Captain Johann A. 158, 171
Kotzebue 174
Kraus 133
Krauskopf, Ludwig 171

Krautz, Jakob 143
Krebs, Christian 66
Kreuzner, Mr. 168
Kronenbold 171
Kröll, Rev. 172, 178
Krugmann, Peter W. 159
Kufer, Daniel 163
Kuhlmann, B. 173
Kühne 132
Kühnle, Captain 193
Kurfis 171
Kyan, Charles 191
Labner, Georg 175
Lafayette 141, 142
    Marquis de 161
Lallemond, Fr. S.J. 7
Lamb Farm 7, 12
Lane, Judge Eb. 165
Lang, Ludwig 143
Lange 171
*Lanman, James H. *History of New France* 7, 12
Lauer, Rev. Baptizan H. W. 172
La Salle, Robert de 6, 7, 9, 12, 22
Laurens, Henry 73
Lauterbach 158
Law, John 10, 11
Lawler, Lieutenant 110
LeBlanc, Fr. Augustine S.J. 84
Leatherlips, Chief 146
Lee
    Arthur. US Commissioner 99
    Colonel Thomas 19, 20
    Henry 122, 129
Leibin, Georg 143
Leitner, Gregor 171
Lenau, Mr. Nicolaus 168, 169
Leon, Count 167
Letner, Gregor 159
Levallier, Francois 89
Lewasseur, Lafayette's secretary 161
Lewis
    Captain Meriweather 182
    Colonel Carl 63
    General Andreas 62, 63
    Major 41
Libeau 171
    Carl 172
Libeaw, Valentin 159
Licht, Jakob 122
Lichtenberg 187
Lignery, Captain Francois de 29, 41

Link 154
    Anton 159, 170
    Brewery 188
    David 53
    Major Franz 155, 193
    J. 159
Linke, Anton 159
Little Turtle, Miami Chief 7, 116, 118, 125
Livingston, Colonel 36
*Löh(e)r, Franz *Germans in America* 42, 110, 160, 179
Löffler
    Gerhard 73
    Jacob Jr 73
Logan
    Cayuga Chief 37, 62, 63
    Colonel 95, 96
    Provincial secretary of Pennsylvaina 15
Long
    Junk dealer 191
    Mr. 192
Longworth 154
    Nicolaus 178
Loramie's Store 79
Loretto 5
Loretz, John 56
Los, Carl 161
*Loskiel, George Henry. *History of the mission...* 5, 40, 66, 81
Louis
    XIV 6, 7, 12
    XV 23
    XVI 131, 153
Lucas, Karl 196
Luckenbach, Rev. 150
Ludlow
    Isreal 106, 107, 133, 148
    John 112, 134
Ludwig, King of Bavaria 181
Luken, Cincinnati Police Captain 186
Lukenbach, Rev. 164
Luth von. Commandant at the fortress of Frontenac 84
Mack, Martin 36
Mahei, Christine 92
Malartin, Count 131, 132
Maltiz, Rudolph. Editor of the *Volksfreund* 177
Mansco, Kaspar 53
Mansfield 162
    Captain of Infantry 152
    Edward D. 145
Marc, J. 160
Marie Antoinette 102
Markgraf, F. 169

Marquette, Fr. 9, 14, 22
Marshe, Witham 18
Martin
    Johann 90
    Thomas 160
Marville, Brissot de 105, 132
Massard, Johann M. 160
Massie, Nathaniel 133
Maunz 133
Maxfeld, Johann 65
Maxwell, William 135
May, John. Surveyor 79
Mays, Jacob 134
McBride 52
McCarthur, Colonel 153
McCarty, Major Hugo 95
McCormick, Alexander 76
McCracken, Captain 96
McDougal, General 114
McIntosh, Colonel Lachlan 81
McKee, Captain Alexander 47, 73, 81, 83, 84, 88, 95
McKinne. A cigar maker 191
McKnight, Dr. John 93
McLaughlin 163
McLean 171
    Levi. Deputy Sheriff 134
McMahan, Major 104
McMillan, William 107, 112
Mehlen, John L. 159
Mehnke, Karl T. 159
Mehrlin. An early trader 17
Meier, Christian 190
Meisner, Jacob 139
Menelaus. Of Greek mythology 109
Menissier, Francois 134
Menkel, Dr. 169
Menken, Salomon 159
Meyer
    Gottlieb 171
    Johann 162, 171
    John 171
    Ludwig Heinrich 156, 159
    Rev. 172
Meyers 159
    John 154
Mifflin, Governor 121
Miller
    Christopher 124, 125
    Jacob 73
    Police Officer. Covington, KY 194
    Thomas 159, 171
Mills, Thomas 103

*Miner, Charles. *History of Wyoming* 58
Mitchell, Captain 178
Mittelberger, Gottlieb 71
Moehring, Mr. M.A. 177
Molitor, Stephan 176
Möllmann, Rev. Wilhelm 172, 173
Monroe
    G.B. 189
    James 170
Montcalm, Marquis de 50
Montraux 161
Moor, August 178, 179, 183, 189
Moreau, General 142
Morgan
    Colonel George 67, 81
    General 129
Moritz of Saxony 22
Morrow, Jeremiah 142, 161
Morse 132
Mortimer, Benjamin 149, 150
Mot, Corporal 120
Mühl, Eduard. Editor of the *Lichtfreund (Friend of Light)* 177
Mühlenberg, Peter 18, 72, 132
Müller
    Bernhard 167
        Captain 193, 195
    Jacob 73
        Mr. 187
Mundhenk
    Caroline 159, 162
    Heinrich 162
Munger, Brigadier General E. 153
Munkel, Friedrich 63
Murphy, Walhter 191
Muselmann, David 143
Myers
    J. 159
    Wilhelm 65
Nall, Nic. 53
Narbonne, French Minister of War 140, 141
Nast, Rev. Wilhelm. Editor of the *Christliche Apologete*. Organ of the German Methodists. 167, 173, 177
Natauge, Rev. 150
Netawetwie, Delaware Chief 67
Neuburg, Karl Philipp von 10
Neville
    John 129
    Morgan 144
Niemann, Rev. 172

Nieswanger 4
    Johann 63
    Peter 63, 72, 102
        Susanna. See Kerr, Susanna. 63
Nitschman. Moravian missionary murdered at Gnadenhütten, PA 38
Nolte, Vincent 144, 145
North, Major 98
Obermeyer, Peter 146
Oberndorf, Dr. Franz Joseph Constantin 156, 159
Obertür, Jakob 146
Oehlmann 170, 185
Oesterle, LT 193
Ohneberg, Sarah 80
Oppermann, Johann 168
Orleans, Count of 10
Ott 133, 158
Otto, J. 182
Owen 127
Palanko, Delaware Chief 54, 55
Panning 171
Paris. Of Greek mythology 109
Parker, Joseph 101
*Parkman, Francis. *Conspiracy of Pontiac*...8, 50
Parsch, Sister 38
Parsons, Judge 105
Passavant
    Mr. 168
    Zerline 168
Patrick, James 165
Patterson 120
    Colonel Robert 76, 106, 107
Paul
    Major 117
    Peter 65
Pauly, Ensign 48
Pendleton, Mr. 178
Penn, William 37, 56, 68, 99, 169
Pepperell, Colonel 18
*Perkins, James H. *Annals of the West* 7, 42
Perrin. Captain of the MS Moselle which exploded at Cincinnati on April 25, 1838. 177
Peschtal, Mrs 107
Peter, Ludwig 165
Peter the Great, Czar of Russia 9
Peyster, Colonel Arent von 83, 84, 88, 89, 93
Pfister, David 171
Philipp 95
    Ludwig 132
Piatt 130
Pierce
    Joseph 152
    President 161

Pierson, Fr. 10
Pipe, Delaware Chief 45, 66, 69, 73, 80, 83, 84, 85, 87, 88, 94
Piselatulpe. Johann Heckewelder's Indian name which means "Turtle" in the Delaware language 45
Pitt, Prime Minster 141
Plaspohl, Heinrich 173
*Poisson, Albert. *Lettres edificantes* 11
Pokanoket, Phillip of 47
Pomoacan, Chief 68, 80, 83, 84, 85
Pontiac, Ottawa Chief 47 48, 50, 95
Pope 145
Posner, Friedrich 193
*Post, Christian F. 4, 36, 39, 40, 41, 42, 44, 45, 46, 47, 54, 55
Powers, Thomas 127
Prim, Eduard 191
Prophet, Brother of Tecumseh 146, 150
Purcell, Rev. Dr. Johann Baptist 173
Puthoff, Adjutant Wilhelm Heinrich 153
Putnam, General Rufus 100, 101, 102, 131, 149
Quagnant, Captain 18
Quinn, Patrick 191
*Ramsay, James Getty Mcready. *The Annals of Tennessee*...53, 63
Randolph, Beverly 75
Rapp
    Friedrich 166
    Johann Georg 166, 167, 168
    Johannes 166
    Wilhelm 193
Raschig, Rev. 172
Rasle, Fr. Sebastion. 47, 84
Rattenkamp 770
Rauch, Christian H. 35, 40
Raumer, Friedrich von 175, 179
Red Hawk, Chief 62, 67, 68
Reeder, Rebecca 107
Rehfuß 171, 185
    Ludwig 172, 194
Reichenbach, Oscar 185
Reidinger, Barbara 158
Reininger, Caspar 159
Reily, John 148
Reis
    Daniel 73
    Johann 168
Reiß
    Jacob 177, 174
    John 155
    Philipp 172, 178
Reiter, Confectioner 168

Renz
    August (Co-editor of the *Deutsch-Amerikaner*. See Georg Walker. Also editor of the *Volksbühne* or *People's Stage*) 174, 176, 177
    Sebastian 158
Rese, Fr. Friedrich 157, 160, 173
Rhoades 191
Rice, Census Reporter 157
Richter, Mr. 179
Riddle
    Colonel 152
    Henry 52
Riek, Wilhelm 171
Riekenbach, Mr. 168
Riese, R. 179
Riesser, Dr. Gabriel 196
Rieter, Johann 171
Rinaldo 102
Riordan. D. 191
Rittenhaus 132
Ritter
    Dr. 156, 160, 162, 171
    Karl G. 158, 170
    Mr. Philadelphia Bookdealer 158
Rittig 184
Rocheblave, Philippe Rastel de 74
Roeder, Heinrich. Publisher of the *Prospect* in 1835. 171
Roedter, Heinrich 172
Röder, George 188
Rogers
    Colonel 77
    Major Robert 47
Roh, Jacob 171
Rohmann, A.B. 173
Rölker, Dr. 176
Roseberry, Tax Collector 128
Rosefeld, Captain 152
Ross. Founder of Franklin County, OH 146
Roth, Moravian Missionary 64
Rothacker 184
Rothe 59
Rothert 185
Rousseau 131, 134
Rowan, sea cadet 161
Rowecraft 193
Röwekamp
    F.H. 183
    Mr. 193
Rüdesel, Michel 139
Rudolph
    L. 158
    Major 123, 124

Ruffin
    Major 152
    Postmaster 138
Rümelin, Karl 171, 172, 178, 183
*Rundthaler, Rev. Edward *Life of Heckewelder* 5, 47
*Rupp, Isreal Daniel. *History of Berks...*15
Rush, Jost 168
Ruß 171
Rymacher, Vincent de 160
Saatkamp, E. M. German baker living in Louisville, KY in the 1850's. 190
Saddler 190
Salis
    Johann Gaudenz von 156
    Julius Ferdinand von 156
Salling, Johann 4, 17
Salomon, Captain Oelmüller 174, 175, 188, 189, 193
Salz, Peter 164
Sammon, Mr. 179
Sample, US Commissioner 69
Sangrain, Dr. 131
Sargent
    Johann 51
    Winthrop 138
Satan 60
Savier, John 100
Schaad, Rev. 172
Schaeffer 148
Schäfer
    Jacob 169
    Ludwig 155, 170
Schahacs, Delaware Chief 57
Schärtel 71
Schaumberg, Lieutenant (later Colonel) B. 4, 120, 123
Schebosch
    Johann 38, 80
    Joseph 90, 111
Scheidler, Mr. 179
Schenck, General Wiliam G. 146
Scheppler, Jakob 147
Scherrer, Daniel 146
Schiele, Joseph 156
Schiff, J.B. 185
Schikellimus, Cayuga Chief 37, 62
Schiller, Friedrich von 196
Schimmer, J. 168
Schingask, Delaware Chief 24, 45, 46, 81, 82, 83, 84, 125
Schloss, Lehmann 185
Schlosser, Captain 48
Schmick, Johann Jakob 4, 60, 63, 68

Schmidt
　　Carl　171
　　Jakob　See Smith, James.
Schmidtlapp
　　Caleb　158
　　Friedrich　155, 158
Schmuck, Daniel　190
Schneß, Georg　174
Schnetz, Jacob　158
Schnittger, Heinrich　173
Schober, Gottfried　171
Schofer, Gottf.　158
*Schoolcraft, Henry R. *History of the Indian Tribes*...6, 7
Schragg, Mr.　179
Schreck　71
Schroeter, Ludwig　158
Schrickel, Theodor Captain　187
Schröder, Captain Johann Jakob. Editor of the Louisville (KY) *Republikaner*　156, 177
Schuck, Michael. Also known as Michael Stoner and Georg Michael Holsteiner.　53, 61, 74
Schuhmacher　188
Schulte, J.　173
Schultze　158
Schulz　71, 171, 185
Schumann　131, 185
Schwarz, Julius　175
Schwegemann, Jos.　173
Schweinitz, Ludwig von　165
Schüz　72
Scott　171
　　General　119, 124, 179
　　Michael　160
Sebastian, Judge　127, 128
Seemann, Joseph　170
Seib, Rev.　173, 176
Seidel, Nathaniel　56
Seidensticker, Mr.　179, 184
Seiz, Heinrich　143
Selker　188
Sellet, Anton　158
Selz　146
Senat, Fr. S.J.　16
Sensemann
　　Anna　85, 87
　　Christian David　85, 88
　　David　4
　　Gottlob　54, 83, 84, 86, 151
　　Sister. Moravian murdered at Gnadenhütten, PA　38
Seyrs, Marie　155
Shaw, Captain　113
Sheffield, Lucy Anna　119

Shelby
    Captain Evan 63
    Isaac 63, 127
Shepherd, Colonel 81
Shirley, William. Governor of Massachusetts. 31
Short, Judge 184
Sicks 130
Siebenthal 161
Sieg, Peter 158
Sigel 185
Sigourd, Fr. S.J. 7
*Silliman, Benjamin. *Silliman's Journal* 3
Sloan, Captain of Cavalry 152
Smith
    Major Campbell 125
    Henry M. 191
    *James (Schmidt, Jakob) *An account of*...30, 46, 47
    John 143
    *William *An Historical Account*...49
Snellbaker, Mayor of Cincinnati 188
Sömmering, Dr. 140
Soto, Hernan de 3
Soucaire, Fr. Joseph 10
Span, Heinrich 63
Spangenberg, Rev. Augustus 32, 37, 38, 39
*Sparks, Jared. *Washington's Writings* 5 21
Speckheinrich (Fat Henry) 158
Speckmann 170
Spencer
    Judge 122
    Oliver M. 122, 158
Spindel, Rev. 172
Spooner 189
Spotswood, Governor Alexander 14
    Mrs. 15
Sprigmann, Mr. 156
St. Ange, Captain Louis de Bellerive de 50
St. Clair, Arthur 4, 61, 102, 105, 112, 115, 116, 119, 120, 121, 122, 127, 128, 132, 133, 135, 136, 137
    Son 148
    Louisa 102
St. Paul 35
St. Peter 35
St. Pierre, Legardier de 24, 25, 28, 37
Stäbler, Jonathan 154, 155
Stael, Mrs. von 34, 140
Stall, Eduard 143
Stallo
    Judge Johann B. 182, 185, 195, 196
    Richard 172
Stanislaus, Mr. 169
Stanley, Major 152

Stanwix, Colonel John 42
Steg, Wilhelm 155
Stegemann 170
Stein
    Albert 156
    David 169
    Freiherr von 166
Steinmaier 172
    Rev. 173
Steinmetz
    Dr 184
    Mr. 179
Sterling 163
Steuben, General Friedrich Wilhelm Rudolf Gerhard Augustin, Baron von, (1730-1794). 97, 98, 99, 113, 121
Stinton, John 56
Stites, Benjamin 115
Stobo, Lt. Robert 27
Stolz 185, 187
Stone, Capt. D.C. 190
Stoner, Michael. See Holsteiner, George Michael and Schuck, Michael. 62
Stopf, Christopher 53
Stowe, Professor Calvin E. 179
Sträter, Rev. 173
Straub, J.N. 168
Stricker, Sheriff. Covington, KY 194, 195
Strickler, Jonathan 155
Strodtbeck, Jacob 171
Strohhuber, Georg 143
Stuntebeck, Ferdinand 173
Suhr, Rev. 173
Sutter, Jakob 158
Suter, Jakob 156
Sutton, James 148
Swartout 140, 142
Symmes, John Cleves 4, 101, 106, 108, 110, 112, 133, 134, 136, 144
    Peyton S. 161
Tanacharison, Wyandot Chief 26, 29
Tartars 7
Tatapachkse, Delaware Chief 150
Tauber, Friedrich 171
*Taylor, James W. *History of Ohio...* 4, 8, 42, 67, 130, 165
Taylor, Pap 185, 187
Techhans, Mr. 156
Tecumseh, Shawnee Chief 42, 95, 146, 150, 153
Tedeuskung, Delaware Chief 39, 40
Tegah Kuita. Also known as Genovesa 84
Tgirhitontie. Augustus Spangenberg's Iroquois name which means "Row of Trees" 37
Thielemann, Christian 179, 181
Thiery, Franz 132
Thole, LT 193

Thomas
    Abraham 106
    Governor of Pennsylvania 31,
Thompson, General 53
Thomson, Charles 149
Thränle, Innocenz 171
Thusnelda 196
Tiete, Peter 18
Tiffin 196
    Governor Edward 143
Tilghman, James 52
Tilly, Wilhelm 143
Timmermann 170
Todd, Colonel John 75, 78, 95
Tolendal, Countess de Laly 141
Tonte 158
Tonti 9
Torrence 148
    Captain 152
Tosso 162
Trainer, Mrs. 191
Trent, William 51
Trigg, Colonel 95
Tron, Fried. 156, 158
Troply, LTC 117
Trotter, Colonel 117
Trumbo 146
Tubal Cain of Virginia. Another name for Governor Alexander Spotswood 15
Tuffly, Peter 158
Turnville 196
Uhland, George 65
Ulry, Jakob 147
Uncle (s) of the Delawares. See Wyandot Indians in PLACENAMES & ORGANIZATIONS index.
    Sam 101
    Tom's Cabin 176
Unzicker 185
Up de Graff, Nathan 136
Vagard, Louis 7, 12, 13
Van Braam, Jacob 27
Van Buren, Martin 171, 172, 178, 179
Van Seggern 185
Vaudreuil, Governor-General Pierre Francois Rigaud Marquis de 21, 47
Verschoot 160
Verrazano 13
Villiers, Captain Coulon de 27
Vincennes, Captain de 7, 12, 16, 22
Virgin Mary 13, 36
Vischer 4
    Captain H.N. 133, 134
Vivier, Fr. 11
Vogelgesang, Mr. 156

Vogler, Mrs. 155
Vogt, Johann 191
Vögtly, Mr. 168
Vollmann
    Caroline 142
    Elisabeth 142
    Erich Justus 140, 141, 142
Volney, Constantin Francois Chasseboeuf, comte de (1757-1820) 116, 127, 131, 132
Volz
    C. 168
    Ferdinand 168
Wachsler, Michael 147
Wachsmuth 184
Wagemun, Chief 84
Waiser
    Friedrich 18
    Philipp 18
Walbach, Adjutant General J. B. 153, 154
Walker
    Georg (Co-editor of the **Deutsch-Amerikaner**. See August Renz.) 173, 174, 177
    Dr. Thomas. Discoverer of the Cumberland Mountains 52
Walle, Rev. Sylvester 165
Waller, Ned 106
Walpole 51, 52
Waltenrath, Jakob 154
Walther
    Bernhard 65
    Conrad 65
Wangomend. Indian shaman 54
Ward, Ensign Edward 26
Warth, Johann 102
Warville, Brissot de 131
Washington 101
    George 101, 114, 115, 117, 121, 122, 124, 126, 127, 128, 129, 162
    Lawrence 20, 52
Watt 146
Wayne, Anthony 118, 122, 123, 124, 125, 127, 133, 135
Weber
    Captain 158, 160
    David 171
Weidig, Mr. 179
Weimann, Georg 158
Weimer, Georg 158
Weise, Julius 174
Weiser
    Conrad 4, 18, 20, 24, 29, 37
    Jakob 102
Weismann 110
    General 101
Weitling, Wilhelm 184, 184
Weitzel, Gottfried 185

Weld 132
Wenz, Johann 182
Werk, M. 194
Wesley
    Charles 34
    John 34, 35
West, Benjamin 49
Westfahl
    Andreas 143
    Susanne 143
Wetterhold, Captain 56
Wetzel
    Jakob 102, 103, 114, 115
    Johann 102
    Ludwig 4, 102, 103, 104, 105, 109, 110, 114, 129, 130, 144, 147
    Martin 102, 103
Whelan 61
White
    Eye Delaware Chief 44, 64, 66, 69, 73, 165
    James 149
    Thomas (Son of Chief White Eye) 149
*Whittlesey. Dissertation before the Historical Society of Ohio 7, 12
Wiegand 71
Wieser 185
Wilde, Mr. 179
Wilkinson, General James 100, 119, 121, 123, 124, 125, 127, 128, 133
Williams
    Elmore 151
    Joel 145
Williamson
    Colonel David 90, 91, 92, 93, 149, 150, 192
    English trader allegedly responsible for the murder of Chief Pontiac 50
Willich 185

Willing 75
Willmann 170
Wilson 146
    Joshua L. 152
    Tax Collector 128
Windeler, Hermann T. 170, 171
Winnitou 3
Wirth, Mr. 179
Wittig 187
Wittmer 144
Wolf 187
    Brothers 171, 181
    Daniel 195
Wolfe, General James 102
Wommeldorf, Daniel 4, 153
Wood, Governor of Ohio in 1853 185
Wrangel 180

Wright
    Commissioner 70
    Moses 163
Wupper, Adolph 155
Wurz, Fr. Mathias 173
Wyllis, Major 11, 118
Yeatman, Griffin 138
York, Duke of 153
Zacharias, Moravian Delaware murdered by whites in 1763. 56
Zane
    Ebenezer 61, 145
    Jonathan 61

Zane (continued)
    Silas 61
Zäslein, Joseph 155
Zeisberger
    Rev. David 4, 5, 36, 37, 54, 55, 56, 58, 59, 62, 63, 64, 66, 67, 68, 69, 73, 76, 80, 81, 83, 84, 85, 86, 87, 88, 89, 90, 92, 95, 149, 150, 164, 165
    Susanna 86
Zenes, Conney 107
Zeumer, August 154, 155, 158
Ziegler
    Bishop of Linz, Austria 181
    David 4, 101, 119, 120, 121, 138, 139, 142, 143, 151, 152
    Lucy Anna 152
Zimmer 171
Zinn, Philip 163
Zinsendorf
    Count Nikolas Ludwig von 33, 34, 37, 150
    Benigna 37
Zöllner, A 182

PLACENAMES & ORGANIZATIONS

The following is the Placename and Organization index of the book
Deutsche Chronik in der Geschichte des Ohio-Thales
by Emil Klauprecht.
(Cincinnati:1864)]

Index

Akron, OH 193
Albany, NY 27, 28, 124
Alexandria, VA 28
Algiers
    Bey of 47
    Pirates 124
Algonquin Indians 7, 8
Allegheny
    City, PA 168
    County, PA 128, 144
    Mountains 3, 6, 8, 13, 14, 15, 18, 26, 43, 44, 47, 49, 77, 97, 102, 105, 160, 182
    River 8, 25, 26, 31, 37, 40, 50, 51, 54, 55, 61, 76, 168
    Territories 22
Allegwi Indians 8
Alsace 7, 26, 169, 198
Amboy, NJ 57
American Reform Party 187
American Turners 180, 184, 185, 186, 189, 192, 193, 194, 195, 196
Andaste Indians 6, 8
Annaheim, CA 174
Appalachian Mountains 9
Appolonian Society 155
Arch Street 4, 109, 155
Arkansas 176
Armbruster Brewery. Louisville, KY Destroyed by Know-Nothing mob in August 1855. 190
Armory Hall 182
Assensipia 101
Athens County, OH 24
Athenäum University 173
Atlantic Ocean 14, 14, 22
Auglaize River 122, 124
Augsburg Confession 33
Austria 31, 142, 159, 166, 198
Aysimik, Indian village 67
Baden, Germany 180, 198
Bald Hill (Cincinnati) 182
Baltimore, MD 153, 154, 163, 166, 168, 193, 196
Bank of
    Cincinnati 178
    Norwalk 169
    Pennsylvania 152
    the United States 158, 178

Bardstown, KY 181
Baring Co. 142
Barthel's Grocery Store 135
Bastille, Storming of 110
Bavaria 71, 181, 198
Beaver Creek 47
Beethoven Society 172
Benedictine Monks 181
Berlin, Germany 141, 162
Bern, Switzerland 156
Berthelsdorf, Germany 33
Bethel
     Gate 175
     OH 147
Bethlehem
     OH 44
     PA 34, 35, 36, 38, 39, 40, 44, 47, 56, 64, 73, 83, 91, 149, 150, 151, 155, 164
Big
     Barren River 53
     Beaver Creek (PA) 54, 55
     Bottom, OH 119
     Kanawha River (WV) 23, 51, 53, 65
     Lick 103
     Miami River (OH) 6, 8, 42, 108, 114, 120, 122
     Sandy River 44
Black
     Forest. Germany 18
     and Gold League 180
Blackhawk Wars 171
Blackwell's Island 179
Blair County, OH 181
Blannerhasset Island 142
Blue
     Licks, KY 76, 95
     Ridge Mountains 14, 15, 31, 37, 38, 39, 43, 71
Board of Health 184
Bolivar, OH 44
Bonn, University of 173
Boonesborough, KY 65, 76
Bowling Green, KY 53
Braddock's Road 70
Bradford
     County, PA 58
     PA 70
Brandenburg 180
Brandywine, Battle of 72
Braunschweig, Germany 168, 179
Braunseifen 142
Brazos River, TX 130
Bremen
     Street 188
     Germany 163, 186

Bretheren Unity (Moravian) 33, 34, 58
Broadway
    Hotel 173
    Street 13, 107, 109, 112, 135, 138, 145, 152, 154, 156, 157, 159, 177
Brooklyn, NY 193
Brothers of Zion Church 71
Bryant's Station, KY 95
Bucyrus, OH 169
Buffalo
    County, WI 196
    Creek 73
    NY 171, 193
    OH 144
    WI 196
Bullit
    Lick, KY 66
Burghold's grocery 190
Burnet House (Cincinnati, OH) 158, 183
Butler County
    PA 54, 168
    KY 121
    OH 148, 185
Bühring and Breuning Co. 155
Cahokia, IL. 50, 74
California 70, 174, 175
Cambria County, OH 181
Campus Martius, Fort 105
Canaanites 37
Canada 7, 9, 13, 17, 20, 21, 28, 37, 38, 41, 42, 47, 61, 84, 98, 99, 136, 149, 153
Cane-land. Early designation for Kentucky 53
Canestoga, PA 57
Canton, OH 193, 196
Cape
    Breton, Nova Scotia 18
    of Good Hope 33
    Horn 174
Capitolium 105
Captina Creek 62
Capua, Italy 124
Carbon County, PA 37
Carlisle, PA 24
Carthage 196
Castripolis 105
Cat
    Indians See Erie Indians. 6
    Lake. See Lake Erie. 9
Catawba
    Indians 22, 41
    Wine 5, 178, 185
Cathedral 138
Catholic Party 185
Cave Creek 93, 95

Cayuga
>Indians 6, 9, 22, 61, 62,
>River 64

Cecilia 105
Center Street 13, 196
Central Market 189
Chamblee, Canada 98
Cherokee Indians 7, 12, 17, 22, 41, 51, 52, 53, 55, 61, 65, 67, 78
Chersonesus 101
Chestnut Mountains 70
Chicago, IL 193, 193
Chickasaw Indians 16, 17, 78
Chillicothe, OH 76, 95, 117, 133, 136, 146, 148, 163
>City of Gamblers and Drunkards 133, 136
>Streets
>>Paint 133
>>Water 133

Chippewa Indians 26, 41, 47, 48, 67, 83, 84, 99, 105, 149, 198
Chocktaw Indians 16
Cholera 96, 167, 168, 170, 171, 177, 182, 184
Christiansbrunn, PA 39
Church Taxes 21
Church of England 21
Cincinnati, OH 3, 4, 8, 13, 79, 83, 96, 106, 107, 109, 110, 112, 116, 117, 122, 124, 127, 133, 134, 135, 136, 137, 139, 140, 142, 143, 144, 145, 151, 152, 153, 154, 157, 158, 159, 160, 161, 169, 170, 171, 172, 173, 175, 176, 177, 178, 179, 180, 181, 182, 183, 184, 185, 186, 193, 195, 196, 197, 198
>Alleys & Streets
>>2nd Street 136, 159
>>3rd Street 13, 134 138, 154, 156, 159, 162, 172
>>4th Street 13, 138, 157, 159, 162, 172, 173, 179
>>5th Street 13, 134, 151, 156, 157, 159, 173, 176, 177
>>6th Street 159, 159, 160, 172, 177
>>7th Street 159
>>8th Street 137, 173, 184
>>9th Street 173, 174, 186
>>12th Street 154
>>13th Street 172
>>Arch Street 4, 109, 155
>>Church Alley 134
>>Bremen Street 188
>>Broadway Street 13, 107, 109, 112, 135, 138, 145, 152, 154, 156, 157, 159, 177
>>Buckeye Street 183
>>Center Street 13, 196
>>Columbia Street 173
>>Congress Street 138, 138, 159
>>Eastern Row 138
>>Elm Street 159, 161, 172, 173, 178
>>Front Street 114, 135, 138, 139, 145, 159
>>Glaser Alley 159
>>Green Street 178
>>High Street 159
>>John Street 159, 172

Cincinnati, OH
    Alleys and streets (continued)
        Lawrence Street 138, 159
        Liberty Street 160
        Lodge Street 181
        London Street 159
        Longworth Street 159
        Lord Street 181
        Loring's Row 159
        Ludlow Street 109, 156, 159
        Main Street 13, 134, 137, 145, 151, 156, 157, 159, 162, 177, 183
        Market Street 134, 154, 156, 159, 160, 172
        Marshal Street 186
        Mercer Street 184, 189
        Mound Street 13, 159
        New Market Street 159
        Pike Street 138
        Plum Street 159, 186
        Race Street 13, 158, 159, 174, 179
        Richmond Street 158
        Smith Street 159
        St. Clair Street 159
        Sycamore Street 13, 115, 138, 156, 157, 159, 160
        Symes Street 159
        Vine Street 13, 134, 154, 159, 160, 161, 173, 184, 186, 189,   189, 196
        Walnut Street 107, 107, 133, 136, 138, 159, 172, 173, 178, 184,   186, 189
        Water Street 107, 134, 159
        Wayne Street 159, 159
        Western Row 138, 159, 161
    Bald Hill 182
    Bank of Cincinnati 178
    Board of Education 5, 197
    Cincinnati and St. Louis Railroad 177
    Cincinnati, Columbus, and Cleveland Railroad 177
    Cincinnati, Hamilton, and Dayton Railroad 185
    Cincinnati Hotel 161, 162
    Cincinnati Liberty Guard 193
    Cincinnati-St. Louis Railroad 182
    Churches
        2nd Presbyterian Church 158, 172
        3rd Street Church 158
        Elm Street Church 178
        Episcopalean Church 172
        Holy Trinity Church 173
        Lutheran Church 173, 179
        Methodist Church 134, 137, 157, 178
        Presbyterian Church 134, 152, 157, 173
        Roman   Catholic Church 160
        St. John's Church 155, 172, 178
        St. Mary's Church 174, 178, 197
        St. Patrick's Church 169
        St. Paul's Church (Founded 1847 at Spring & Abigail Streets) 173, 178, 185

Cincinnati, OH
- Churches (continued)
  - St. Peter's Church 172, 177
  - Unitarian Church 179
  - United Bretheren 150
  - United Brotherhood in Christ 155
  - United Reformed Church 123
- City Council 145, 157, 182
- City Hall 138
- Courthouse 155, 157
- Historical Society 85
- Jackson Hill 183, 188
- Mayor Snellbaker 188
- Order of the Cincinnati, The 112, 114, 152

Cincinnati, OH (cont'd)
- Periodicals
  - *Catholic Telegraph* 173
  - *Central Watchman* 182
  - *Cincinnati Directory* 157, 158
  - *Cincinnati Gazette* 142, 153, 154, 155, 160
  - *Cincinnati Volksblatt* 1, 172, 177
  - *Christian Apologet* 177
  - *Deutschen im Westen.* See *Germans in the West.*
  - *Friend of Light.* See *Lichtfreund.*
  - *Germans in the West* (*Deutschen im Westen*-published by Christian Burghalter & Hefley. Later became *Volksfreund* edited by Rudolph Maltiz) 177
  - *Hochwächter (High Watchman).* Organ of the Freemen's Club 184, 186
  - *Lichtfreund (Friend of Light)* 177
  - *Ohio Chronicle, The*; Cincinnati's first German newspaper 162
  - *Prospect* 171
  - *Protestant* 173
  - *Republican.* 177
  - *Sentinel of the North Western Territory, The.* William Maxwell, Editor. 135
  - *Spring Messengers* 186
  - *Times* 183, 189
  - *United States Catholic Magazine* 160
  - *Volksbühne (People's Stage)* Edited by Walker and Renz 177
  - *Volksfreund.* Edited by Rudolph Maltiz. See *Germans in the West* above.
  - *Wahrheitsfreund. (Friend of Truth)* Founded by Fr. John Martin Henni in 1837. Ended publication in 1907. 173
  - *Western Mercury (Westlicher Merkur).* Edited by Christian Burghalter. 156, 177
  - *Western Spy* 139, 143, 151, 152
  - *Westlicher Merkur.* See *Western Mercury.*
  - *Workers' Republic, The* 184
  - *World Citizen* 172

Cincinnati, OH (cont'd)
    Queen of the West 3, 152, 183
    Rhein area of Cincinnati 177
    Ross Hill 193, 196
    Texas area of Cincinnati 178
    Wards
        9th Ward 183
        11th Ward 188
        12th Ward 137, 138, 143
Circleville, OH 146, 193
City Guard 178
City of Gamblers and Drunkards, The. Refers to Chillicothe, OH 133, 136
Clara, Order of Poor 162
Clearfield County, OH 181
Clermont County, OH 147
Cleveland, OH 177, 187, 193, 193, 196
Clinch, NC 53
Colerain Station, OH 114
Columbia 122
    Garden 154
    Hotel 154
    OH 110, 115, 152
    Street 173
Columbiana
    County, OH 146
    OH 147
Columbus, OH 146, 163, 164, 176, 183, 184, 185, 192, 193, 196
Common Pleas Court 185
Communism 167
Company of the West 10, 11
Concordia 196
Congress Street 138, 159
Conneaut, OH 3
Connecticut 14, 35, 100, 159
    Indians 40
    River 35
Constantinople 196
Constitution of 1772 4
Continental
    Congress 66, 73, 102, 149
    Dollars, Devaluation of 79
    Certificates 107
Corinth 196
Cornett's Station, OH 114
Coshocking, OH 3, 73
Coureurs des Bois 7, 12
Covington and Lexington Railroad 177
Covington, KY 77, 161, 183, 187, 189, 193, 194, 195
    Streets
        Orchard 195
        York 194
Crawford County, OH 169, 169

Creek Indians 21, 150
Creoles 75
Crimea 101, 193
Crooked Creek 63
Crown Point, NY 28 31
Crystal Palace, London 185
Cumberland
    Ford 52
    Gap 52
    MD 26, 29
    Mountains 52, 78
    River 53, 65, 100
Cumminsville 183
Dark and Bloody Ground (Common reference to Kentucky) 62, 66
Darke County, OH 120, 132
Darmstadt, Germany 168
Davenport, IA 193
Dayton, OH 133, 152, 153, 174, 179, 18, 185, 193, 196
Death Hallow 86, 87
Declaration of Independence 182
Deer Creek 122, 154, 158, 159, 172
    Bottom 174
    Valley 156
Delaware 100, 159
    Indians 8, 9, 24, 26, 32, 37, 38, 39, 40, 41, 42, 44, 45, 46, 47, 49, 51, 54, 55, 56, 57, 58, 62, 63, 64, 66, 67, 68, 69, 73, 76, 80, 81, 83, 84, 86, 87, 89, 92, 93, 94, 99, 105, 111, 115, 149, 150, 153, 197
    Language 67, 151
    Leni Lenape (Delaware) Indians 8
    Nation 60, 68
    River 8
    Turtle Clan 8, 119, 150
    Welch Cock Clans 8
    Wolf Clans 8, 54, 62, 64, 66, 68, 69, 73, 83, 85, 93
Delhi 114
Detroit, MI 7, 8, 9, 13, 16, 22, 44, 47, 48, 49, 50, 72, 74, 75, 76, 79, 81, 83, 85, 86, 88, 89, 93, 98, 106, 124, 132, 135, 136, 165, 173, 193, 193, 196
Dierdorf Mill 148
Dirty Dogs. A social club in Indianapolis 187
District
    Court 66
    of Columbia 159
Dominican Order 160
Donnegal, NY 7
Dorcass Society 152
Dorfeuille's Museum in Cincinnati. 13
Dragoons 193
Dresden, Germany 180
Dreybach 84
Dunkers 18, 19
Dunkirk, (France) Battle of 153
Duquesne Borough (Pittsburgh, PA) 168
Durlach 71

Düsseldorf Society 175
Dutch Station, KY 66
Earthquake of 1811. See New Madrid, MO.
East-West Highway 163
Eastern Row 138
Easton, PA 31, 39, 42
    Treaty of 43
Ebenezer, GA 35
Economy, PA 167
Edenau, PA 166
Edinburgh, University of 102
Eel River 119
Eggers and Wilde Publishing House 179
Einsiedeln Abbey 181
El Dorado 11
Elk County, OH 181
Elkhorn Creek 95
    River 62
Ellwanger 171
Elm Street 159, 161, 172, 173, 178
Elysium 75
Emigrants' School 174, 175
Emitsburg, MD 173
England 18, 21, 22, 31, 38, 41, 77, 97, 143, 154, 158, 180, 197
English Language 67
Erfurt, Germany 174
Erie Indians 6, 8
Erie, PA 196
Esopus, NY 36
Europe 22, 41, 179
Fairfield 151
    OH 122, 146, 146, 148
    Canada 149
Fairmount 183
Falls of the Ohio 78, 96, 123
Farlowe House 189
Fayette County
    KY 78
    OH 146
Fincastle County, VA 53, 63
Fish Creek, VA 181
Five Nations. See Iroquois. 7, 8, 14, 18, 19, 22, 36, 37
Flag of Lillies 41
Flanders 22
Flogging Frolic 134
Flood of 1832 171
Forks of
    the Delaware 35
    the Ohio 9, 13, 24, 26, 27, 40, 43

Fort
    Assumption, TN 16
    Campus Martius, OH (Original name for Marietta, OH) 105
    Charlotte, OH 63
    Defiance, OH 124
    Deposit, OH 125
    Dunmore, PA 61
    Duquense, PA 13, 28, 29, 30, 40, 4,, 42
    Fincastle, WV 72
    Frontenac 41, 84
    Greenville, OH 124, 125
    Hamilton, OH 120, 123
    Harmar, OH 100, 102, 105, 109, 119
    Henry 72
    Jefferson, KY 78, 79, 120, 121
    Junandot, OH 24
    Laurens, OH 69, 74, 76, 167
    Ligonier, PA 70, 102
    Machault 24
    Massac, IL 7, 12, 74, 127, 142
    McHenry, MD 154
    McIntosh, PA 74, 76, 84, 99, 100, 102, 116
    Miami, OH 23, 24
    Michillimacinac, MI. 47, 48
    Necessity, PA 27
    Niagara 48
    Piqua, OH 40, 41, 42, 133
    Pitt, PA 42, 45, 48, 49, 55, 61, 79, 84, 102, 129
    Ponchartrain, MI. (Detroit) 7
    Prudhomme, TN 21
    Reis, WV 73
    St. Joseph, OH 126
    Stanwix, NY 51, 52,53, 58, 99
        Treaty of 61, 65, 105
    Steuben 116
    Venango, PA 40
    Washington, OH 109, 110, 112, 116, 117, 118, 119, 121, 122, 123, 124, 127, 135, 138, 183
    Wayne, IN 22, 23, 42, 196
        Treaty of 1809 153
    Woodstock, NY 72
Fox Indians 198
France 6, 7, 10, 18, 25, 27, 28, 31, 40, 77, 114, 115, 127, 132, 134, 141, 144, 166, 180, 183
Franciscans 10
Frankfort, KY 53
Frankfurt am Main, Germany 167, 168
    Parliament 196
Frankland 100
Franklin 172, 173, 196
    County, OH 146
Franklinton, OH 146
Franks 71
Franzburg 181

Free
- German Schools 197
- Mason Hall 196
- Lodge Nr 208 196

Freedom Tree 162
Freemens' Club 184, 186, 187, 193
- Hall 187, 189

Freiburg 196
French
- Creek 13, 24, 26, 40
- Grant 132
- Indians 10
- Lick, TN 53
- Margarets 24
- Revolution 127, 165, 166
- and Indian War of 1756 18 27

Friedensdorf
- OH 55
- PA 62

Friedenshütten, PA 58, 59, 60
Front Street 114, 135, 138, 139, 145, 159
Fulneck, Moravia 33
Fulton, OH 177
Gallia County, OH 153
Gallipolis, OH 123, 131, 132, 134
Garrard's Station, OH 114
Gekelemukpechink 55, 58, 67, 103
Gellertsburg 158
General
- Athony Wayne Inn 133
- Assembly 136
- Locator 65
- Settlers Club of Cincinnati 196

Georgetown, DC 178
Georgia 33, 34, 35, 150
German
- Immigration 180
- Indians 84, 91, 149
- Language 67
- Low German 173
- National Fund 185
- Singers Union of North America 181, 193, 196
- Society 172
- Station, OH
- Wolfhunters 139

German-English Free School 175, 185
Germania 193, 196
- Lodge 181
- Lodge. Union of Special Brothers 196

Germanna, VA 15
Germantown, PA 158
- Battle of 72

Germany 10, 21, 40, 51, 72, 139, 145, 156, 158, 166, 168, 169, 173, 174, 180, 185, 197
Gerrety's cooperage (Louisville KY) 191
Geschecking. Indian name for Coshockton, OH 67
Gettheim 181
Ghent, Belgium 10
Glaser Alley 159
Gnadenborn, PA 55
Gnadenhütten
    PA 37, 38, 39
    OH 60, 63, 68, 76, 80, 81, 82, 83, 84, 85, 86, 87, 89, 90, 91, 93, 95, 128, 149, 165
    Monument Society 165
Gnadenthal, PA 39
Golgatha 4
Gonsenheim, a suburb of Mainz, Germany 161
Goschgosching. Ohio Indian village 54, 55
Goschocking, OH 68, 69, 80, 88
Goshen, OH 149, 150, 164, 165
Granville County, NC 52
Gray's Military Company 178
Great Britain 7, 22, 99, 115, 126, 18, 152
    British Army
        42nd Highland Regiment 49
        44th Regiment 28
        48th Regiment 28
        77th Highland Regiment 49
        Parliament 16, 21
Great Lakes 22, 185
Green
    River 78, 100
    Street 178
    Tree Inn 133
Greenland 33
Greenville
    Creek 152
    North Carolina 68
    Ohio 120, 134, 141
    Treaty of 134, 149, 150
Grenadiers 192
Guernsey County, OH 153
Gulf of Mexico 6, 17, 22
Guttenberg, IA 179
Göttingen, Germany 168
    University 140
Hair River. Better known as the Scioto River 20
Halle, Germany 33
Hambach Festival 171, 174, 182
Hamburg, Germany 145, 176, 196
Hamilton
    OH 123, 148
    Road 188
Hannover, Germany 154, 160, 168, 170
Harbor Collector 152

Harmony
    Lodge. Freemasons #2 159
    PA 166, 167
Harrison County, PA 147
Harrodsburg, KY 55, 65, 66, 79
Hart's Shoestore 154
Hazard's Register 18
Heidelberg, E. 168
Hermann Lodge # 208. Union of Special Brothers 196
Hermann, MO. 177
Hermitage, TN 178
Herrenberg, Germany 18
Herrenhut 33
Hessia 198
High
    Springs, KY 65
    Street 159
Highland 196
Highlander regiment 57
Hispaniola 3
Hockhocking 67
    River 145
Hocking River 24, 28
Hohenlinden 143
Holland 21, 52, 166
Holstein
    River 65
    North Carolina 53
Holy Trinity Church Originally constructed in 1837 on West 5th Street in Cincinnati. 173
Horticultural Society 154
House of Friends 157
Hoya, Hanover 140
Hudson River 8, 18, 112
Humboldt
    City 196
Hunters and Sharpshooters. A German military club 193
Huron
    Indians 7 See Wyandot Indians.
    River, OH 149
Hussites 33, 40
Hutberg, Germany 33
Hütten, MN 196
Illenoia 101
Illinois 9, 21
    District of 75
    Indians 17
    River 6, 126
    Territory 74, 198

Indian
    Creek 62
    Spring 103
Indiana 7, 9, 12, 75, 101, 135, 159, 167, 187, 189, 197, 198
    Counties
        Jefferson 139
        Switzerland 182
    Territory 136
Indiana County, OH 181
Indianapolis, IN 193, 196
Introductory German English School 5
Iowa 179
    Indians 84
Iptingen, Germany 166
Ireland 99, 145, 197
Iroquois
    Confederation 6, 28, 38, 41, 55, 58, 83
    Indians 8, 9, 20, 22, 24, 36, 37, 39, 42, 47, 48, 49, 61, 62, 63, 66, 76, 99, 102
    Five Nations 8, 14, 18, 19, 22, 36, 37
    Six Nations 37, 51,5, 66, 83, 115, 151
Jackson
    County, OH 148, 164
    Guard. A German military club 178, 193
    Hill (Cincinnati) 183, 188,
Jacobinists 140
James River, VA 43, 126
Jamestown, VA 13
Jefferson
    County, KY 78
    County, IN 139
    County, OH 146
    County, PA 147
Jeffersonville, IN 116
Jena, University of 35
Jerusalem 167, 175
Jesuits 21, 35, 44, 58, 83, 160, 176
Jewish Congregation 162
Jewish Synogogue 177
John Street 159, 172
Jupiter 3
Justice of the Peace 18, 168, 183, 195
Kambach. Swabian village 9
Kanawha
    Big Kanawha River 23, 51, 53, 65
    Kanawha River 43, 52, 62, 63, 68
    Kanawha Valley 80, 81
    Little Kanawha River 51, 62
Kansas River 79, 197
Karlsruhe, Germany 140
Kaskaskia
    Indians 50, 198
    Illinois 17, 74, 75, 132, 135

Keaton's Station, TN 53
Kelly's Island 6
Kennebec Bay, ME. 22
Kent River 36
Kenton County (KY) Court 195
Kentucky 8, 9, 13, 44, 51, 52, 53, 54, 55, 61, 62, 63, 65, 75, 76, 77, 79, 90, 95, 96, 106, 122, 124, 126, 127, 145, 146, 159, 166, 182, 198
    Counties
        Butler 121
        Fayette 78
        Jefferson 78
        Kenton 195
        Lincoln 78
        Mason 66
    District of 66, 102, 105, 117
    House of Representatives 128
    Militia 101, 117, 120
    River 52, 62, 65
Kentucky County, VA 65, 78
Kickapoo Indians 116, 119
Kingston
    Jamaica 142
    Ontario, Canada 41
Kittatinny Mountains 37, 58
Know Nothing Party 187
Knownothings 188
Knox County, OH 135
Kosziusko Guard 178
Kuschkuschky. Delaware Village on Big Beaver Creek, PA 40, 54, 55
La belle Riviere. French term for the Ohio 10
Labrador 33
Lachaise 127
Lafayette 141, 142
    Guard 178, 193
    Indiana 193, 196
Lake
    Allemand, LA 11
    Champlain 98
    Erie 6, 7, 8, 9, 13, 66, 177, 185
    George, NY 31
    Huron 7, 48
    Michigan 6, 47
    Ontario 9, 31
Lamb Farm 7, 12
Lancaster
    Seminary 157
    OH 122, 146, 160, 163, 163
    PA 18, 18, 19, 45, 47, 57, 144, 145, 147
    Treaty of 18, 20, 24, 61
Land Patent of 1798 164
Latrobe Monastary, PA 181

Laurel Mountains (MD) 70
Lausatia (Lausitz) 33, 150
Lawrence Street 138, 159
Lawrenceburg 177
Lawunakhannock. Indian village in Butler County, PA 54
Lebanon, OH 133
Legion of the United States 122
Lehigh
    River 39, 56
    Valley, PA 37
Leipzig, Germany 161
Leni Lenape (Delaware) Indians 8
Leopold Institute 160
Letton's Museum (Cincinnati) 13
Lexington, KY 66, 76, 77, 95, 105, 106, 161, 182
Liberty Street 160
Lichtenau, OH 67, 68, 69, 73, 76, 80, 82
Lichtenberg 187
Licking
    County, OH 146
    River 52, 53, 76, 77, 79, 95, 96, 106, 107, 133, 194
Liedertafel 179, 181, 184, 193
Ligonier Valley, PA 102, 137
Limestone, KY 106
Lincoln County
    KY 78
    NC 52
Lititz, Germany 80
Little
    Kanawha River 51, 62
    Miami River 76, 79, 115, 118, 133
    Miami Railroad 177, 194
    Sandy River 132
Lockland 183
Lodge 113. Union of Special Brothers 196
Logtown, OH 9, 25
Lombardy 139
London
    Street 159
    England 28, 51, 141, 145, 158, 185
Long
    Hunters 53
    Knives 81, 82
Longworth Street 159
Lorain County, OH 7, 12
Loramie's Store 79
Lord Street 181
Loring's Row 159
Lorraine 26, 198
Los Angeles, CA 174
Losantiville, OH 106, 107, 109, 12, 114
Louisburg, NS 18, 22

Louisd'or (French currency) 141
Louisiana 9, 13, 28, 47, 127, 130, 144, 166
    Territory 77
Louisville, KY 53, 66, 78, 102, 116, 157, 177, 178, 180, 183, 184, 185, 187, 189, 190, 192, 193, 196, 198
    Church
        St. Martin's Catholic Church 190
    Streets
        11th 191, 192
        Chapel 191
        Clay 191
        Green 190
        Jefferson 190
        Madison 190, 191
        Main 191, 192
        Shelby 190, 191
        Walnut 190
    Wards
        1st Ward 190
        3rd Ward 190
        5th Ward 191
        6th Ward 191
        8th Ward 191
Low German Language 173
Ludlow Street 109, 156, 159
Ludlow's Station, OH 114, 120
Lumenkamp Creek VA 181
Lutheran Church 15, 71, 173, 179
MS
    Bee 195
    General Pike 157
    Moselle (exploded at Cincinnati on April 25, 1838, killing 136 passengers, many of them German immigrants.) 176, 177
    Natchez 129, 130
    Vesta 158
Mackinaw, MI 48
Mad River 96, 133
    and Lake Erie Railroad 177
Madison 193
    County, OH 164
    Indiana 158
Madrid, Spain 78, 126
Mahony Creek, PA 37
Main Street 13, 134, 137, 145, 151, 156, 157, 159, 162, 177
Maine 22, 159
Mainz, Germany 140
Manchester, KY 133
Mansco, Kaspar 53
Marietta, OH 102, 105, 106, 109, 110, 119, 131, 135, 140
Market Street 159
Marshal
    County, VA 181
    Street 186

Martin's Station 79
Marville, Brissot de 105, 132
Maryland 18, 19, 31, 70, 71, 100, 159
    Militia 129
Mason County, KY 66
Masonic Hall 181
Massachussetts 14, 159
Mastodon Skeleton, discovery of 169
Mauer's Wood. Columbus, OH 192
Maulbronn, Germany 166
Maumee River 7, 12, 23, 24, 42
Maysville, KY 106, 107, 110, 133, 145, 157, 193
McMahon's Creek 103
McPherson's Volunteers 153
Measles 59
Mechanic's Institute 138
Mecklinburg County, NC 52
Memphis 193
Mendelheim, Swabia 9
Mennonites 18
Mercer
    County, OH 132
    Street 184, 189
Merchant's Exchange 157
Methodism 173
Methodist Church 134, 137, 157, 178
Methodists 177
Metropotamia 101
Mexico 140, 175
    War, with 179
Miami
    Confederation 6, 22
    County, OH 41, 152, 185
    and Erie Canal 185
    Exporting Company 145, 152, 178
    Indians 7, 17, 23, 28, , 41, 42, 47, 66, 115, 153
    Purchase 107
    River 7, 64, 96, 97, 101, 102, 106, 124, 125, 133, 134
    Valley 96, 185
Miamisburg, OH 156, 171
Michigan 101, 135, 149, 160
    Peninsula 48
    Territory 153, 165
Michigania 101
Middletown, OH 148
Milan, OH 149
Military Reserve 138
Mill
    Creek 114
    Creek Station, OH 133
Milwaukee, WI 193, 196
Mingo Bottom, OH 104

Mingo Creek, PA 129
Ministry of War 102, 137
Mississippi River 6, 7, 12, 13, 16, 21, 22, 74, 77, 78, 101, 126, 127, 128, 135, 144, 152, 160, 171, 182
    Company 51, 52
    Territory 22
    Valley 3, 10, 11, 55
Missouri River 79
Mobile, AL 49
Mohawk Indians 6, 7, 18
Mohican
    Indians 35, 37, 38, 39, 60, 66, 84
    Mohican River 164
Monmouth, NJ Battle of 72
Monongahela River 25, 26, 29, 51, 61, 70
Monterey, Mexico 179
Montgomery County, OH 148, 185
Montraux 161
Montreal, Quebec 7, 10
Moravia 33, 150
Moravian
    Bretheren 33
    Brotherhood 71, 164
    Congregation 149
    Directorate 40, 44, 165
    North America 35
    Synod 34
Moravians 34, 35, 36, 38, 39, 53, 54, 57, 81, 93, 155
Morgan County, OH 160
Morrisville, PA 143
Mound Street 13, 159
Mount
    Ada 96
    Auburn 183
    Easton 193
    Vernon, VA 52
Mozart Hall 138, 196
Munich, Germany 181
Munjay Indians 86
Munsey Indians 62
Muskingum River 4, 8, 23, 44, 45, 49, 58, 62, 66, 67, 69, 76, 80, 83, 84, 85, 89, 93, 94, 100, 101, 102, 104, 109, 112, 116, 119, 145, 149, 165, 192
Nain. Indian village in PA 56
Nashville, TN 9, 53, 156
Nassau 198
Natchez
    Indians 16
    MS 16 (Also see the ship under MS Natchez.)
Natchitoches 167
National Reformers 181, 184
National Theater 196
Navy Yard, Washington, DC 142
Nazareth, PA 39, 150

Netherlands 153
Neutrality Laws, Violation of 194
New Barnabas, OH 160
New Bremen, OH 172
New England 10, 37, 47, 100
    Company 101, 102
New France 3, 7, 9, 12, 13, 16, 22, 22, 28, 84
New Gnadenhütten, MI 149
New Hampshire 159
    Province 47
New Harmony, IN 167
New Jersey 8, 38, 100, 101, 106, 107, 134, 139, 145, 158, 159
    Militia 129
    Province 57
New Lancaster, PA 145
New Madrid, MO. Earthquake of 1811. 152
New Market Street 159
New Milford, NY 36
New Orleans, LA 11, 16, 21, 22, 26, 127, 128, 130, 135, 144, 145, 151, 152, 156
New Philadelphia, OH 164, 165
New River, NC 53
New Salem, OH 149
New Ulm, MN 196
New York 6, 18, 29, 31, 35, 37, 57, 58, 66, 97, 106, 124, 158, 169, 176, 182, 196
    Counties
        York 57
    Immigration Commission 193
    Province 25, 25, 27, 36, 50, 57
New York, NY 161, 169, 193, 194
Newark, OH 146
Newport, KY 183, 193, 194, 195
Niagara, NY 31, 83
    River 7, 28
Nibelungen 196
Norfolk, VA 124
Norridgewock 47
North American Singers' Union. See Singers' Union.
North Bend, OH 108, 109
North Carolina 47, 52, 53, 65, 70, 95, 100, 159
    Counties
        Granville 52
        Lincoln 52
        Mecklinburg 52
        Stokes 52
Northern Liberties 159, 183
Northumberland County, PA 37
Northwest
    Department 16
    Territory 105, 108, 112, 115, 123, 129, 133, 135, 136, 160
Nova Scotia 28
Nürnberg, Germany 9
Offenbach, Germany 167

Ohezu. Wyandot word for Ohio River 10
Ohio 7, 8, 9, 12, 13, 23, 44, 56, 70, 83, 96, 101, 102, 109, 133, 135, 136, 148, 151, 153, 155, 159, 160, 161, 165,168, 169, 178, 198
    Canal 163, 165, 170
    Company 20, 21, 25, 28, 51, 52
    Counties
        Athens 24
        Blair 181
        Butler 148, 185
        Cambria 181
        Clearfield 181
        Clermont 147
        Columbiana 146
        Crawford 169,
        Darke 120, 132
        Elk 181
        Fairfield 122, 146
        Fayette 146
        Franklin 146
        Gallia 153
        Guernsey 153
        Hamilton 112, 135, 143, 148, 152, 164, 171, 177, 185, 197
        Jackson 148, 164
        Jefferson 146
        Knox 135
        Licking 146
        Lorain 7, 12
        Madison 164
        Mercer 132
        Miami 41, 152, 185
        Montgomery 185
        Morgan 160
        Perry 146, 160
        Pickaway 146
        Ross 133, 146
        St. Clair 135
        Stark 44
        Tuscaroras 147, 167, 173
        Urbana 153
        Washington 128, 135, 146, 164
        Wayne 135
        Warren 133, 181, 185
    Department (French) 20
    Historical Society 22
    House of Representatives 185
    Land Company 152
    Legislature 149, 157, 163
    Militia Adjutant General 152
    Province (English) 51
    Republic of 179

Ohio (continued)
  River 6, 7, 8, 9, 10, 12, 14, 21, 24, 25, 26, 28, 32, 37, 39, 41, 50, 51, 52, 53, 55, 56, 58, 59, 62, 63, 65, 68, 69, 70, 76, 77, 78, 79, 93, 95, 97, 100, 101, 103, 104, 106, 110, 114, 116, 120, 129, 130, 131, 135, 144, 145, 152, 154, 167, 196, 198
  Territorial Legislature 138
  Valley 3, 6, 19, 40, 42, 43, 44, 69, 71, 92, 95, 97, 99, 128, 142, 150, 151, 158, 165, 168, 171, 196
Ohiopeckhanne. Delaware name for the Ohio River 10
Ojibwa Indians 48
Old Chillicothe, OH 118
Ollmütz Prison 141, 142, 162
Oneida Indians 6, 66
Onondago, NY 37
  Indians 6, 22, 41
  Language 151
Orchard Street (Covington, KY) 195
Order of
  Druids 181
  Tramontines 15
  the Mustard Seed 33
  the Cincinnati, The 112, 114, 152
Ordinance of 1787 101, 105, 136
Oregon 179
  Guard 179
Osnabrück, Germany 172, 173
Ottawa
  Indians 6, 9, 40, 41, 47, 48, 68, 83, 84, 99, 105, 198
  Language 7
Ouabache. French for Wabash 9
Oyo River 9
Oyster Street 175
Pacific Ocean 3, 14
Paint
  Creek, OH 146
  Street. Chillicothe, OH 133
Palatinate, Germany 10, 11, 14, 15, 71
Papists 36, 38
Paris, France 28, 97, 102, 110, 131, 136, 140, 158
  Peace of 43
Parker, Joseph 101
Pawnee Indians 136
Paxton, PA 57, 58, 92
Peace (Treaty) of
  1763 102
  Aachen 22
  Utrecht 22
Peach Grove 138
Peaked Mountains 15
Pearl Street 172
Pegasus and the Fallen Poet 134

Pelisipia 101
Pennsylvania 6, 8, 15, 17, 18, 19, 20, 21, 24, 31, 32, 33, 35, 36, 37, 40, 51, 52, 56, 68, 70, 71, 80, 116, 128, 137, 139, 145, 150, 158, 159, 166, 167, 198
- Canal 169
- Counties
  - Allegheny 128, 144
  - Bradford 58
  - Butler 54, 168
  - Carbon 37
  - Harrison 147
  - Jefferson 147
  - Northumberland 37
  - Schuykill 56
  - Westmoreland 102, 181
- German Language 8, 146
- Legislature 49, 92
- Militia 117, 118, 129
- Province 24, 25, 25, 27, 48

Pentecost Monday 194
Perry County, OH 146, 160
Philadelphia, PA 28, 31, 39, 40, 52, 56, 57, 71, 101, 117, 121, 129, 132, 135, 137, 142, 151, 152, 166, 167, 168, 193, 196
Philippsburg 167, 174
Piankeshaw Indians 6, 23, 24, 198
Pickaway County, OH 146
Pickawillany, OH 23, 79
Pietists 166
Pike Street 138
Pike's Opera house 13
Pilgrims Rest, OH 149
Piqua
- Indians 6, 197
- OH 40, 41, 42, 133

Pittman's Hall 143
Pittsburg, PA 25, 42, 44, 46, 47, 54, 61, 62, 66, 68, 69, 70, 73, 74, 76, 79, 80, 81, 90, 91, 92, 93, 95, 99, 115, 116, 121, 122, 124, 128, 129, 130, 135, 144, 151, 152, 166, 168, 169, 174, 180, 193, 196, 198
- Duquesne Borough 168
- Periodicals
  - *Pittsburg Eagle* 168
  - *Pittsburg Gazette* 150
  - *Pittsburg Observer* 168
- Wards
  - 3rd Ward 168
  - 4th Ward 168

Plato's Republic 140
Plum Street 159, 186
Plymouth Rock 4
Po River, Italy 139
Podagra 84
Point Pleasant, WV 63, 67, 72
Poland 117

Polypotamia 101
Ponks Uteney. Indian for "Abode of the sand flies" 59
Pontiac Wars 56
Pope 145
Portland Avenue 192
Portsmouth, OH 193
Potomac River 8, 15, 52, 126
Pottowatami Indians 48, 105, 198
Poughkeepsie, NY 36
Praying Indians 82, 83, 84
Presbyterian Church 134, 152, 157, 173
Princeton
    College, NJ 149
    NJ 102
Probate Court of Hamilton County, OH 152
Process Verbal 23
Protestant
    Monks 34
    Reformation 33
Province Island 57
Prussia 21, 141, 158, 168, 169, 170, 171, 180, 198
Pulasky's Legion 100
Purgatory, Banning belief in 36
Puritans 34
Quakers 21, 35, 56, 59, 167
Quartermaster
    Department 120
    General 134
Quebec, Canada 38, 102, 171
Queen of the West 3, 152, 183
Race Street 13, 158, 159, 174, 179
Ramsthal, PA 166
Randorf Church 71
Rapidan River, VA 15
Reborn Church 71
Red
    Hawk, Chief 62, 67, 68
    Men; a social club 185
    River 130
Redstone River 51
Reeder, Rebecca 107
Reformed Church 71
Rehoboth, OH 160
Revolutionary War 52, 60, 97, 102
Rhein
    River 5, 153
    Wine 178
Rhein area of Cincinnati 177
Rhode Island 159
Richland, OH 164
Richmond Street 158

Riddle's Station KY 79
Riga, Latvia 139
Rochester, NY 193
Rocky Mountains 6, 162
Roman Catholic Church 71, 160
Rome 75
    People of 3
Ross
    County, OH 133
    Hill (Cincinnati) 193, 196
Rossville, OH 148
Round Bottom 114
Royal
    American Regiment 16, 42
    Bank 10
    Highlanders 56
Russia 31
SS Cadmus 161
Sac Indians 105, 198
Salem
    NC 34
    OH 80, 82, 83, 84, 85, 86, 87, 90, 91, 149, 165
Salt Lick, Kentucky 17
San Lorenzo 145
Sans Souci House 178
Sandusky 69, 89
    Bay 6, 9
    Creek, OH 88
    Indians 80, 164
    Ohio 8, 48, 76, 80, 84, 88, 89, 91, 93, 116, 193, 196
    Plateau 169
    River 24
Santo Domingo, Hispaniola 16, 153
Saratoga 101
    Battle of 106
Sausage Street 175
Savannah
    GA 34, 49, 100
    River 8, 9
Saxons 15
Saxony, Germany 33, 170, 179
Schaller's Brewery 161
Schamockin. Indian village later renamed Sunbury, PA 37
Schekomeko 35, 36, 40
Scheschequon, PA 55, 58
Schoharie River 18
Schoharies 66
Schönbrunn, OH 59, 63, 64, 66, 67, 73, 74, 76, 80, 83, 84, 85, 86, 88, 93, 149, 164, 165
Schuykill
    County, PA 56
    Grapes 182
    River 118

Scioto
- Bottom 133
- River 6, 8, 9, 20, 23, 28, 52, 53, 63, 69, 88, 101, 131, 133, 145, 149, 163
- Valley 131, 146

Scotland 99, 102, 197
Secession, War of. (Civil War) 185
Secretary of State, Ohio 15
Sedamsville 183
Seneca
- Indians 6, 9, 22, 41, 46, 55, 61, 62, 66, 68, 69, 76, 197

Tribe #7, a lodge of the Red Men, a social club 185
Settlers' Club. American Turners 195
Seven Years' War 27
Sharpshooters. A German military club 193
Shawnee Indians 6, 8, 9, 23, 24, 26, 32, 41, 42, 47, 49, 51, 53, 61, 62, 63, 64, 66, 67, 68, 69, 73, 76, 78, 79, 84, 95, 102, 108, 114, 115, 117, 125, 150, 153, 197
Shenandoah
- River 17
- Valley 15

Sheriff 169
Short Creek, WV 110
Sidney, OH 193
Signpost Hall 159
Silesia, Germany 142
Singers' Union (North American Singers' Union or *Sängerbund*) 181, 193
Sioux Indians 6
Six Nations. See Iroquois. 37, 51,5, 66, 83, 115, 151
Small Pox 7
Smith and Nixon Hall 186
Smith Street 159
Society
- for the Arts 145
- of Jesuit Missionaries 84

Sohio River 9
Somerset
- OH 160
- PA 147

Sonnenhof 181
South Carolina 141, 159
Spanish Claims on the Mississippi Valley 126
Spanish dollars 135
Sparta 196
Spencer House 135
Spotsylvania County, VA 15
St. Aloysious Orphans' Society 173
St. Asaph, KY 65, 78 (Also called Logan's Fort, Standing Fort. Near present-day Stanford, KY)
St. Bernard 183
St. Bernard Parish, LA 11
St. Cecilia Society 155
St. Charles Parish, LA 11
St. Clair County, OH 135

St. Clair Street 159
St. Clairsville, OH 103
St. Ferdinand, IN 181
St. Ignatious, Canada 7
St. Ildefonso, Treaty of 144
St. John's Church 155, 172, 178
St. John's, Canada 99
St. Joseph County, VA 181
St. Joseph River 48, 116, 117, 119
St. Joseph's Chapel 160
St. Lawrence River 13, 22, 171
St. Louis, MO 50, 170, 177, 193
St. Martin's Catholic Church (Louisville, KY) 190
St. Mary River 116, 119, 197
St. Mary's Church 174, 178, 197
St. Mary's College, Emitsburg, MD 173
St. Patrick's Church 169
St. Patrick, OH 160
St. Paul's Church (Founded 1847 at Spring & Abigail streets) 173, 178
St. Peter's Church 177
St. Peter's Parish 172
St. Xav(i)er
    Collegium 176
    Seminary 173
Stark County, OH 44
Stars and Stripes 188
Staunton, VA 15, 63
Steak Street 175
Steam Navigation 144
Sterling 163
Steuben Guard; a German military club 193
Steubenville, OH 9, 104
Stissik Mountains 35
Stites, Benjamin 115
Stokes County, NC 52
Stony Point 123
Storrs 114
Strassburg, VA 15
Strode's Station, KY 66
Stuttgart, Germany 169
Suhr, Rev. 173
Superior Court 122
Surinam 33
Susquehannah River 8, 31, 37, 37, 40, 50, 55, 56
Swabia 14, 166, 167
Swabians 156, 157
Sweden 31
Swiss Cheese Street 175
Switzerland 71, 158, 159, 168, 170, 171, 180, 198
    County, IN 182
Sycamore Street 13, 115, 138, 156, 157, 159, 160
Sylvania 101

Symmes
    Creek, OH 148
    Street 159
Synagogue Bnei Ischurun 181
Syracuse, NY 193
Talmud Yelodim Institute 197
Tartars 7
Tawightee Indians 6
Te Deum 6
Telegraph Office 193
Tell City, IN 196
Tennessee 9, 63, 100, 159, 179, 198
    River 17, 78
Terre Haute, IN 193
Territorial Code 135
    Court 135
Teutonia 196
    Lodge # 177. Union of Special Brothers 196
Texas 70, 168
    Area of Cincinnati 178
Thames River, Canada 149, 165
Thrappich. Indian magic spells 60
Ticonderoga, NY 102
Tippecanoe, OH Battle of 153
Titans 3
Tivoli 174
Toledo, OH 145
Tomahawk Law 70
Tombechbee River 16
Transylvania 65
    Company 65
Trappist Monks 181
Trenton, NJ 102
Tübingen, University of 173
Tuffly & Co. 158
    Tunkers 35
Turnville 196
Turtle Clan, Delaware Indians 8, 119, 150
Turtle Creek 26, 49
Tuscararas
    County, OH 147, 167, 173
    River 44, 58, 74, 82, 111
Tuscarara Indians 44, 46, 66
Ulrichshain 196
Uncle
    (s) of the Delaware 55 (Refers to the Wyandot Indians)
    Sam 101
Union of Special Brothers 180, 196
    Lodges

Union of Special Brothers (continued)
    # 113. 196
        Hermann Lodge # 208. 196
        Humboldt Lodge #247 196
        Germania Lodge 181, 196
        Teutonia Lodge # 177. 196
        William Tell Lodge # 335. 196
Unitarian Church 179
United
    Bretheren 150
    Brotherhood in Christ 155
    Reformed Church 123
United States 77, 78, 95, 97, 98, 105, 139, 141, 142, 144, 153
    Army 113
        1st Infantry 120
        1st Regiment 101
        2nd Regiment 120
        4th Regiment 179
    Congress 69, 97, 98, 99, 100, 115, 128, 131, 132, 133, 136, 137 145, 158, 161, 164, 165, 198
    Marshal 129
    Mint 135
United States Hotel. Columbus, OH 192
Urbana, OH 164
Urbana County, OH 153
Valley of Josaphat 175
Valparaiso, Chile 174
Venango, PA 24
Verbice 33
Vermont 159
Verrazano 13
Vevay, IN 5, 155, 160, 161, 161, 182
    Artillery Company 161, 162
    Palladium 182
Via Sacra 105
Vienna, Austria 141, 160, 180
Vincennes, IN 7, 12, 50, 74, 75, 101, 102, 116, 126, 132, 135, 136
Vine Street 13, 134, 154, 159, 160, 161, 173, 184, 186, 189, 196
Virginia 14, 17, 18, 19, 20, 24, 25, 28, 31, 38, 48, 51, 52, 53, 61, 65, 70, 71, 74, 78, 79, 90, 95, 97, 99, 100, 101, 103, 116, 122, 124, 126, 133, 159, 182
    Counties
        Fincastle 53, 63
        Kentucky 65, 78
        Marshal 181
        Spotsylvania 15
        St. Joseph 181
        Wetzel 181
    Government 43, 49
    Militia 26
        8th Regiment 72
    Reserve 133
Vöringen, Germany 154
Waadt, Swiss Canton 139

Wabash
- Indians 102, 119
- River 7, 12, 16, 24, 28, 42, 101, 116, 119, 126, 149, 67
- Territory 74
- Valley 22

Wales 197
Walhonding River 88, 149. See White Woman Creek.
Walnut Street 107, 107, 133, 136, 138, 159, 172, 173, 178, 184, 186, 189
Wampano Indians 35, 37
Wapakonetta, OH 197
War of 1812 164
Warren County, OH 133, 181, 185
Washington 101
Washington
- County, OH 128, 135, 146, 164
- DC 142, 153, 182, 194
- OH 146, 169
- PA 147

Water
- Street 107, 134, 159
- Street (Chillicothe, OH) 133

Wayne
- County, OH 135
- Street 159, 159

Wea Indians 116
Welch Cock Clan. Delaware Indians 8
Wequetani. Indian village in PA 56
West Point 185
West Virginia 9, 44, 53, 61, 76, 198
Western
- Museum 145
- Reserve 3, 14, 145
- Row 138, 159, 161
- Sanitary Fair 83

Westmoreland County, PA 102, 181
Wetstone Creek (VA) 181
Wetzel County, VA 181
Wheeling, WV 61, 62, 72, 84, 93, 104, 110, 111, 116, 121, 144, 45, 147 181, 187, 193, 196
Whig Party 170, 171
Whiskey Rebellion 129, 130
White
- River 149
- Water Canal 177
- Woman Creek (Walhonding River) 49

White's Station, OH 114
Whitehall, Covington, KY 194
Wieling 61
Wilhelm Tell Exchange 160
Will's Creek, MD 29
William Tell Lodge # 335. Union of Special Brothers 196
Williamsburg, VA 17, 70, 193
Winchester, VA 15, 24, 72

Winnenden, Germany 169
Wisconsin 101, 192
    Buffalo County 196
Wittenberg, University of 33
Wolf Clan, Delaware Indians 8, 54, 62, 64, 66, 68, 69, 73, 83, 85, 93
Wommeldorf, PA 18
Wood's Theater 172
Woodland Garden 191
Workers' Club 181, 184, 193
    Hall 184
Württemberg, Germany 71, 168, 198
Wyalusing. Delaware name for Friedensdorf, PA 55
Wyandot Indians 6, 7, 8, 9, 10, 26, 32, 40, 41, 47, 48, 55, 62, 66, 68, 69, 78, 80, 83, 84, 85, 86, 87, 89, 90, 93, 99, 102, 105, 115, 146, 197
Wyandott 196
Wyoming Valley, PA 56, 58
York
    County, NY 57
    Street (Covington, KY) 194
Youghiogheny
    PA 102
    River 29
Zanesville, OH 147, 160, 163, 163
Zäslein, Joseph 155
Zelionopel, PA 168
Zion's Gate 175
Zoarites 167
Zorndorf, Battle of 41

BIBLIOGRAPHY

The following is the Periodicals and Publication index of
the book *Deutsche Chronik in der Geschichte des Ohio-Thales*.
by
Emil Klauprecht.
(Cincinnati:1864)

PERIODICALS

Allegheny Democrat 168
American Register 150
Boston Courier 155
California Democrat 174, 175
Catholic Telegraph 173
Central Watchman 182
Cincinnati Directory 157, 158
Cincinnati Gazette 142, 153, 154, 155, 160
Cincinnati Volksblatt 1, 177
Christian Apologet (*Christliche Apologete*). Edited by W. Nast 177
Deutschen im Westen. See *Germans in the West*.
Enquirer 188
Friend of Truth (See *Wahrheitsfreund*)
German American 174
Germans in the West (*Deutschen im Westen*-published
    by Christian Burghalter & Hefley. Later became the
    Volksfreund,) edited by Rudolph Maltiz   177
Hazard's Register (PA) 18
Historical Note of Pennsylvania 18
Hochwächter. Organ of the Freemen's Club 184, 186
Indianapolis Free Press 187
Kentucky Gazette 105, 182
Lancaster Eagle, The. (*Der Ohio Adler*-first German newspaper in Ohio) 146
Lichtfreund. (*Friend of Light*). Edited by Eduard Mühl. 177
Missouri Intelligencer 5
Ohio Chronicle, The; Cincinnati's first German newspaper 162
Pennsylvania Gazette 27, 92
People's Friend. See *Volksfreund* 177
Pittsburg Eagle 168
Pittsburg Gazette 150
Pittsburg Observer 168
Prospect 171
Protestant 173
Republikaner. (*Republican*) Edited by Capt. J.H. Schröder in Louisville, KY 177
Sentinel of the North Western Territory, The. William Maxwell, Editor. 135
Spring Messengers. Edited by Friedrich August Hobelmann 186
Troy Times 106
Times 183, 189
United States Catholic Magazine 160
Volksblatt 172, 177
Volksbühne. (*People's Stage*) Edited by Walker and Renz. 177
Volksfreund. 177 See *Germans in the West* above.

Wahrheitsfreund. (Friend of Truth) Begun by Fr. John Martin Henni in 1837. Ended publication in 1907. 173
Westbote 163
Western
    Agriculterist 148
    Intelligencer 163
    Mercury. Edited by Christian Burghalter. 156, 177
    Monthly Review 53
    Spy 139, 143, 151, 152
Westlicher Merkur. See *Western Mercury.*
Workers' Republic, The 184
World Citizen 172

PUBLICATIONS/DISSERTATIONS

Bowen. Wheeling, WV *City Directory of 1839.* 61

Brown, Henry. (1789-1849) *The History of Illinois from its first discovery and settlement to the present time.* J. Winchester (New York:1844) 7, 12

Burnet, Jacob. *Notes on the Settlement of the North-western Territory.* Derby, Bradley and Company, (Cincinnati:1847) 136, 109, 123, 127, 135, 136, 143, 156, 158

Butler, Mann. (1784-1852) *A History of the Commonwealth of Kentucky.* Wilcox, Dickerman and Company, (Louisville, KY:1834) 66

Byrd, J. *Progress to the Mines of Virginia* (1732) 15, 79

Casseday, Ben. *The History of Louisville from its earliest settlement to 1852.* Hyull & Bros. (Louisville, KY:1852)

Cist, Charles. *The Cincinnati Miscellany; or, Antiquities of the West and Pioneer History and General and Local Statistics.* C. Clark, Printer, (Cincinnati:1845-56). 121

Collins, Lewis. (1797-1870) *Historical Sketches of Kentucky.* (Cincinnati:1847) 53, 55, 66

Craig, F. *An Account of the Remarkable Occurences in the Life and Travel's of Col. James Smith.* (Philadelphia: 1831) 66

Craig, Neville B. (1787-1863) *The Olden Time: A Monthly Publication, Devoted to the Preservation of Documents and Other Authentic Information in Relation to the Early Explorations and the Settlement and Improvement of the County Around the Head of the Ohio.* Vols. I-II Printed by Dumars & Co. Chronicle Buildings. (Pittsburgh:Jan. 1846-Dec. 1847). 40, 47

Doddridge, Rev. Joseph. (1769-1826) *Notes on the Settlement and Indian Wars of the Western Parts of Virginia and Pennsylvania, from the Year 1763 until the Year 1783 Inclusive. Together with a View of the State of Society and Manners of the First Settlers of the Western County.* (1824) 71, 92

Drake, Daniel Dr. (1785-1852) *Information About Cincinnati* (Cincinnati:1810) 151

Drake, Daniel Dr. *Picture of Cincinnati and Miami County* (Cincinnati:1815) 151

Drake, Dr. Benjamin. (1794-1841) *Cincinnati in 1815* 154

Drake, Dr. Benjamin and E.D. Mansfield. *Cincinnati in 1826*. (Cincinnati:1827) 162

Ellet, Elizabeth F. *Pioneer Women of the West*. Porter & Coates, (Philadelphia:18--). 66

Flügel, Johann Gottfried (1788-1855). *Flowers of German Poetry*. J. Klinkhardt (Leipzig:1835). 161

Gordon. *History of Pennsylvania* 16

Hall, James. (1793-1868) *The Romance of Western History or Sketches of History, Life and Manners in the West*. Harrison Hall.(Philadelphia:1835) 7, 12

Hazard's *Pennsylvania Register* 18

Heckewelder, Johann (1743-1823). *History, manners, and customs of the Indian nations who once inhabited Pennsylvania and the neighboring states*. S. Small (Philadelphia:1818) 8

Hennepin, Louis. *Amplissimae Regiones Mississippi, seu Provinciae Ludovicianae a R.P. Ludovico Hennepin Francise miss in America Septentionali, anno 1687 delectae, nunc Gallorum coloniis et actionum negotiis toto orbe celeberrimae, nova tagbula edita a J. Bapt Homanno*. (Nürnberg:1759) 9

Hildreth, S.P. (1783-1863) *Pioneer History: Being An Account of the First Examination of the Ohio Valley, and the Early Settlement of the Northwest Territory. Chiefly from Original Manuscripts; Containing the Papers of Col. George Morgan; those of Judge Barker; the Diaries of Joseph Buell and John Matthews; the Records of the Ohio Company, etc., etc., etc.* H. W. Derby & Co. New York: A.S. Barnes & Co. (Cincinnati:1848). 3, 9, 23, 63, 72, 101

Historical Notes of Pennsylvania; included in *Hazard's Register* 18

Homann, Johann Baptist (1664-1724) et. al. *Regni Mexicani seu Novae Hispaniae, Ludoviaianne, N. Angliae, Caroliniae, Virginiae et Pennsylvaniae [sic], nec nun insularum archipelagi Mexicani in America Septentrionali accurata tabula*. (Nürnberg:1720) 9

Howe's *Historical Collection of Ohio* 42

Jones, Hugh. (1669-1760) *The present state of Virginia. Giving a particular and short account of the Indian, English, and negroe inhabitants of that colony. Shewing their religion, manners, government, trade, way of living, &c., with a description of the country. From whence is inferred a short view of Maryland and North Carolina* **(1725)**. 15

Kapp, Friedrich, 1824-1884. *Leben des amerikanischen Generals Friedrich Wilhelm von Steuben*, von Friedrich Kapp. Mit Steuben's Portrait. Duncker & Humbolt. (Berlin:1858). 97

Kercheval, Samuel, 1786-1845? *History of the Valley of Virginia*. (Winchester:1833). 71

Lanman. *History of New France* 7, 12

Lossing, Benson. *Fieldbook of the Revolution*. Harper & Bros. (New York:1860). 71

Löher, Franz von. (1818-1892) *Geschichte und Zustände der Deutschen in Amerika. (History and Condition of the Germans in America)*. Eggers and Wilde (Cincinnati:1847). 42, 110, 178, 179

Loskiel, George Henry. (1740-1814) *History of the mission of the United Brethren among the Indians in North America*. Published by the Brethrens' society for the furtherance of the gospel. (London:1794) 37, 38, 40

Miltenberger, Gottfried. *Journey to Pennsylvania in the Year 1750*. F. Jenisch. (Stuttgart:1756) 71

Minor, Charles. (1835-1903) *History of Wyoming* (Philadelphia:1845) 58

Parkman, Francis Scott. (1823-1893) *History of the Conspiracy of Pontiac, and the War of the North American Tribes Against the English Colonies, after the Conquest of Canada*. Little and Brown. (Boston:1851). 8, 50

Perkins, James H. (1810-1849) *Annals of the West*. J.R. Albach (Cincinnati:1847) 51

Plato. *Republic*. 140.

Poisson, Albert. (1633-1690) *Lettres edifiantes*. (Paris:1781). 11

Post, Christian F. (1710-1785) *Diary of a Trip from Philadelphia to the Ohio*. (London:1759). 40

Ramsay, James Getty Mcready. *The Annals of Tennessee to the End of the Eighteenth Century: Compromising Its Settlement, as the Watanga Association, from the 1769 to 1777; a part of North Carolina, from 1777 to 1784; the State of Franklin, from 1788 to 1790; the Territory of the United States, South of the Ohio, from 1790 to 1796; the State of Tennessee, from 1796 to 1800*. (Charleston:1853). 53, 63

Rundthaler, Edward. *Life of Heckewelder* 47

Rupp, Isreal Daniel. (1803-1878) *History of the counties of Berks and Lebanon: containing a brief account of the Indians...and the numerous murders by them; notices of the first Swedish, Welsh, French, German, Irish, and English settlers, giving the names of nearly five thousand of them, biographical sketches, topographical descriptions...religious history...statistical information, notices of the press and education*. G. Hills (Lancaster, PA:1844) 15

Schoolcraft, Henry R. *Information Respecting the History, Condition, and Prospects of the Indian Tribes of the United States, Collected and Prepared under the Direction of the Bureau of Indian Affairs*. Lippincott, Grambo and Co. (Philadelphia:1851). 6

Smith, James. *An Account of the Remarkable Occurances in the Life and Travels of Col James Smith (now a citizen of Bourbon County, Kentucky), During his captivity with the Indians, in the years 1755, 56, 57, 58 & 59*. John Bradford, (Lexington, KY:1799); F. Craig, (Philadelphia:1831). 66

Smith, William. *An Historical Account of the Expedition Against the Indians, in the year 1764, under the Command of Henry Bouquet, Esq*. (London:1766). 49

Sparks, Jared. (1789-1866) *The Writings of George Washington: Being His Correspondence, Addresses, Messages, and Other Papers, Official and Private, Selected and Published from the Original Sources; With a Life of the Author*. American Stationers Company, (Boston:1837). 21, 26

Taylor, James Wickes. (1819-1893) *History of the State of Ohio, First period 1650-1787*. H.W. Derby & co. (Cincinnati and Sandusky:1854) 4, 8, 42, 67, 130, 165

Thousand and One Nights 148

Transactions of the Historical Society of Ohio 9, 13

Volney, Constantin Francois Chasseboeuf comte de (1757-1820). *Voyages from Montreal, on the river St. Lawrence, through the continent of North America, to the frozen and Pacific oceans; in the years 1789 and 1793. With a preliminary account of the rise, progress, and present state of the fur trade of that country.* W. Creech (Edinburgh:1802) 116, 127, 131, 132

Whittlesey. Dissertation before the Historical Society of Ohio. 12

Other books by Don Heinrich Tolzmann:

*Amana: William Rufus Perkins' and Barthinius L. Wick's
History of the Amana Society, or Community of True Inspiration*

*Americana Germanica: Paul Ben Baginsky's Bibliography of
German Works Relating to America, 1493-1800*

*Biography of Baron Von Steuben, the Army of the American Revolution and
Its Organizer: Rudolf Cronau's Biography of Baron von Steuben*

CD: German-American Biographical Index (Midwest Families)

CD: Germans, Volume 2

CD: The German Colonial Era (four volumes)

Cincinnati's German Heritage

Covington's German Heritage

*Custer: Frederick Whittaker's Complete Life of General George A. Custer, Major General of Volunteers, Brevet Major General U.S. Army and
Lieutenant-Colonel Seventh U.S. Cavalry*

*Dayton's German Heritage: Karl Karstaedt's Golden Jubilee History of the
German Pioneer Society of Dayton, Ohio*

Early German-American Newspapers: Daniel Miller's History

German Americans in the Revolution

German Immigration to America: The First Wave

German Pioneer Life and Domestic Customs

German Pioneer Lifestyle

German Pioneers in Early California: Erwin G. Gudde's History

German-American Achievements: 400 Years of Contributions to America

German-Americana: A Bibliography

Germany and America, 1450-1700

Kentucky's German Pioneers: H.A. Rattermann's History

*Lives and Exploits of the Daring Frank and Jesse James: Thaddeus Thorndike's
Graphic and Realistic Description of Their Many Deeds of Unparalleled
Daring in the Robbing of Banks and Railroad Trains*

Louisiana's German Heritage: Louis Voss' Introductory History

Maryland's German Heritage: Daniel Wunderlich Nead's History

*Memories of the Battle of New Ulm: Personal Accounts of the Sioux Uprising.
L. A. Fritsche's History of Brown County, Minnesota (1916)*

*Michigan's German Heritage: John Andrew Russell's History of the
German Influence in the Making of Michigan*

Ohio's German Heritage

*Outbreak and Massacre by the Dakota Indians in Minnesota in 1862: Marion P. Satterlee's
Minute Account of the Outbreak, with Exact Locations, Names of All Victims, Prisoners
at Camp Release, Refugees at Fort Ridgely, etc. Complete List of Indians Killed in
Battle and Those Hung, and Those Pardoned at Rock Island, Iowa*

The German Element in Virginia: Herrmann Schuricht's History

The German Immigrant in America

The Pennsylvania Germans: James Owen Knauss, Jr.'s Social History

The Pennsylvania Germans: Jesse Leonard Rosenberger's Sketch of Their History and Life

www.ingramcontent.com/pod-product-compliance
Lightning Source LLC
Chambersburg PA
CBHW081417230426

43668CB00016B/2272